AF477037

British Life Photography Awards

"…the British Life Photography Awards are a journey of discovery. They are about meeting people, going to places, getting up before dawn, going to bed too late, being out there, experiencing, learning, thinking on your feet and trying to understand how we live, work and play. They record interesting and meaningful aspects of daily life; the things that we like, and find most interesting."

British Life Photography Awards

Portfolio 2

dewi lewis publishing

BRITISH LIFE PHOTOGRAPHY AWARDS

Published in the UK in 2016 by
Dewi Lewis Publishing
8, Broomfield Road
Heaton Moor, Stockport SK4 4ND
www.dewilewis.com

ISBN 978-1-907893-88-9

Based on an original design
© Octopus Publishing Group Ltd 2015

Printed in Italy by EBS, Verona

5 4 3 2 1

CONTENTS

INTRODUCTION

Britain is an interesting place to photograph. In my career I have been repeatedly drawn back to photograph aspects of UK life centred around England, and it does not lose its fascination. The length and breadth of the human condition, the main driver of any artistic enterprise, as manifest by our British culture and identity, and the whirlwind manner of its changing, along with the metal of its durability are a heady brew for any committed photographer.

This competition draws together some of these photographs looking at life in the UK. Attracting thousands of entries from both amateurs and professionals, I think the judges have managed to select a winning image that holds up formally and also comments on how we collectively make and consume our experiences as images. Overall the judges have edited a selection that give us a sense of place, both in individual photographs and in photo essays, not of an idealised sceptred isle, but of the country I live in and would not wish to live in any other.

CHRIS STEELE-PERKINS

ABOUT THE
BRITISH LIFE PHOTOGRAPHY AWARDS

Welcome to the second portfolio of the British Life Photography Awards.

The British Life Photography Awards is a showcase for contemporary and imaginative images that capture the essence and spirit of British life, documenting real life through original, illuminating, thought provoking, humorous and poignant imagery.

Covering everything from; street life, rural life, portraiture, weather and a special award for the best documentary feature, the awards celebrate British life and culture, whilst also highlighting the relevance and importance of photography to raise awareness and inform.

It is a celebration of photographs that capture the very spirit and essence of British life – spontaneous and arresting images of our nation and people.

The inspiration for these awards is the renewed interest in photography that has been enabled by digital technology, along with a desire to revive a greater awareness of documentary photography.

Documenting daily life has been a tradition for over a century, so just like the great documentary photographers of the past (and present), we want to encourage photographers to elevate the commonplace and familiar into something compelling or fascinating through the craft, creativity and discipline of photography. Whether it's a personal vision, an intimate portrait, a visual pun or a sequence of innovative images telling a story.

The competition is a voice for all photographers and open to all photographers both amateur and professional.

MAGGIE GOWAN
BLPA Director

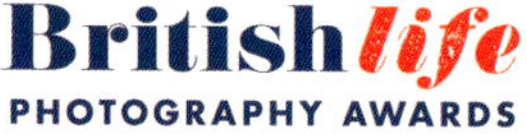

The aim of the awards:

- To showcase contemporary and imaginative images that capture the spirit of British life.

- To revive an interest in documentary and reportage photography.

- To highlight the relevance and importance of photography in raising awareness and informing about social issues.

- To inspire and motivate young people to develop a passion for photography.

For further information about the annual competition and exhibition, visit: www.blpawards.com

Categories

Overall Winner

Rural Life

Urban Life

Street Life

Life at Work

Brits on Holiday

Portraiture

British Weather

Historic Britain

Documentary Series

Young British Life Photographer

With thanks to:

All the photographers who have participated in the awards, as well as the sponsors, supporters and judges

Matthew Chatfield
Website Manager, Facilitator
and Chair of the Judging Panel

Clare Webb
Technical Adviser and Manager

Victoria Skeet
Assistant Judge and Administrator

Jennie Hart
Assistant Judge and Administrator

Adam Sanders
Exhibitions Manager

Rebecca Moran
Social Media

Chris Hart
Design

SUPPORTERS

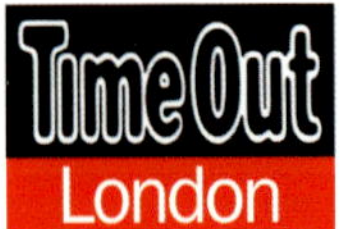

Time Out is the ultimate insider guide for inspiring you to keep up and join in with all that's new and best in your city. Founded by Tony Elliot, in London in 1968, *Time Out* has grown into a global media group that spans 70 cities across 37 countries with a monthly combined audience in excess of 33 million people. No one knows the city better than *Time Out*. The business is uniquely positioned to provide the platform and marketplace for inspiring people to make the most of their own city. This is achieved through a distribution network that includes a growing online presence, mobile applications, magazines, events and partnerships.

COUNTRY LIFE

Since its launch in 1897, *Country Life* has been the world's most celebrated magazine of the British way of life, its countryside, properties and gardens. Its matchless authority, exquisite photography and world-class writing have ensured its position as one of the nation's truly great magazines. *Country Life's* readers have always sought the best things in life from food and antiques to the finest properties and estates.

SPONSORS

SONY

Sony is a global leader in photography offering a comprehensive range of digital cameras from the professional quality Alpha line of digital compact system cameras through to the point and shoot Cyber-shot range, there is a camera for every occasion. Whether you are photographing your child's first steps, capturing a sunset on holiday, or your friends at a picnic, Sony helps you record the image just the way you want it.

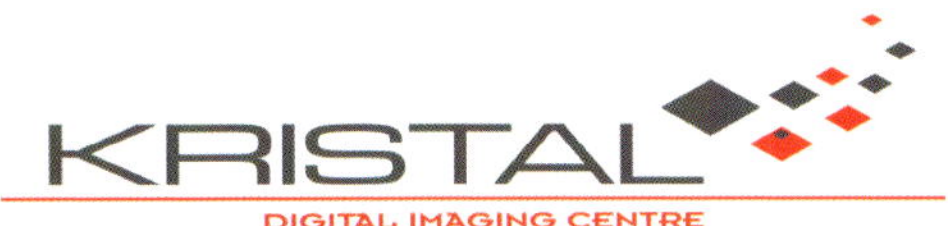

Kristal Digital Imaging Centre is Surrey's premier professional processing laboratory. A family-run independent business established in 2003, providing the best products and services. With an ever-growing product range, including professionally bound photo books, right up to very large high quality exhibition prints. Kristal uses the latest wet-lab HD print processors, a range of 12 colour printers including flat-beds for direct to substrate printing, allowing the presentation of your work onto a wide range of materials, including Foamex, Acrylics, MDF and Aluminium.

THE JUDGING PANEL

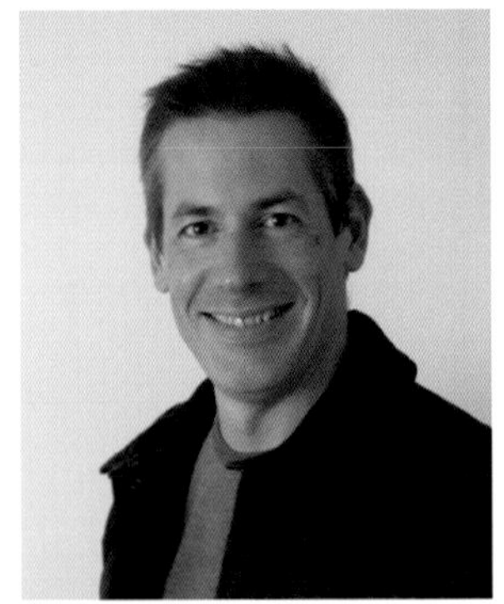

JASON KEENE

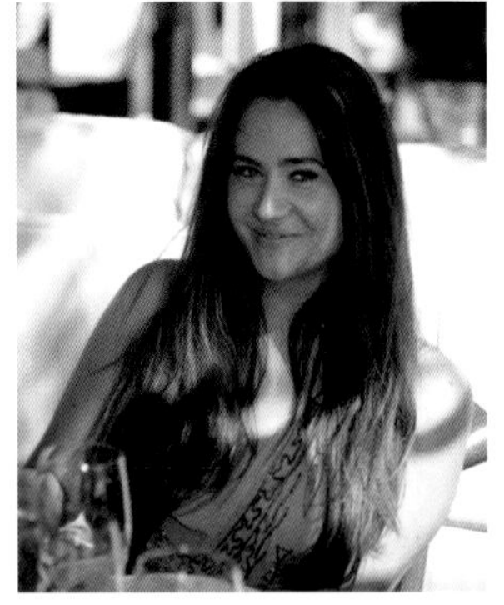

OLIVIA LADBROOKE-CHARTRES

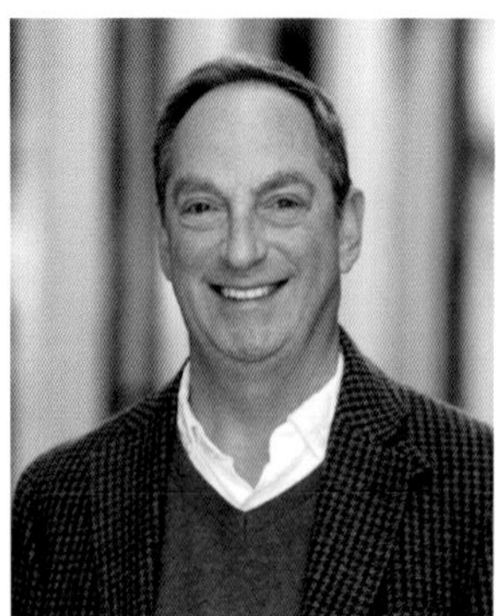

GLEN MARKS

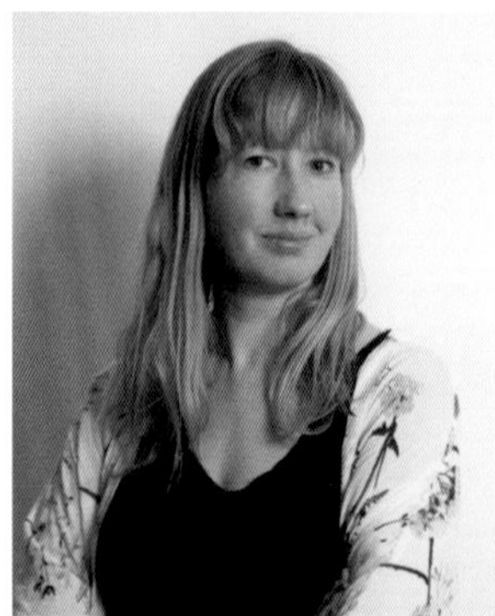

JAEL MARSCHNER

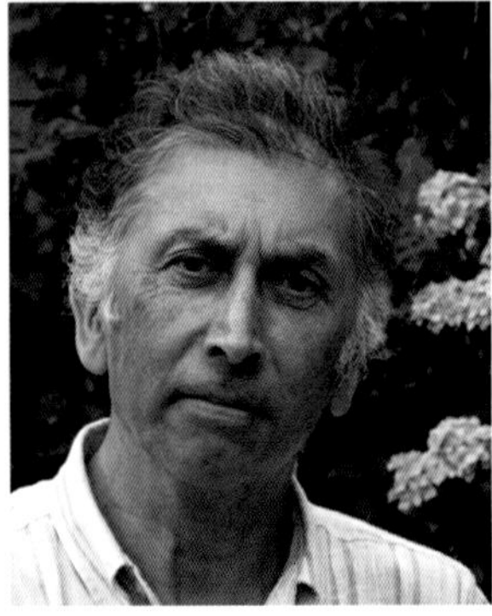

CHRIS STEELE-PERKINS

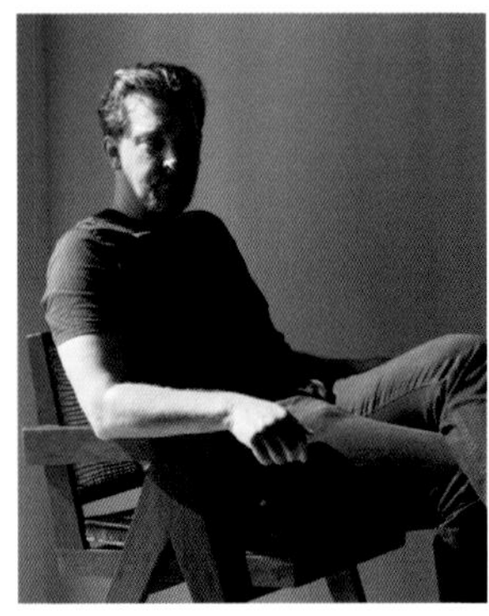

MIKE TROW

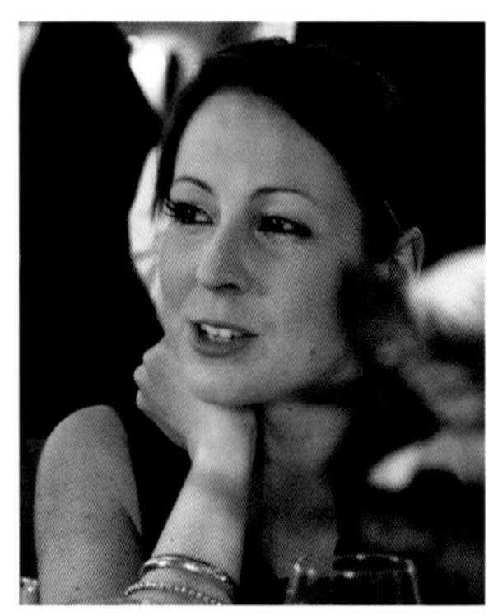

VICKY WILKES

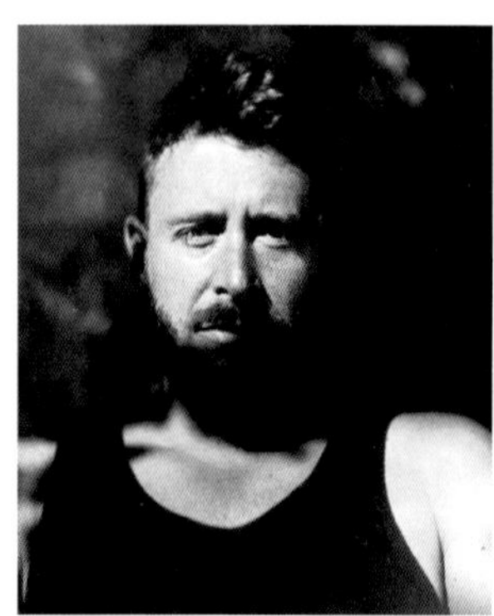

DAVID YEO

JASON KEENE
Area Sales Manager, SONY

Jason has 25 years' experience in the photography business. Initially from a photographic retail background, experiencing the transition from manual to autofocus and film to digital. Jason took a sales role within wholesale photographic supply and then the photographic processing industry. For the past 7 years, Jason has been part of the Sony digital imaging division, during which time Sony has introduced a broad range of professional and amateur cameras bringing innovative technology to a wider audience.

OLIVIA LADBROOKE-CHARTRES
Artist

Olivia is an accomplished artist, graduating from Wimbledon College of Art with a BA in Fine Art Painting, using photography as a key element of her practice. She understands the inherent appeal of the visual arts. Her work develops the traditional fresco genre beyond the context of painting, key elements of which are used to explore the fragility of life and our transition through it. This visual representation illustrates how connections, their associated meaning and suggested narrative, deteriorate over time. Reversed photographic images from a pre-digital era, paint and symbols are juxtaposed, creating conflict and synergy between past and present. She has worked at the prestigious Mall Galleries, Federation of British Artists, running contemporary exhibitions, private views and events including Threadneedle Prize and ING Discerning Eye. Currently she works for PAM Insight.

GLEN MARKS
Photo Industry Professional

Glen Marks is a photo industry veteran who has worked with a wide range of photographers, archives, publishers and major media corporations over his thirty year plus career with Rex Features photo agency, which is now a division of Shutterstock. He hosted the inaugural BLPA event in March 2015 and was a judge on this year's panel.

JAEL MARSCHNER
Group Picture Editor, *Time Out*

Most of Jael's work at *Time Out* focuses on researching, commissioning and art directing photography for the magazine, but also includes website imagery, travel guide photography and stints on *Time Out New York* magazine. In the past she has been the Picture Editor for *The Sunday Times Travel Magazine* and worked on the *Evening Standard Magazine* Picture Desk. Jael has always had a keen eye for striking imagery and has worked with some of the best photographers in the business. However, she is also always on the lookout for new talent. As a food and travel photographer herself she can sometimes be found behind the camera as well, if time allows.

CHRIS STEELE-PERKINS
Photographer

Born in Burma in 1947, the son of an English colonel and a young Burmese woman, Chris Steele-Perkins came to England when he was a small boy and went to school at Christ's Hospital. He studied Psychology at the University of Newcastle-upon-Tyne, and in his spare time learnt photography working on the student newspaper. After graduating in 1970 he followed his interest in photography and started to work as a freelance photographer,

moving to London in 1971. Steele-Perkins joined Magnum Photos in 1979. Throughout his career he has always been concerned to be an independent author, with his own photographic voice, exploring the aspects of the world that mattered most to him. This is best described as following twin obsessions: on one hand a continual dissection of Englishness from youth culture through urban poverty to the elderly and rural life. On the other hand he has always explored the rest of the world which has taken him from the war zones of El Salvador, Lebanon and Afghanistan to the cities and plains of Africa; from the shadow of Mount Fuji to the new face of Burma. From this work he has produced many books, the most recent of which is *A Place in the Country*, an examination, and a celebration, of the great English estate, Holkham Hall.

MIKE TROW
Picture Editor, *Vogue*

Having completed a degree in philosophy, Mike Trow started out in fashion working on *Bizarre* magazine as photo editor and photographer. He later worked on *Jack* magazine with James Brown, as photo director and occasional feature writer. He has been picture editor of *British Vogue* since 2005 – responsible for commissioning, production and art direction of most of the portraits, reportage and house shoots of the magazine. He shoots some portraits for the magazine himself. He cycles everywhere.

VICKY WILKES
Picture Editor, *Country Life*

Vicky has worked on the *Country Life* picture desk for six years, having previously been at *The*

Saturday Telegraph Magazine. Commissioning and researching high standard photography is key to the picture editor's role and she is always looking for new photographers and different styles of photography which will compliment *Country Life*. Vicky has a strong passion for the British countryside and the people who call it their home.

DAVID YEO
Photographer

David Yeo is an award winning cross-genre photographer working in both stills and film. He was the overall winner of BLPA 2014. David's work has been exhibited extensively and his published work appears in *Vogue* and *Elle* magazines internationally, *GQ Style*, *iD*, *Vanity Fair* and major national editorials and magazines. David's diverse portfolio spans corporate, editorial and film commissions. Some of his portraits include: Al Murray, All Saints, Boris Johnson, Christopher Kane, Christopher Bailey, David Mitchell, Earl Spencer, Editors, Henry Holland, Heston Blumenthal, Manolo Blahnik, Mark Hix, Martin Parr, Mary Portas, Mollie King The Saturdays, Ralph Fiennes, Rick Stein, Rosamund Pike, Rosie Huntingdon-Whiteley, Sandra Choi, Simon Russell-Beale, Victoria Pendleton, Will Smith, Will Young, Jamie Woon, Zaha Hadid, Zandra Rhodes.

OVERALL WINNER

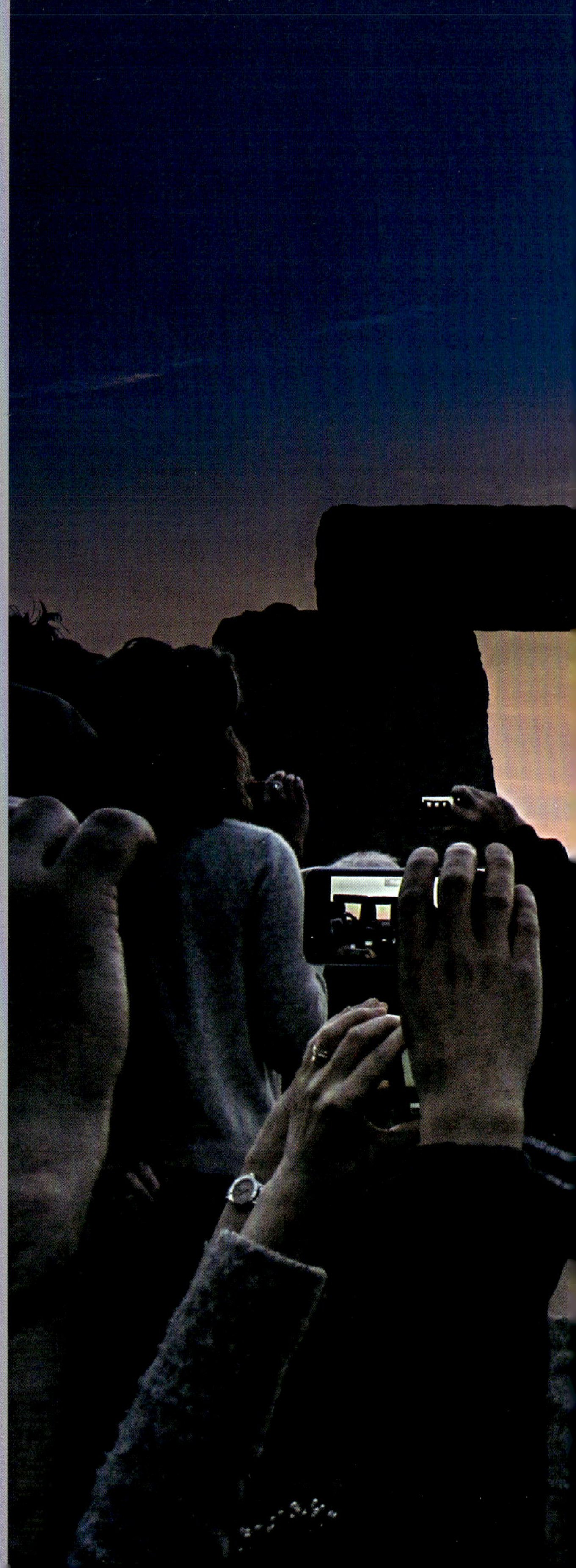

ELENA MARIMON MUNOZ

Past Present
Stonehenge, Wiltshire, England

Sunrise at Stonehenge during the summer solstice festival.
By the time the sun started to rise above the stones, hundreds,
if not thousands of people had gathered, phones and cameras
up in the air ready to record the magical moment. In the
picture, I wanted to capture the mixture of ancient history
and modern technology, fused together: past and present.

With thanks to English Heritage

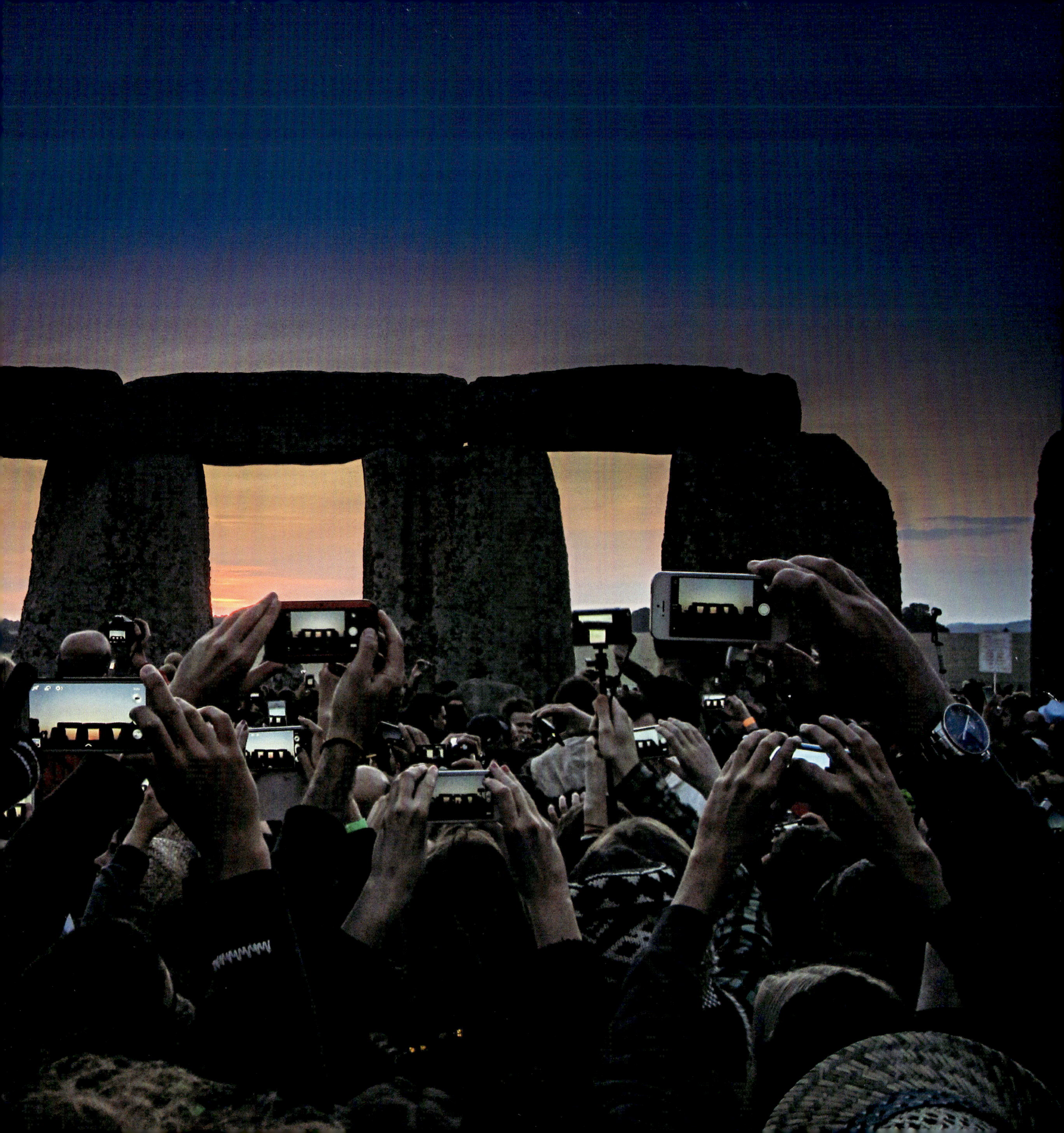

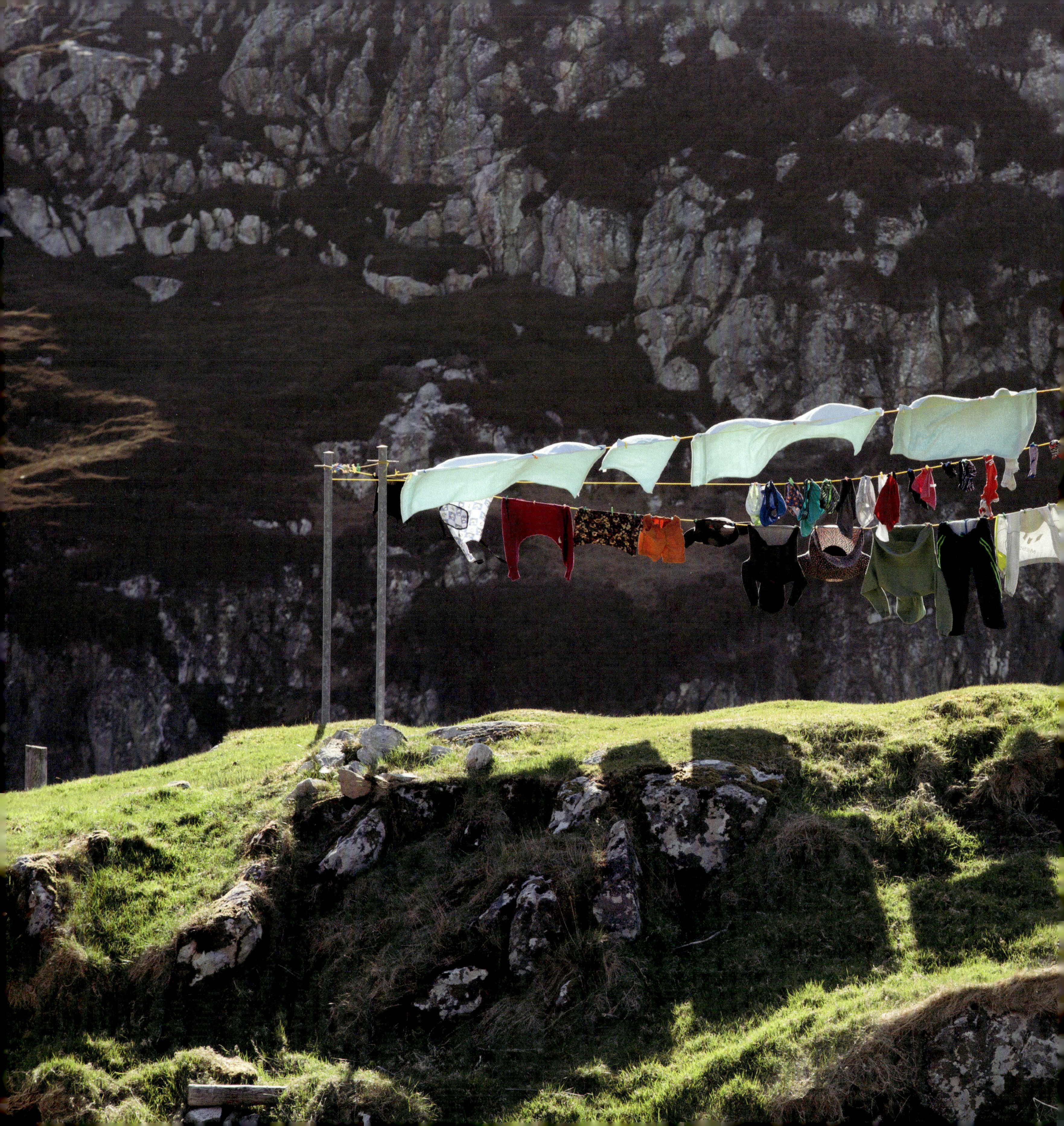

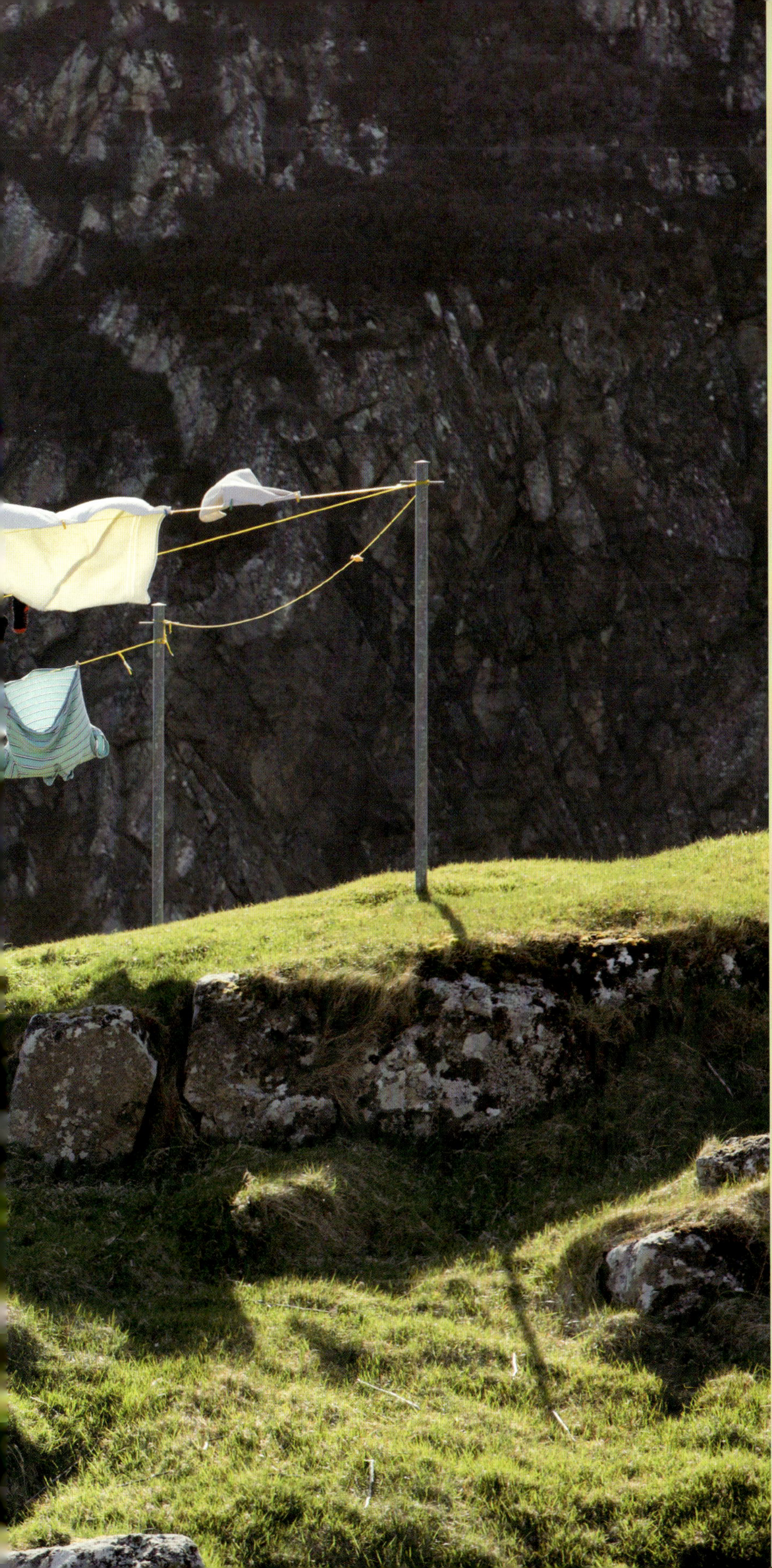

1 RURAL LIFE

Rural Life covers all aspects of life within the villages and small communities outside our towns and cities.

It captures the relationship between people, the land and the coast, including agriculture, farming, fishing, local trade, country fairs, crafts, events, traditions, customs, culture, sport and leisure.

◗ STEVE MORGAN / WINNER

Blown washing
Isle of Lewis, Outer Hebrides, Scotland

Washing drying on a blustery day next to a croft on South Harris in the Outer Hebrides. After spotting it whilst driving along the Golden Road on the east coast of Harris, I jumped out of the car on the single track road to catch the backlit scene before the sun disappeared behind the clouds again.

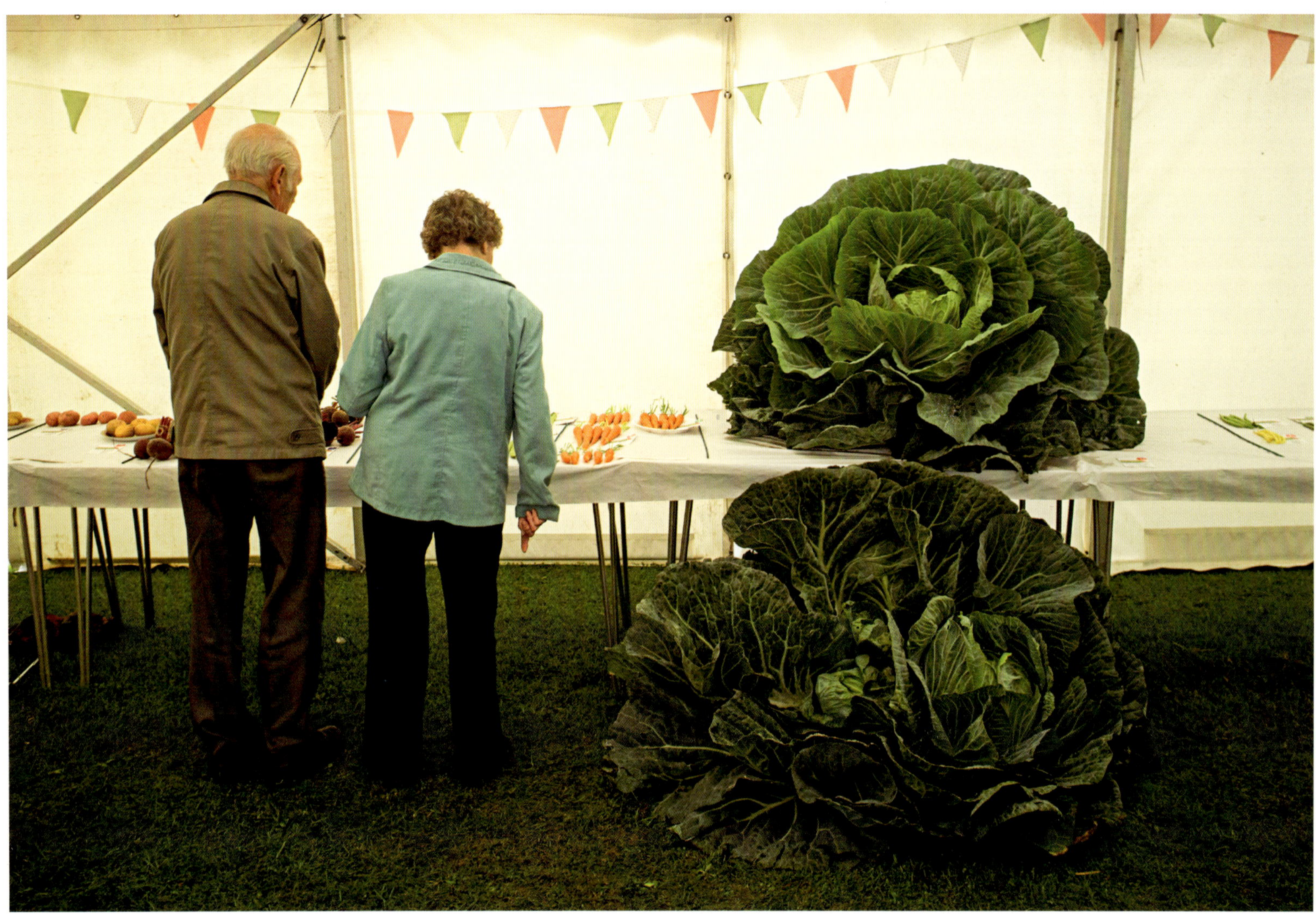

MARK HARRISON / HIGHLY COMMENDED

Best in show
Ewelme, Oxfordshire

Clearly the quite extraordinary cabbages could easily have been the subject of this picture but I wanted to try and capture something of the simple timeless tradition of the local horticultural show and the couple looking at the carrots under the bunting helped to do that for me.

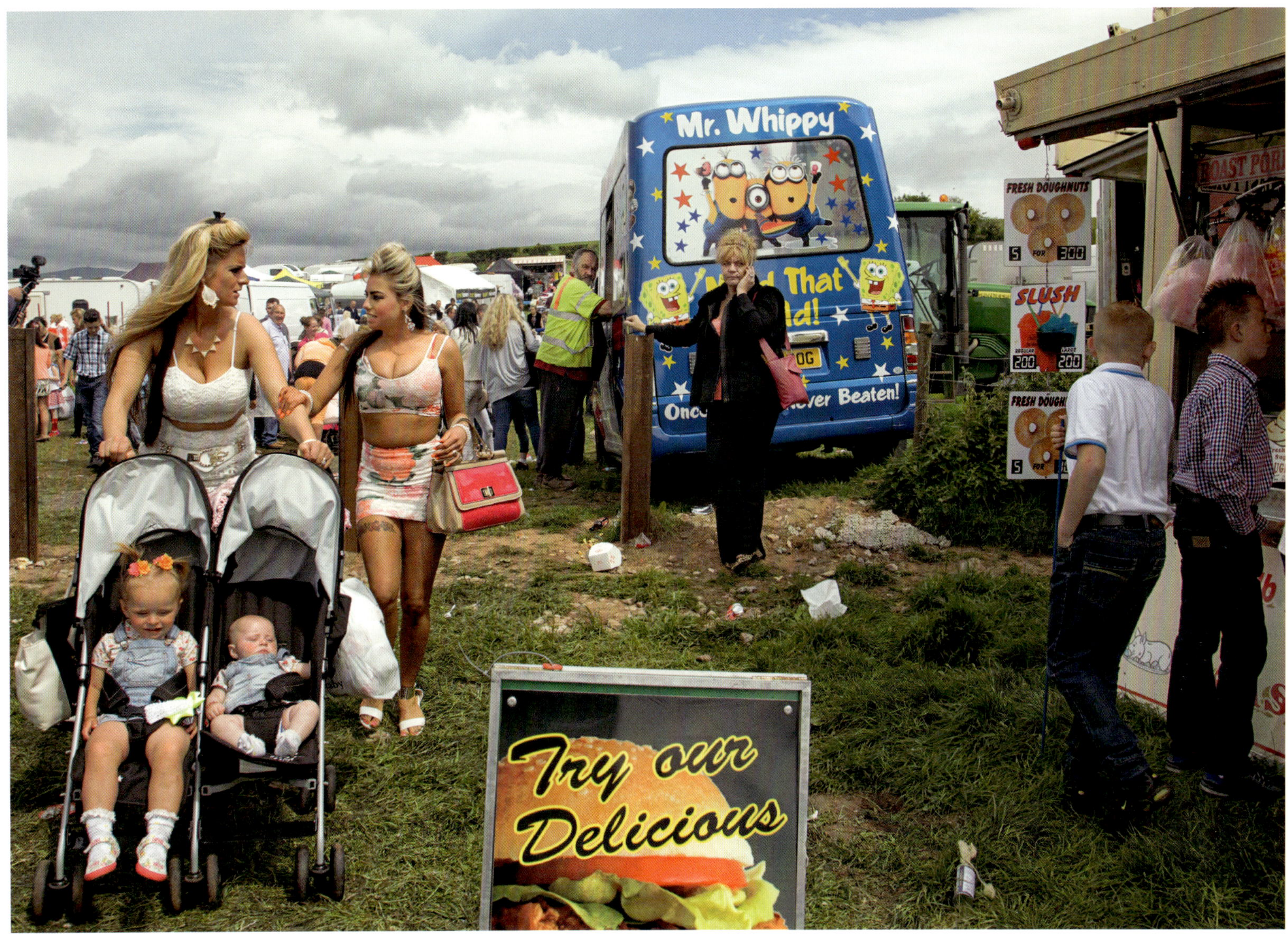

⬥ CHRISSIE WESTGATE / HIGHLY COMMENDED

All the fun of the Fair
Appleby Horse Fair, Cumbria

Taken at the annual Horse Fair where Gypsy Travellers and their families gather to buy and sell horses, enjoy time together and celebrate their culture.

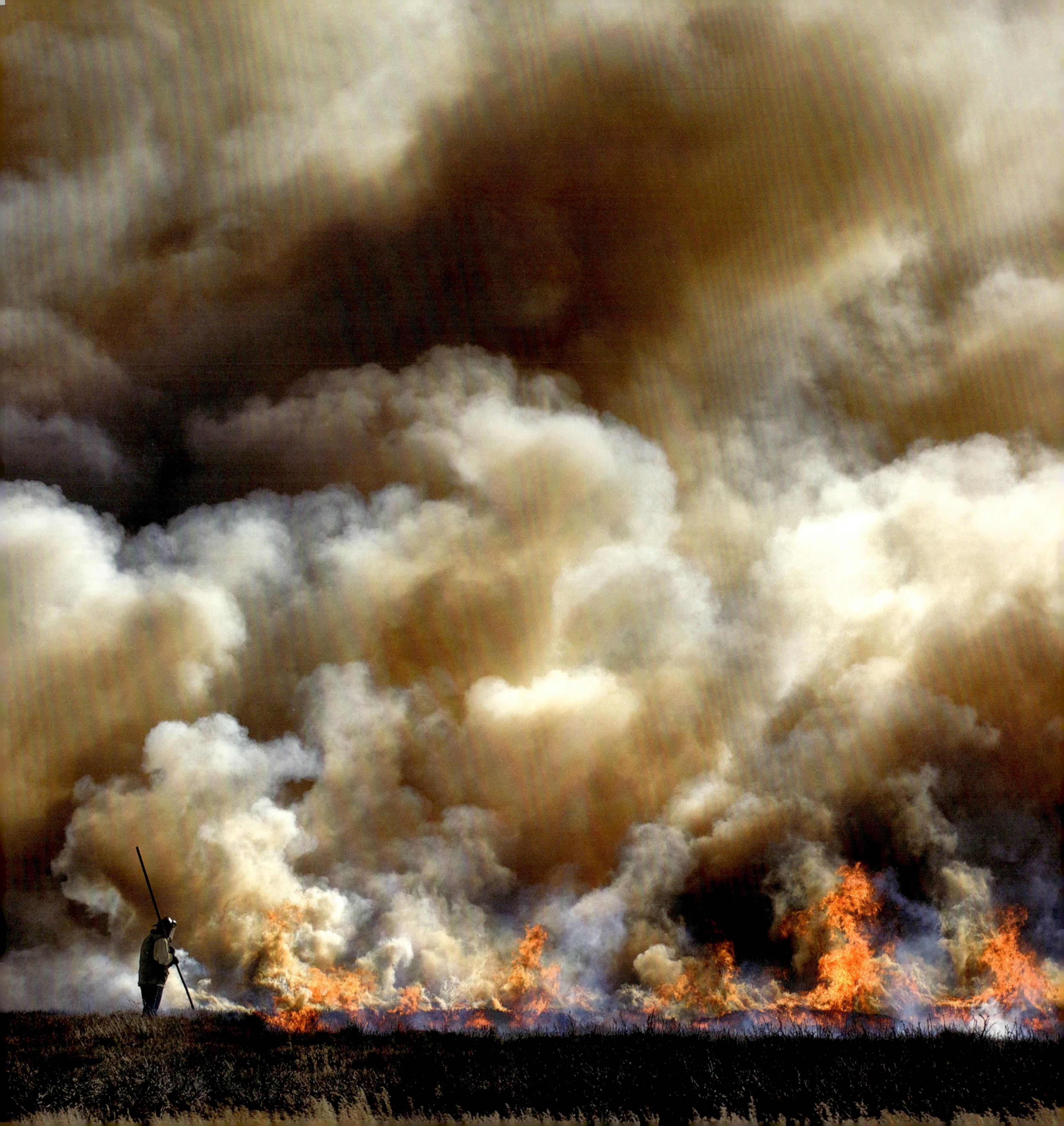

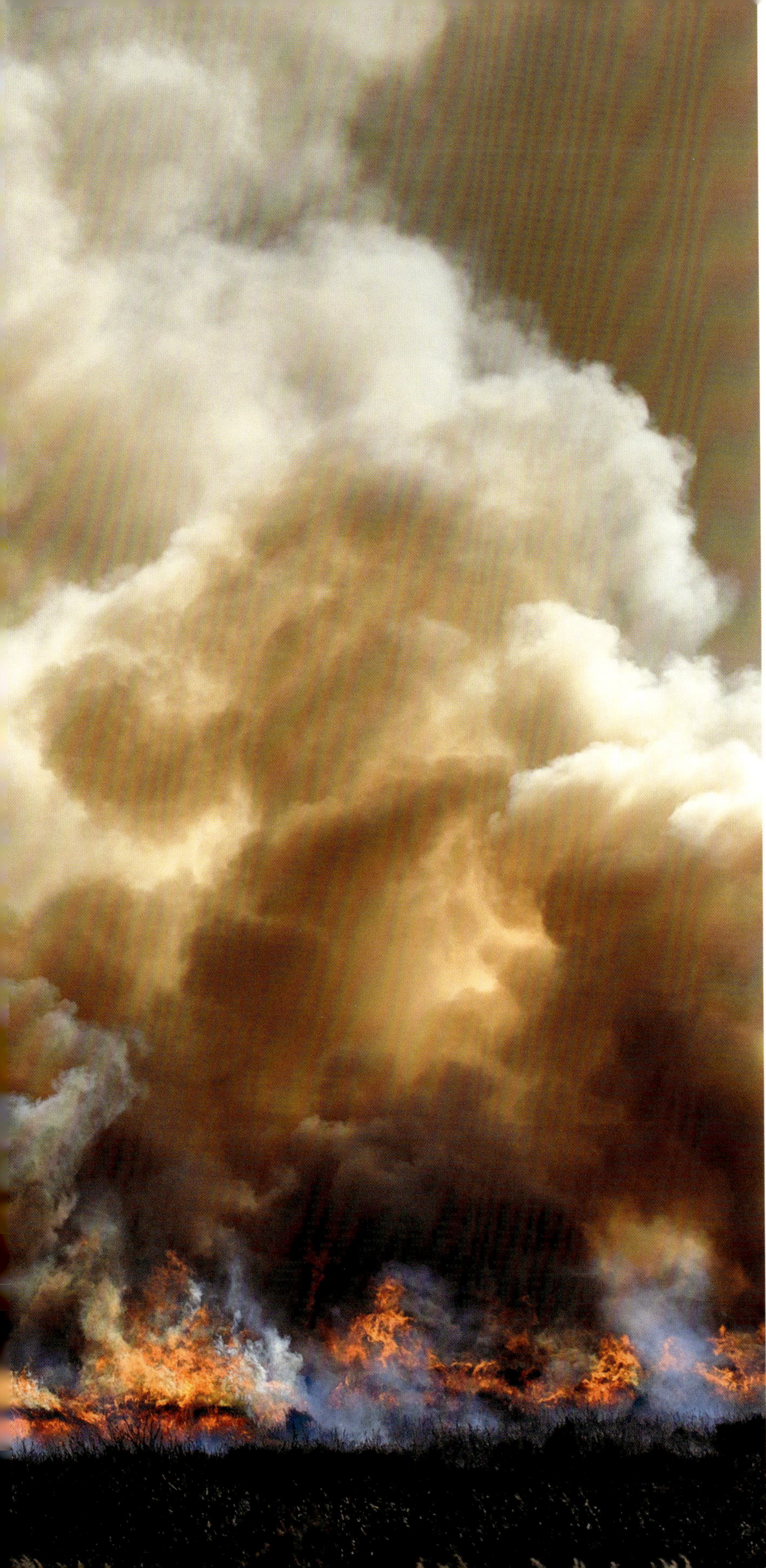

PAUL ANTHONY WILSON
HIGHLY COMMENDED

Burning The Heather
North Yorkshire Moors

Travelling towards Middlesbrough on the North Yorkshire Moors I noticed huge plumes of smoke billowing into the air, it turned out to be controlled heather burning. Carried out between April and October this stimulates new growth, providing good grazing for sheep and an ideal habitat for wild birds. I placed the 'beater' in the bottom corner to provide scale and show the enormity of the scene.

Country Mists
South Downs

I shot this image in the South Downs, knowing that summer mists can be quite beautiful in this part of the country, especially in the rural areas. To get to this vantage point, it took a 2am train ride, a rather frustrating drive through thick fog and a 1 hour trek in the dark – absolutely worth it!

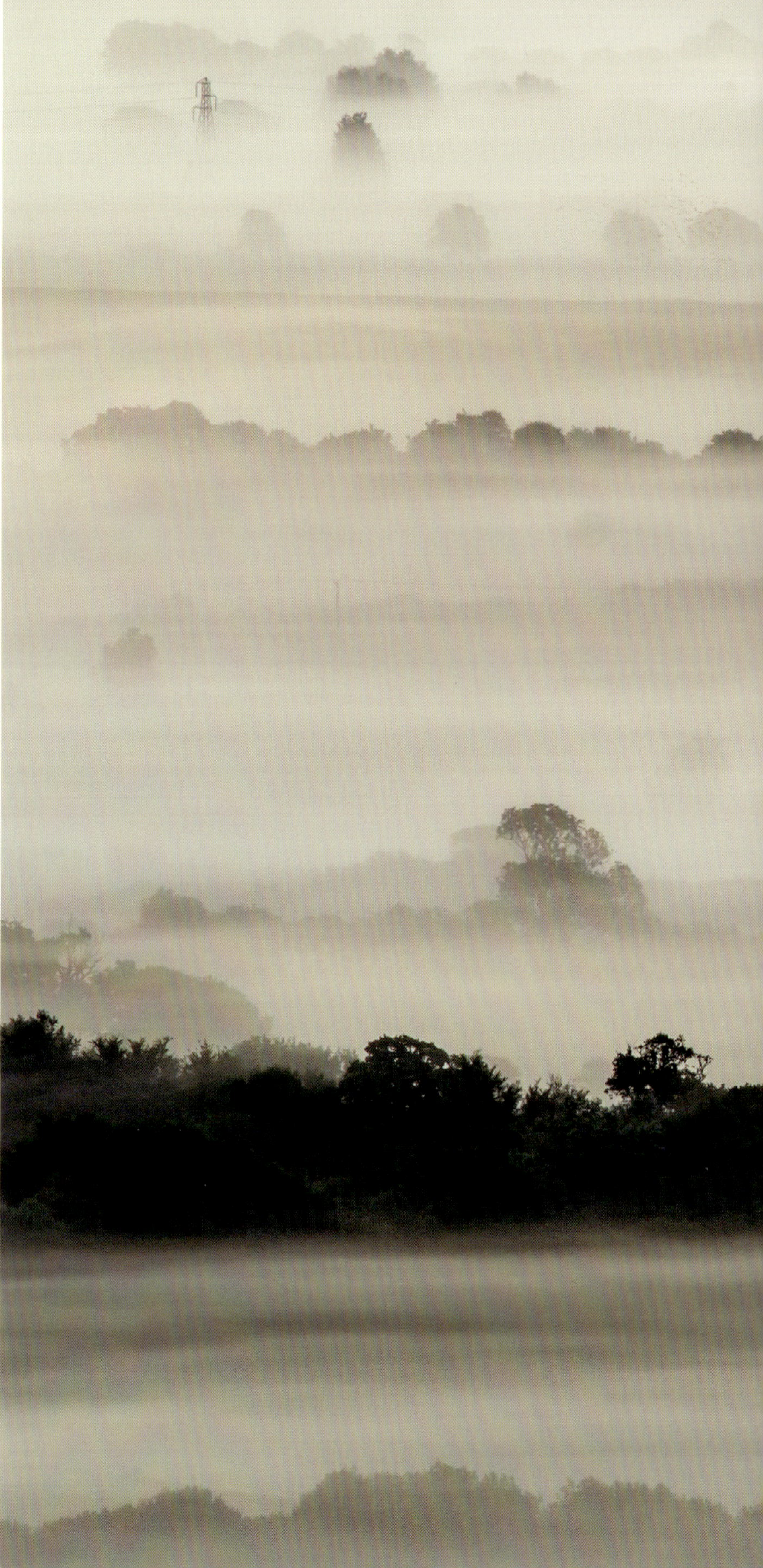

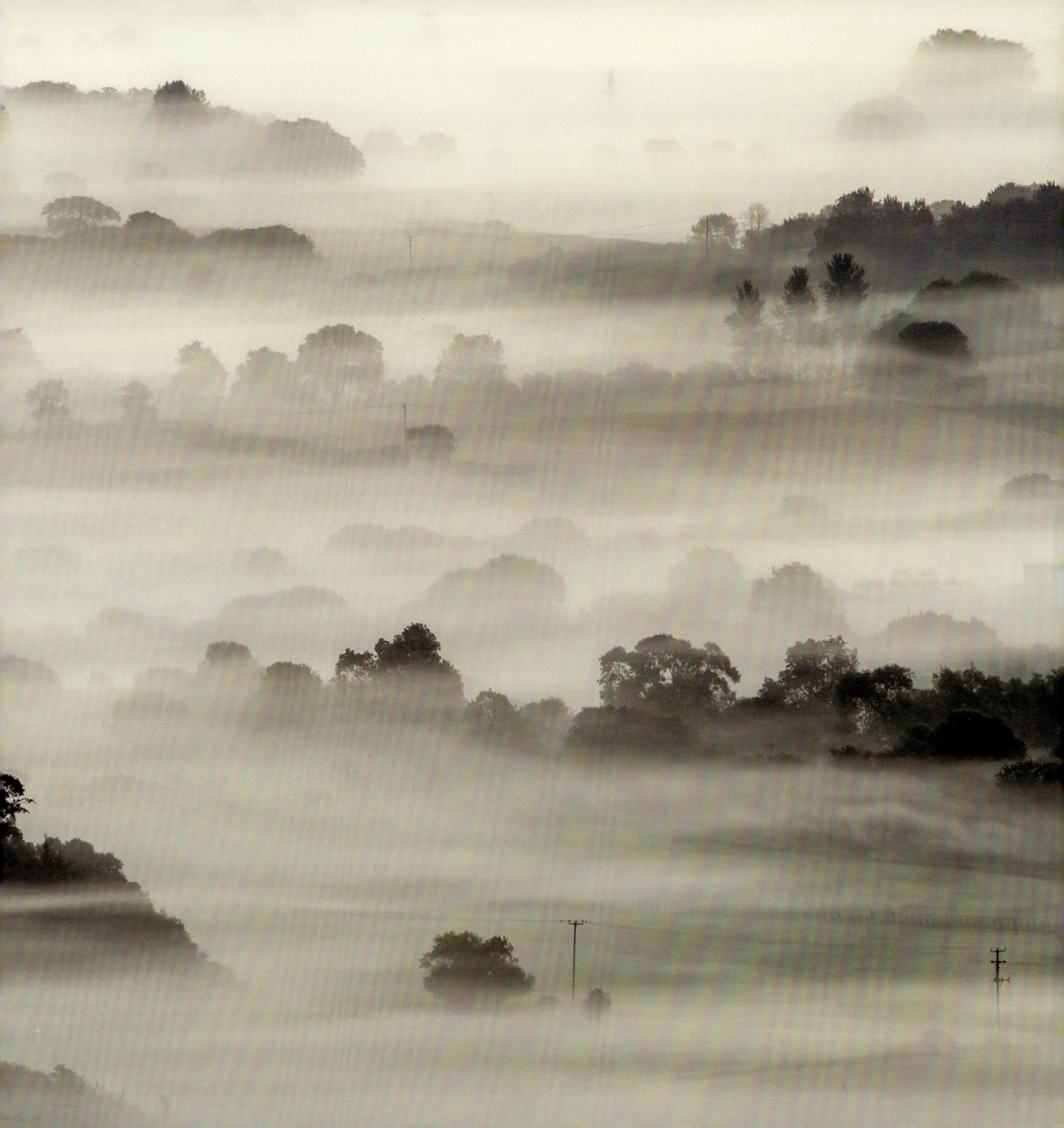

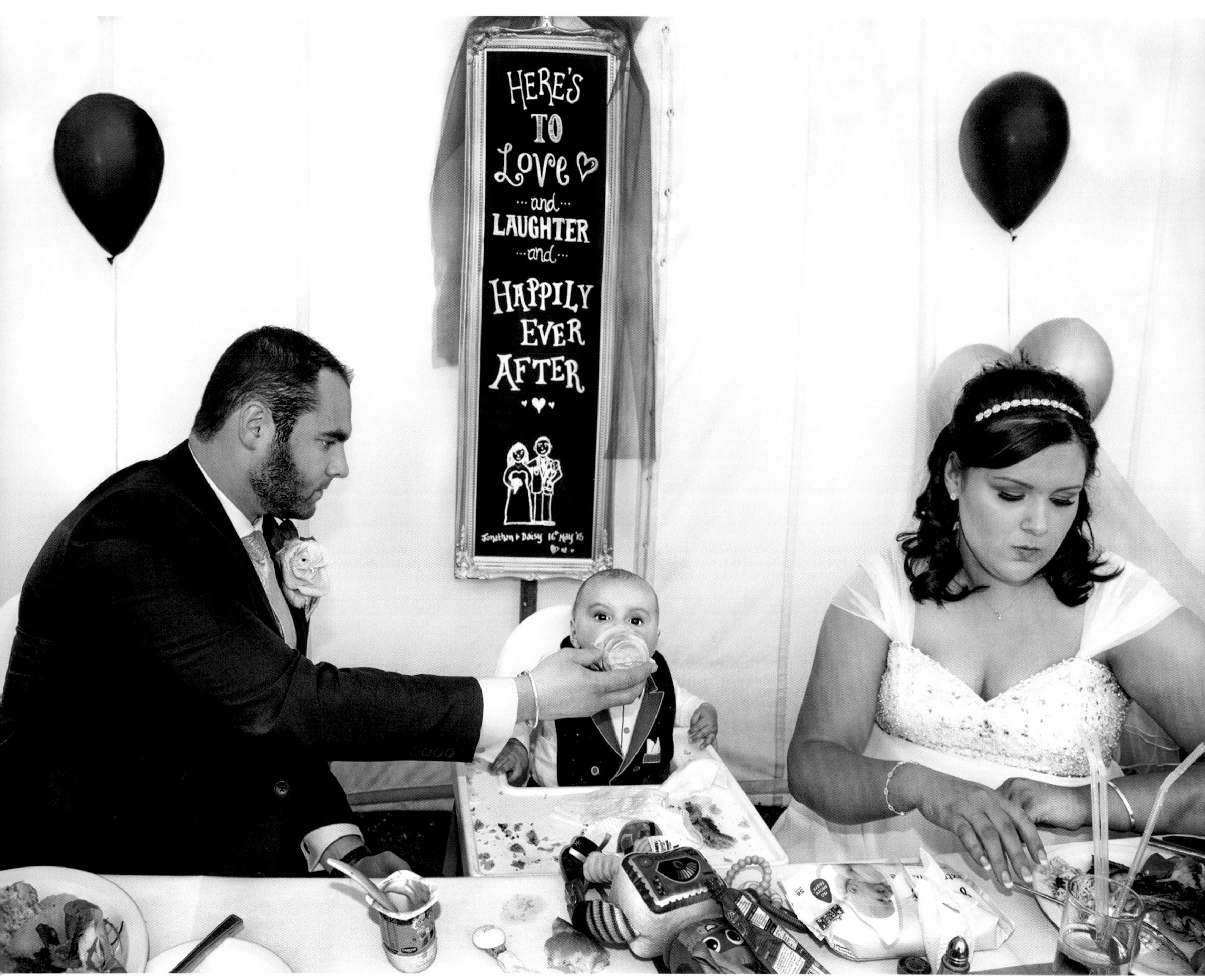

HERE'S
TO
LOVE
...and...
LAUGHTER
...and...
HAPPILY
EVER
AFTER
Jonathon & Daisy 16th May '15

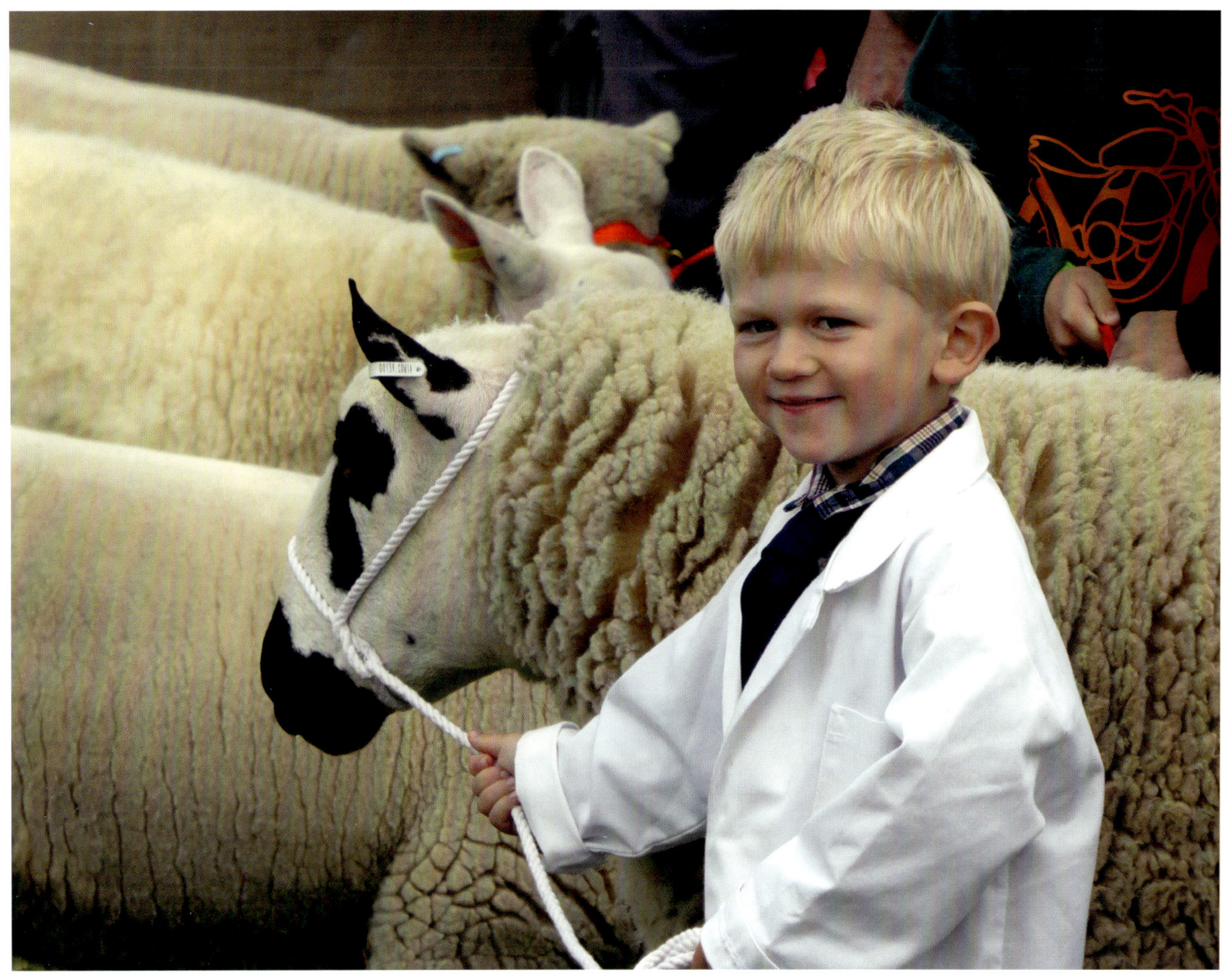

The Wedding Day
Wedding Marquee, Essex

Here's to love, laughter and happily ever after for Daisy,
Jonni and baby Woody.

◔ JANE JARVIS

At the Show
Bucks County Show
Aylesbury, Buckinghamshire

A day out at Bucks County Show. A young lad holds
on tightly to his lamb in the show ring while the
judging takes place in the junior livestock class.

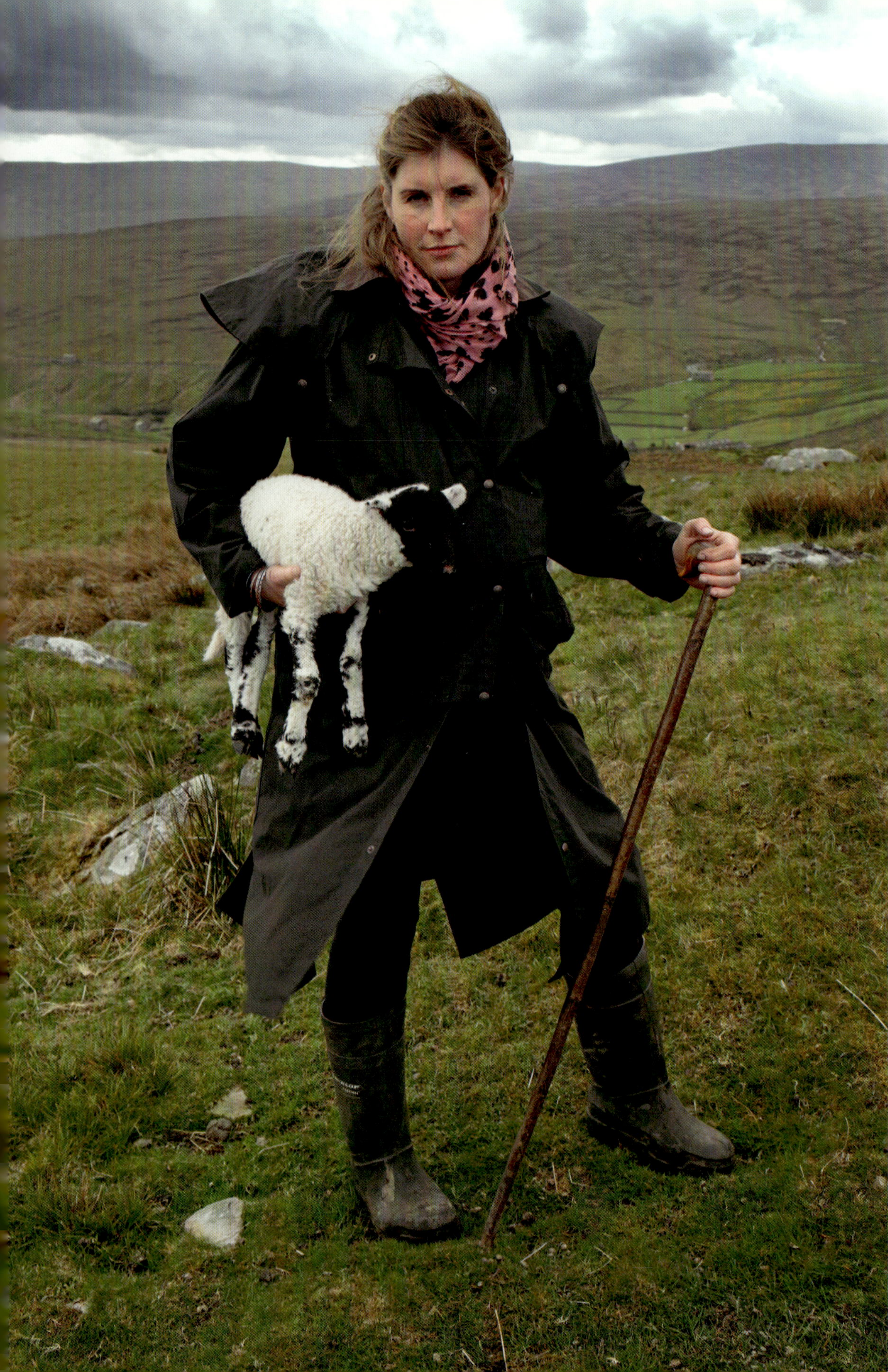

○ PAUL BERRIFF

Amanda Owen, shepherdess
Ravenseat, North Yorkshire

Yorkshire shepherdess Amanda Owen on the windswept moorland high above her farmhouse at Ravenseat in the Yorkshire Dales. Amanda was 8 months pregnant with her eighth child when I took this photograph. Apart from caring for her children, Amanda has almost 1000 sheep to look after 24/7 every day of the year. I was captivated by Amanda's love of life and her determination, which inspired me to take this photograph.

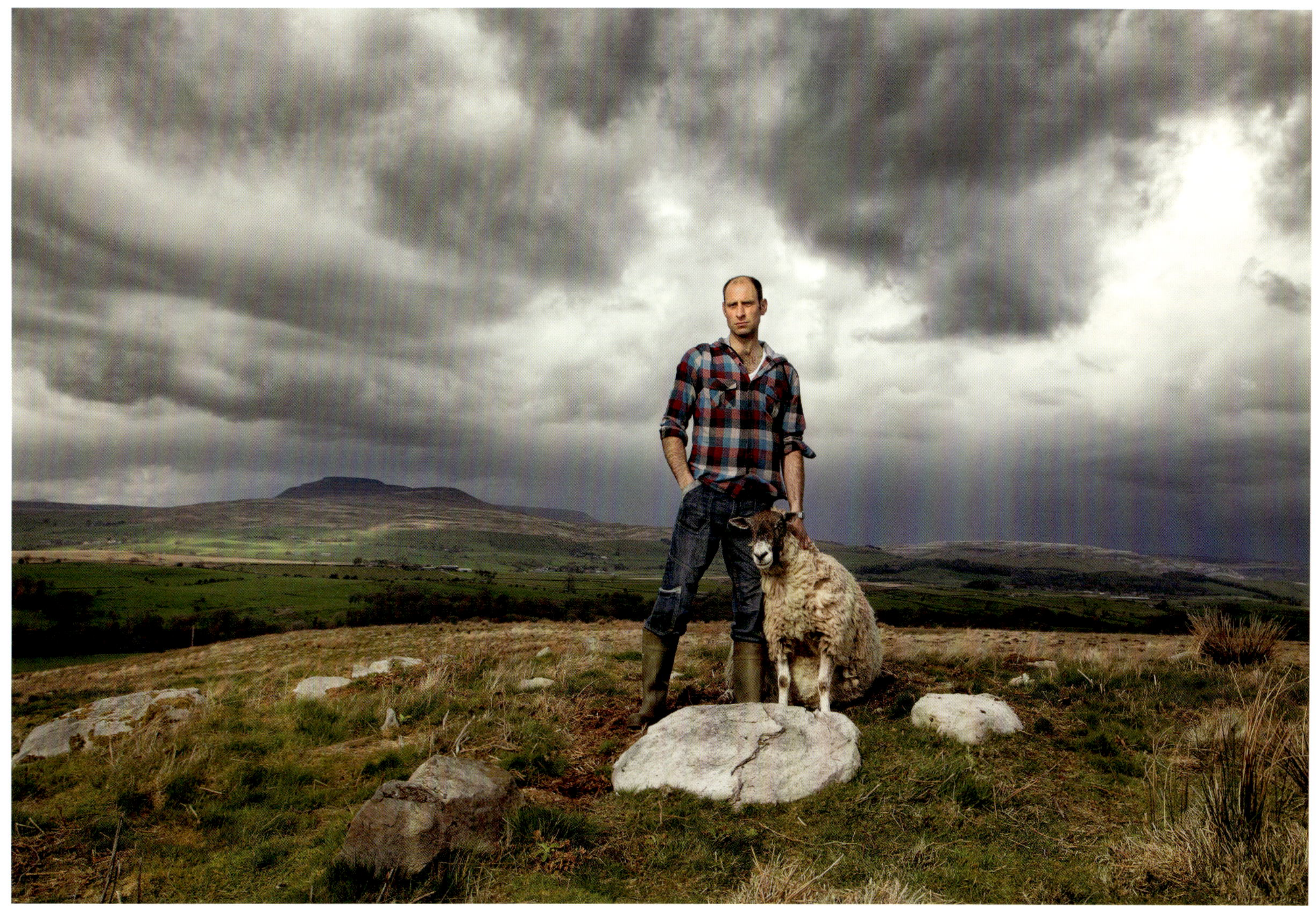

The Escapee
Bentham, North Yorkshire

This sheep had escaped from its field and been recaptured
by the farmer close to my house. I noticed the approaching
storm and asked him to pose. I asked one of his children to
hold a flash off camera for me and got a couple of shots
before it started to rain.

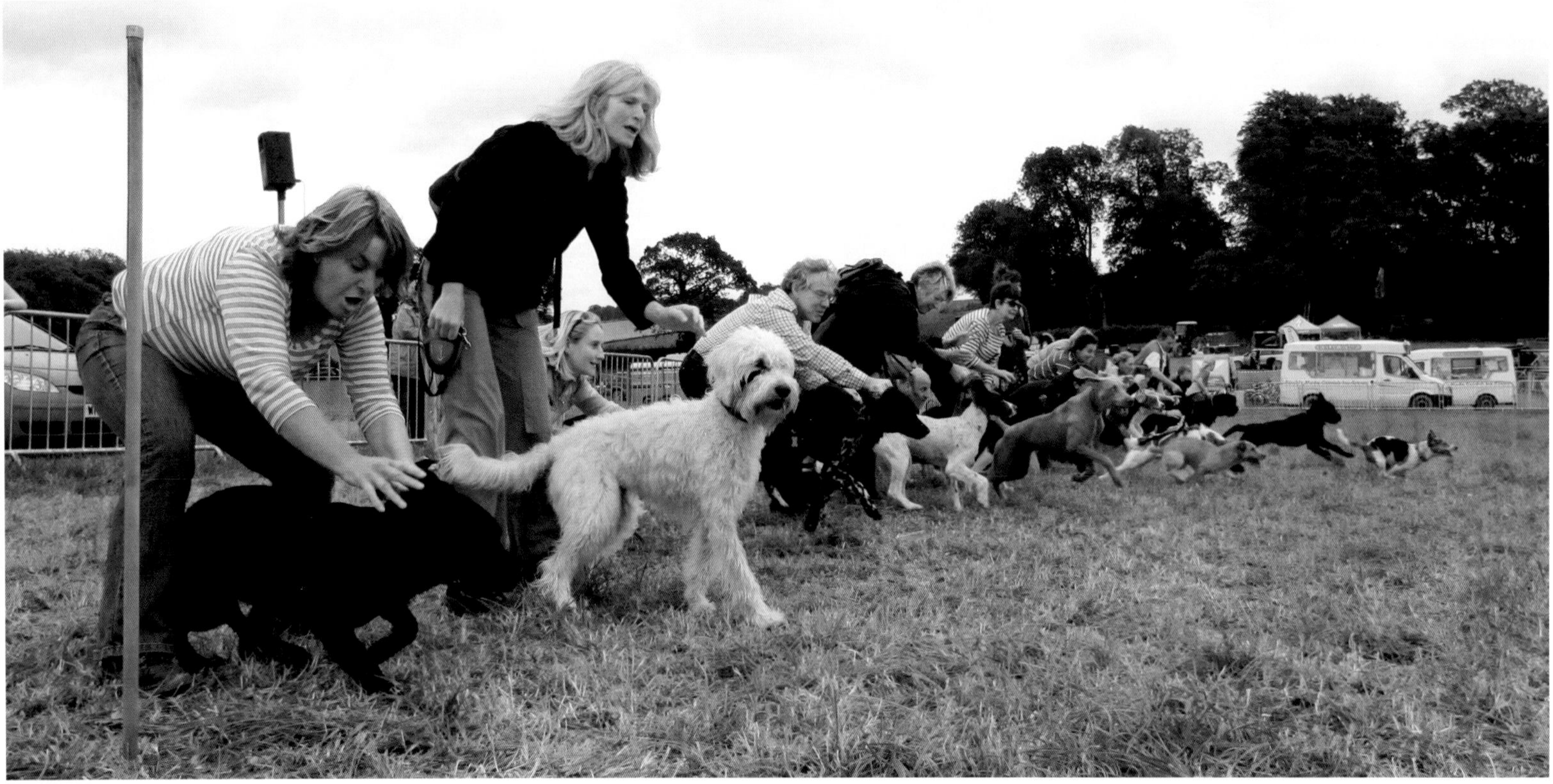

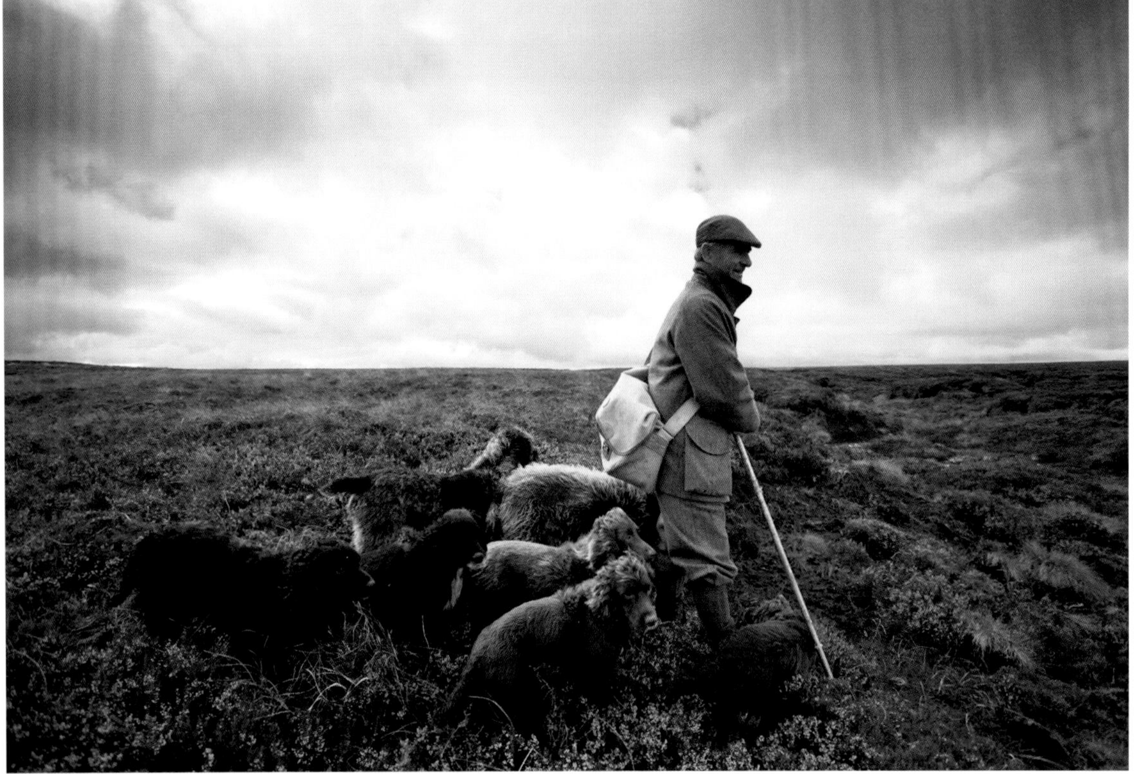

The Race
Totnes, Devon

The dog race at the annual Totnes Agricultural show. The enthusiasm of both owners and canine participants amused me!

JAKE EASTHAM

Gamekeeper
Upper Teesdale

A gamekeeper and his gundogs survey the moor between drives.

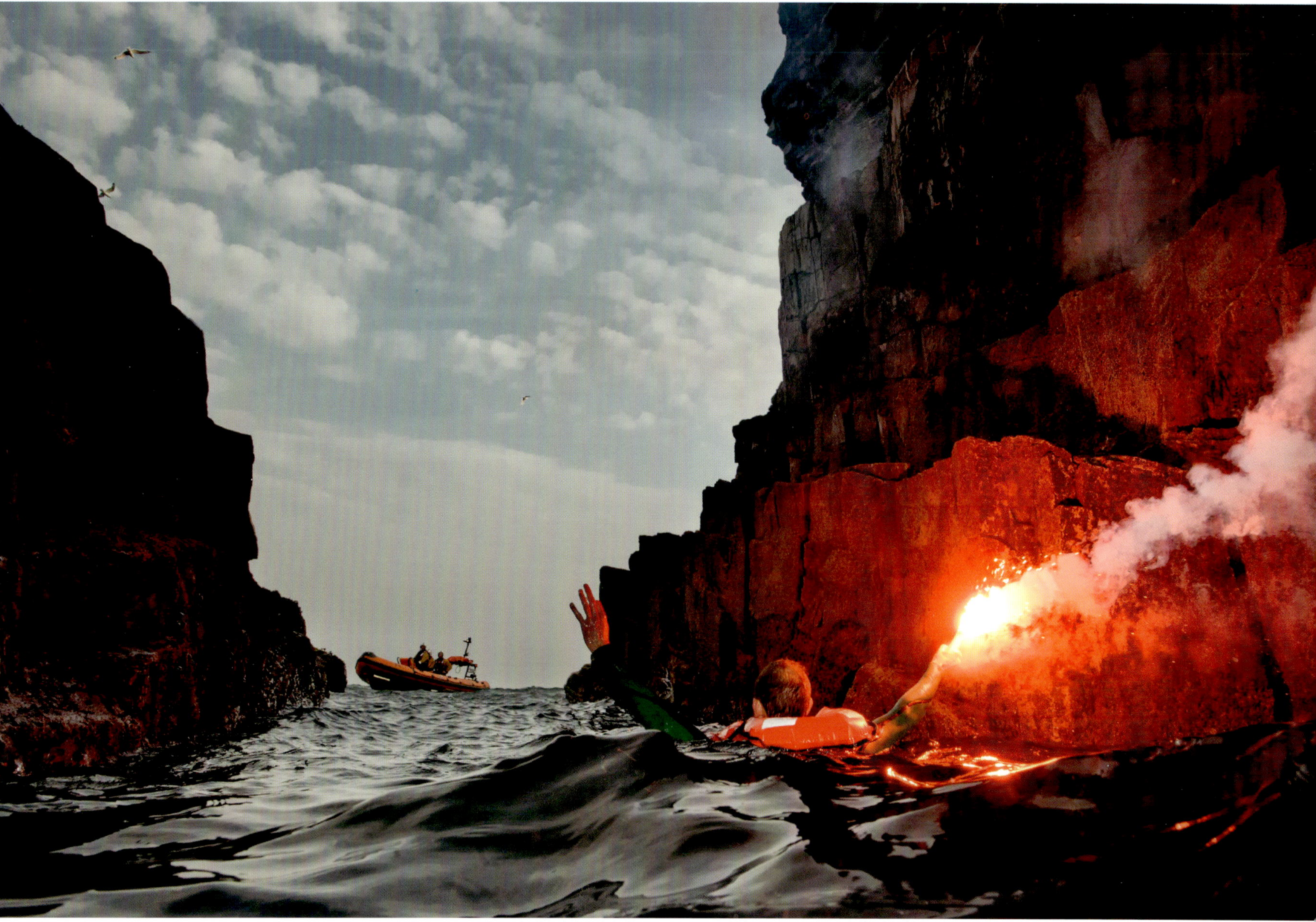

⬡ GRAHAM EATON

I'm In Here!
Abersoch, Gwynedd, Wales

I wanted a view from within a sea cave of someone in the water, with
an approaching or searching lifeboat. I wanted to capture the drama,
and light with the cave illuminated by a flare, the sense of desperation,
stress, hope. The volunteers of the RNLI have saved many lives, often in
horrendous conditions and deserve our appreciation and support.

2

URBAN LIFE

Architecture and the built environment are an integral part of urban society, conveying mood, atmosphere and history.

Urban Life illustrates our towns and cities at work.

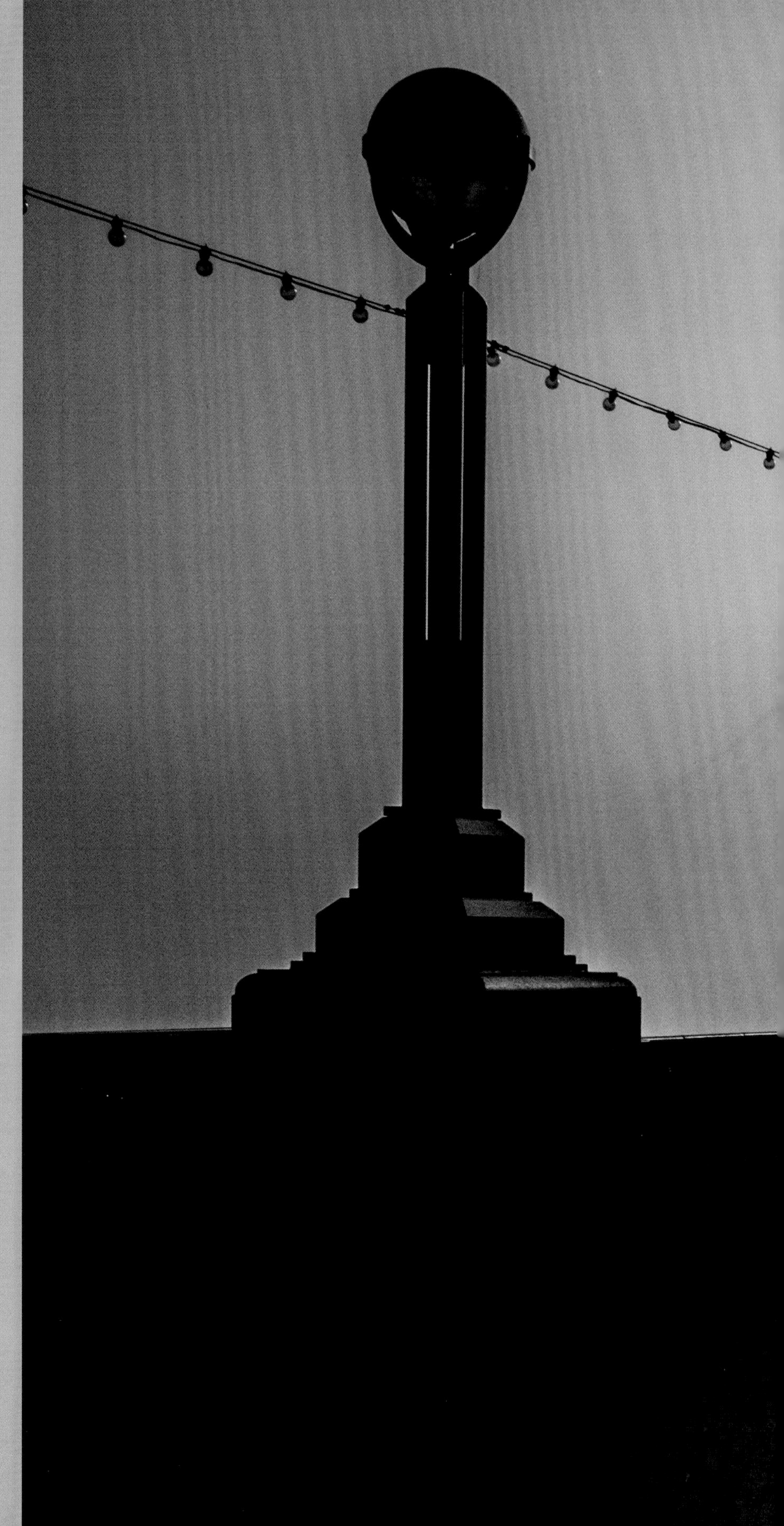

NICK ISDEN / WINNER

Morning Fog over Tower Bridge
London

An early morning fog envelops Tower Bridge as commuters make their way to work.

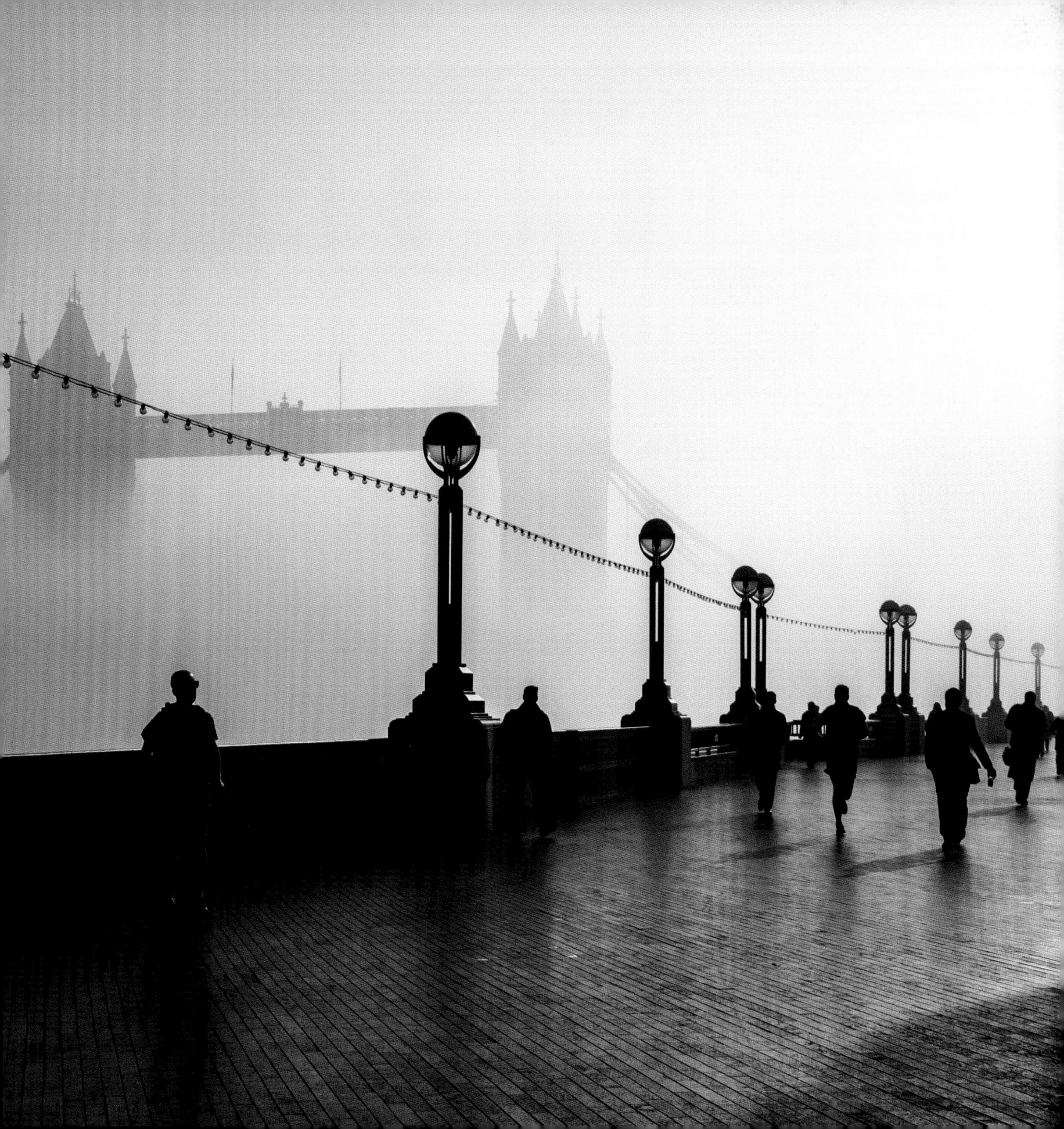

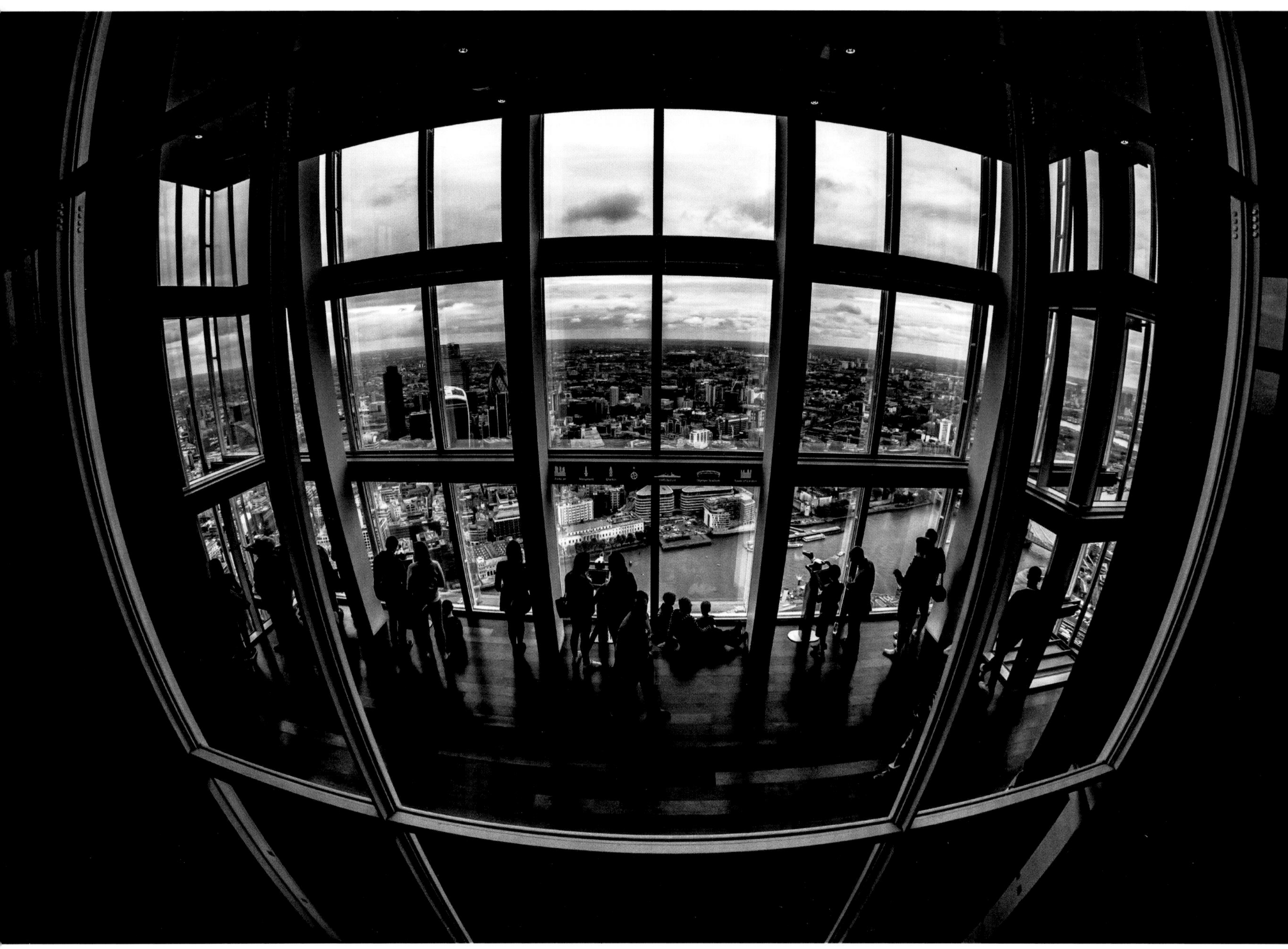

○ SIMON HADLEIGH-SPARKS / HIGHLY COMMENDED

Eyes on London
The Shard, London

The view from The Shard wasn't as scary as I had anticipated but I still couldn't go near the windows. I'd won tickets to go up otherwise I may not have done so – fear of heights. This is from the floor above the viewing floor. I love the collection of people looking and relaxing – almost as if watching the whole of London, and all that goes on, like impartial witnesses.

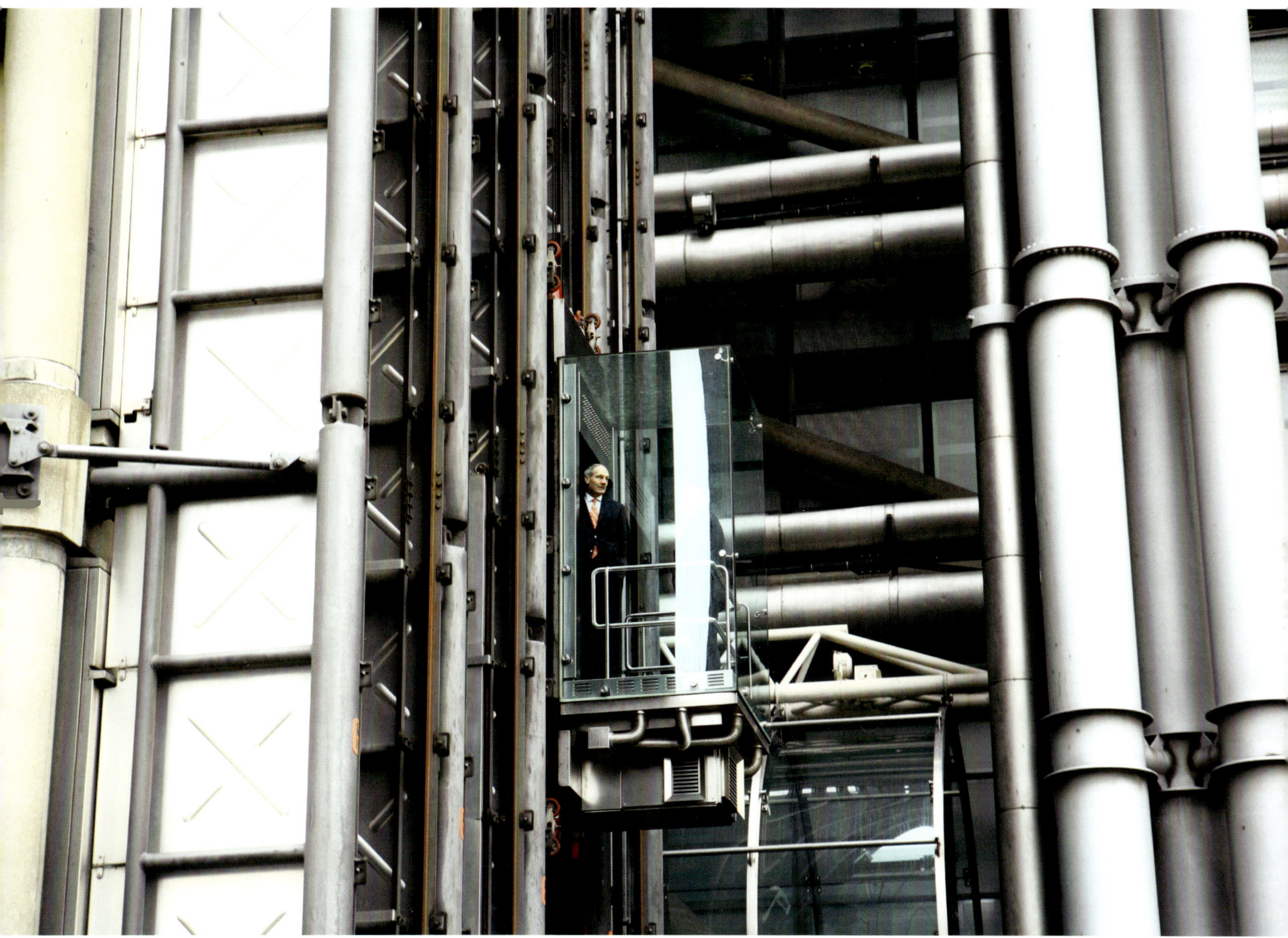

City of London

This picture is part of a project about the City of London and the people working in that area.

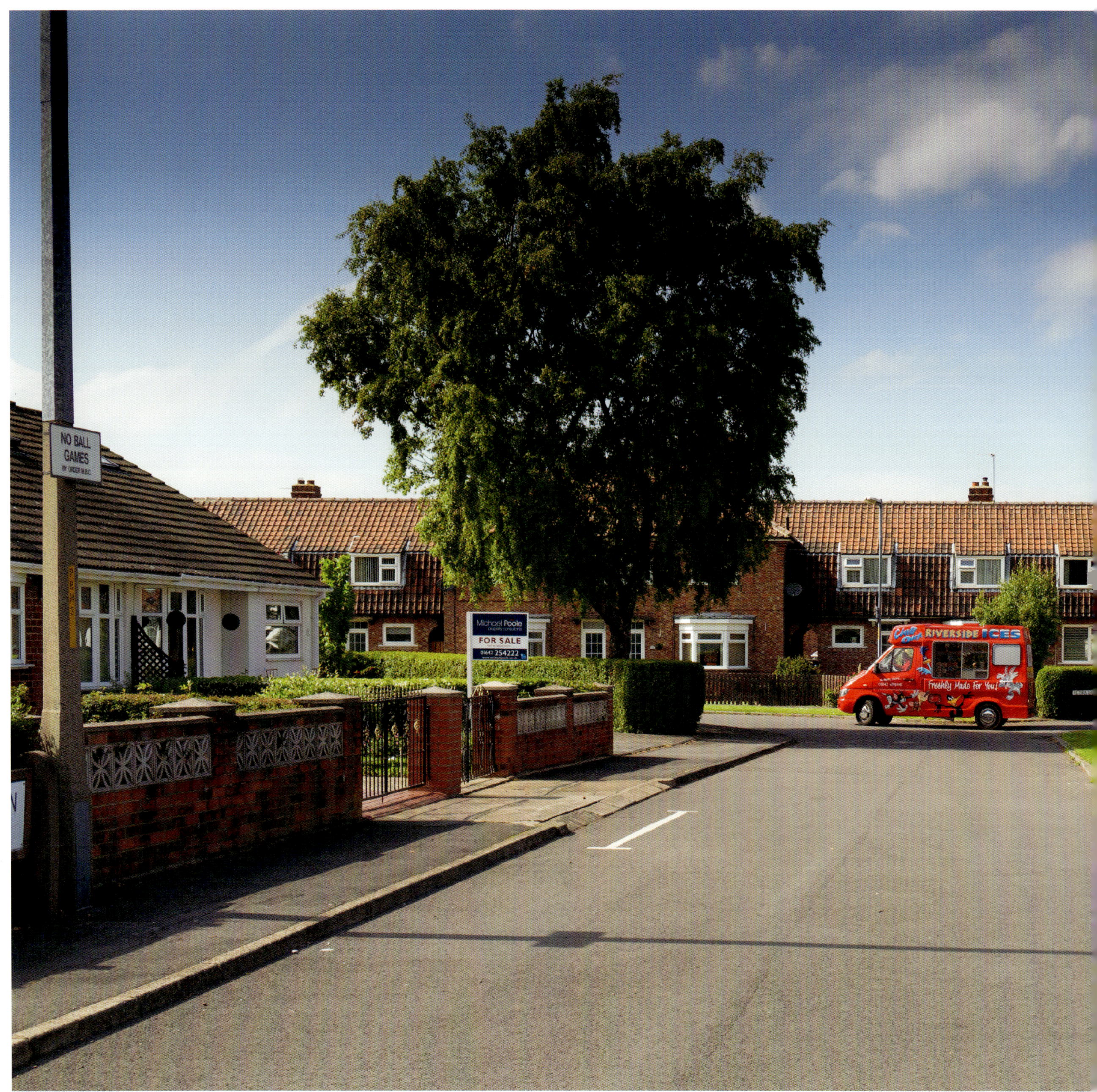

NO BALL
GAMES
BY ORDER M.B.C.

Michael Poole
FOR SALE
01642 254222

RIVERSIDE ICES
Freshly Made for You!

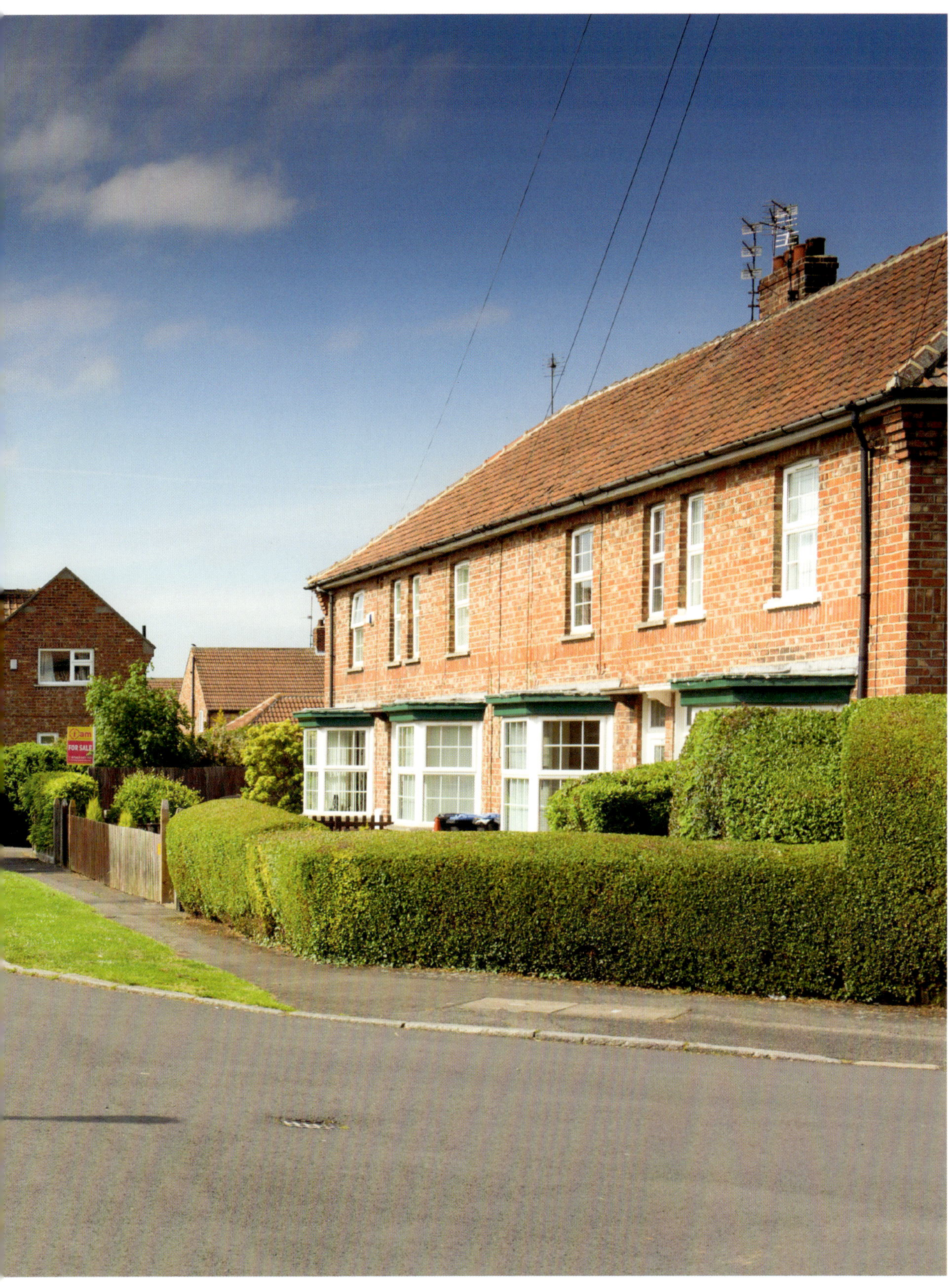

○ STEVE MORGAN
HIGHLY COMMENDED

Ice Cream Van
Middlesbrough, Teesside

An ice cream van from Riverside Ices plying its trade on a council estate in Middlesbrough.

A UK institution for over 100 years the ice cream van now faces stiff competition from supermarkets and home freezers. Apparently home double glazing has also hit the business as residents are no longer able to hear the chimes from the street as a van passes by outside.

◖ STEPHEN TAYLOR / HIGHLY COMMENDED

Reflections on the Tyne
Newcastle Quayside, Newcastle

The combination of slack water, and clear skies with only high level clouds and low winds meant that conditions were perfect for this wonderful reflection of the old and new architecture that makes up the Newcastle quayside. The photograph was taken at dusk.

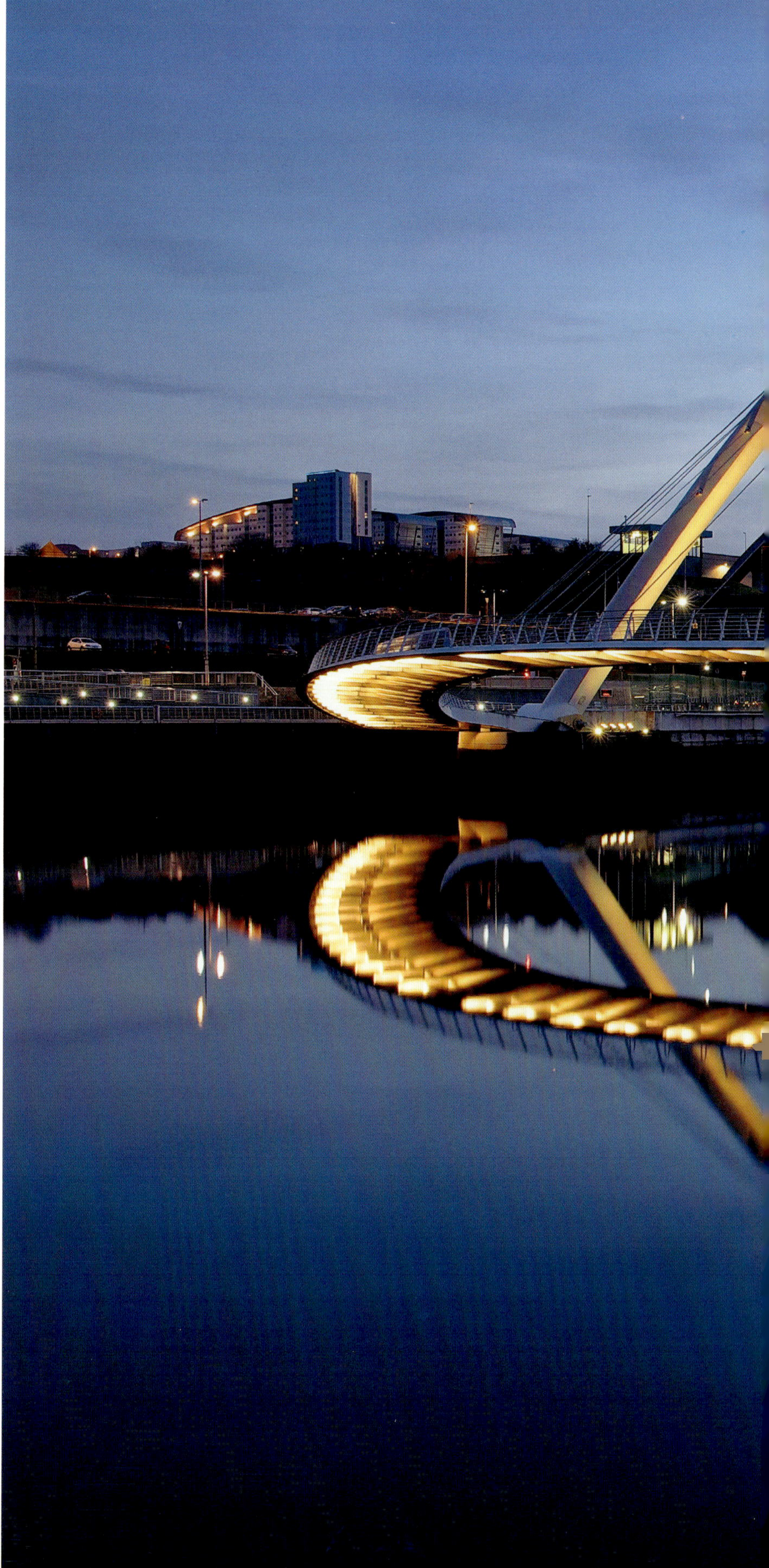

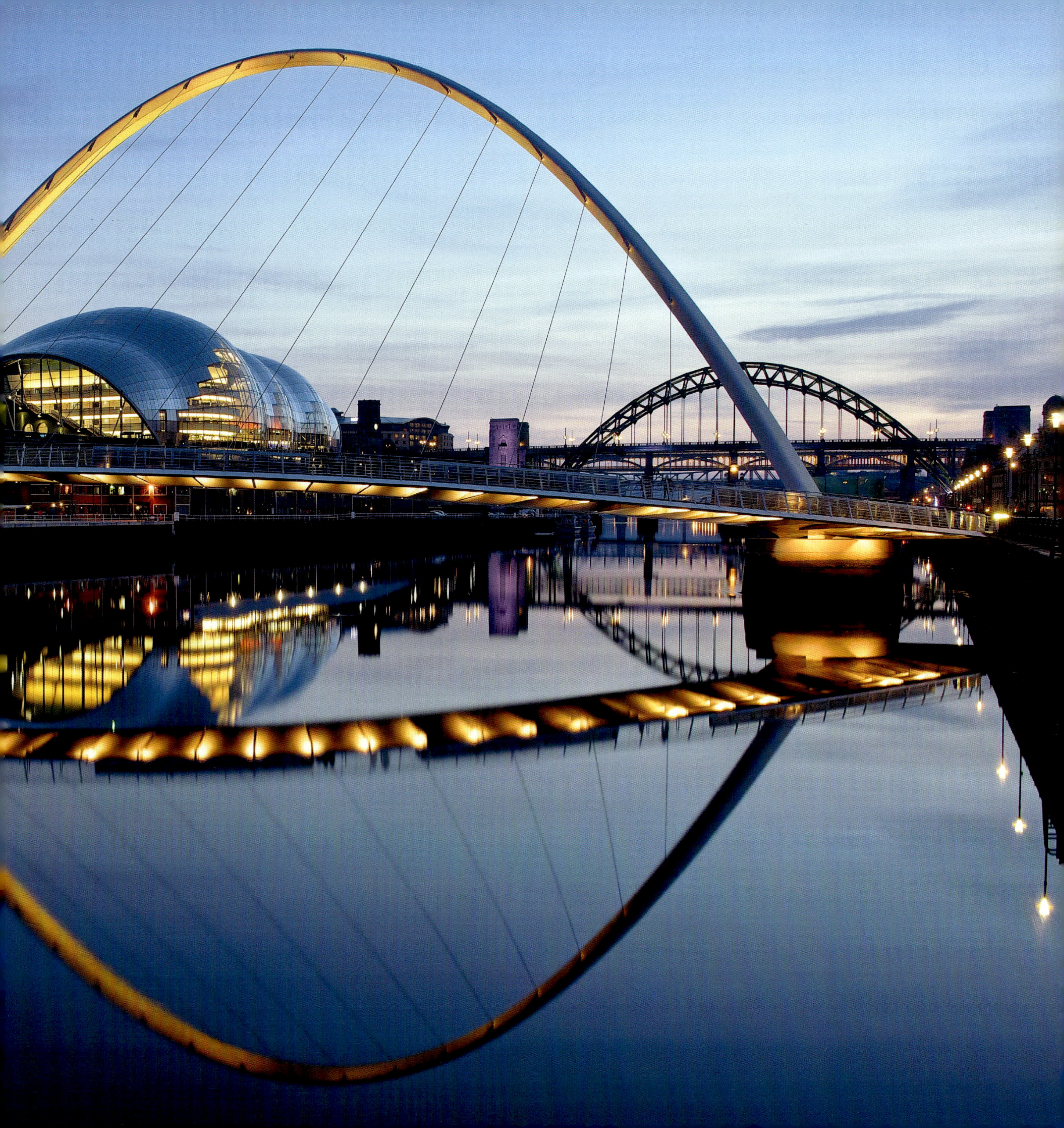

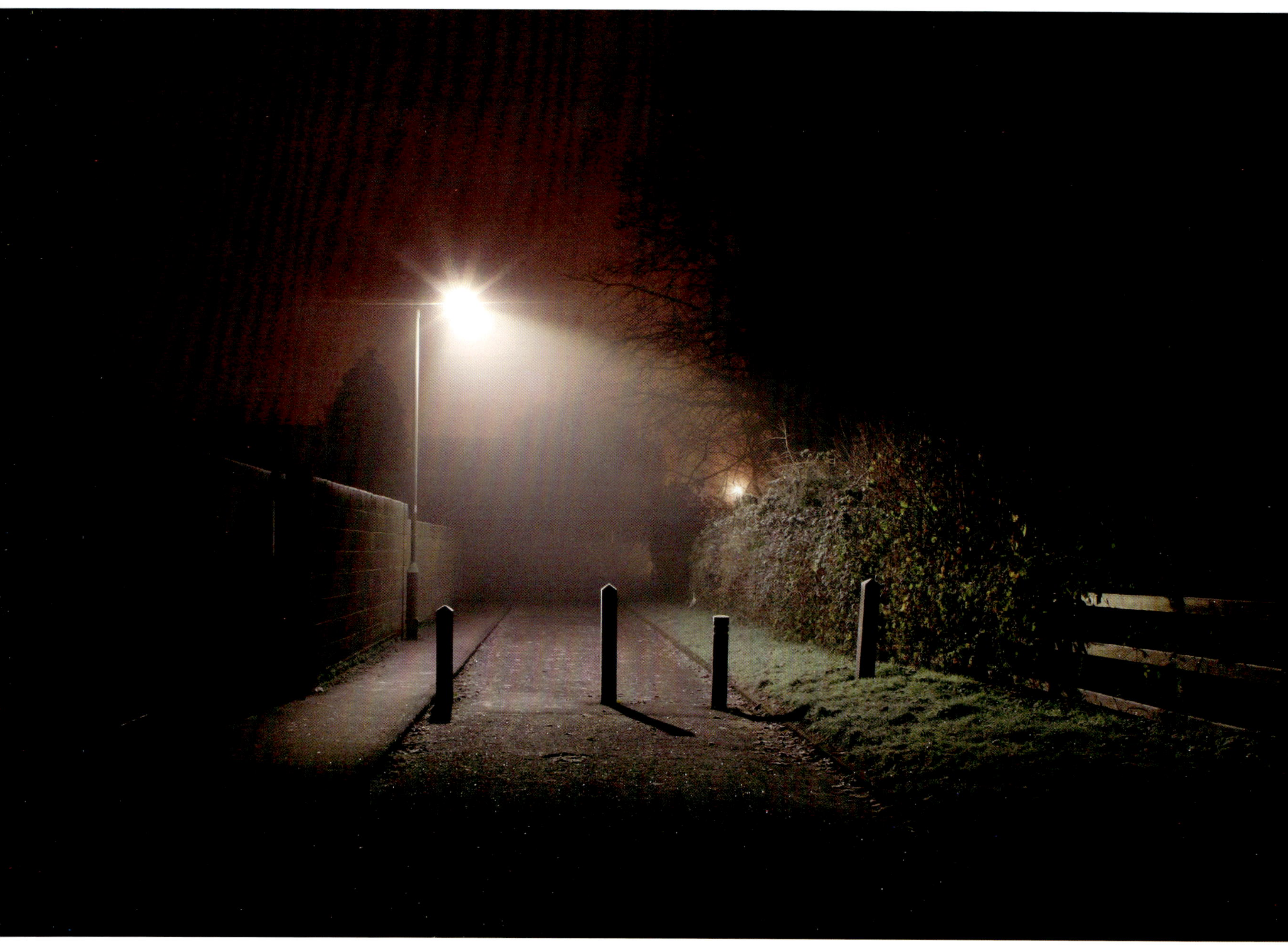

◔ ANDY MCKAY / HIGHLY COMMENDED

Early morning in Marston
Marston, Oxford, Oxfordshire

I was out photographing in my local area early one morning.
I liked the tunnel-view of the shot and the juxtaposition
between the bollards and the street light.

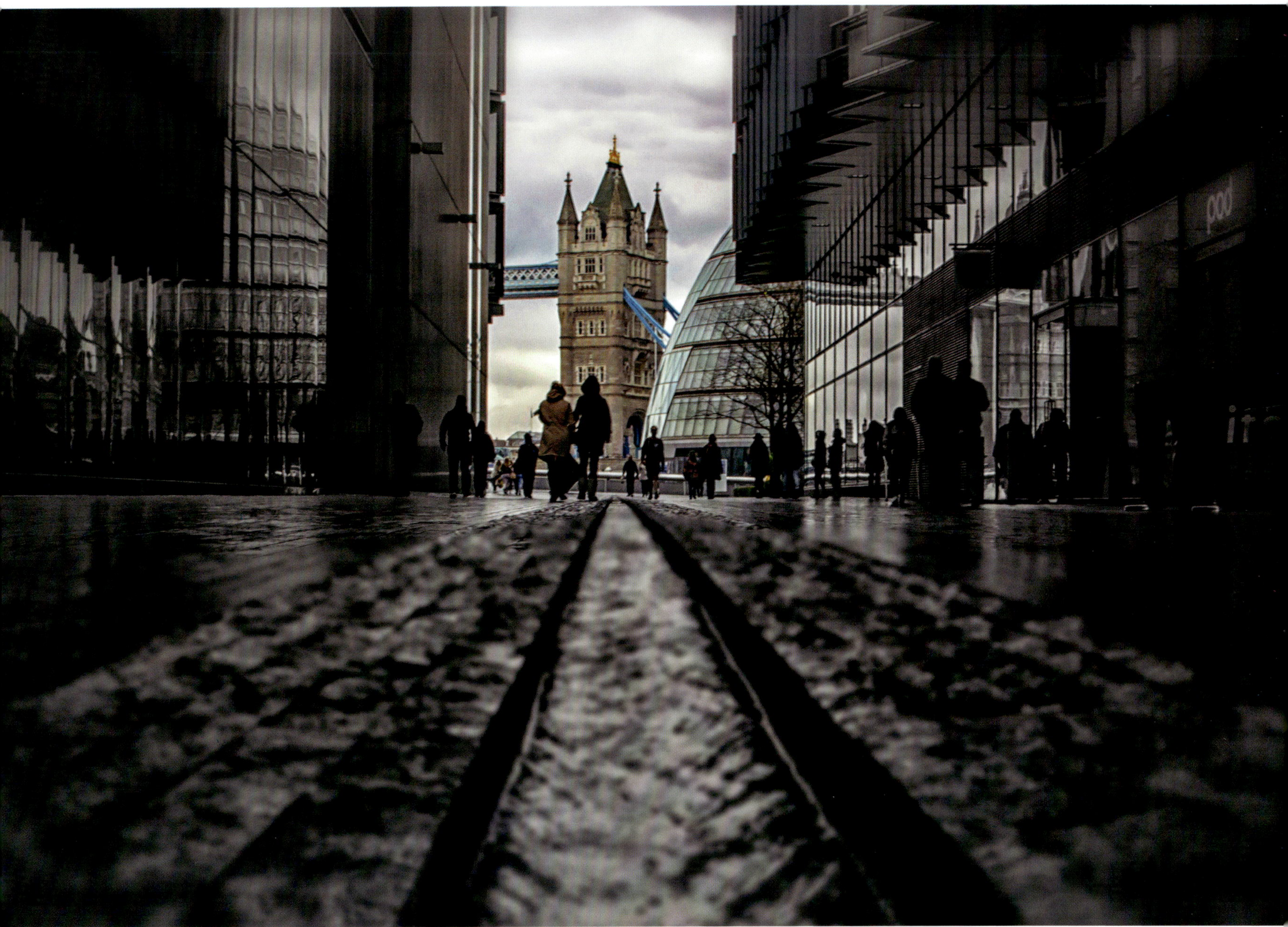

⬤ GEORGE GRIFFIN

More London
near Tower Bridge, London

More London has this water track running the length of it,
with little crossing points. I placed the camera on one of these
points and took a few pictures. I like the way the leading line
of the water track draws you to Tower Bridge and also the way
the people seem drawn to City Hall as if it was a spaceship.

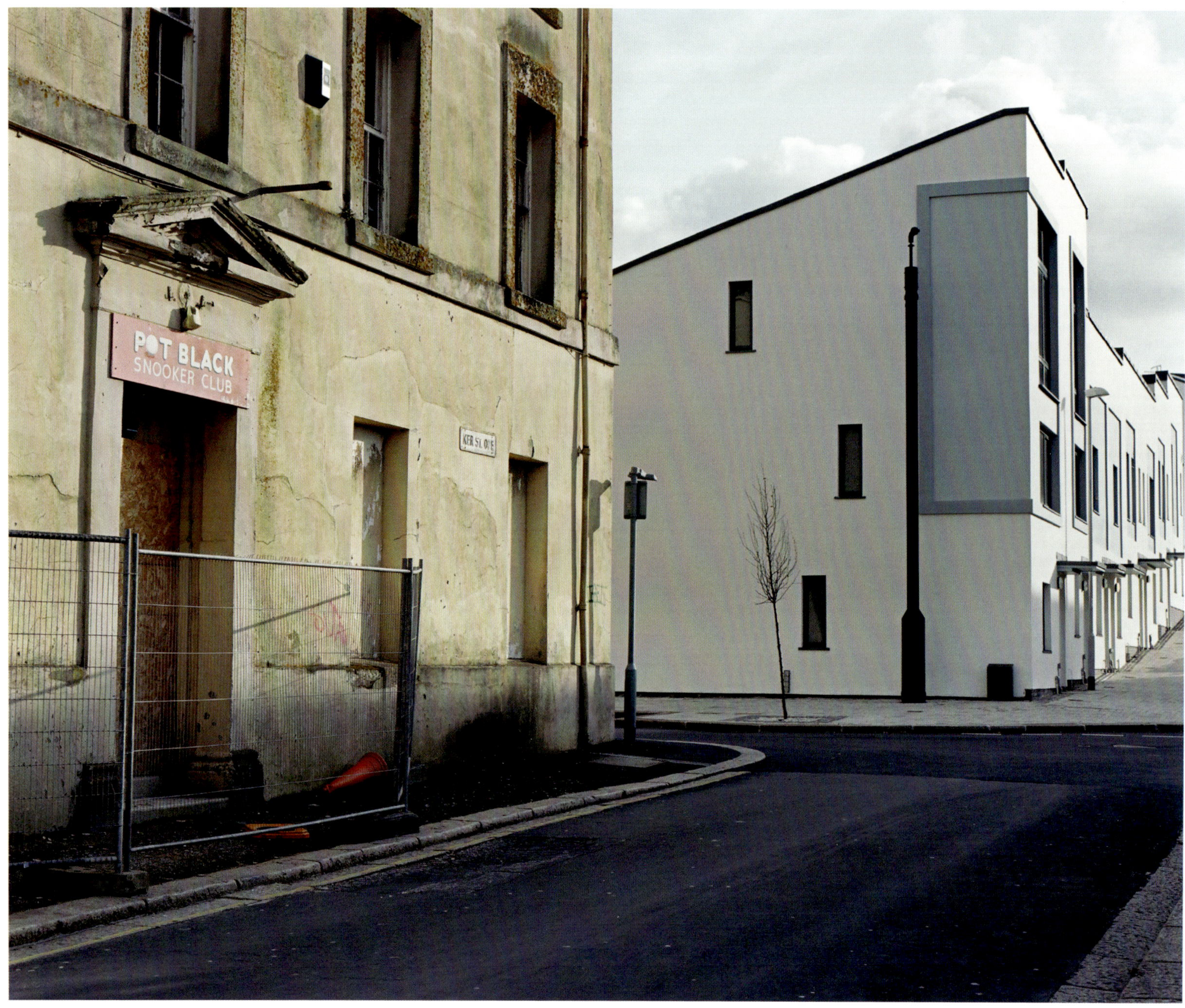

DOM MOORE

Regeneration of Devonport
Devonport, Plymouth

As an ongoing series I have been documenting the regeneration
of Devonport in Plymouth. With this image I wanted to capture
the juxtaposition in architectural style from old to new.

● NIGEL SAWYER

A misty London morning
Palace of Westminster, London

The mist was clearing rapidly when I reached Southbank and I had to take this shot using the wall to brace myself (tripods not allowed). I liked the layered effect created by the mist and the people crossing the bridge. I could say otherwise but the birds flying at the top left were fortuitous and not planned. They make the shot work for me.

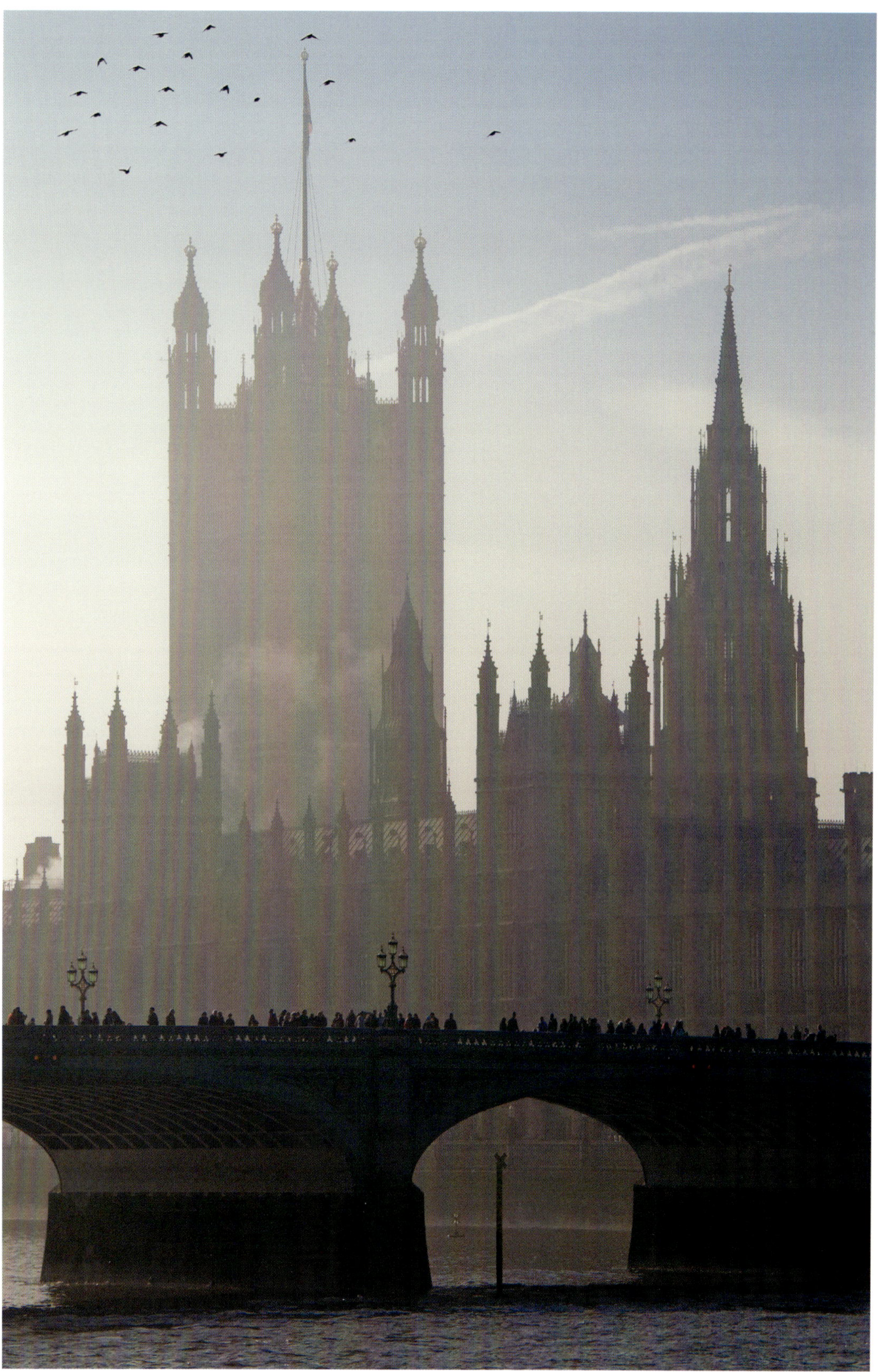

3
STREET LIFE

Candid Images of everyday life on the street, be it a crowded market, city park or lively café culture.

Street Life provides us with a true reflection of people from all walks of life within our multicultural and cosmopolitan society.

◎ SAM MELLISH / WINNER

East London Street Art
Holywell Lane, East London

I was out in East London documenting the streets. Walking along Holywell Lane, infamous for street graffiti, I stumbled across this team freshly designing a unique urban fresco. I really like the symmetry between the artists in relation to the characters they are painting.

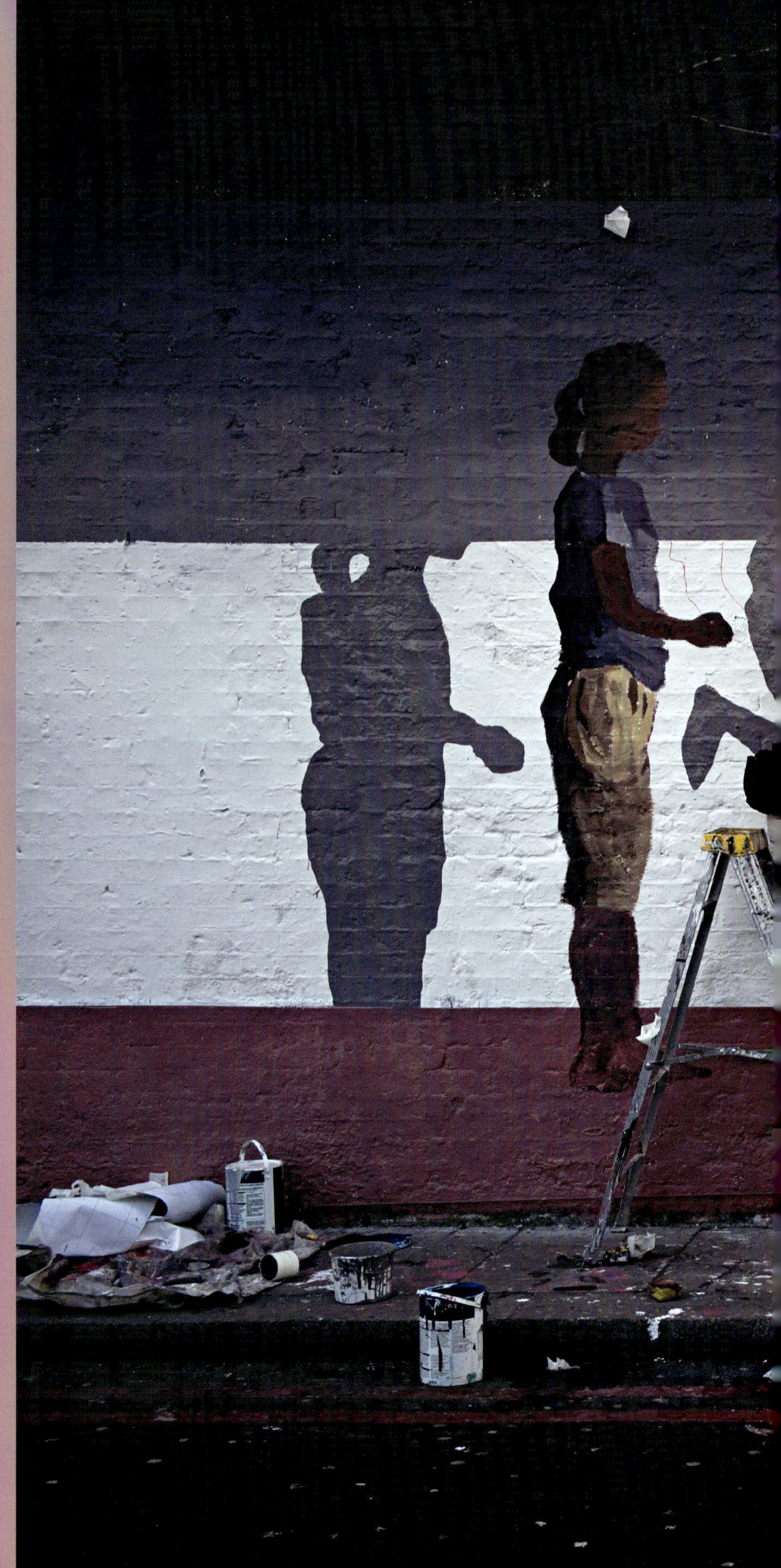

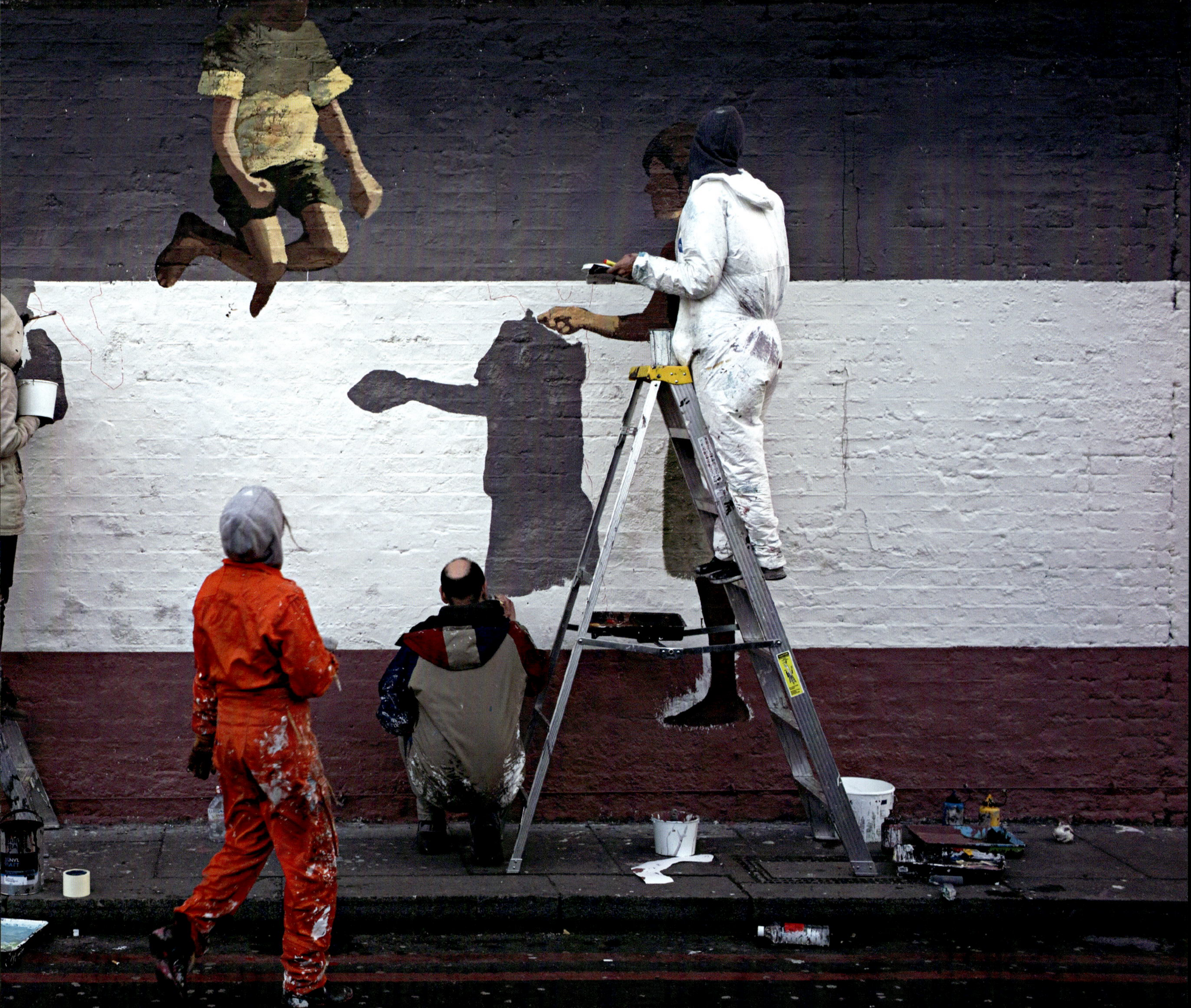

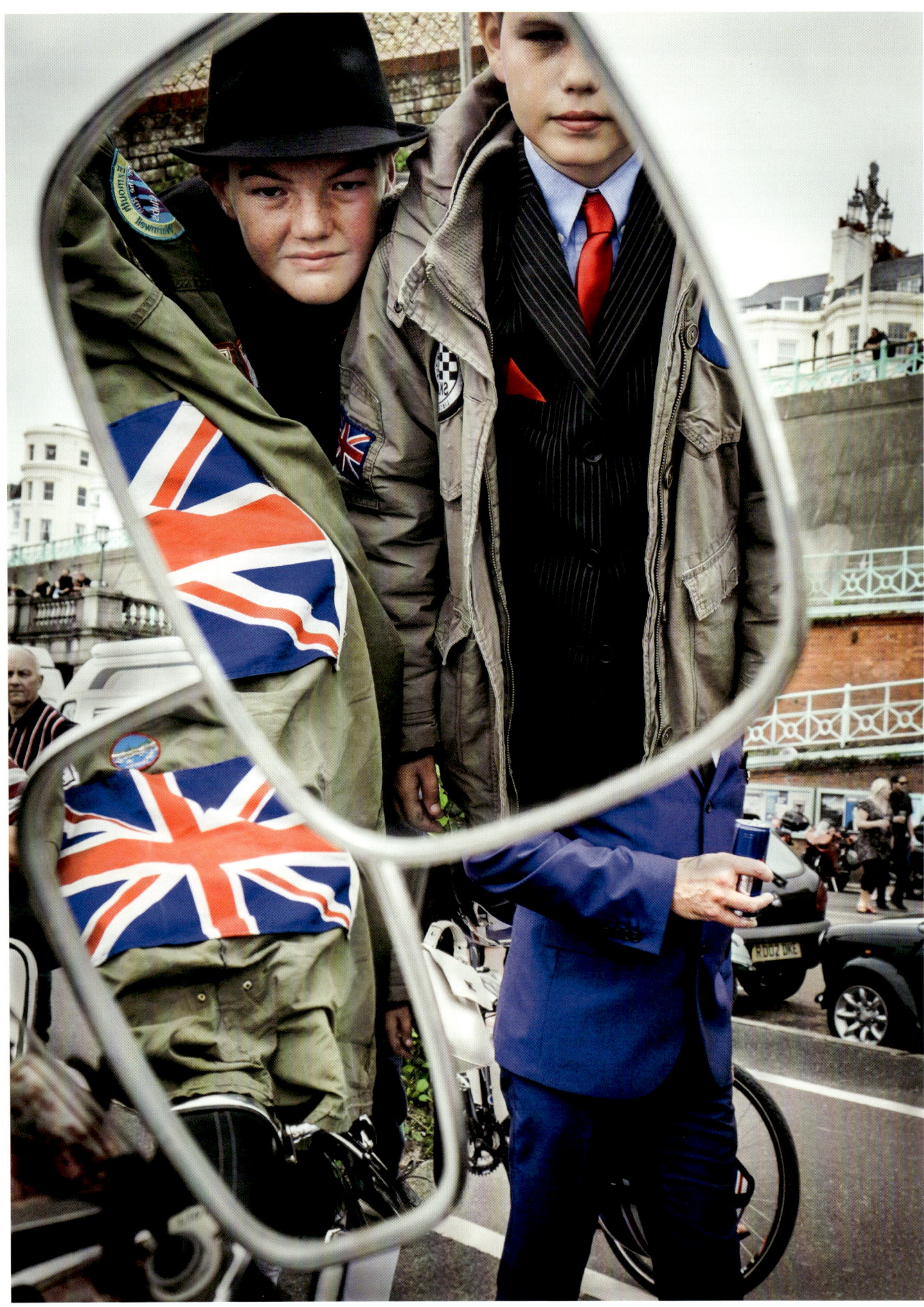

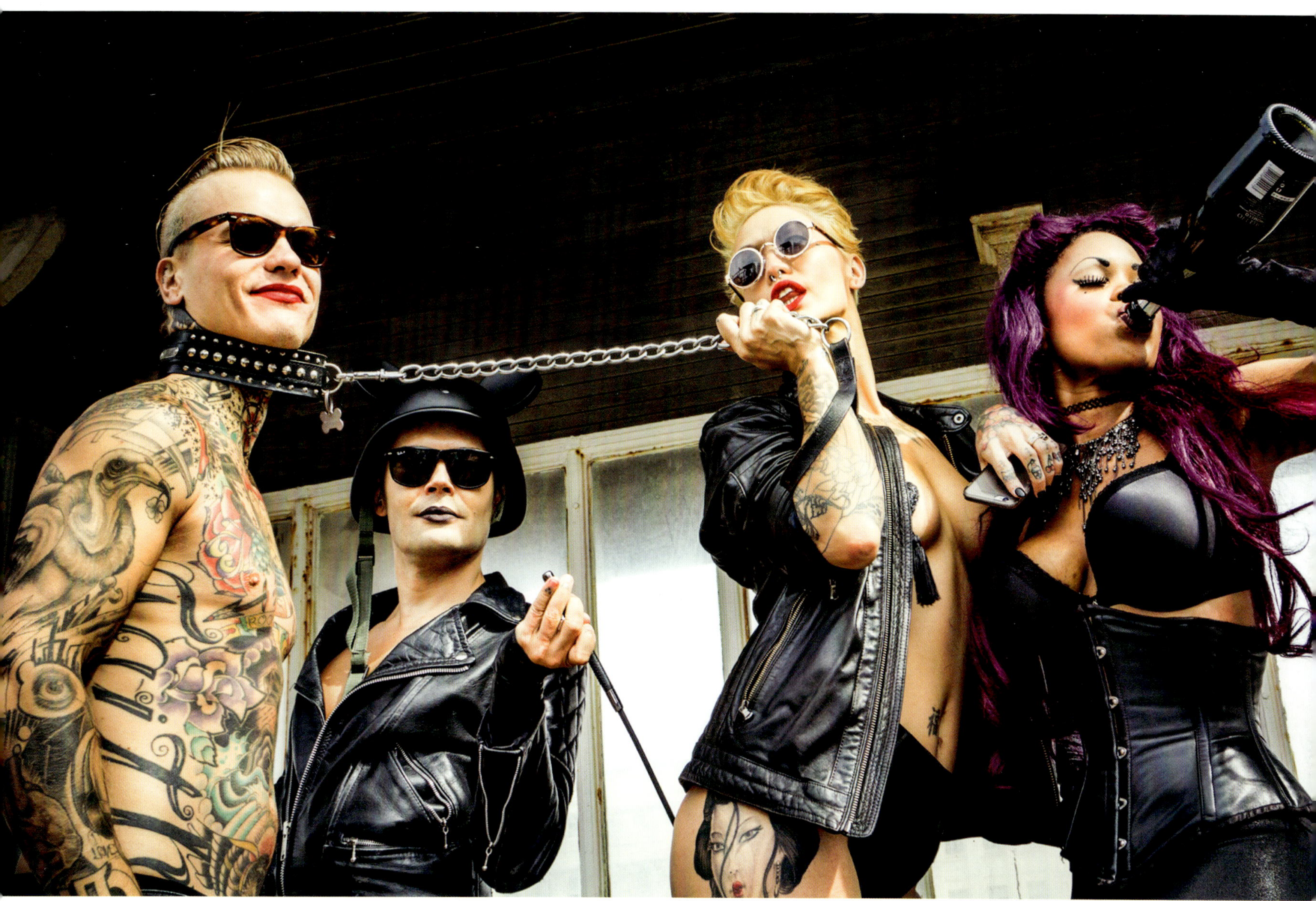

Reflecting the Younger Generation
Brighton, Sussex

These two young lads had come to Brighton for the first time to be a part of the Mod weekender. Mod culture is really big in Brighton and people travel from far and wide to be a part of the gatherings. I happened to be looking at the scooter when I noticed the boys' reflection in one of the mirrors. Then the Mod in the blue suit walked past and I knew I had the picture I wanted.

JO TEASDALE / HIGHLY COMMENDED

Lead On
Brighton, Sussex

This was taken before the Brighton Pride Parade started, on Hove Lawns Promenade. Everyone was getting ready and warming up before getting on their floats. It was a really big weekend in Brighton, celebrating 25 years of Pride, so everyone made a really huge effort and I thought these people looked amazing.

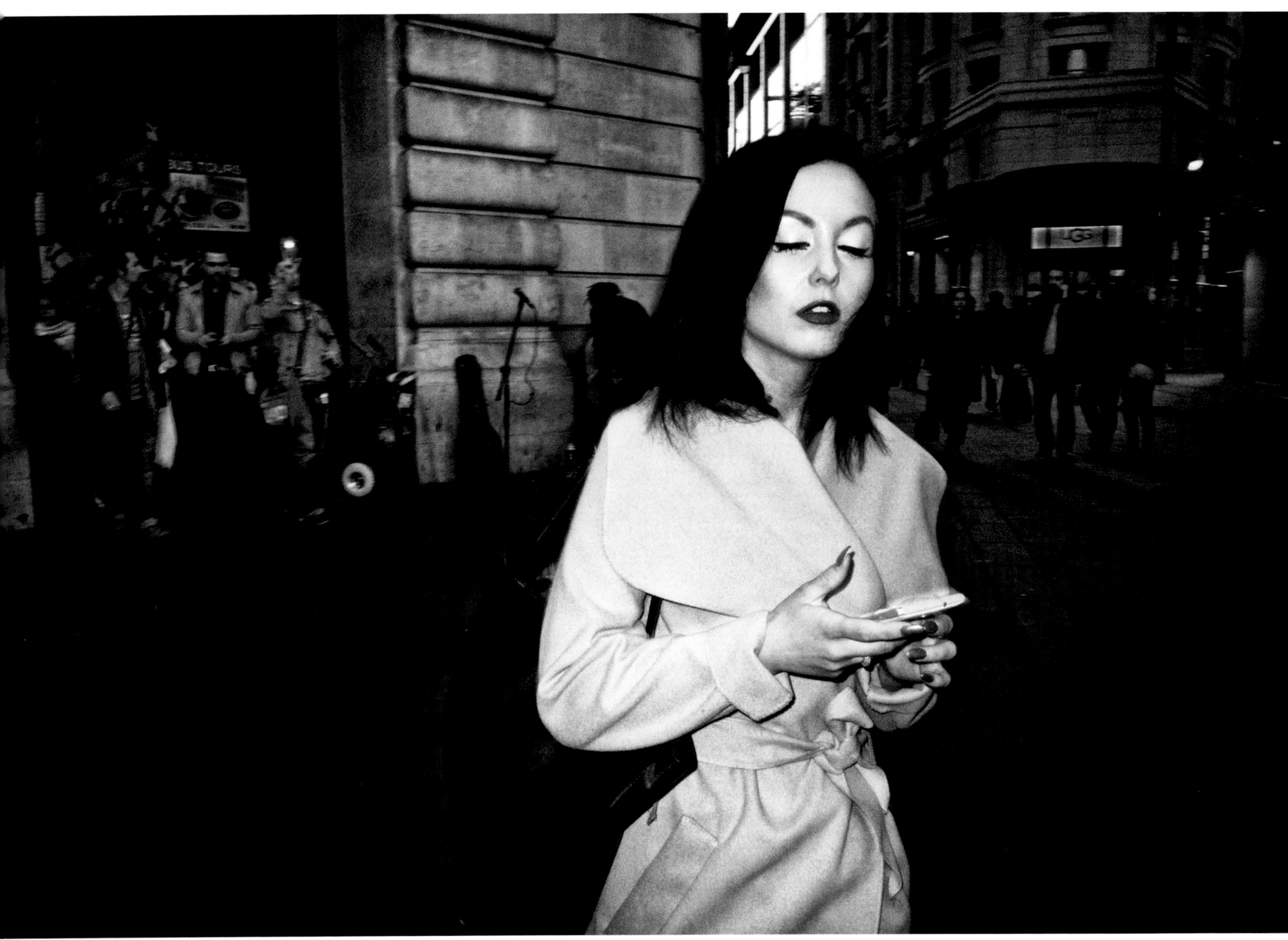

○ SIMON PEACOCK / HIGHLY COMMENDED

Woman standing out in a crowd
Piccadilly Circus, London

I don't often use flash when photographing in the street.
Camera flashes inevitably draw attention and can change the
nature of the photograph. I usually reject photographs when
the subject's eyes are closed, however, with this one I felt that
she looked serene and dreamy.

⊙ JACEK OBLOJ
HIGHLY COMMENDED

Dickensian London
Trafalgar Square, London

A man walking through Trafalgar Square.
I was trying to get through a crowd of
people on a zebra crossing and pressed
my shutter almost instinctively as I
spotted this gentlemen in the corner of
my eye. I like its Dickensian feeling. This
picture is part of my ongoing project
portraying people of London, using flash
for a more theatrical effect.

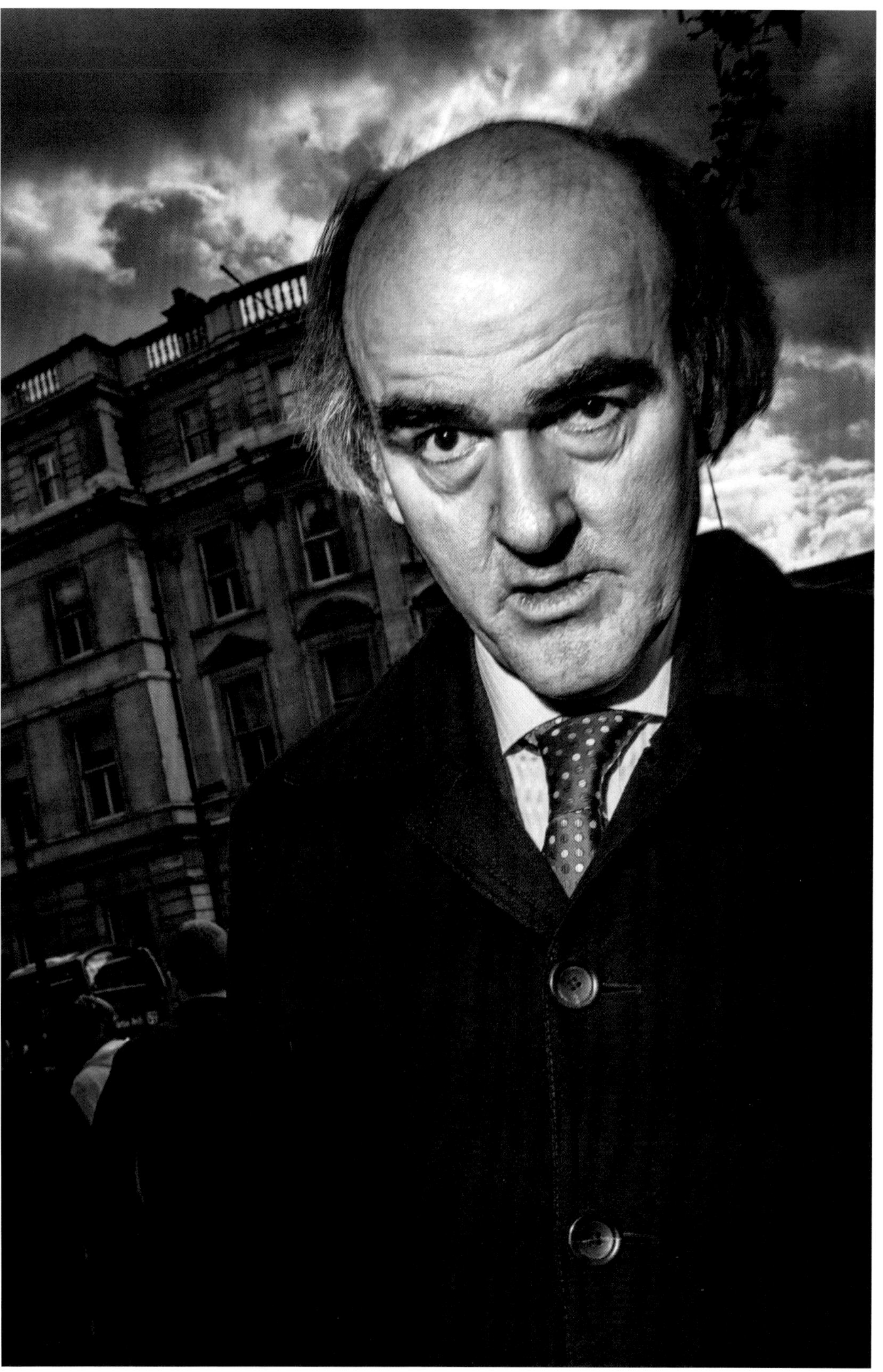

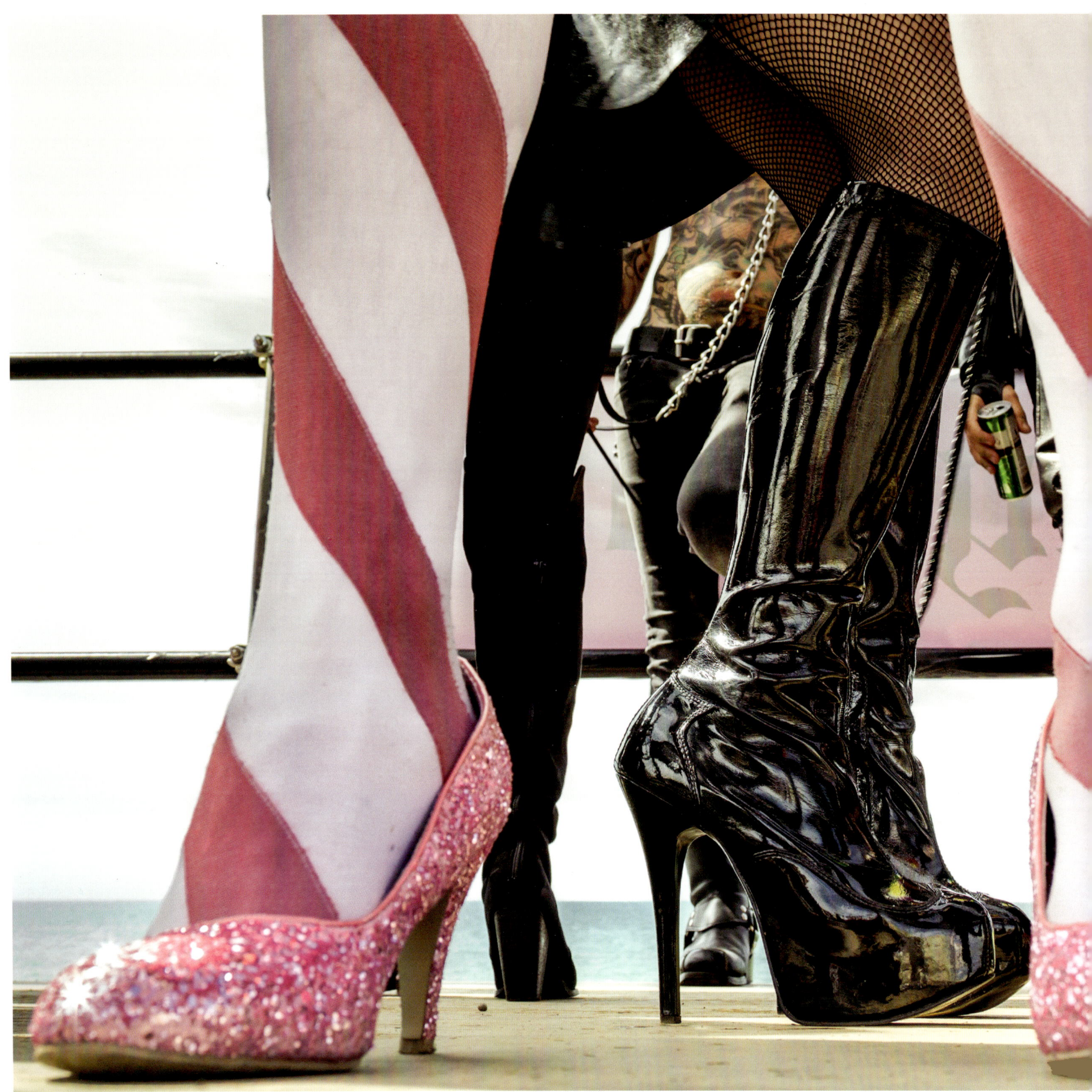

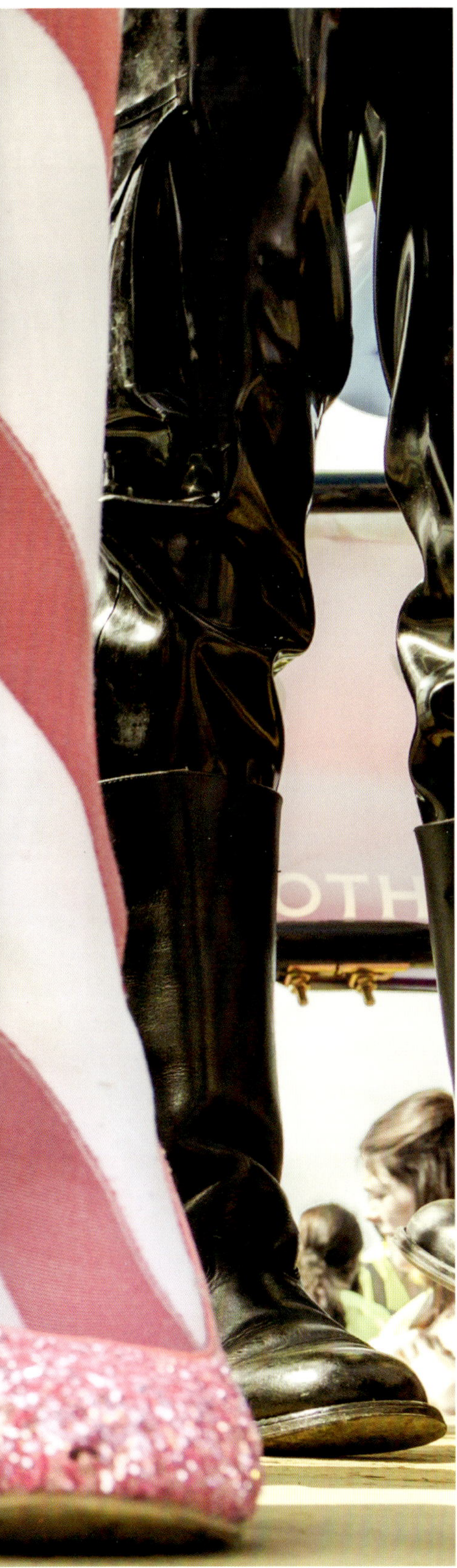

◐ JO TEASDALE
HIGHLY COMMENDED

Brighton Rock
Brighton, Sussex

This year at Pride in Brighton, it was the 25th Anniversary, so there was a huge party atmosphere. Just before the parade began down at Hove Lawns, various groups were onboard their floats. I was drawn to the array of legs, shoes and boots that were at eye level. I particularly liked the pink and white striped tights; they looked like sticks of rock; set against the patent black boots.

◐ NEIL PROCTOR
HIGHLY COMMENDED

Tweed Run
London

I had never heard of the Tweed Run until it was announced on BBC Radio London on the morning of the event. I dashed off to Trafalgar Square where I was met by a large informal gathering of tweed-clad vintage cyclists waiting for the off. Not a stitch of lycra in sight. This image was taken as they were about to depart. When this lady appeared with her Jack Russell in a pannier as a passenger, along with all the other participants scanning the traffic, the picture came together.

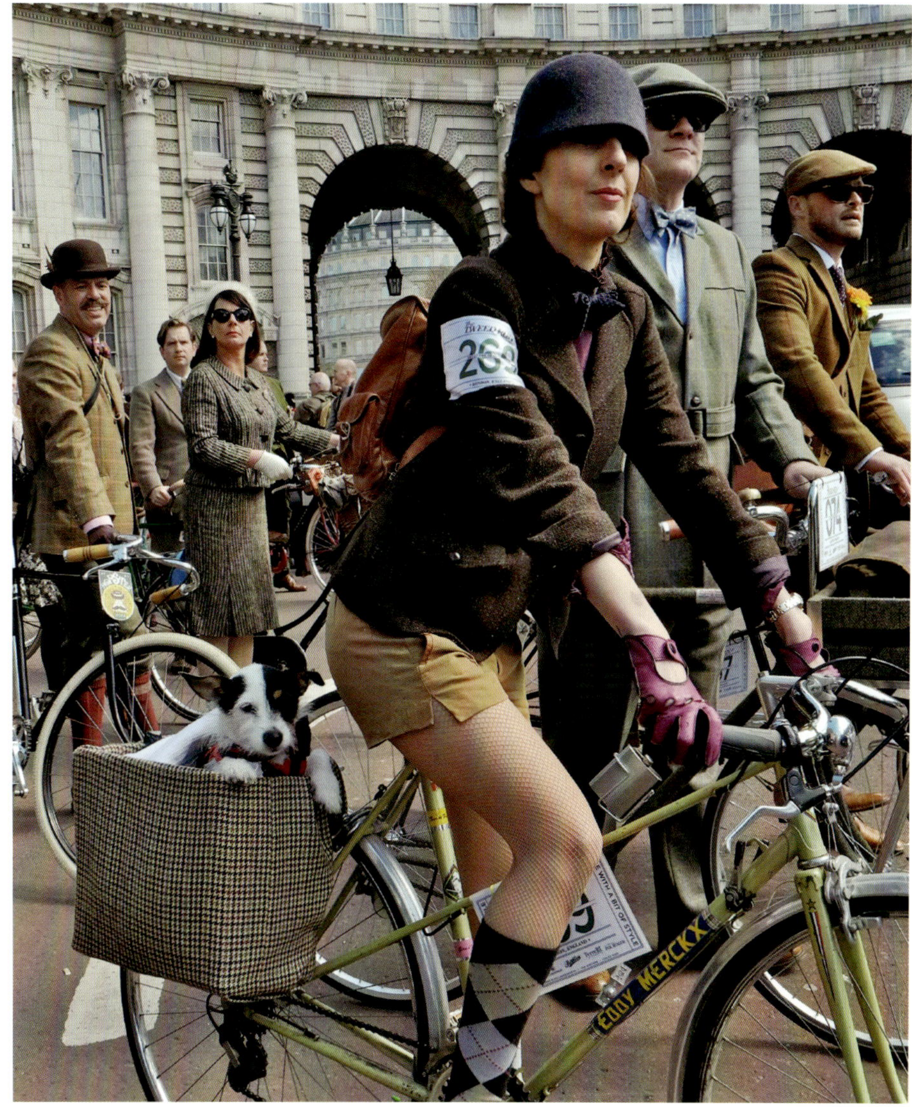

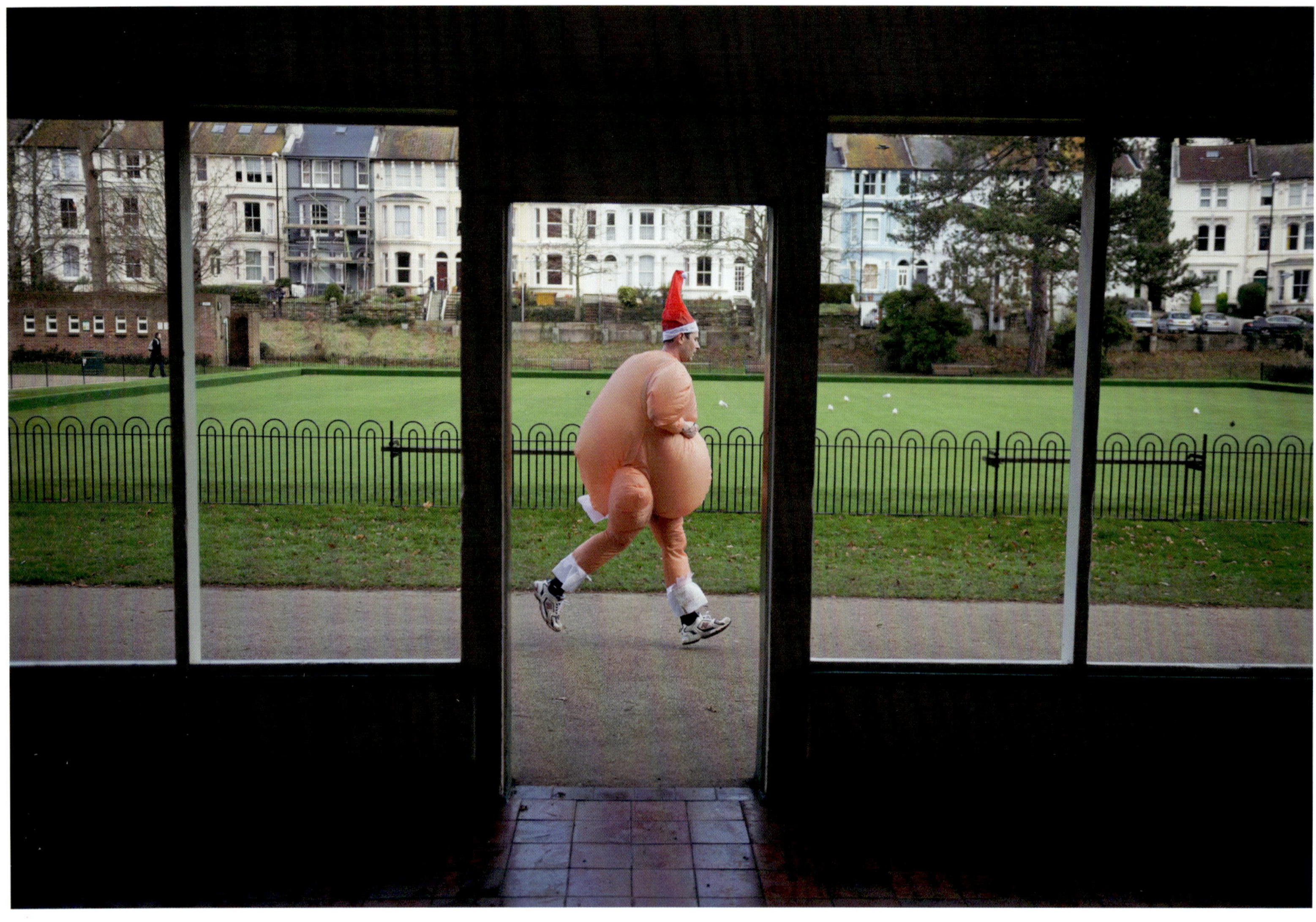

Santa Fun Run Turkey
Alexandra Park. Hastings. E Sussex

I spotted this turkey amongst a gathering of Santa Claus charity fun runners. I wanted to isolate him from the rest and frame him through the hut. Luckily for me, the competitors had spread out by the time they passed and I grabbed my solitary turkey in full flow.

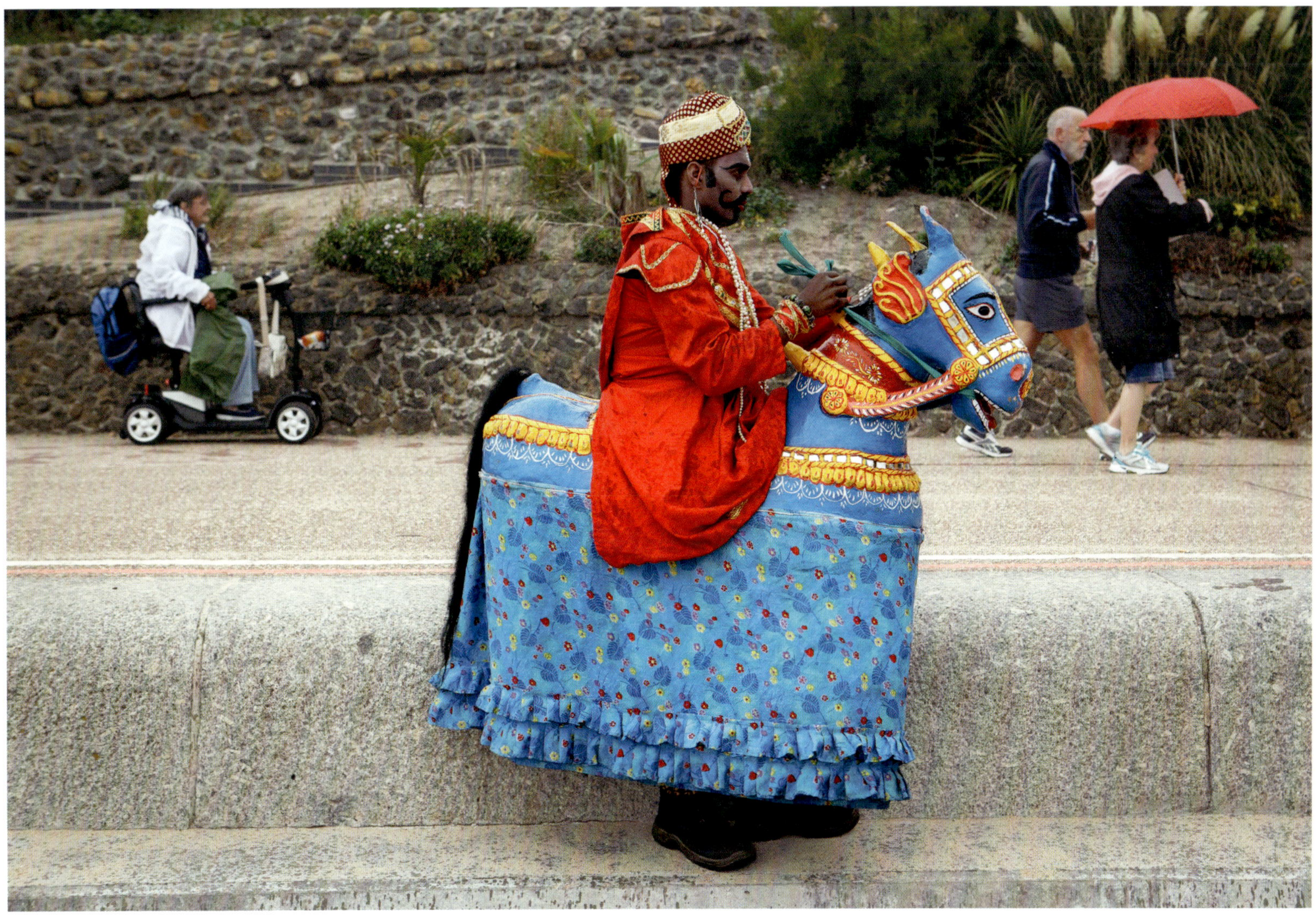

◐ JACEK OBLOJ / HIGHLY COMMENDED

Ganesh Festival
Clacton on Sea

The annual event is organised by London Ganesh temple and
attracts a large crowd of people from the south east of England.
I captured a moment when the entertainer mixed with some
local on-lookers. This is part of my ongoing project exploring
multicultural London.

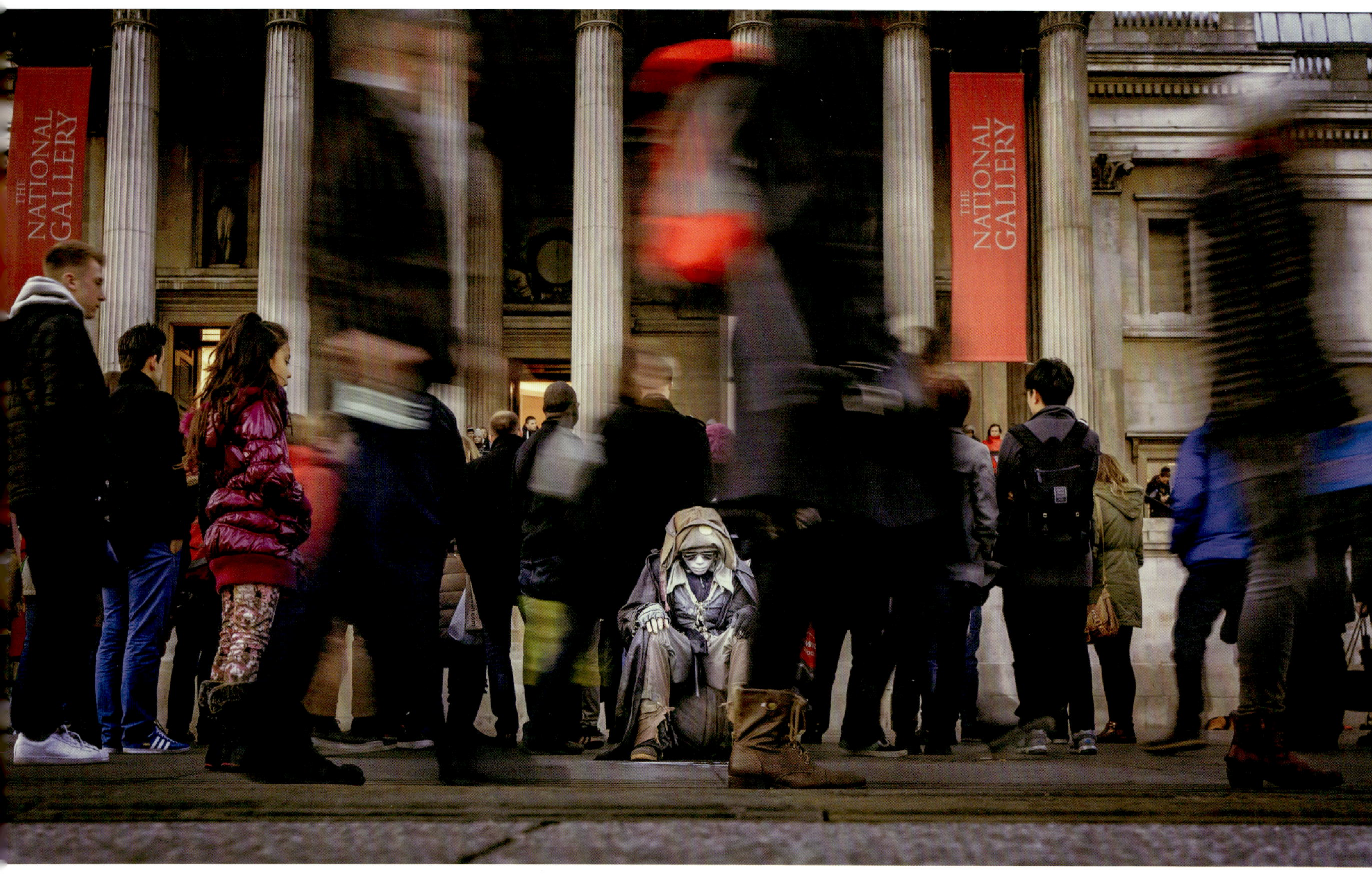

◑ NAF SELMANI / HIGHLY COMMENDED

Petrified
London

Alone in the middle of a busy Trafalgar Square, and among many other buskers who have gathered more attention, a street performer in pirate's dress waits in the hope of being noticed and appreciated for her work.

DAVID JONES
HIGHLY COMMENDED

Ferry 'cross the Mersey
River Mersey, Liverpool

It had been a busy day at the festival at Liverpool Pierhead, and a number of people were making their way home on the ferry. I had been looking at the reflection of the sea in the glass, when a child suddenly appeared at the window. Her pose and expression fitted in with the reflection of the sea. I included the passengers, and a little of the background to give it context.

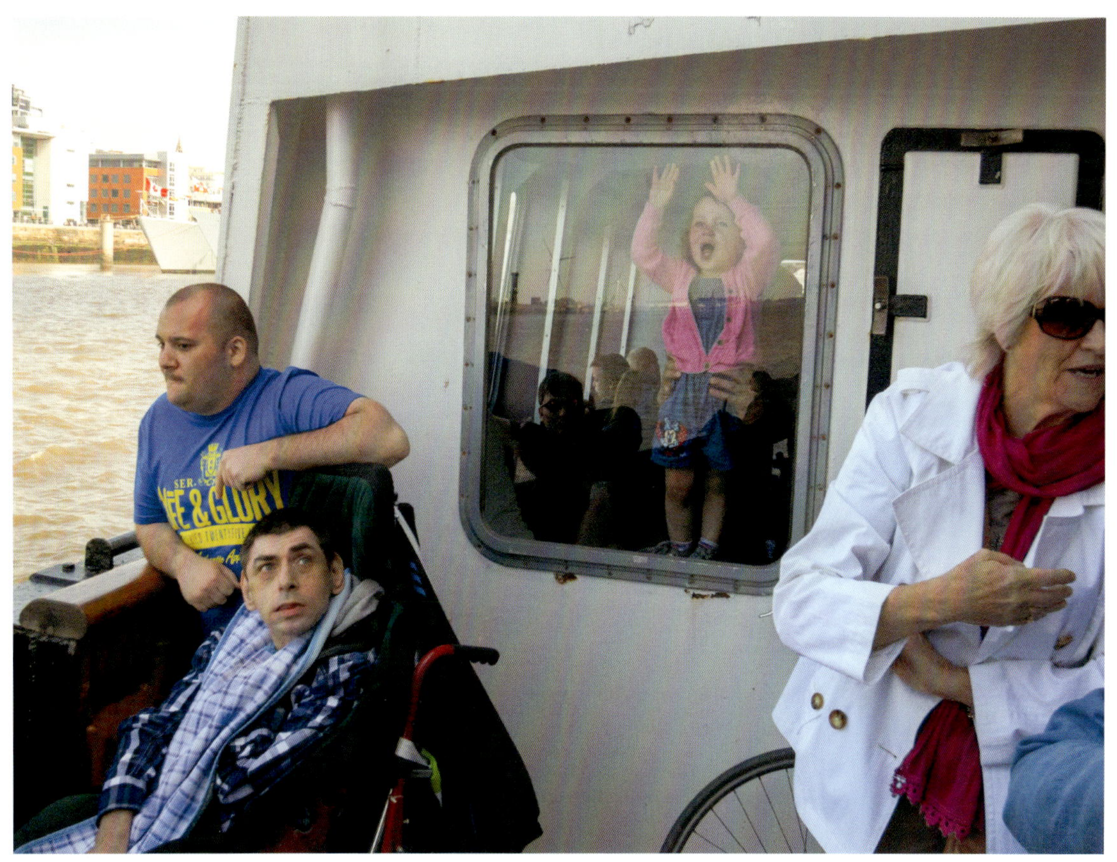

SARA NICOMEDI
HIGHLY COMMENDED

Picnic outside London
Public park outside London

I like to go out of London, especially on sunny days, and feel myself in Britain. In London, sometimes you can forget that you're in England. This picture was taken in a café in a public park.

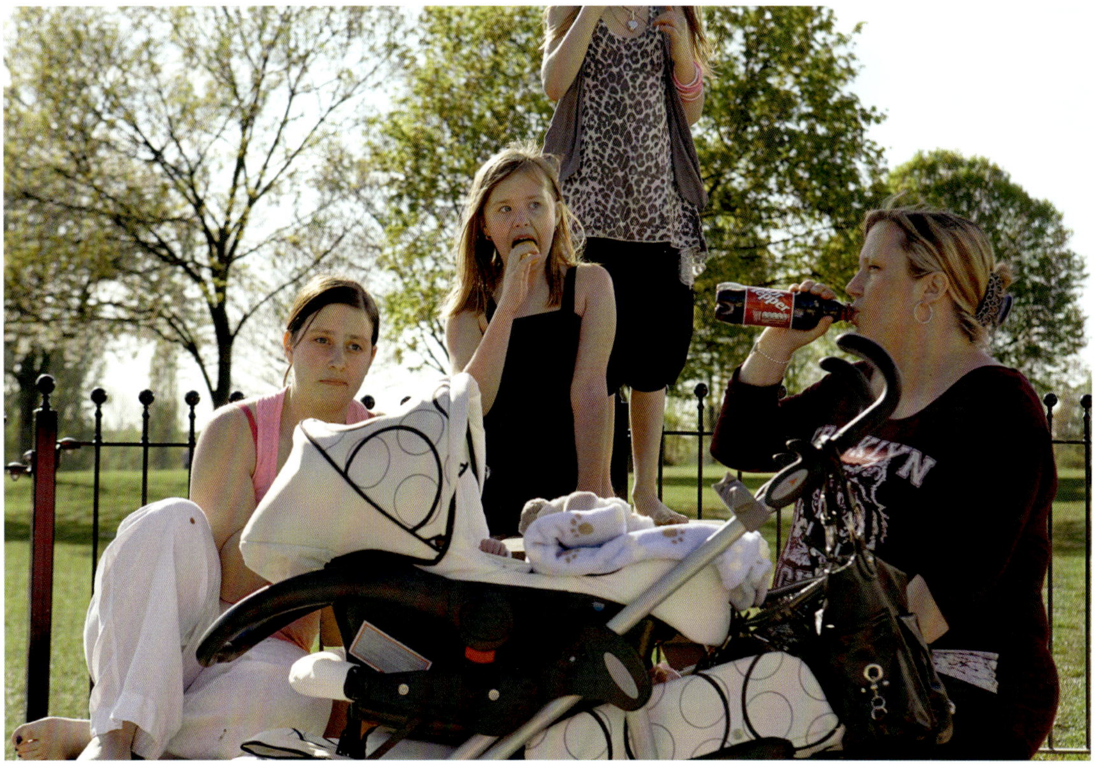

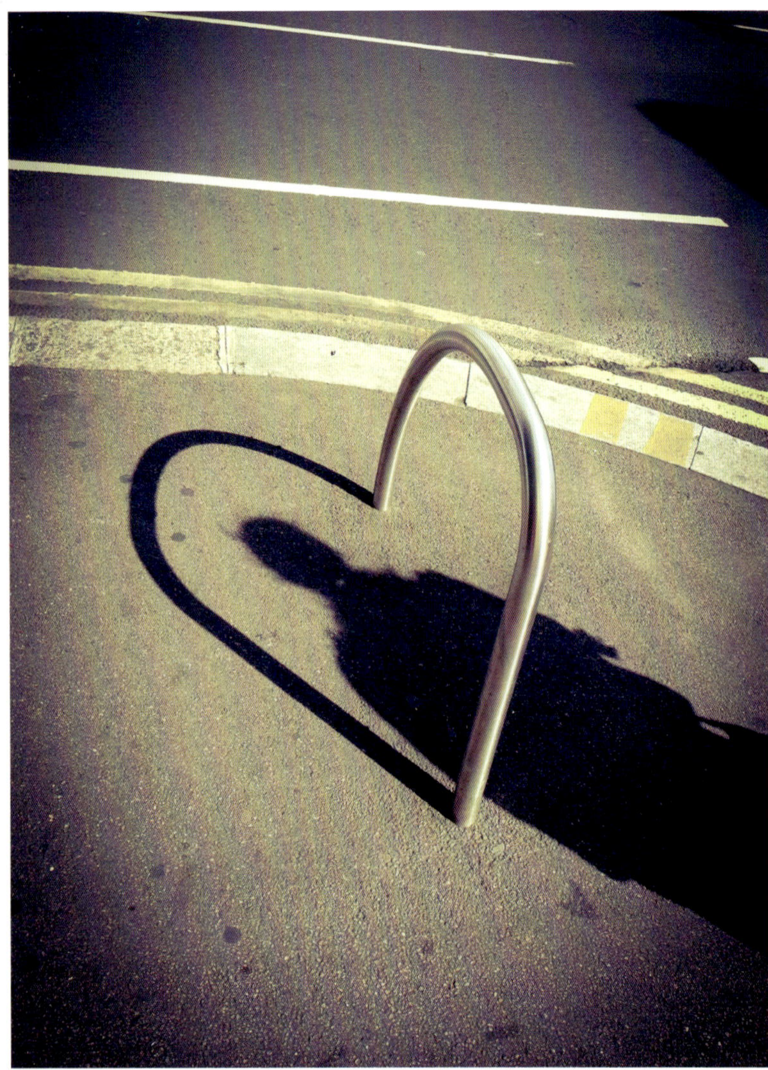

JOHN GREENE / HIGHLY COMMENDED

My Love
Leytonstone High Road, London

I caught this photo whilst in my local neighbourhood of Leytonstone. Shadows often strike a creative chord with me and this chance discovery was definitely no exception. This universal symbol of love was so simply created by this ordinary bicycle parking hoop and the sun being low in the sky. The love of my life was also perfectly positioned for me to capture this memorable image.

PAUL ANTHONY WILSON
HIGHLY COMMENDED

Mind The Gap
Cheltenham

It was one of those moments when you knew something was about to happen. I was on the other side of a busy road and could see these window dressers were going to move the mannequin by holding its bottom. I had a wide lens on the camera and was too far away, I ran across the road (dodging traffic) and managed one shot before they realised. They both laughed. When I arrived home I sent a copy to the shop. They later replied that it was framed and on the shop wall.

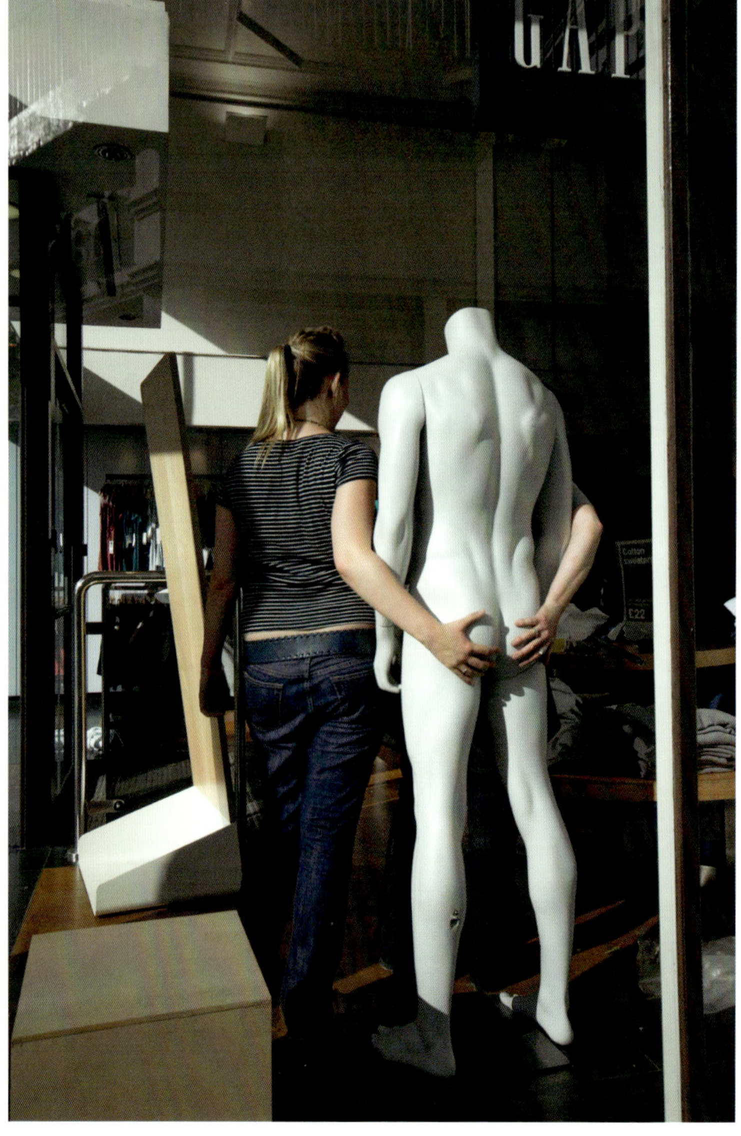

◐ GEORGE GRIFFIN
HIGHLY COMMENDED

Smiles
Montague Close near London Bridge

I had been out all day shooting 'Street'
and this was at the end of the day.
I happened to see the smiley face on
the bollard and as I shot the picture,
the lady with the smiley bag walked
past. A lucky 'decisive moment'.

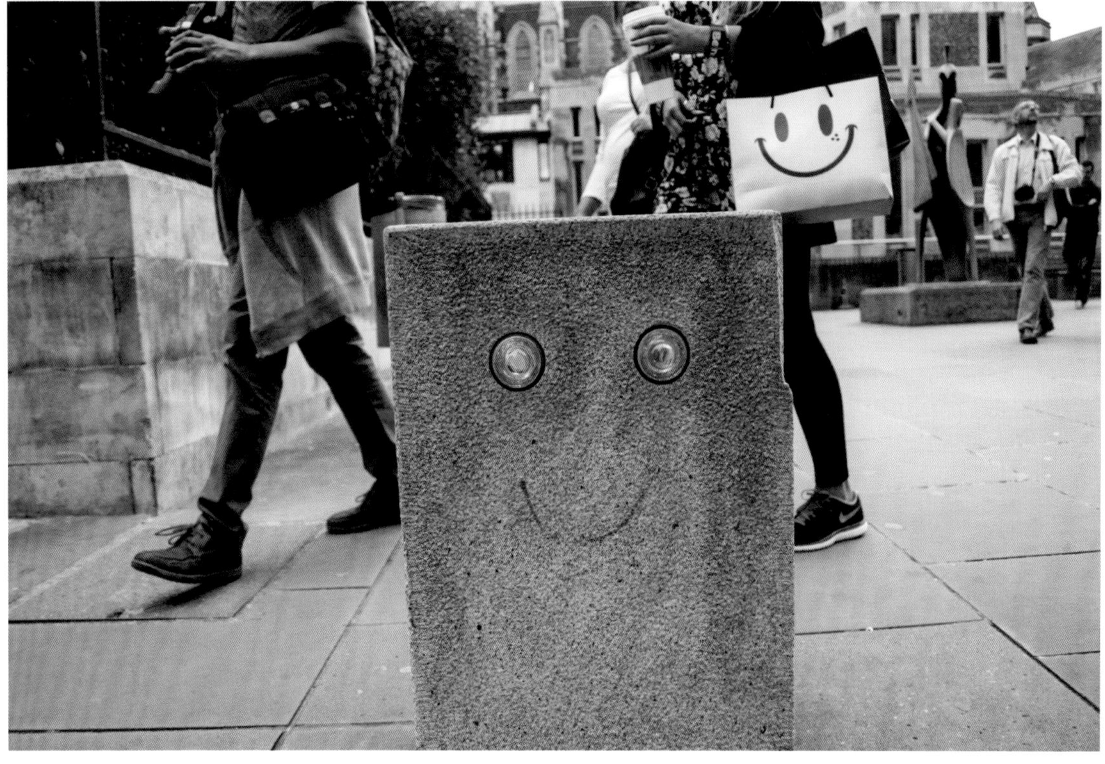

◐ FRED WILKINSON
HIGHLY COMMENDED

London

I was about to descend to the Crypt Café
in St Martins in the Fields. The scenario
seemed almost surreal – a half human
half zebra figure walking an empty street,
yet so close to the hustle and bustle of
Trafalgar Square. For me, it demonstrates
one of the fundamentals of street
photography "always remain observant"
(even when going for a coffee)!

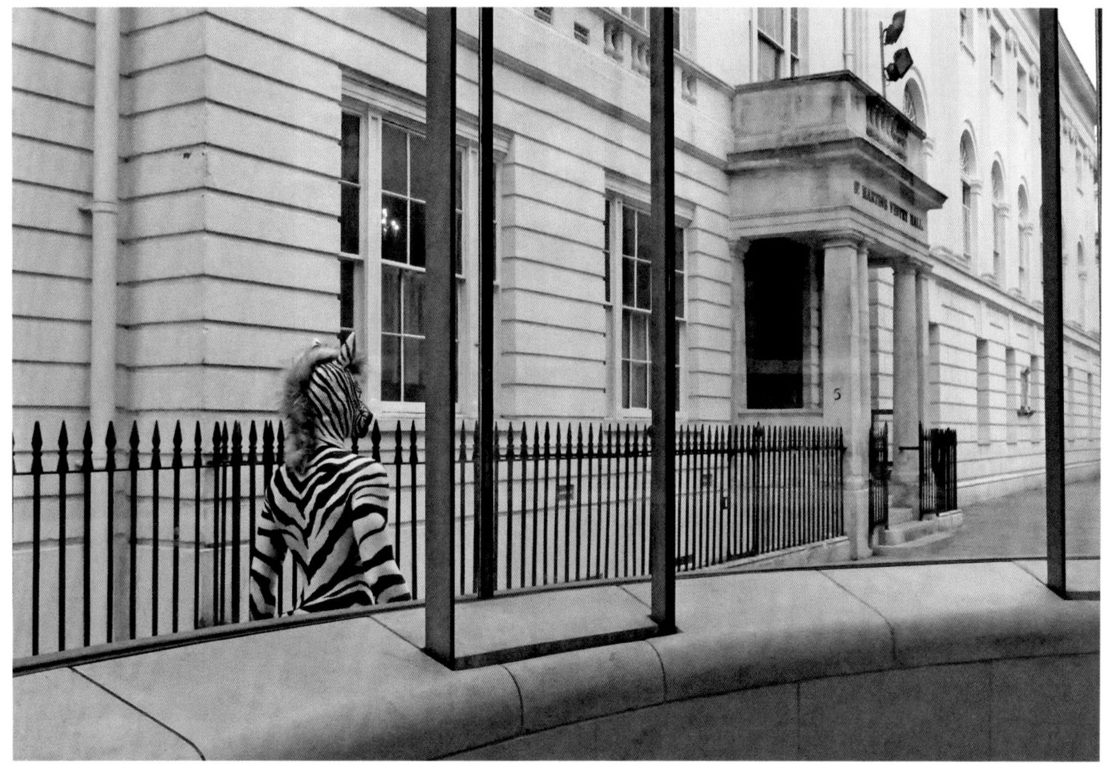

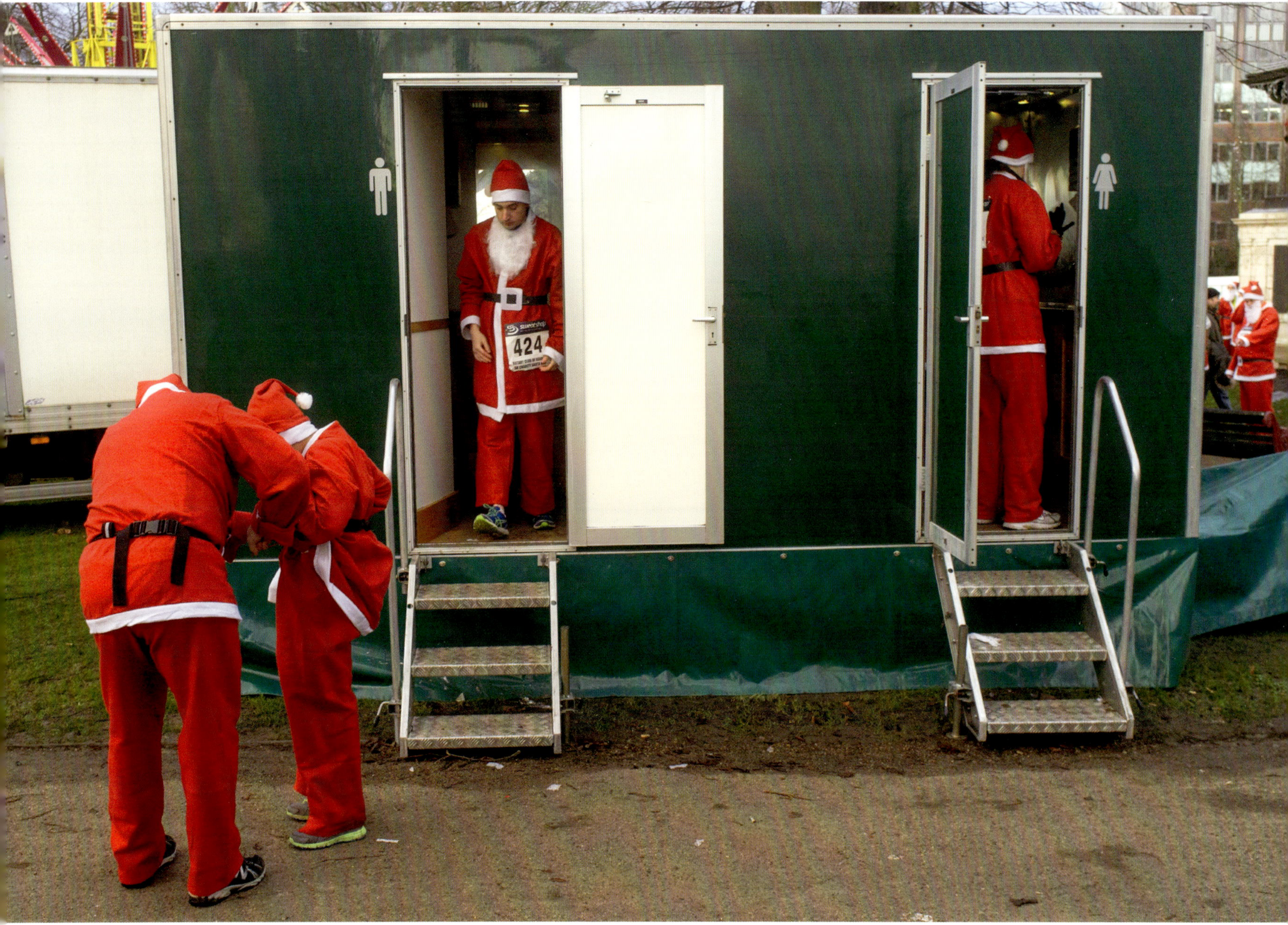

⏶ MARK HARRISON

Final preparations

The Forbury, Reading, Berkshire

This was the first year that the local Rotary Club organised a Santa Charity
Run and, of course, everyone who entered was given a Santa Claus outfit.
In fact there were hordes of Santas of all shapes and sizes and most of
them seemed to be streaming past in front of me to the starting line. Just
for an instant there was a gap and this scene presented itself to me.

○ PAUL ANTHONY
WILSON

No Dogs Allowed
Whitby, North Yorkshire

Last minute shopping, two
days before Christmas, the
owner went in to buy something from the shop, the dog
tried to follow but wasn't
allowed in, I approached
quietly and close to the wall
so that I didn't spook the
animal. I managed one shot
before the dog was ushered
back out to wait in the street,
luckily there were no other
people around to clutter and
spoil the background.

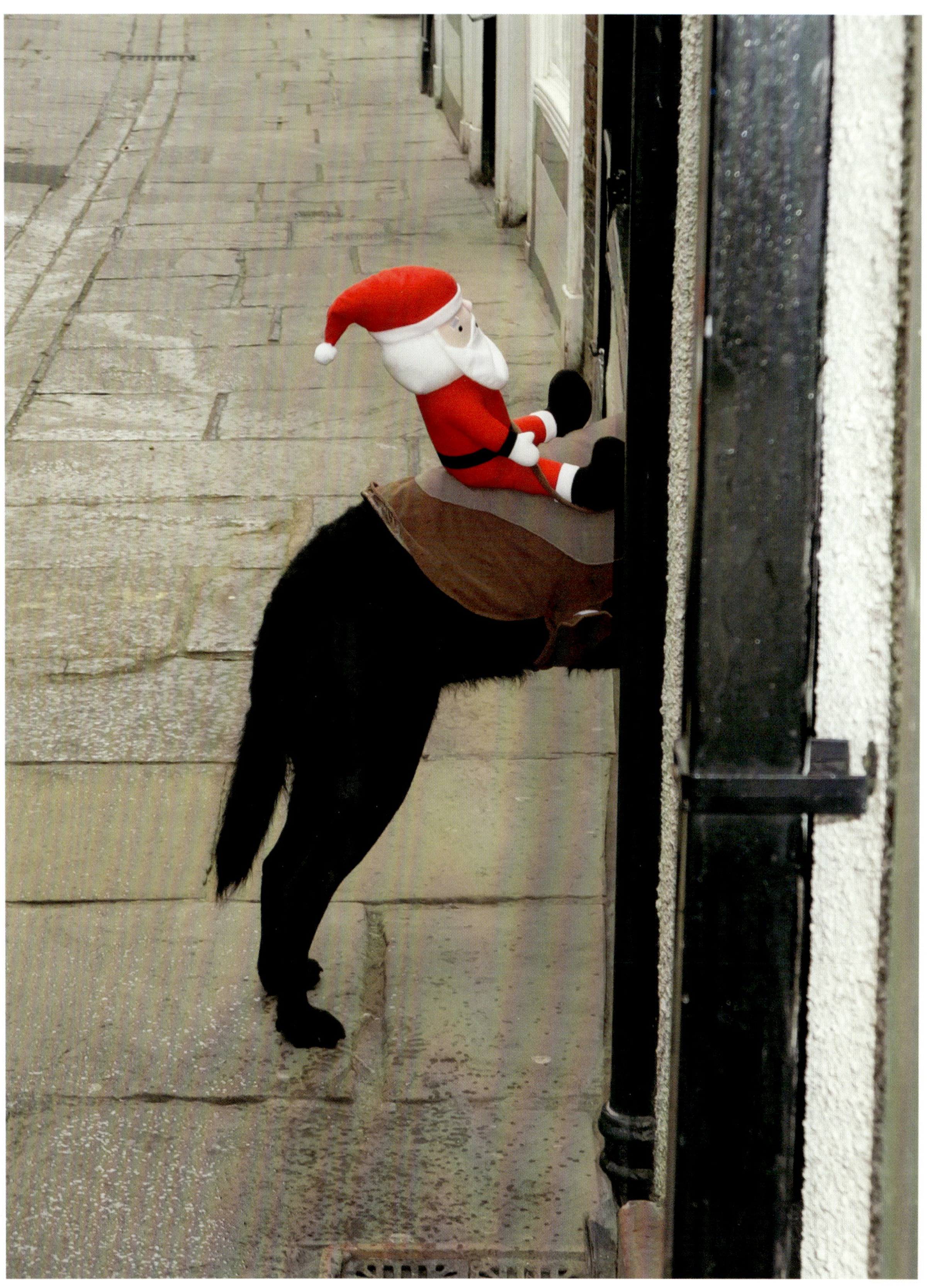

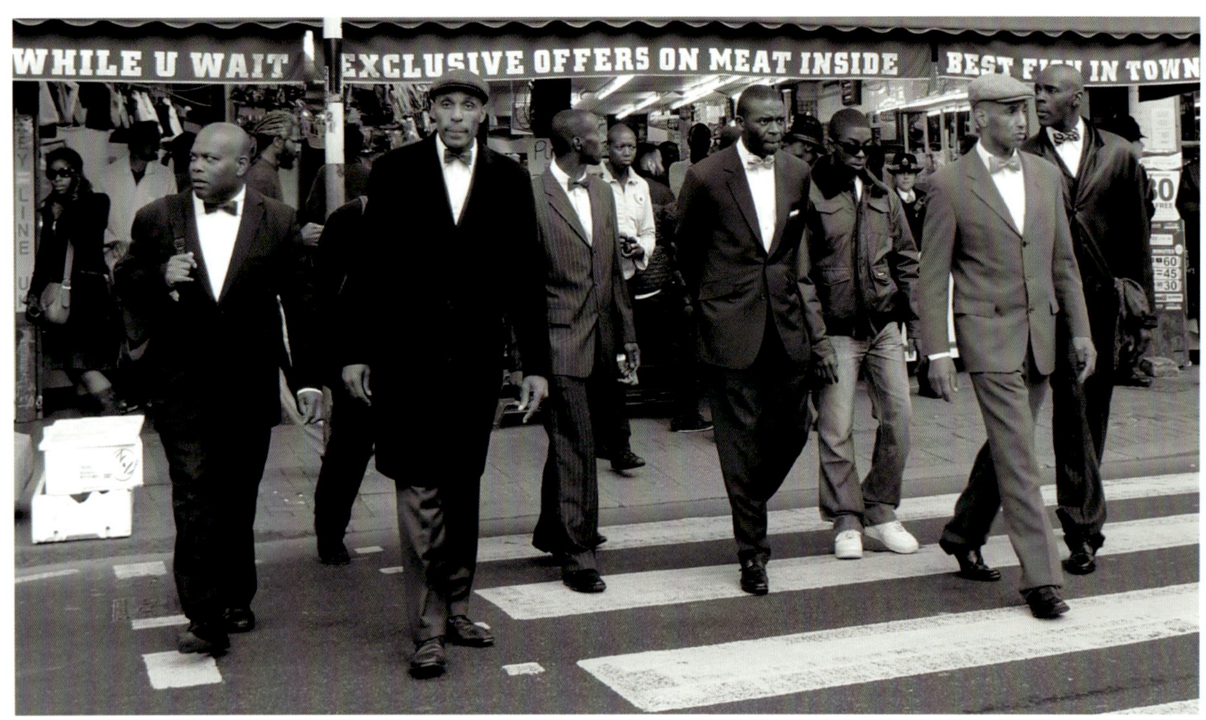

IAN BRUMPTON

The Nation of Islam
Peckham High Street, London

Members of The Nation of Islam,
Peckham High Street.

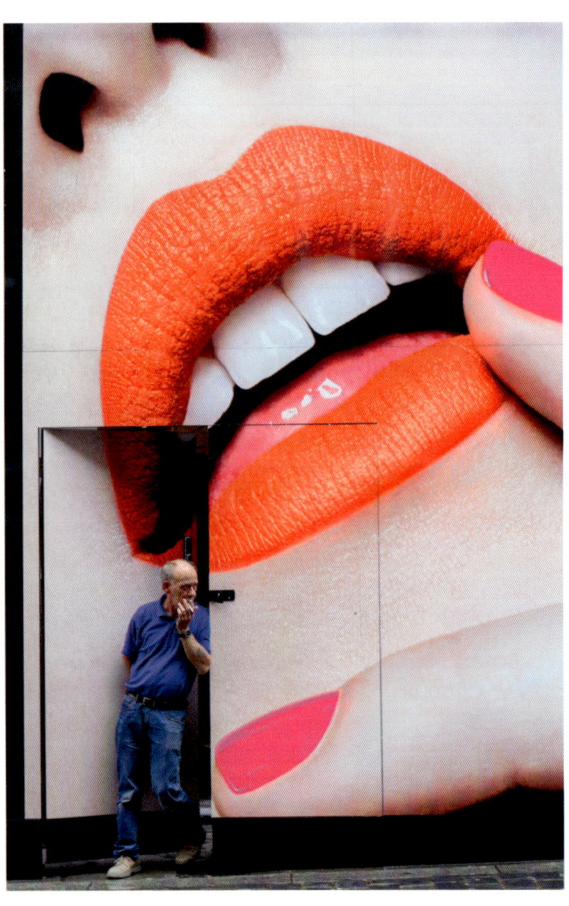

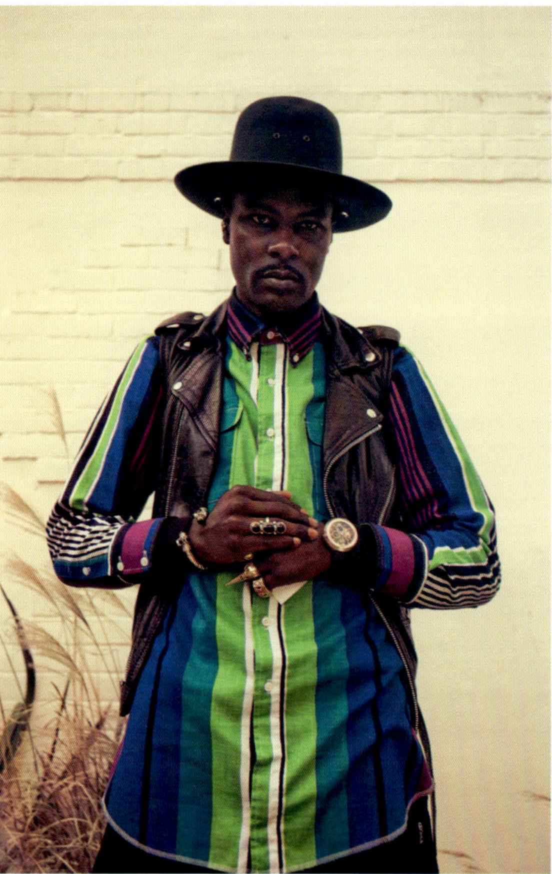

NAF SELMANI

The Kiss
London

The glamour of airbrushed
advertising is all around us on
city streets, and this shot
juxtaposes the glossy, artificial
world of ads with the reality of a
normal person sneaking out for
a quick smoke.

SAM MELLISH

A portrait of East London
Whitecross Street, East London

I met Empy on Whitecross Street
in the late afternoon. As the
myriad of food traders packed
down for the day, I rolled off a
series of portraits. A stylist by
trade, Empy was more than
happy to spend a little time with
me capturing some street photos.

● JANINE WIEDEL

Evicting St Agnes
St Agnes Squat, Kennington, South London

Between 2003 and 2007, I documented the final years of St Agnes Place, a South London back street notable for its status as the longest running squat in London. For over 30 years the street was occupied by a fluid and diverse range of groups and individuals who established a community outside the bounds of governmental control. In 2005, the riot police moved in and left 150 people homeless and 21 houses demolished.

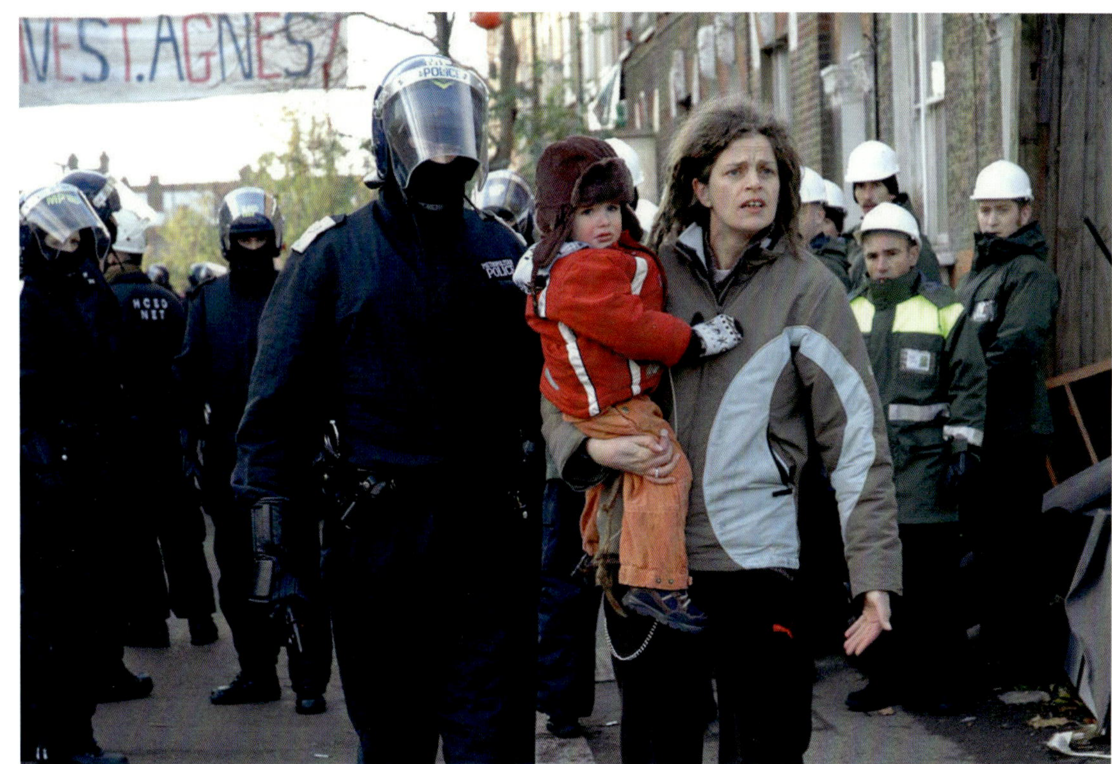

● RUDOLF ABRAHAM

The Lord Mayor's Show
Guildhall Yard, London

The 684th Lord Mayor of London, David Wootton, in the Lord Mayor's Coach, at Guildhall. In a tradition stretching back 800 years and enshrined in a charter by King John, the Lord Mayor of London travels across the City of London – in a supremely elaborate 18th century stately coach, with a procession three miles long – to the Royal Courts of Justice, to swear an oath of allegiance to the Sovereign.

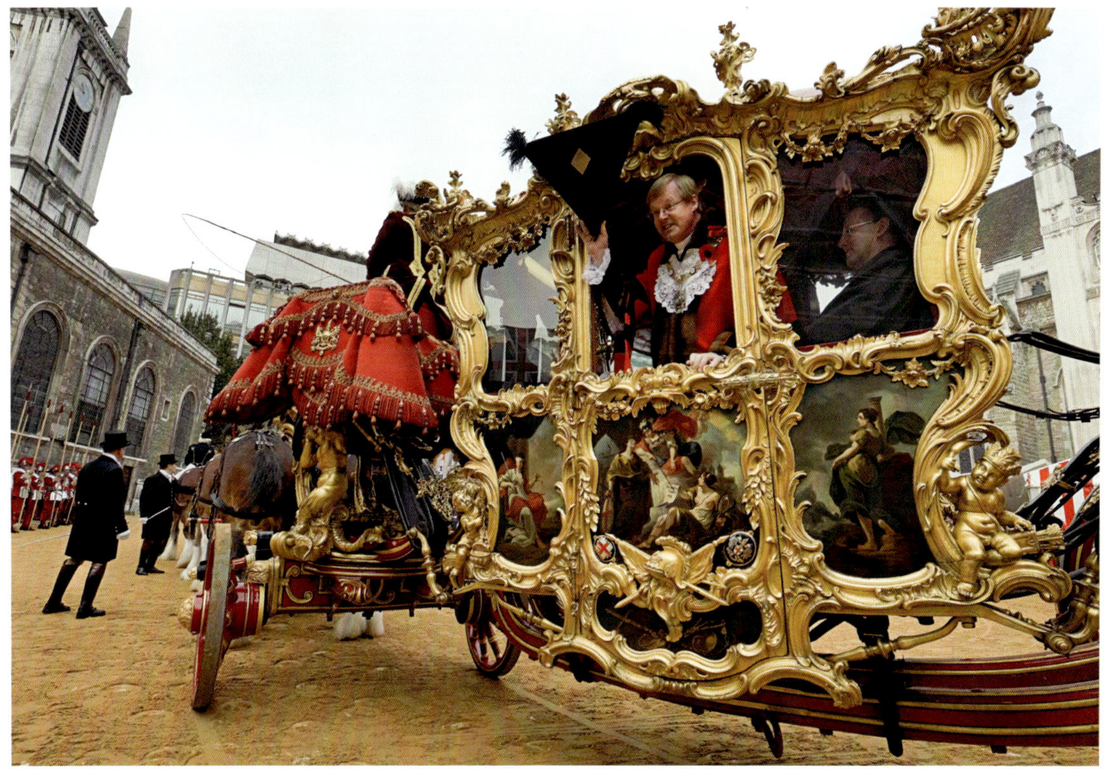

4

LIFE AT WORK

Whether it's industry and trade, communications, the arts, science and technology, health education, transport or the Leisure industry, *Life At Work* documents the essence of working life, its diversity, and its relevance within the community.

▷ JANINE WIEDEL / WINNER

Throwing and Winding
Gainsborough Silk Weaving Company, Sudbury, West Suffolk

Gainsborough Silk Weaving Company was established in 1903 and is now one of the oldest and last remaining commercial mills in England. Awarded the Royal Warrant in 1980 it has produced many fabrics for the Royal Family as well as State buildings worldwide.

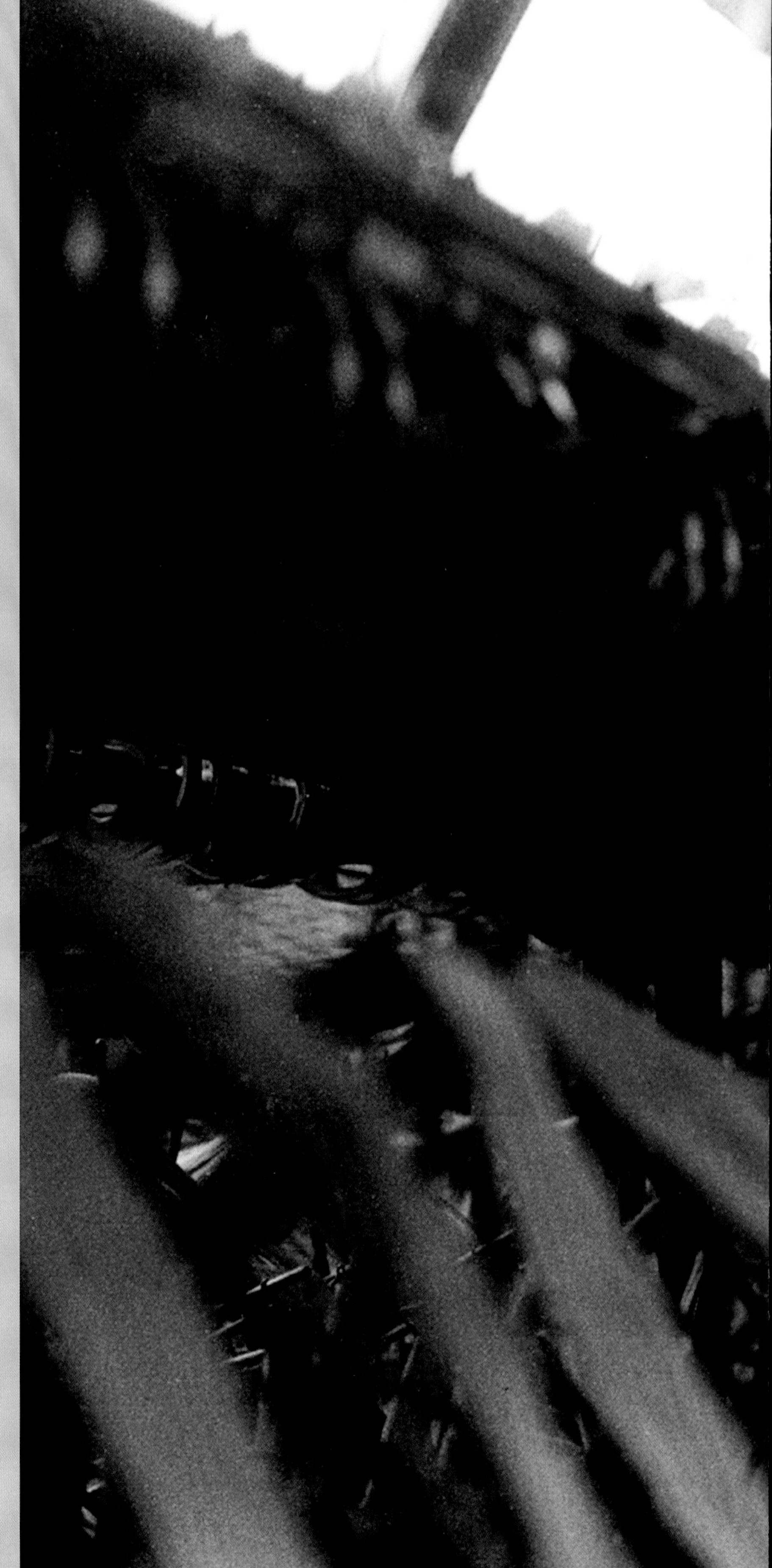

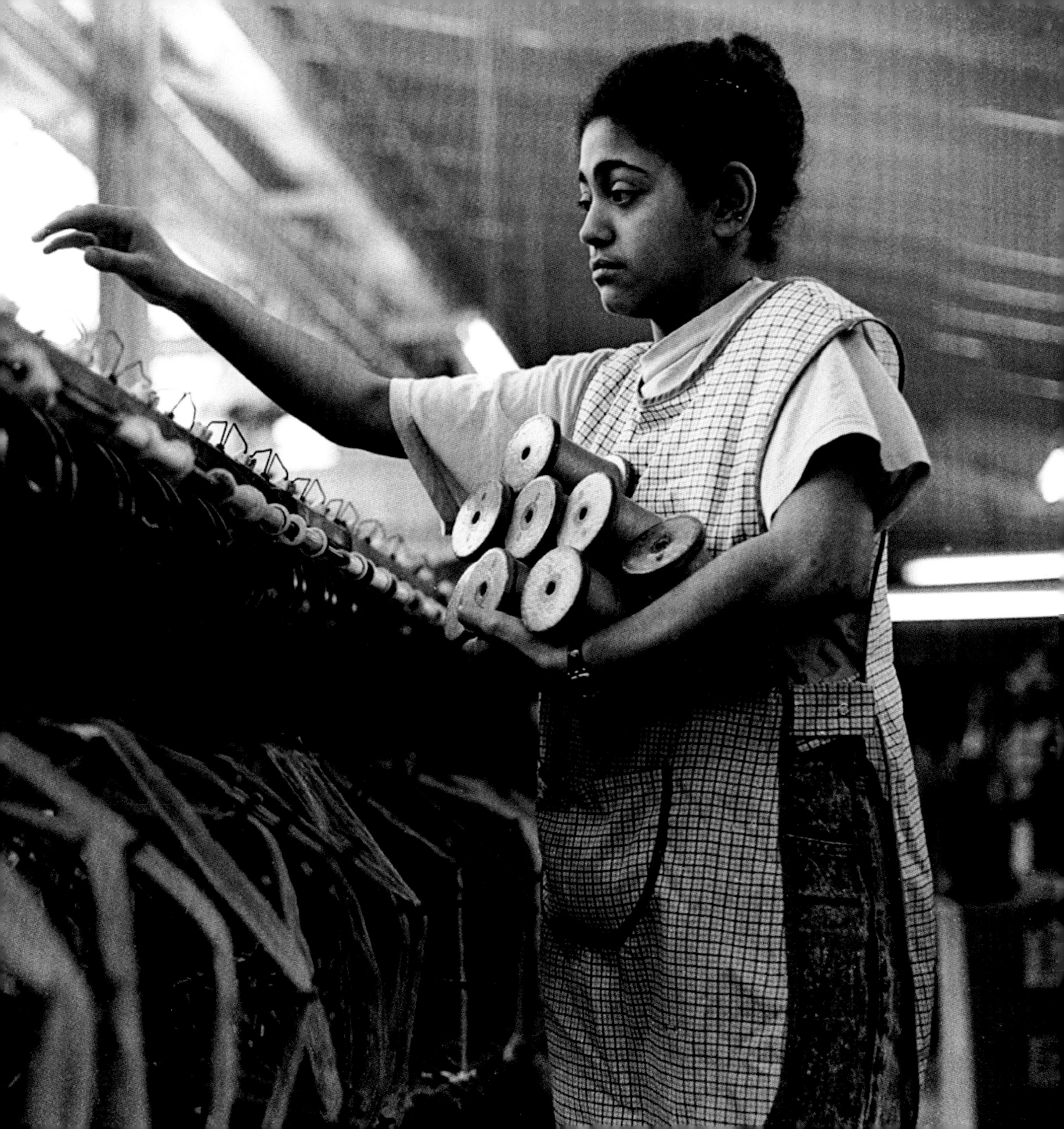

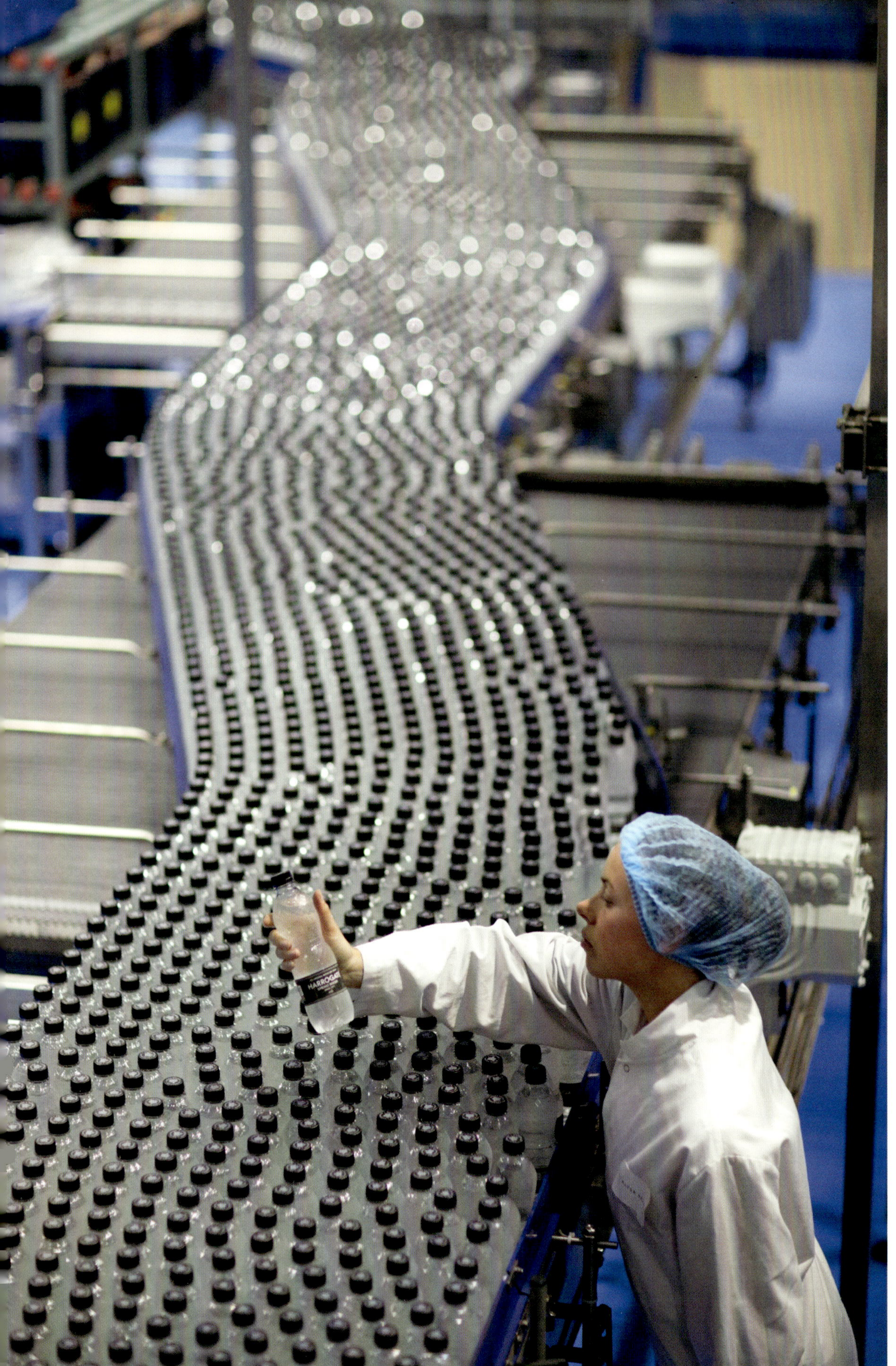

○ STEVE MORGAN
HIGHLY COMMENDED

Production Line
Harrogate, Yorkshire

A Production line and worker at Harrogate Spring water. The water is sourced locally. The first mineral spring in Harrogate was discovered in 1571 by Queen Elizabeth's physician who recommended its medicinal properties to his patients and the town became christened 'The English Spa'.

○ AMIT LENNON
HIGHLY COMMENDED

Scallop fisherman
Borough Market, London

Here he is preparing and cleaning scallops. He agreed to be photographed as part of a larger series about London life.

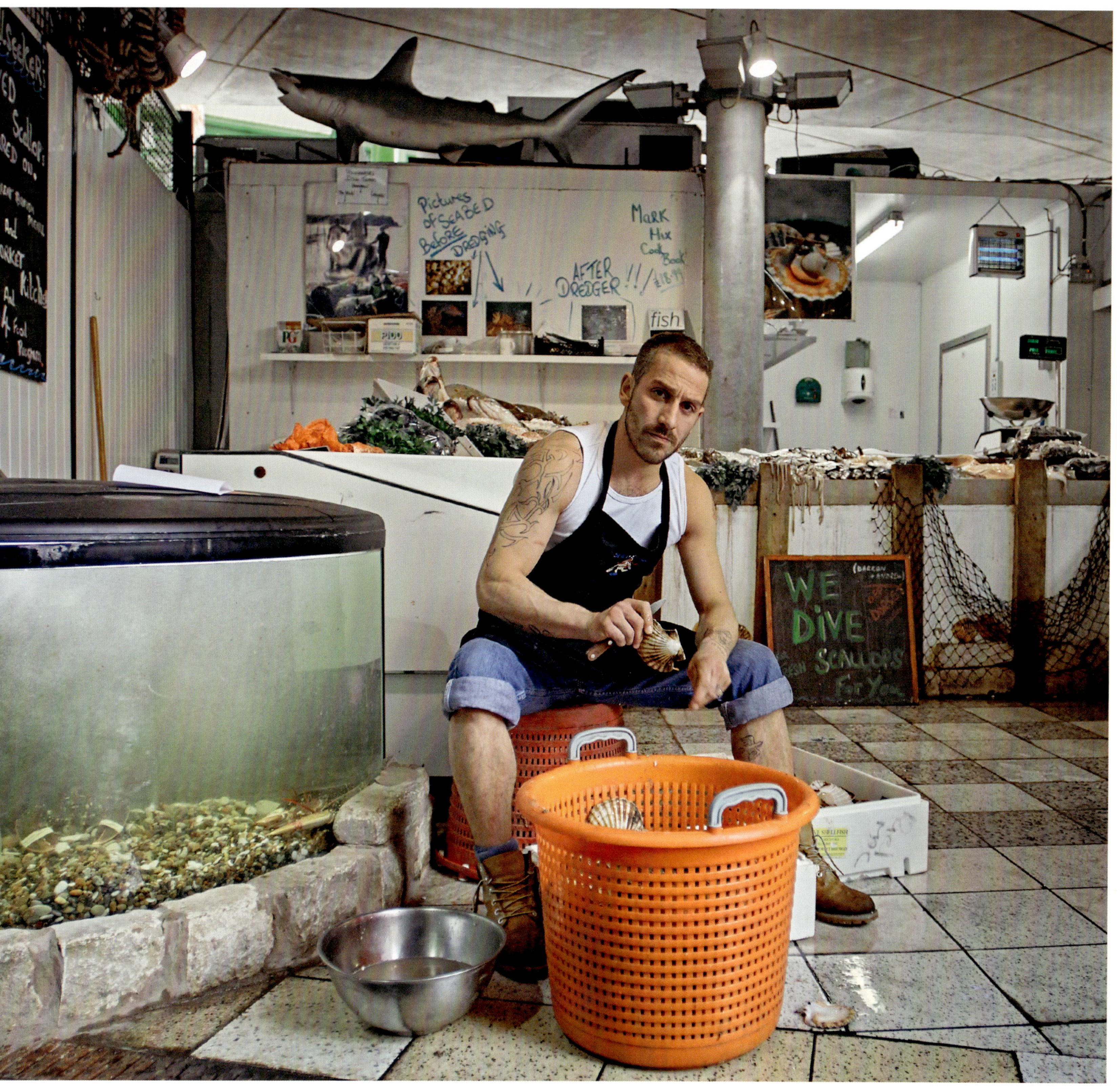

Pictures
of SEA BED
BEFORE DREDGING
MARK
HIX
Cook
Book
£18.99
AFTER DREDGER !!!
fish
WE DIVE
FOR SCALLOPS
FOR YOU

5

BRITS ON HOLIDAY

Brits on Holiday captures British people away from work, whether that's a day trip, weekend break, Easter, Christmas, or a traditional 'bucket-and-spade' trip to the coast.

ELENA MARIMON MUNOZ
OVERALL WINNER & CATEGORY WINNER

Past Present
Stonehenge, Wiltshire, England

Sunrise at Stonehenge during the summer solstice festival. By the time the sun started to rise above the stones, hundreds, if not thousands of people had gathered, phones and cameras up in the air ready to record the magical moment. In the picture, I wanted to capture the mixture of ancient history and modern technology, fused together: past and present.

With thanks to English Heritage

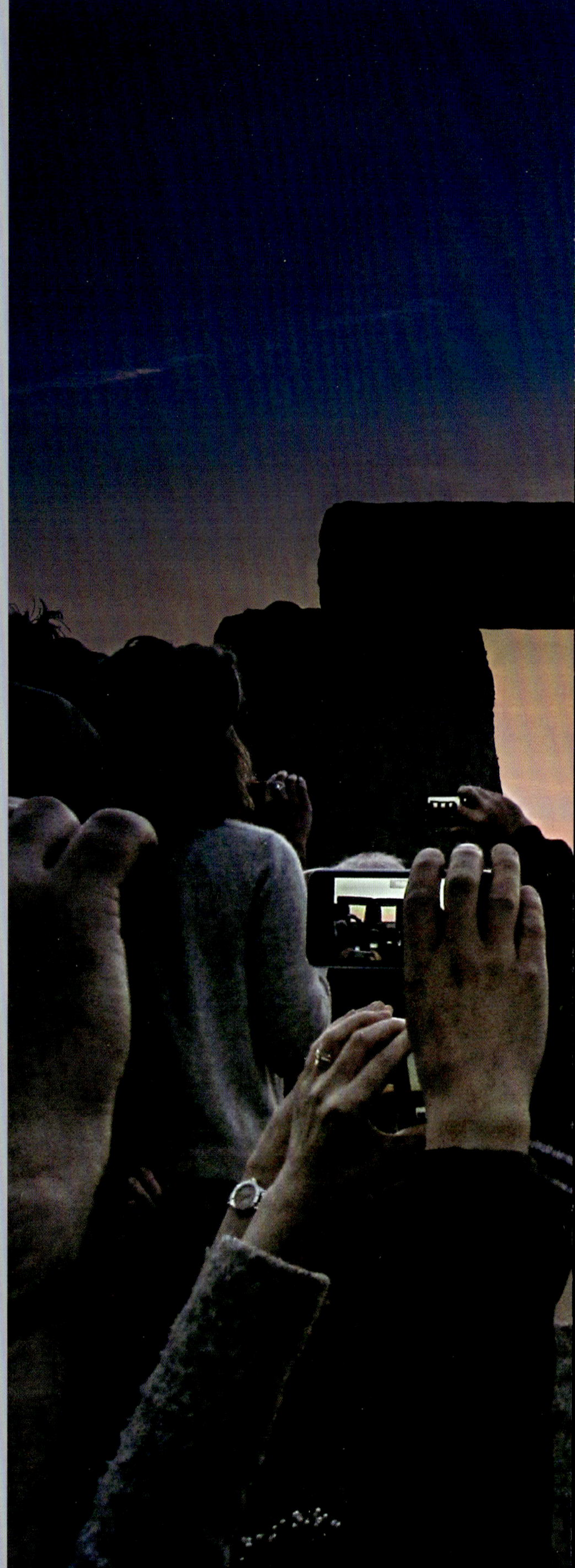

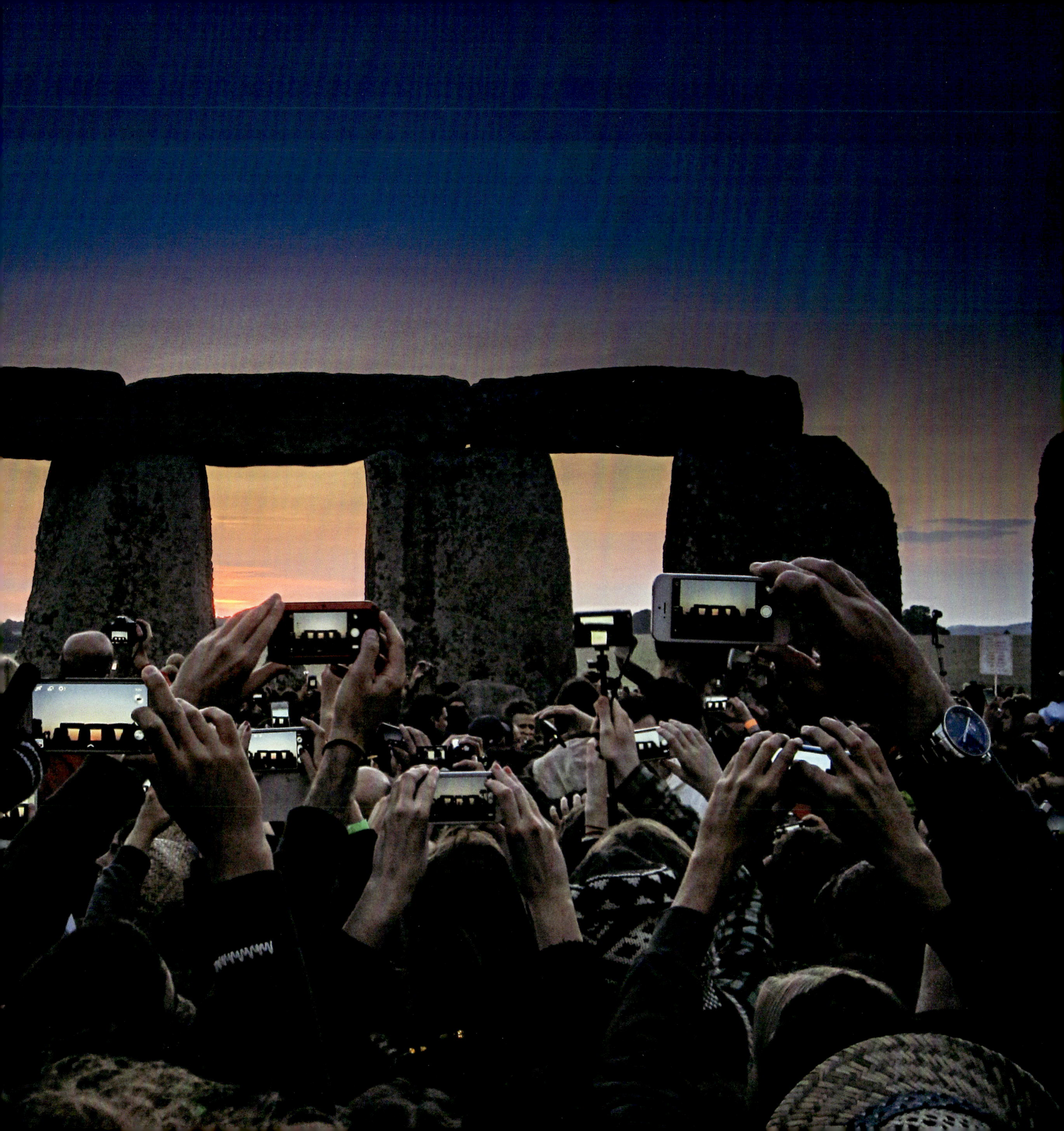

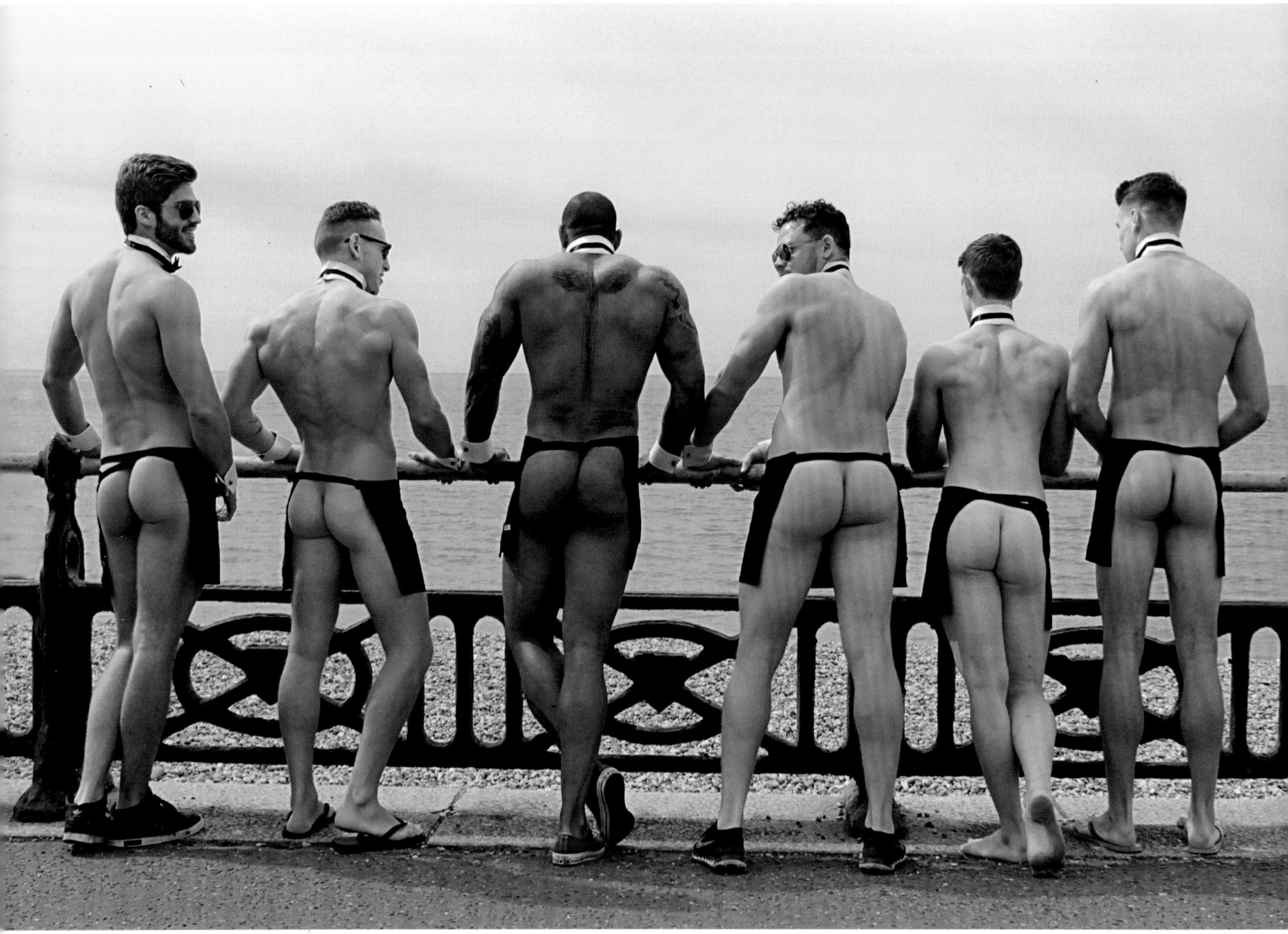

 CHRIS BARBARA / HIGHLY COMMENDED

Oh I do like to be beside the seaside (The Bottom Line)
Brighton, East Sussex

As soon as I saw these guys getting out of a car on Brighton Promenade I saw the photo opportunity. I quickly asked them if they'd mind standing in front of the railings looking out to sea. A voice from behind said 'hang on, I'm not in the picture' and a well-built guy placed himself on the end unbalancing my line up. I asked if he'd mind moving to the centre to balance the image and I clicked.

○ RICHARD CHERRY
HIGHLY COMMENDED

Threesome
Walton-on-the-Naze, Essex

This is from a project photographing people on the beach. I try to capture images that suggest relationships between people and perhaps have a certain ambiguity. In this image, the posture of the man and the triangular composition with the two women were what caught my eye.

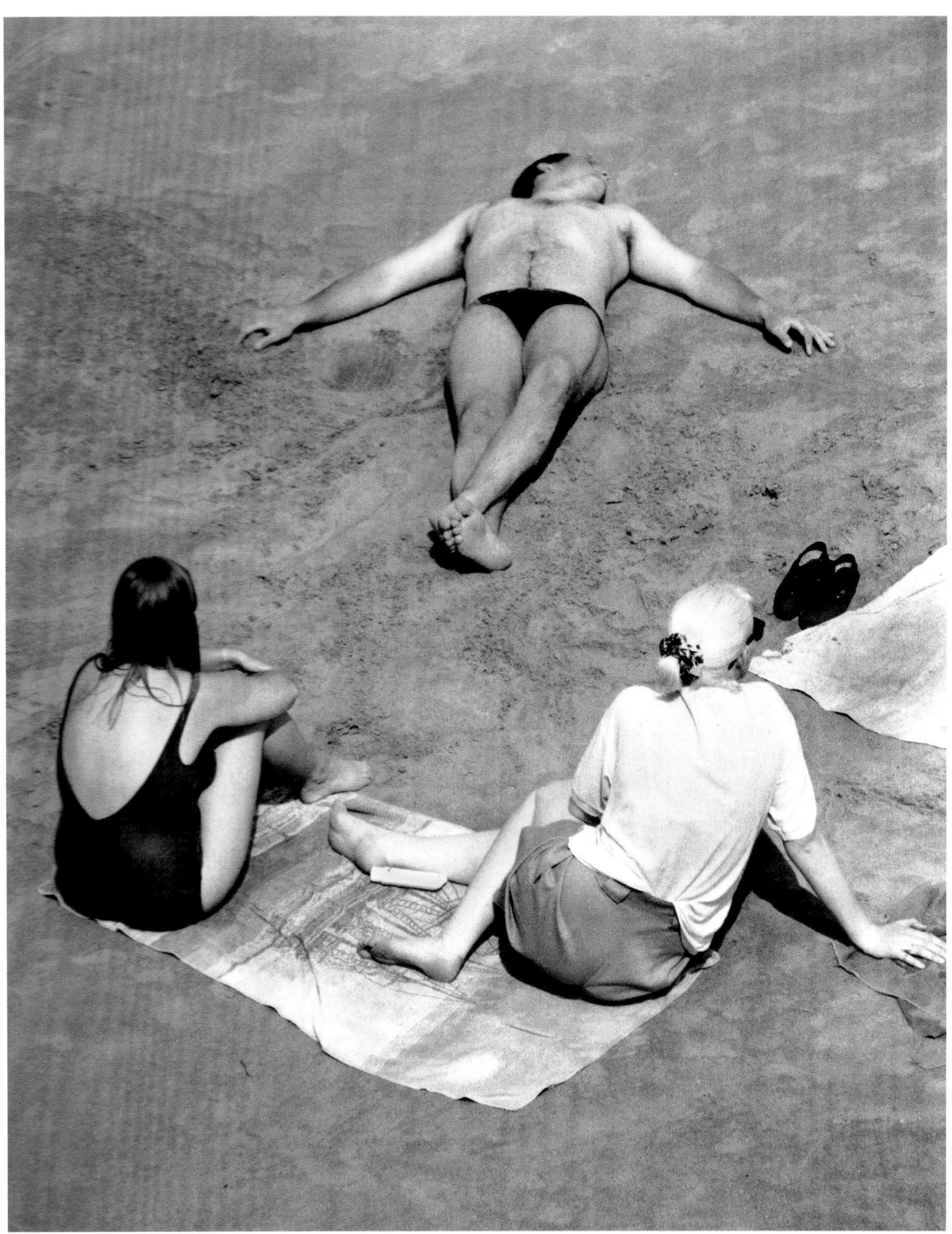

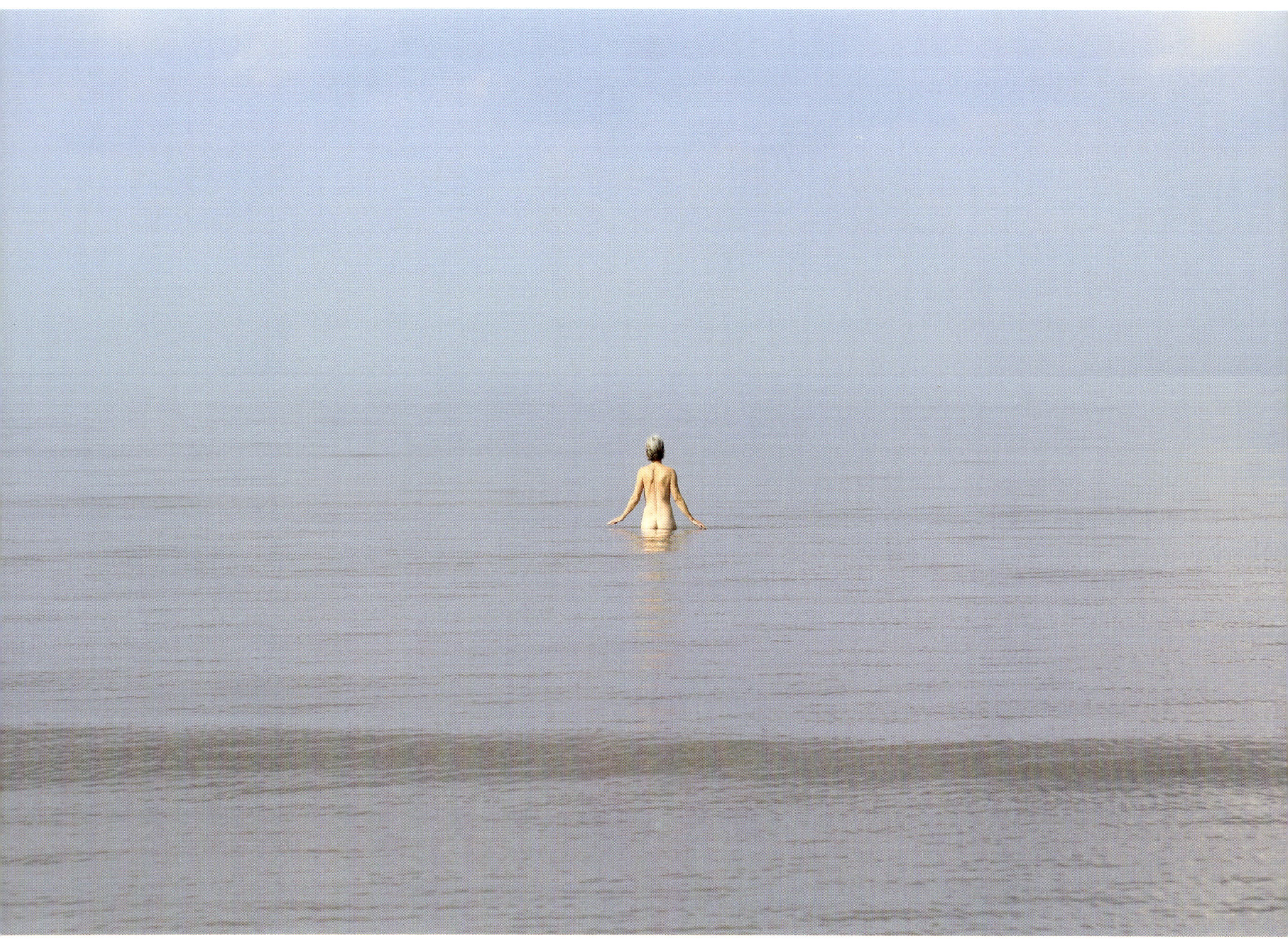

There is no end to the sea and sky
Old Hunstanton

Sept 20th 2015. A delicate but glorious east coast day,
barely touching the sea and sky.

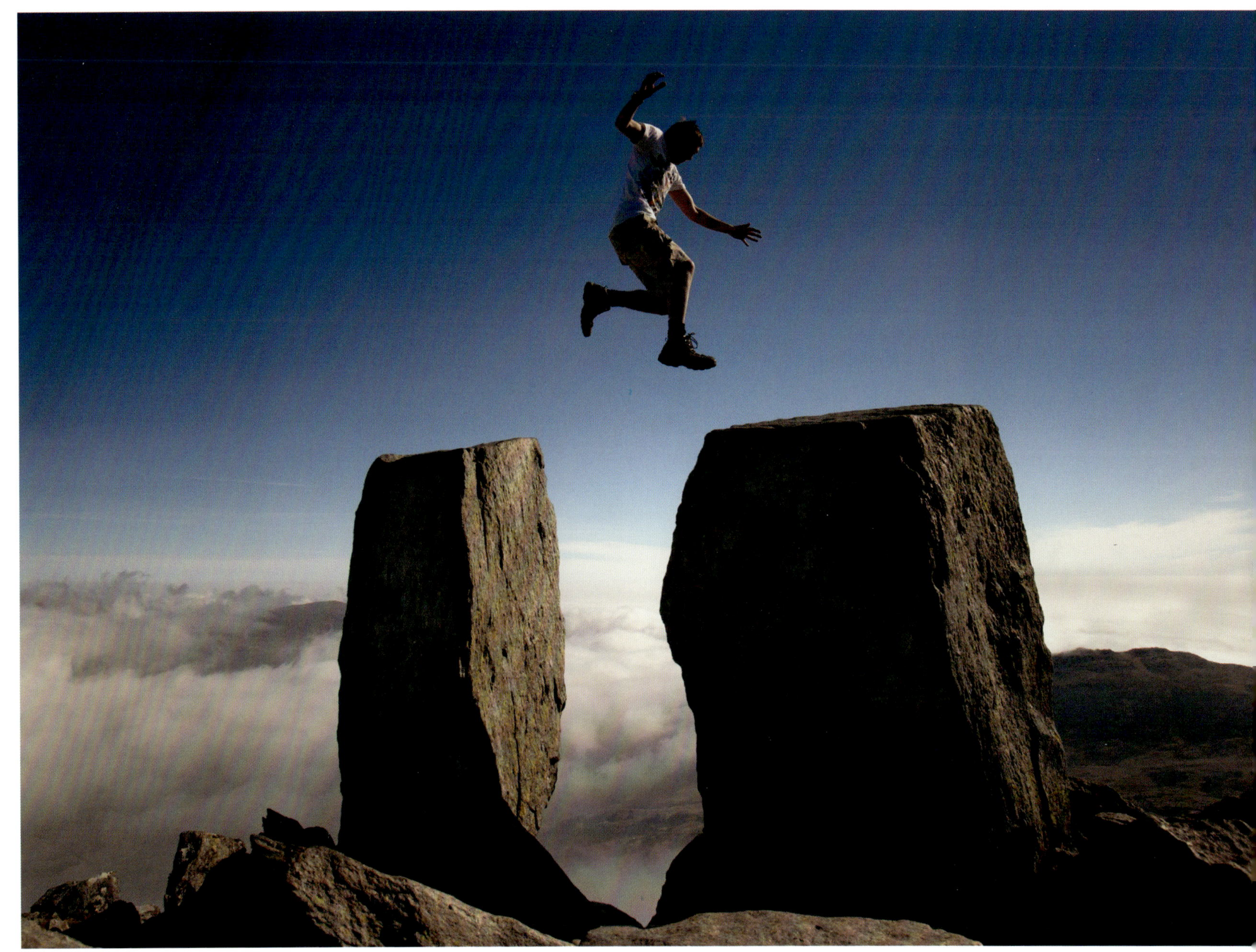

Over Adam and Eve
Tryfan, Snowdonia, Gwynedd, Wales

Two large rock columns on top of Tryfan are called Adam and
Eve. If you make the precarious jump from one to the other
you gain the 'freedom of the mountain'.

Walker on Malham Cove Limestone Pavement
Malham Cove, North Yorkshire

Hannah pictured on the Limestone Pavement above
Malham Cove in North Yorkshire with the view of
Malham Dale in the winter morning sunlight. Taken
for WALK Magazine to mark the 50th anniversary of
the opening of the Pennine Way. Whilst many exotic
foreign destinations are a short aeroplane journey away,
rambling remains a favourite British holiday pastime.

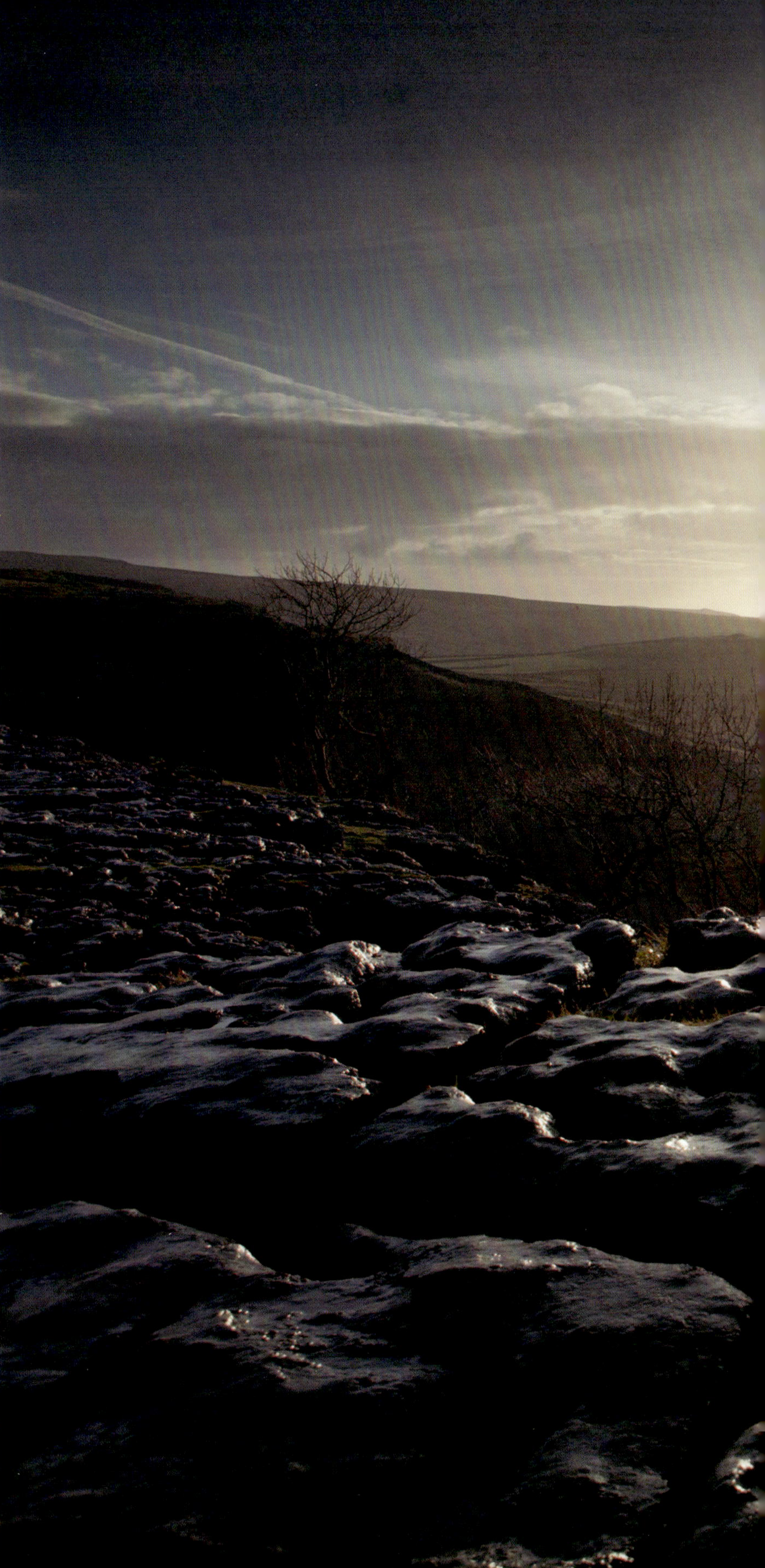

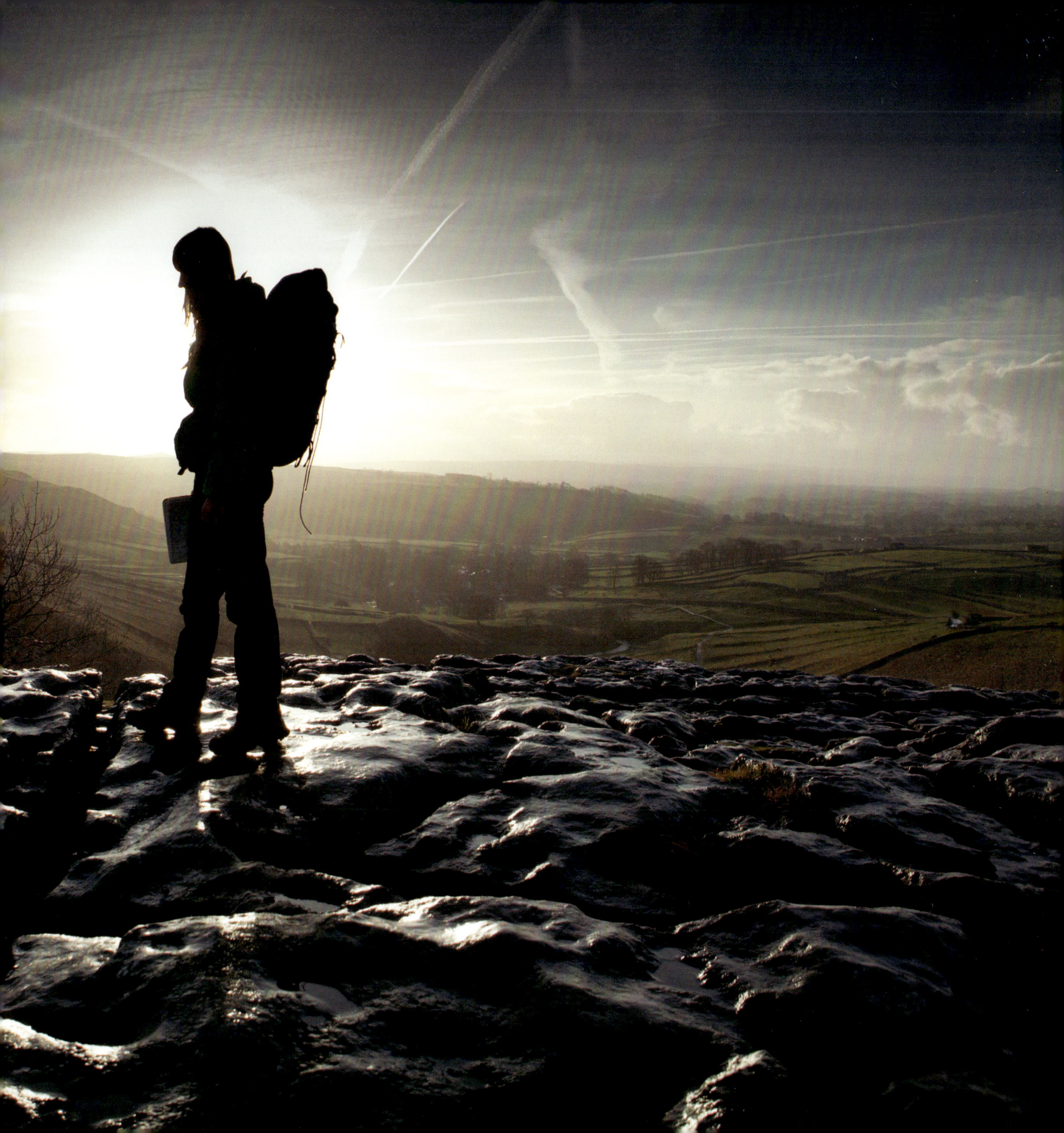

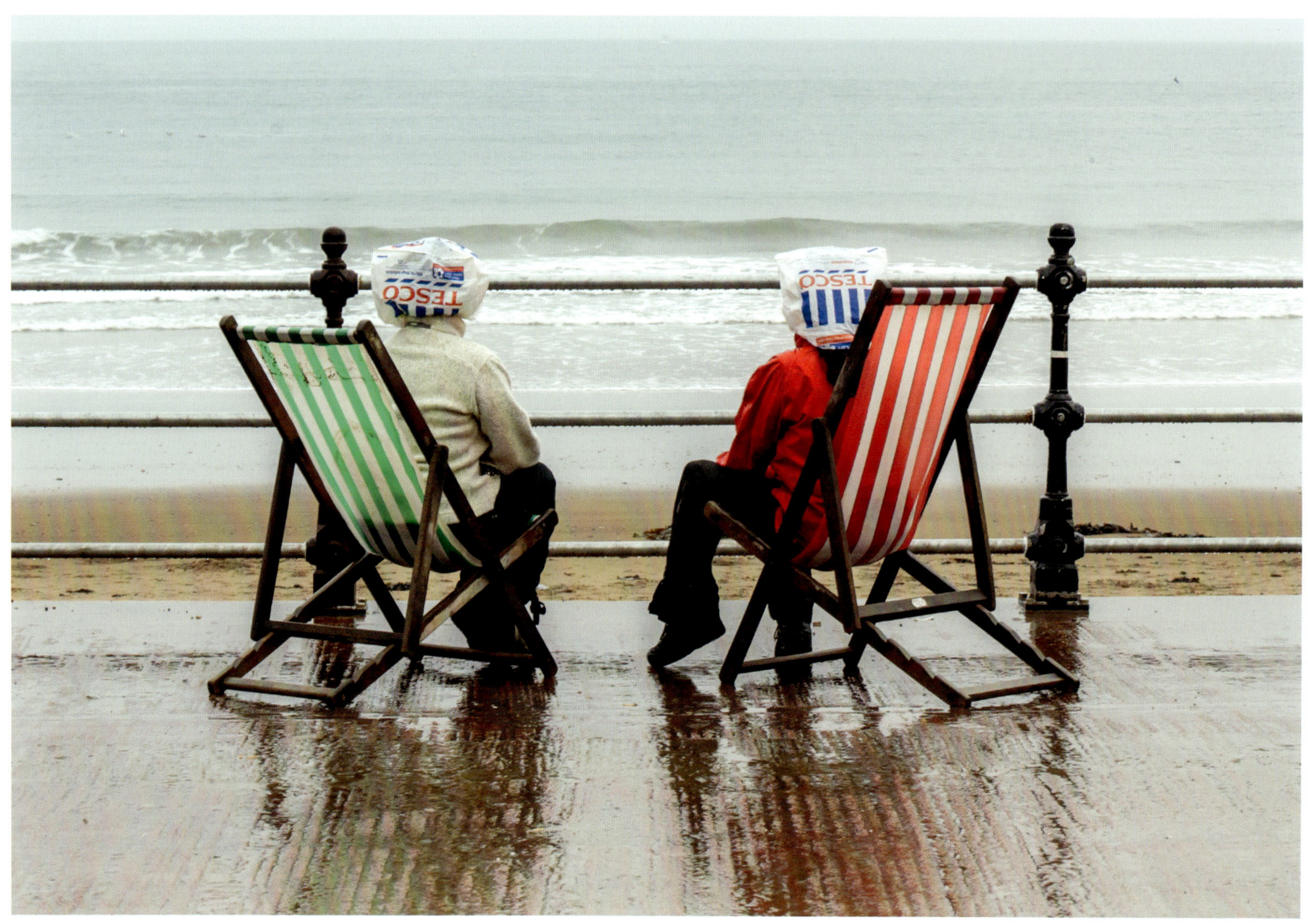

○ PAUL ANTHONY WILSON / HIGHLY COMMENDED

Very Little Helps
Scarborough Seafront, North Yorkshire

A visit to the seaside can be often marred by the weather, some
people, however, are determined to brave the elements. I saw these
two holiday makers making the best of a wet day on Scarborough's
promenade. Perhaps this will catch on as a way of recycling used
carrier bags.

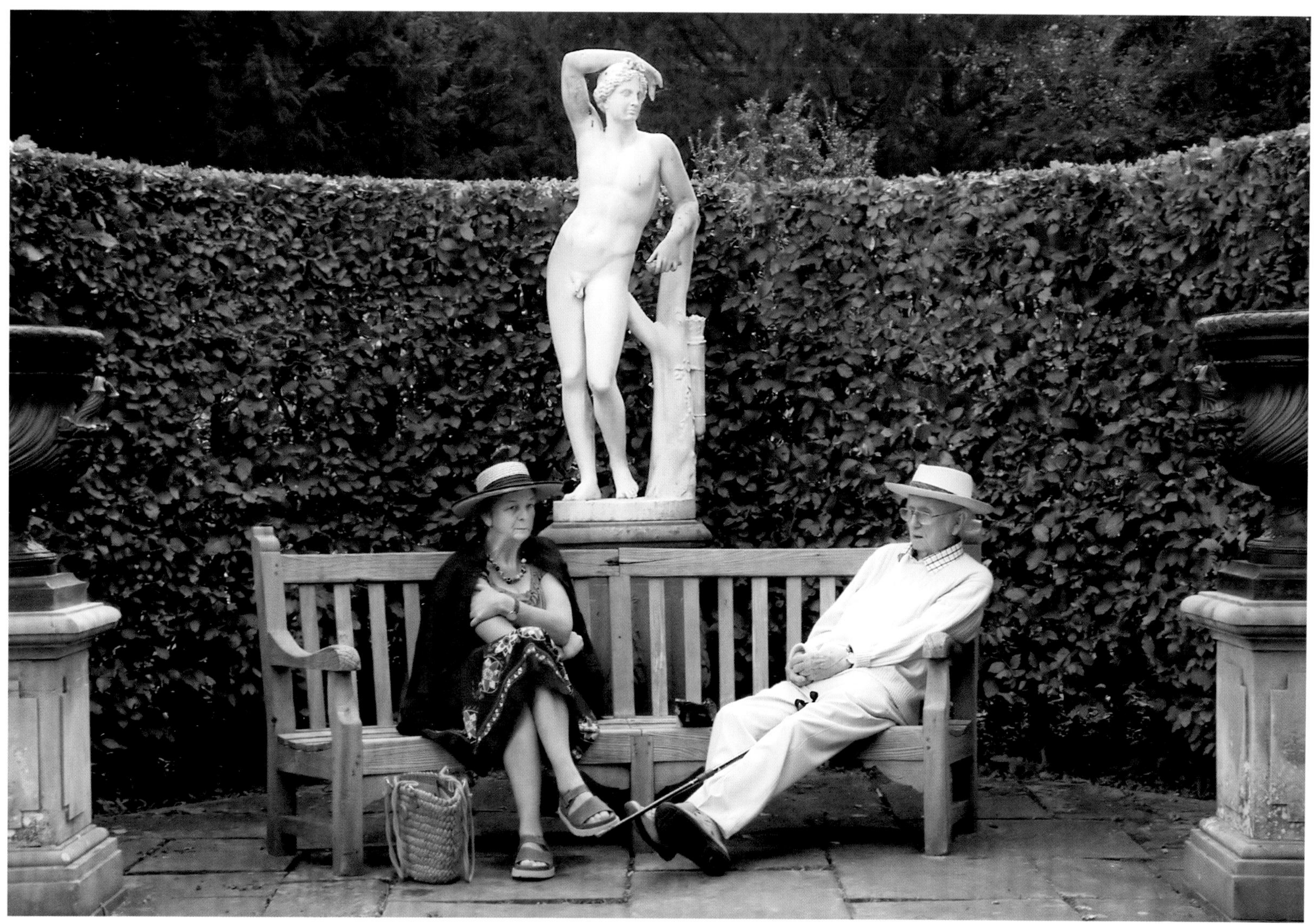

Cambridgeshire

I am always on the lookout for people pictures and this couple
caught my eye. I liked the juxtaposition of the figure of the
statue with the rather thoughtful looking couple.

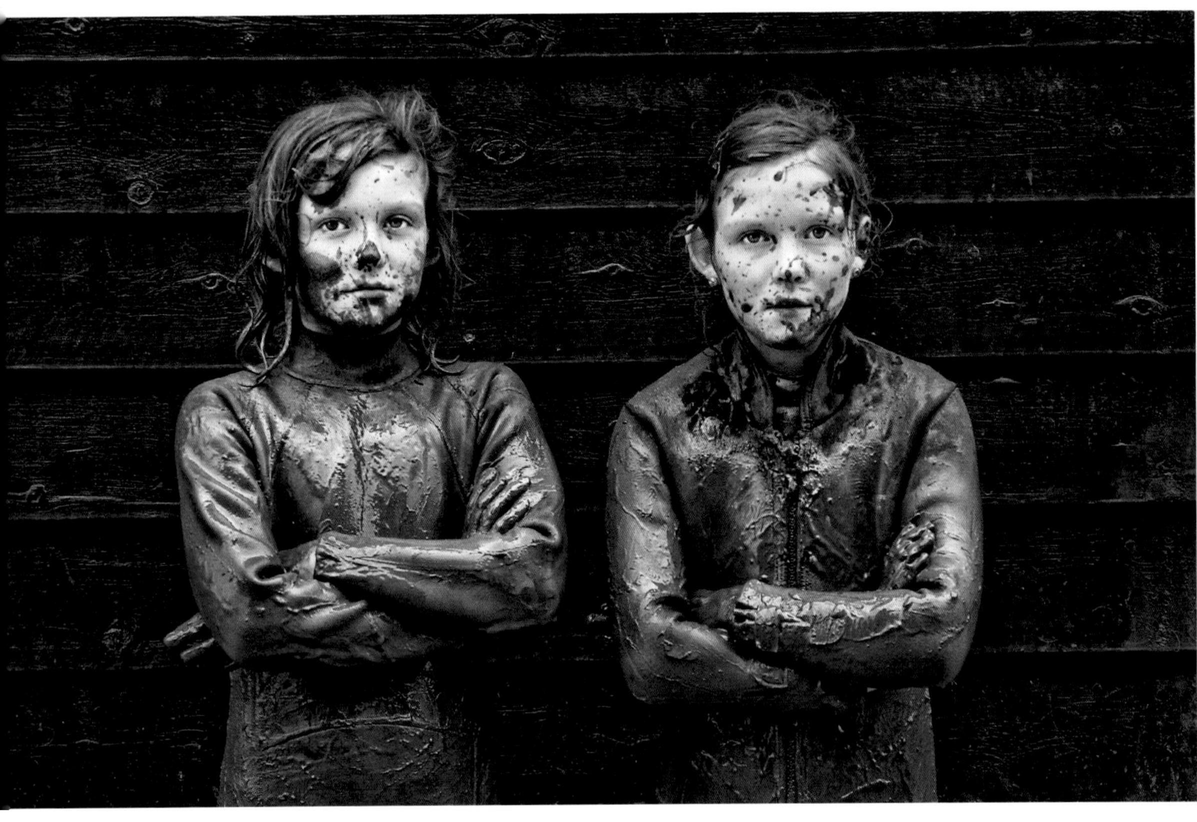

Mud Twins
Mersea Island, Essex

I was sitting in my front garden and became aware of a rather disgruntled voice
saying 'what am I going to do with you'.
I looked up to see these two young girls
walking by, with mum behind. I said
'please just wait there and let me get my
camera!' I took this image as the girls
stood by my garage. The family now have
a large print of this over their fireplace.

● IAN BRUMPTON

The day I became a jive fan
South Bank, London

A free concert at the South Bank featuring
the Jive Aces and the Flirtinis, which went
down very well.

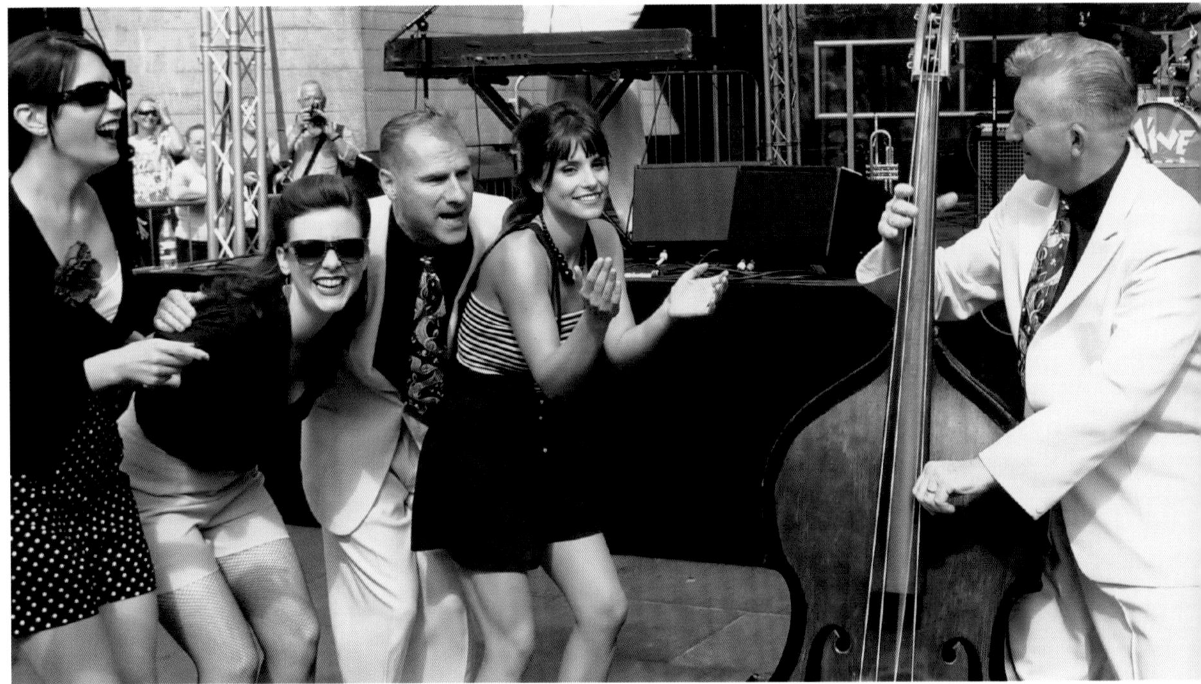

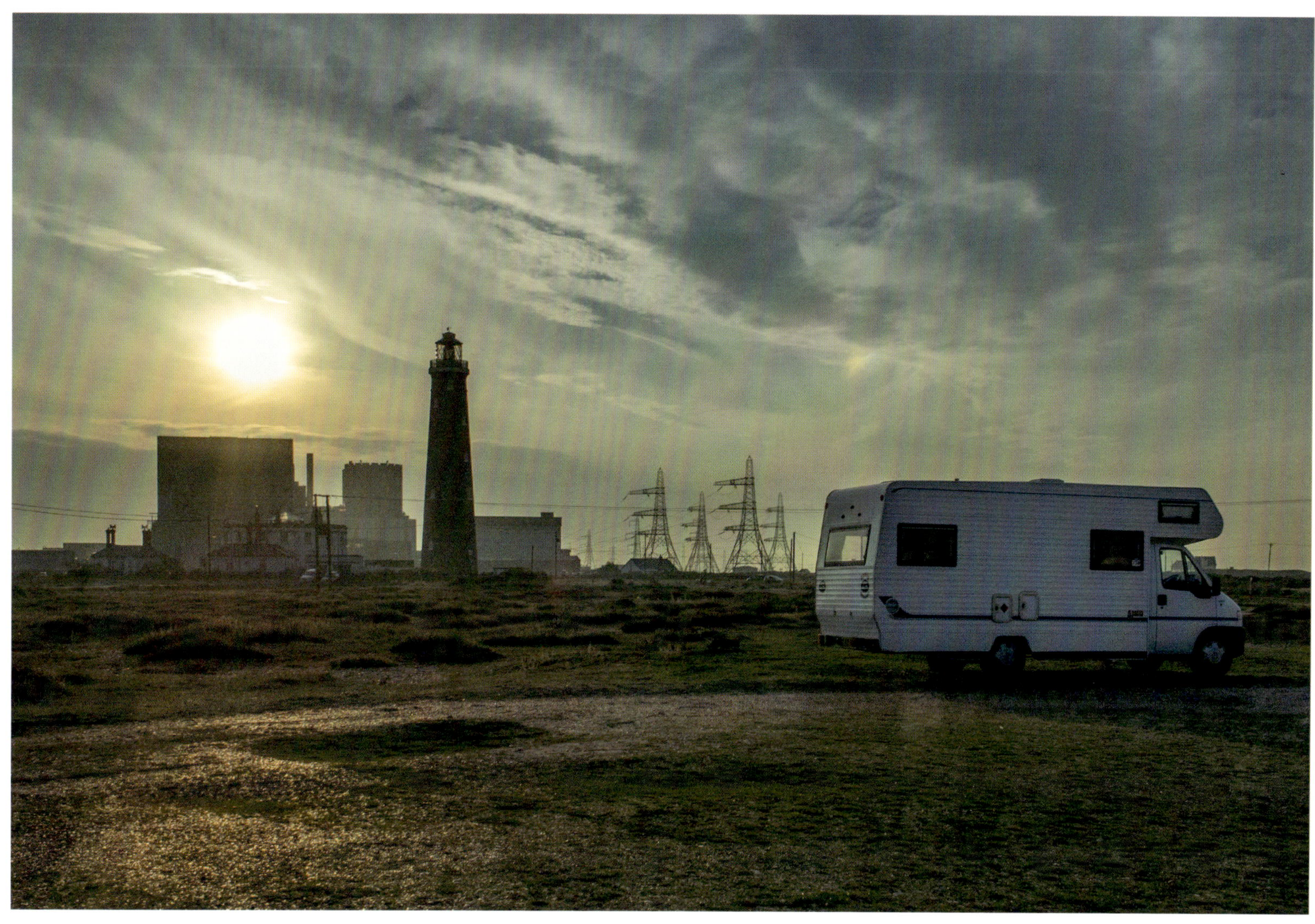

A week in Dungeness
Dungeness, Kent

I saw this juxtaposition between the usual
holiday sunset shot and the mundanity of the
nuclear power station behind the camper van.
I wanted to capture that scene, to feel how the
people inside felt, and why they chose this
spot and location for a holiday.

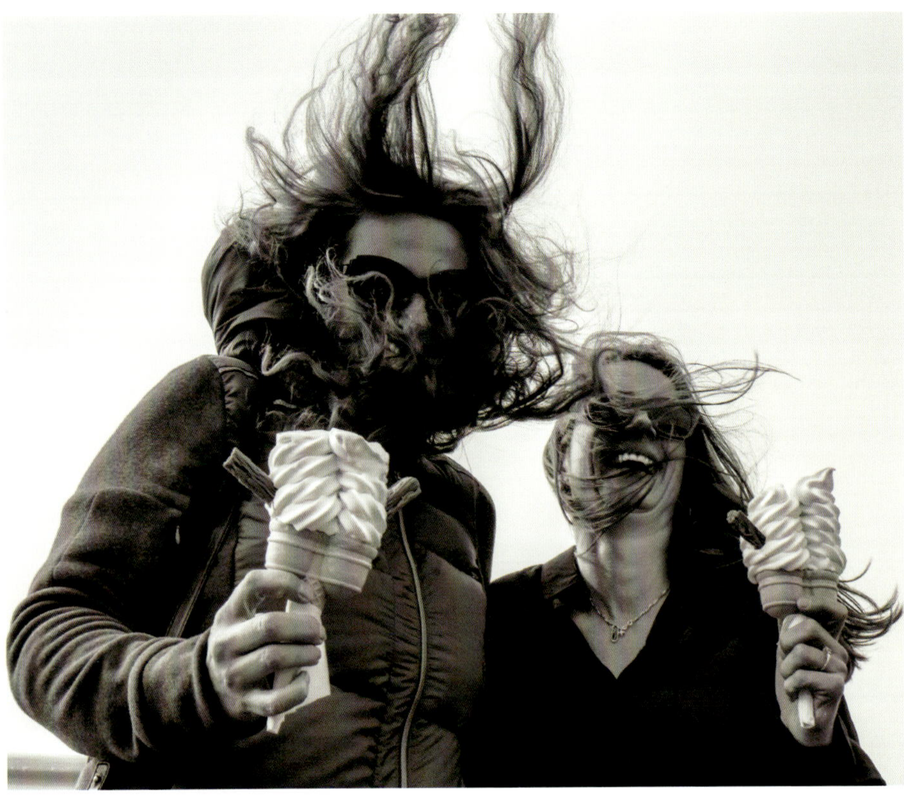

◔ JO TEASDALE

Brighton, Sussex

I was on Brighton Pier in the summer when I spotted these two girls. The wind was so fierce it was blowing their hair all over the place and they were really struggling to eat their ice creams. I loved that, for a brief moment, the girl's hair looked like horns. Despite the cloudy, cold day they still managed to laugh about their ice-cream problems and enjoy their day out at the seaside.

◔ CHRISSIE WESTGATE

Betty
Mersea Island, Essex

A book, a bear, blue sky and a beach hut named Betty – what more could anyone want?

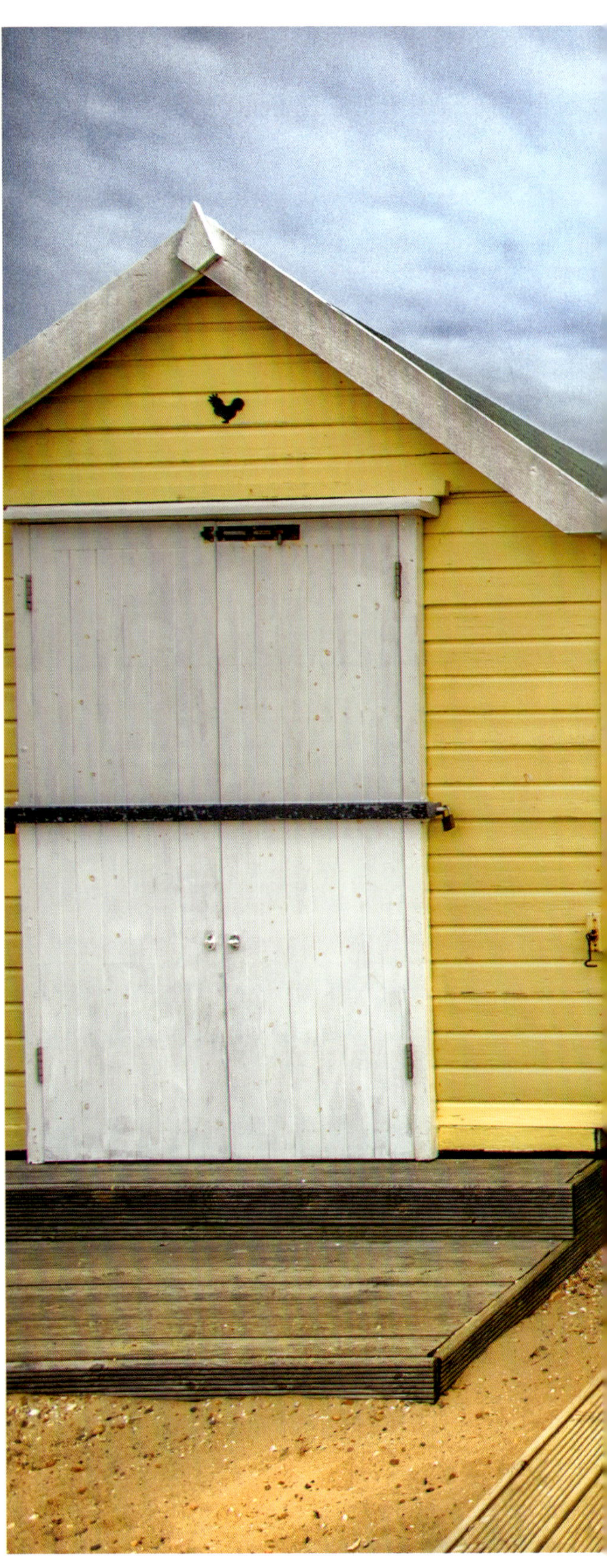

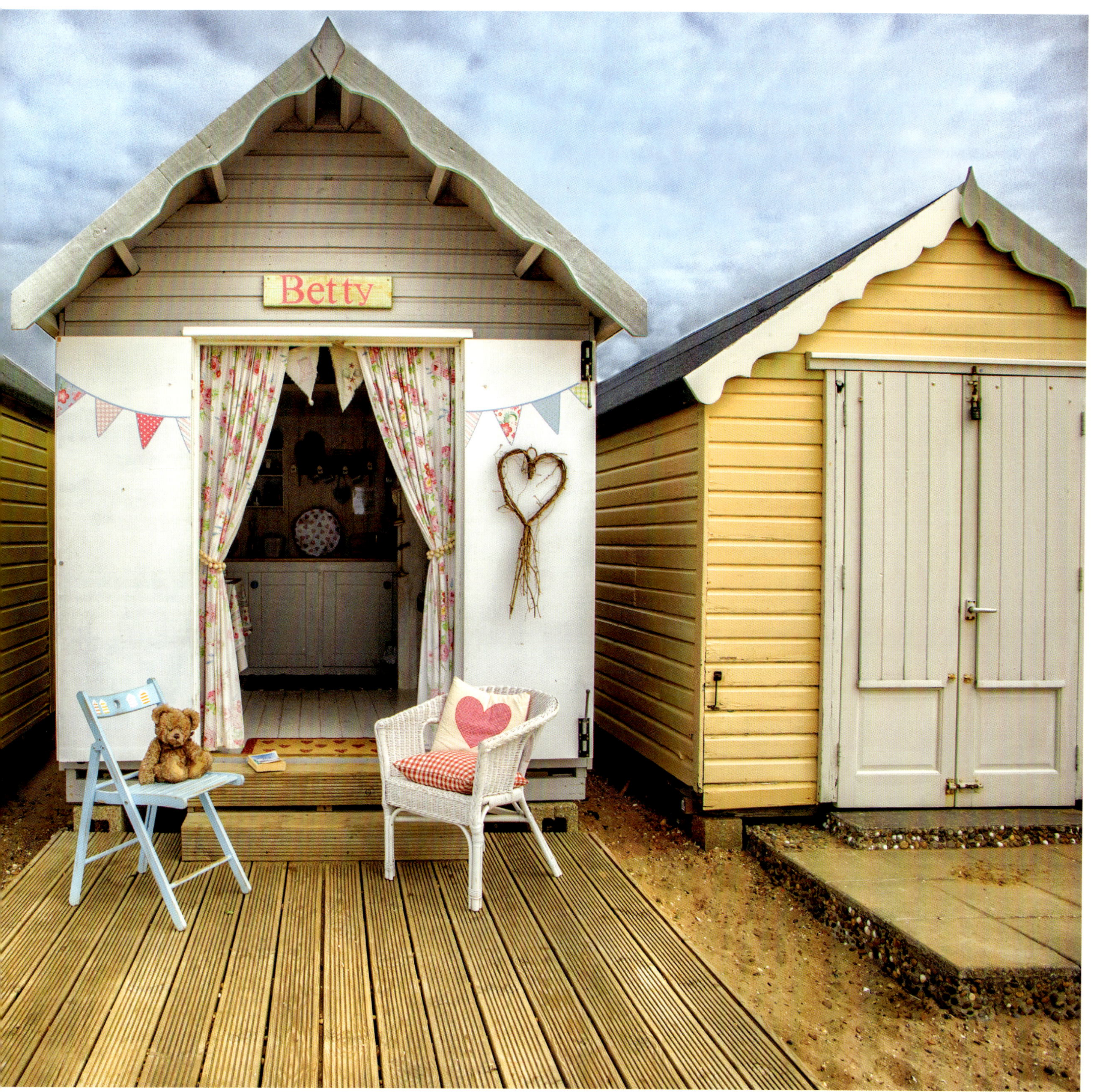
Betty

6 PORTRAITURE

The face of Britain: portraits of any age that capture character, spirit, and soul.

◯ CLAUDIA JANKE / WINNER

George
Packington Square Estate, Islington, London

George, 84, lived in this flat for forty two years, sharing it with his sister Doris until she was moved into a care home. George has also now moved to new accommodation as the result of a regeneration programme. The image was part of an installation challenging common prejudices about people living on council estates as well as exploring the sense of loss and gain that irreversible change brings with it.

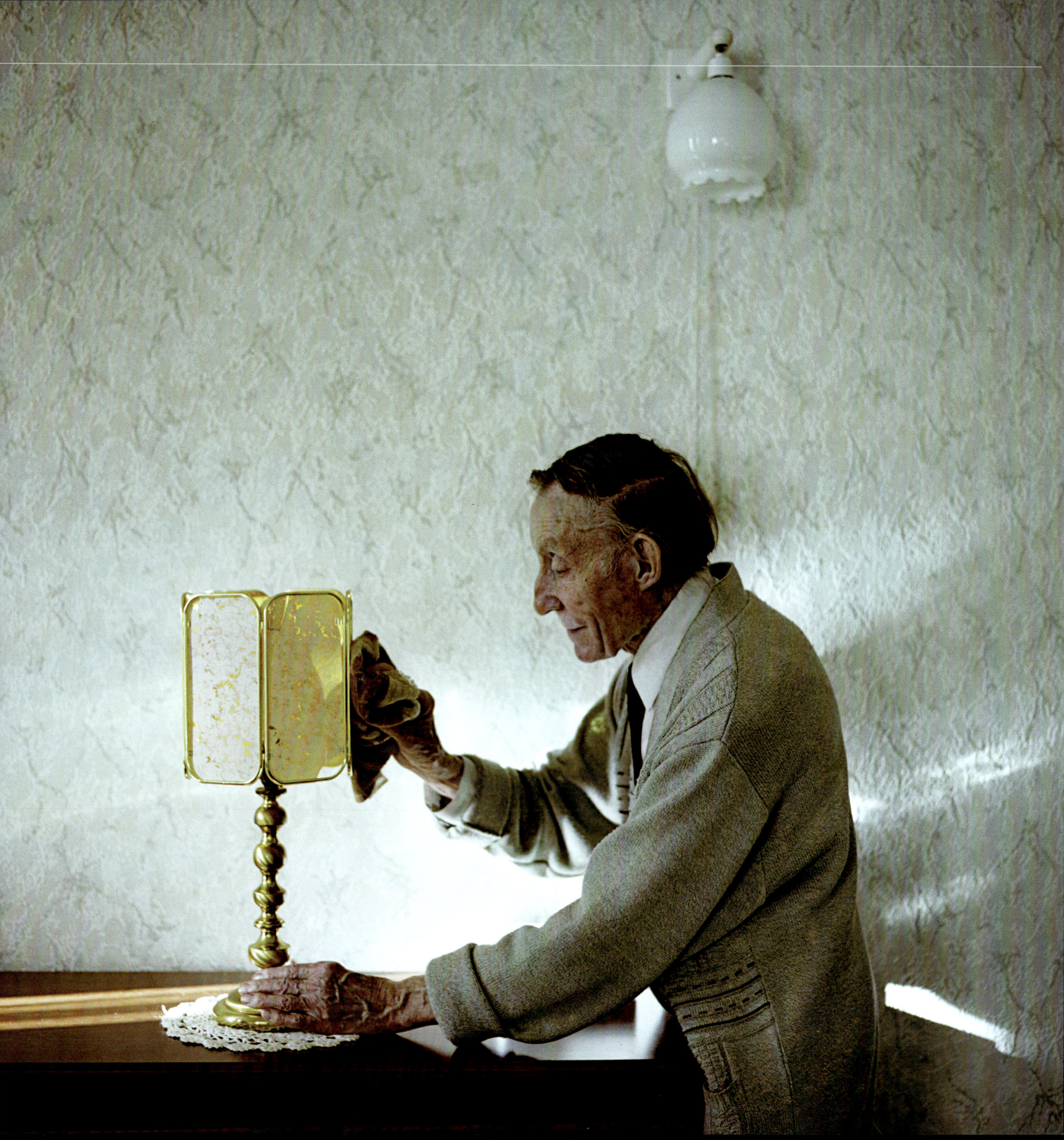

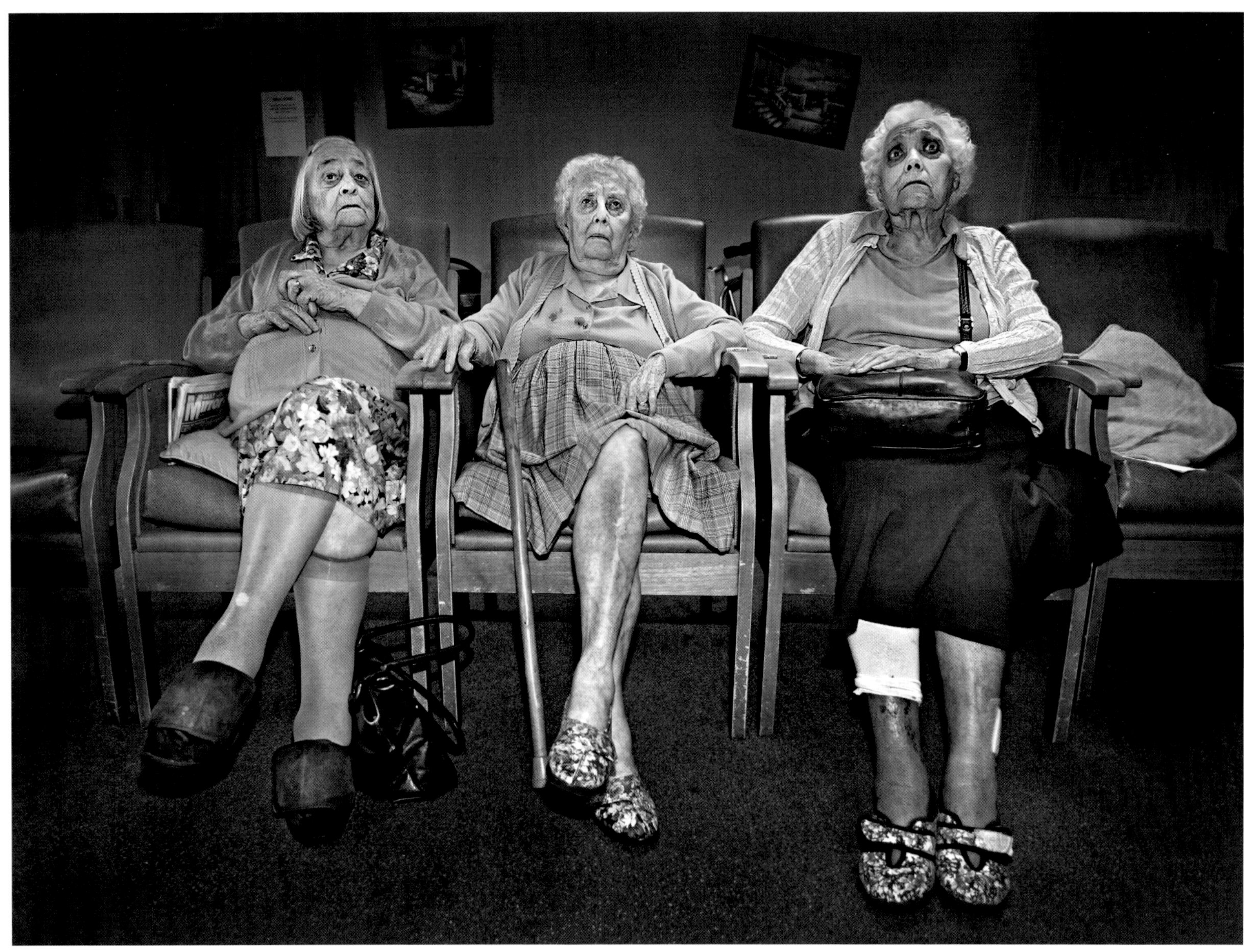

◌ CHRISSIE WESTGATE / HIGHLY COMMENDED

Waiting
Colchester, Essex

This image is part of a body of work I called 'Forgetting my
Memory'. The focus was on my lovely Aunt who was in a
residential home. One evening I arrived to find my aunt, sitting
with two of her fellow residents forlornly staring into space.
For some while they were completely unaware of my presence
as they just sat there waiting!

▷ DANIEL LEWIS
HIGHLY COMMENDED

**Jonathan Mercer,
wood engraver**
Chiswick, London

Jonathan was a dream subject for
me and my artist project. Not only
does he have an amazing face, full
of character, but his studio was a
treasure trove of detailed trinkets
that he, with his immense talent,
had created by hand. He was a
thoroughly lovely man too. Of all
the portraits in the series his was
the quickest to shoot, everything
fell into place, taking a mere thirty
minutes from start to finish.

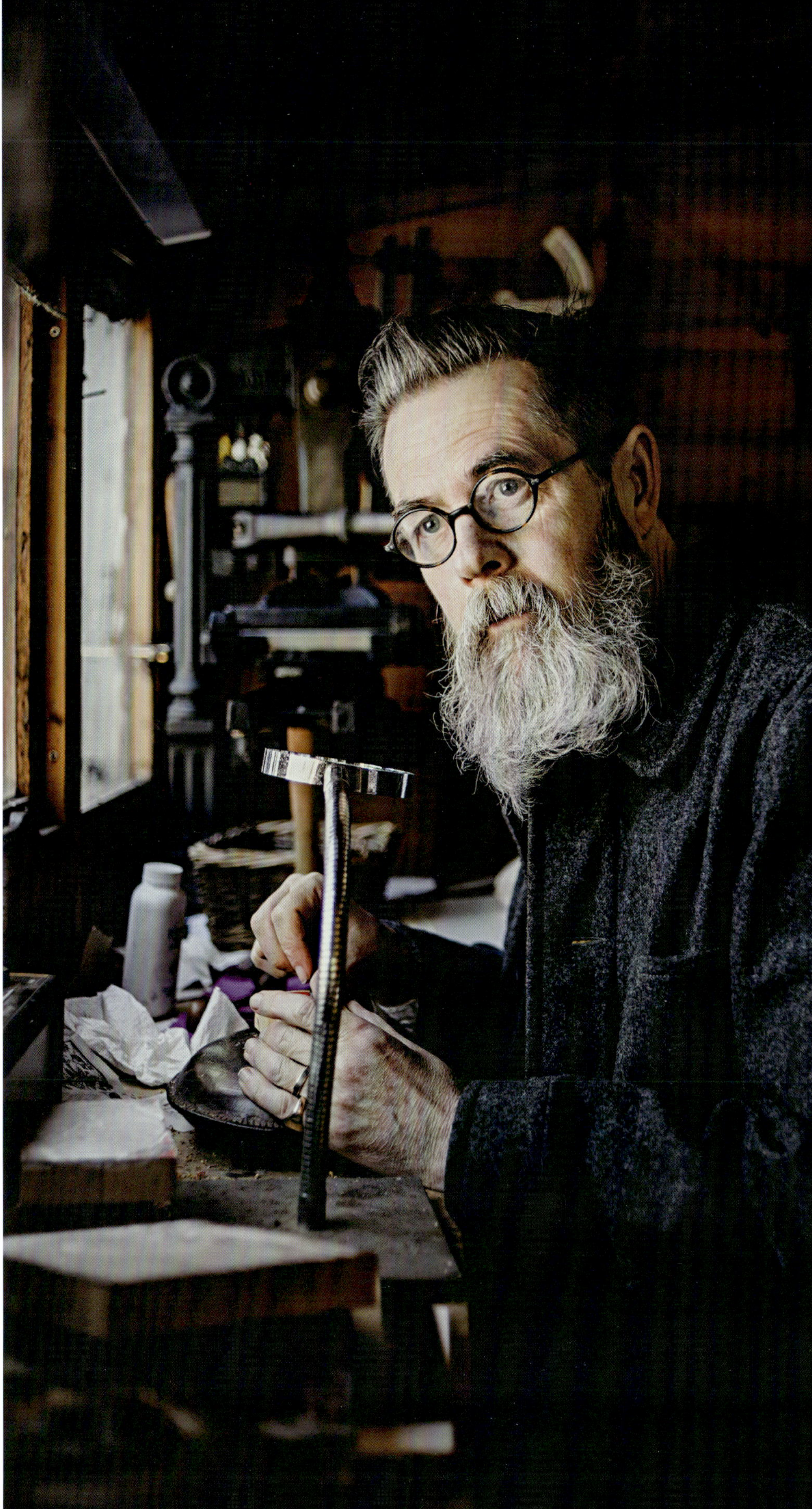

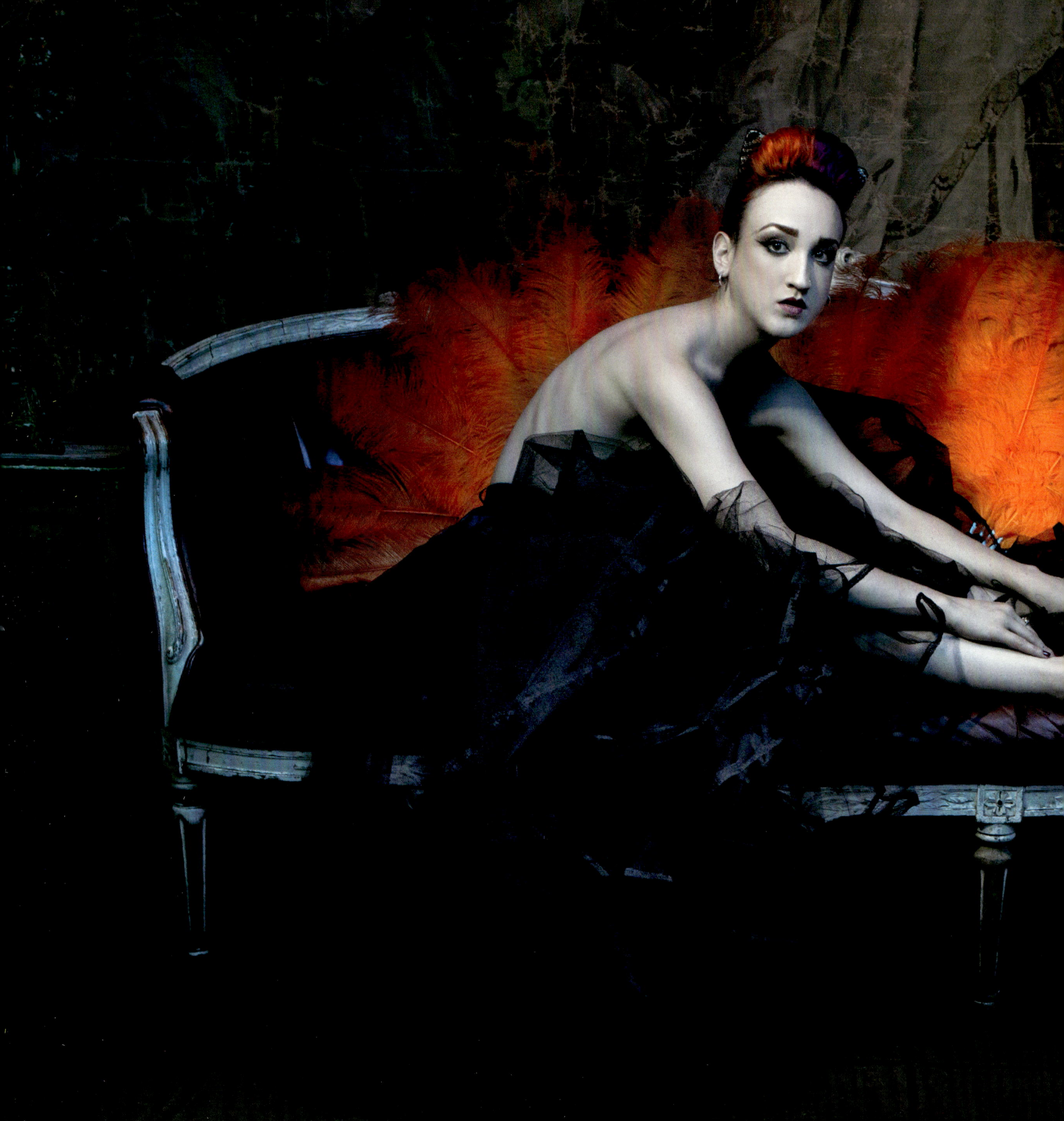

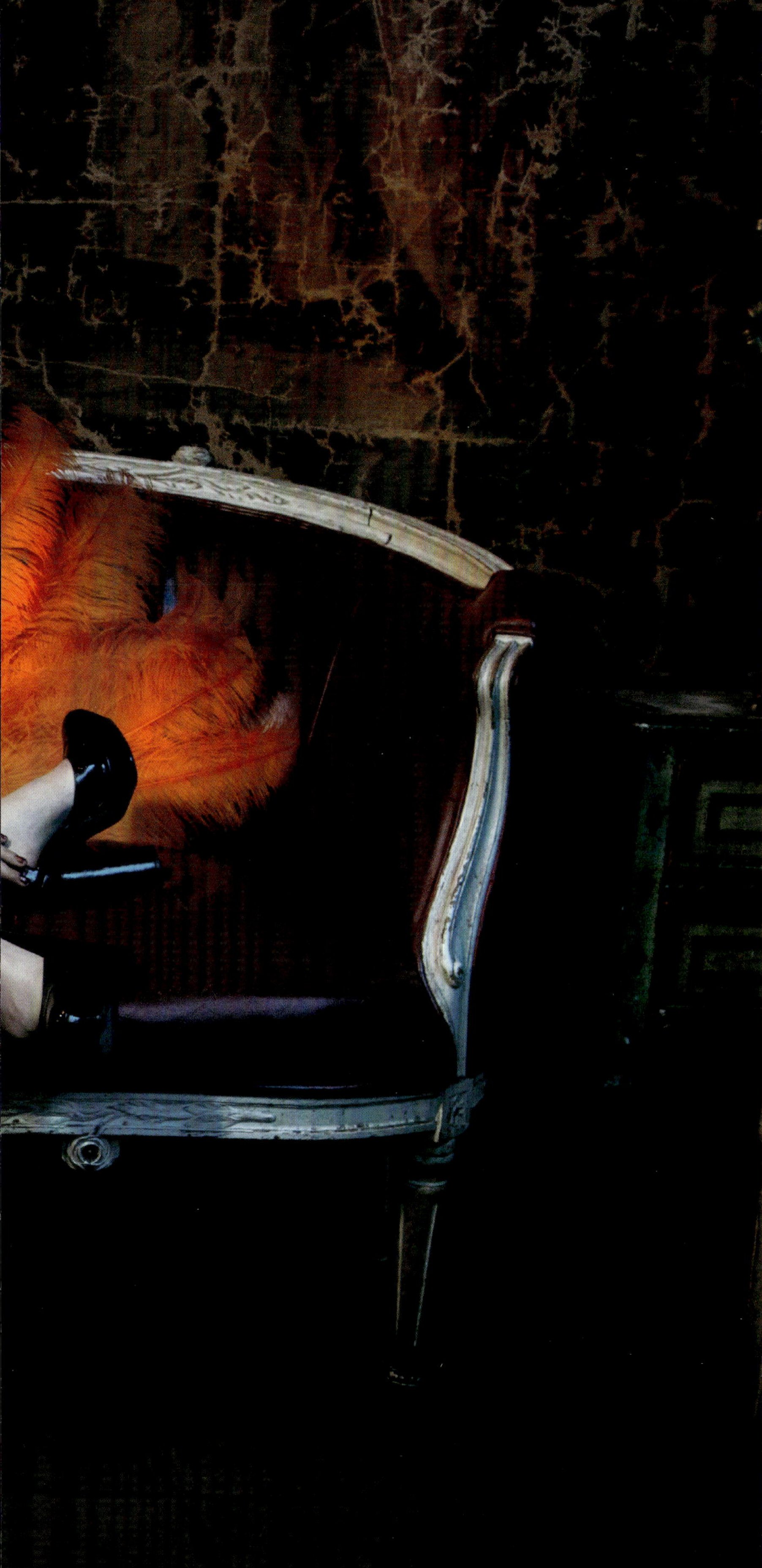

MAURIZIO MELOZZI / HIGHLY COMMENDED

Portrait of Tiger Rose
Brick Lane, London

The singer and perfomer Tiger Rose, contacted me to do the
portraits for her new music performance CD. We did these
photographs inside a restaurant in the Brick Lane area. I used
only the light available in the dining room, the ambient spotlight
was perfect – it was like being in a theatre.

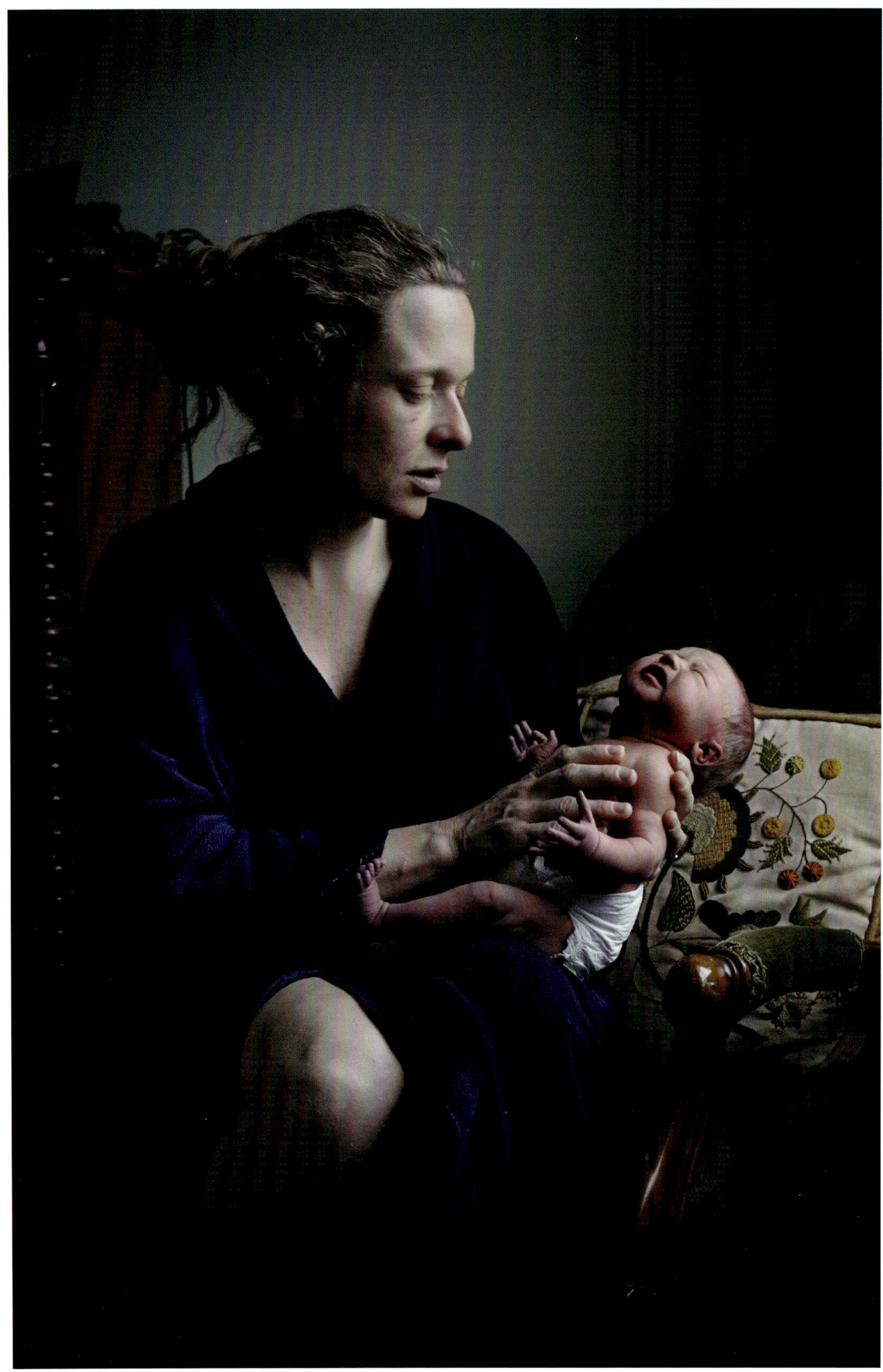

Nicola and Jemima
London

This portrait was shot for 'One Day Young', a series of portraits of women taken within twenty four hours of the birth back in their own homes. A moment usually only seen by the family, caught in a family album, but I wanted to capture this strength and beauty of the women in their triumph over the challenges of birth.

The series raises many questions on the subject of motherhood in art and aims to support and empower women. Over five years I shot 150 subjects.

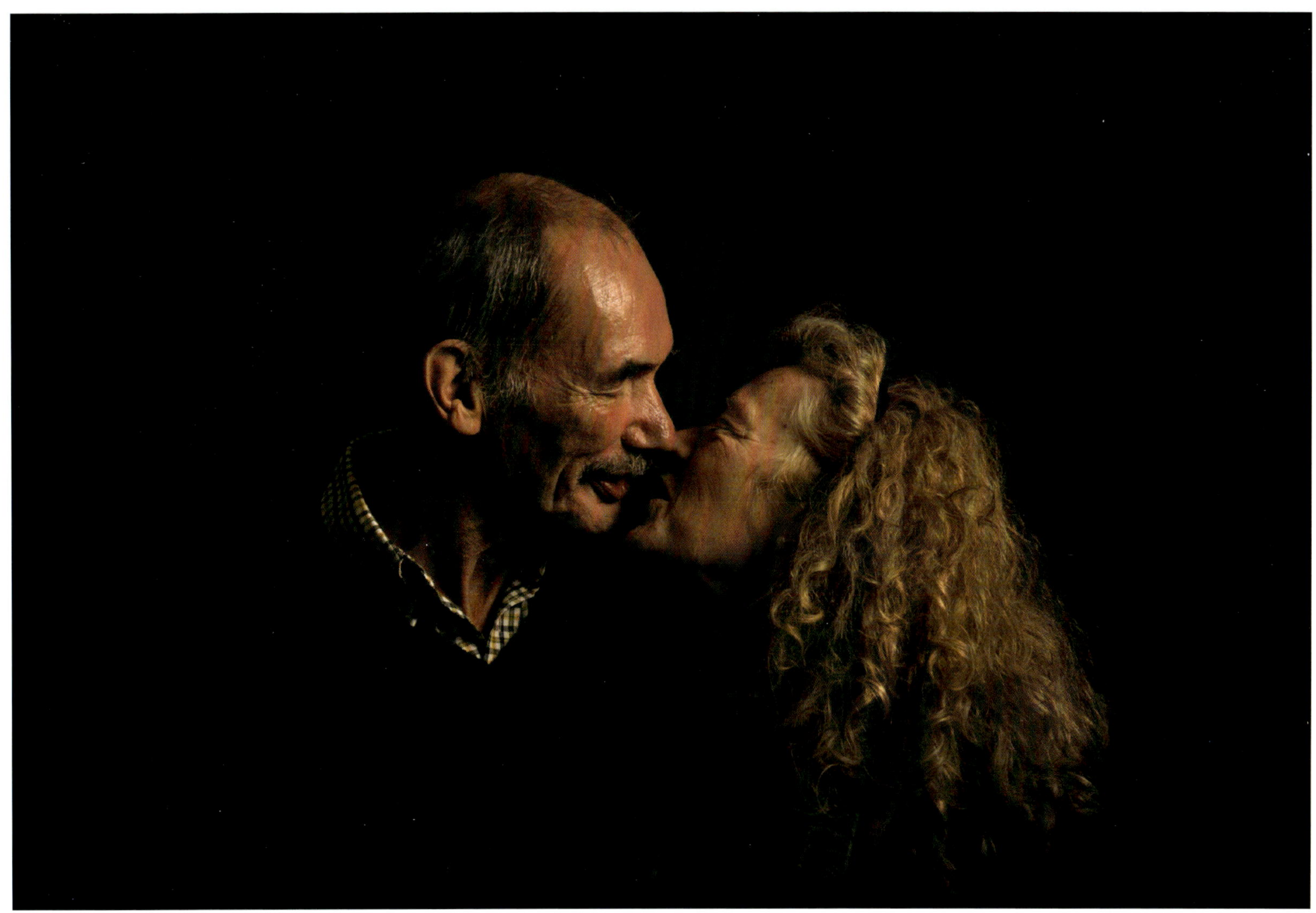

Until death do us part
Streatham, London

Katie and Michael are my friends. Michael has been diagnosed
with motor neuron disease. They came together for this kiss quite
spontaneously and as they did I took a couple of shots. However,
for this, the second shot, the flash lights had not had time to fully
recharge resulting in an under exposed image that seemed to
convey the drawing to an end of their time together.

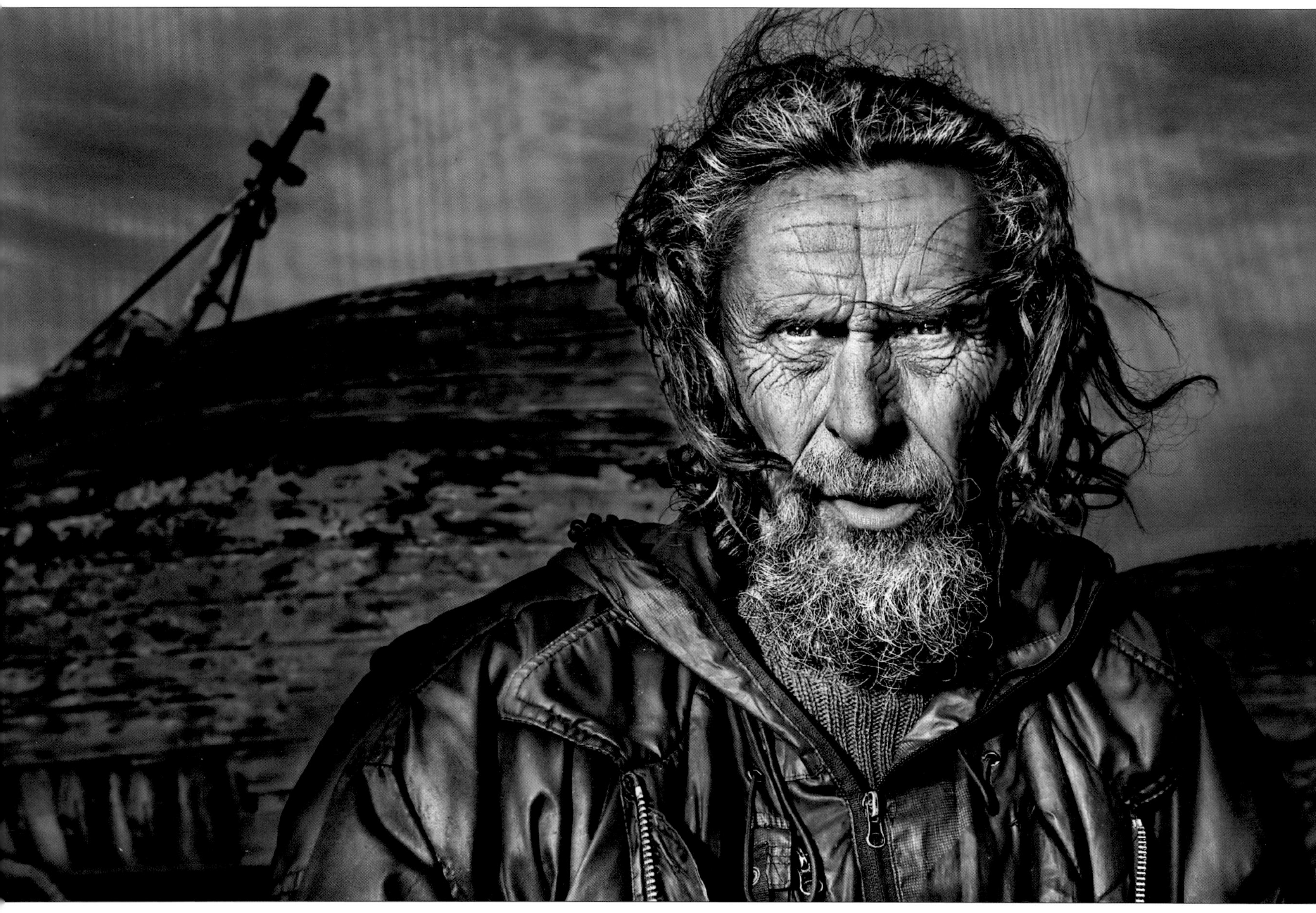

Gerry The Boat Gypsy
Mersea Island, Essex

Gerry is a bit of a travelling man and lives on a very old dilapidated boat called the 'May Celeste'. He has moored up on the River Blackwater for the last few years. Always a pleasure to spend time with, he enjoys telling passers by of the many scrapes and adventures he has encountered.

Grayson Perry
London

Shot at the British Museum where he had exhibited his work alongside pieces that he had selected from the Museum's collection.

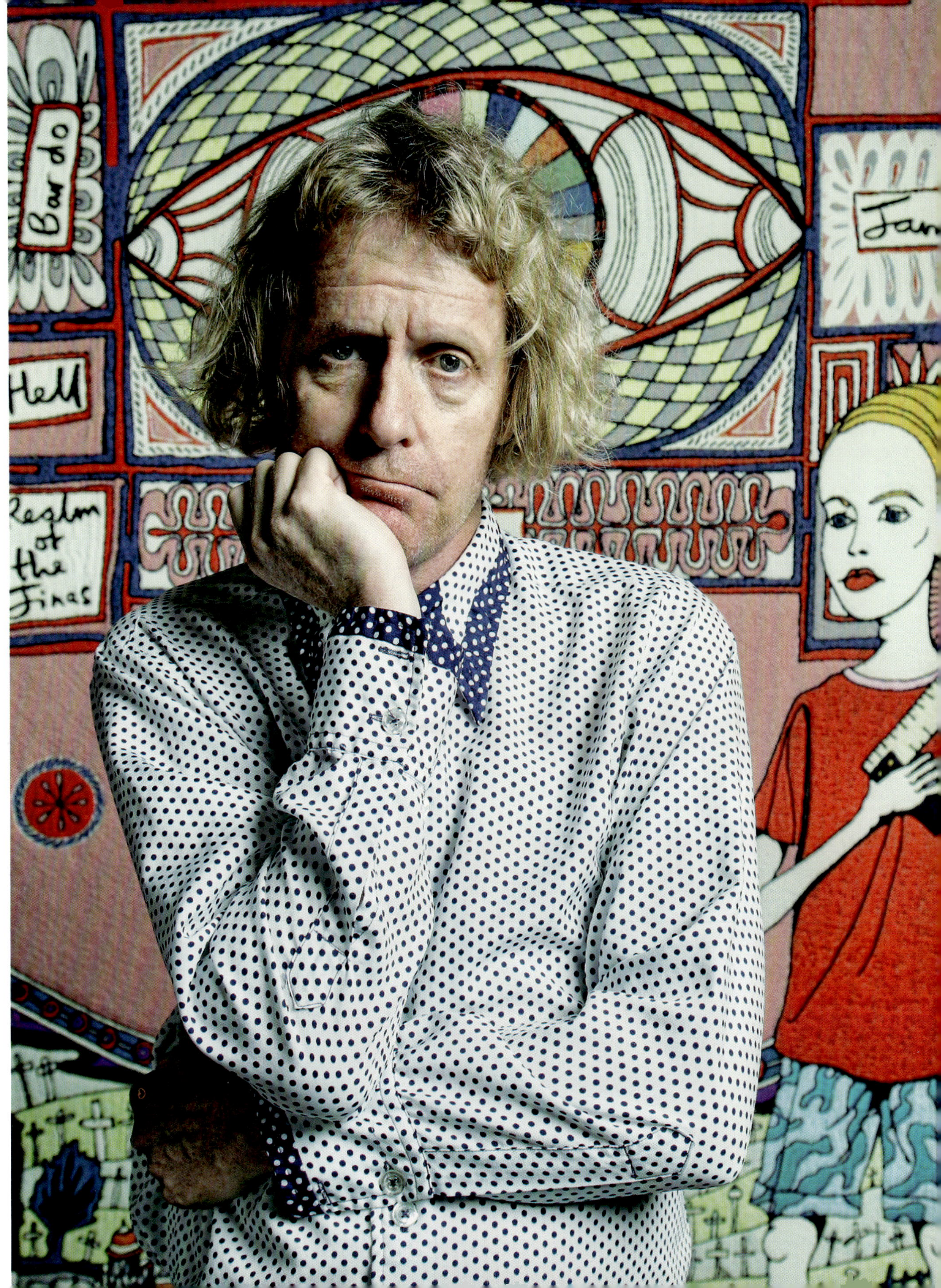
Bar do
Hell
Realm
of
the
Jinas

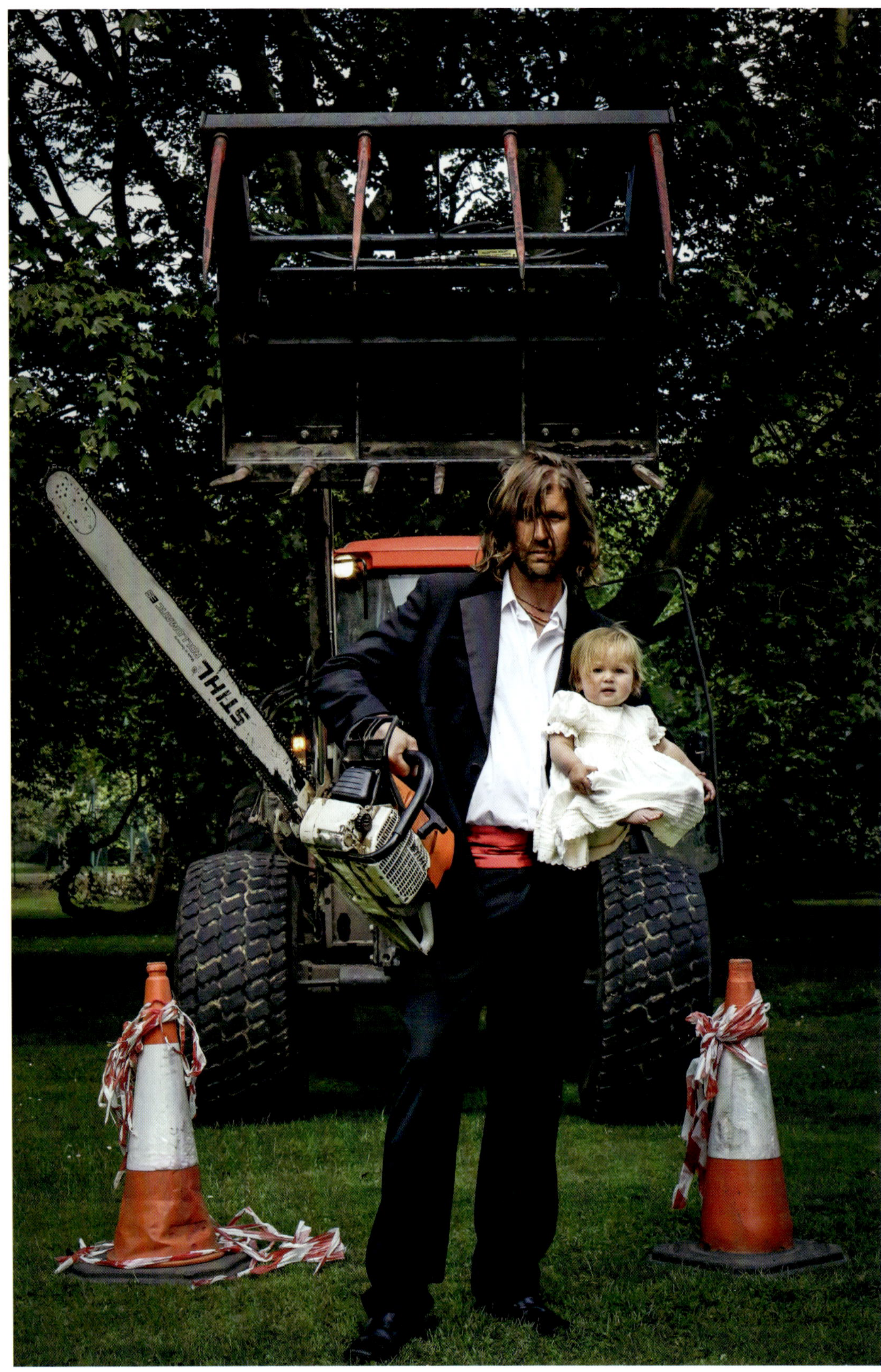

○ SIMON HADLEIGH-SPARKS
HIGHLY COMMENDED

**Gardener's Don't Do It In Wellies
– Mackenzie**
Syon Park, London

Part of a series – an unusual and light-hearted
idea strongly influenced by gardens and
gardening. The basic concept concerns
garden workers at the stately home, Syon
House, their roles and interests and how they
take their joy of work to the extreme. It sounds
tacky but all the workers love their jobs and
look forward to each new morning. Most of the
staff also live at Syon. Mack is one of the
team and the image shows how job and
family interrelate as a result of him living
and working on the estate.

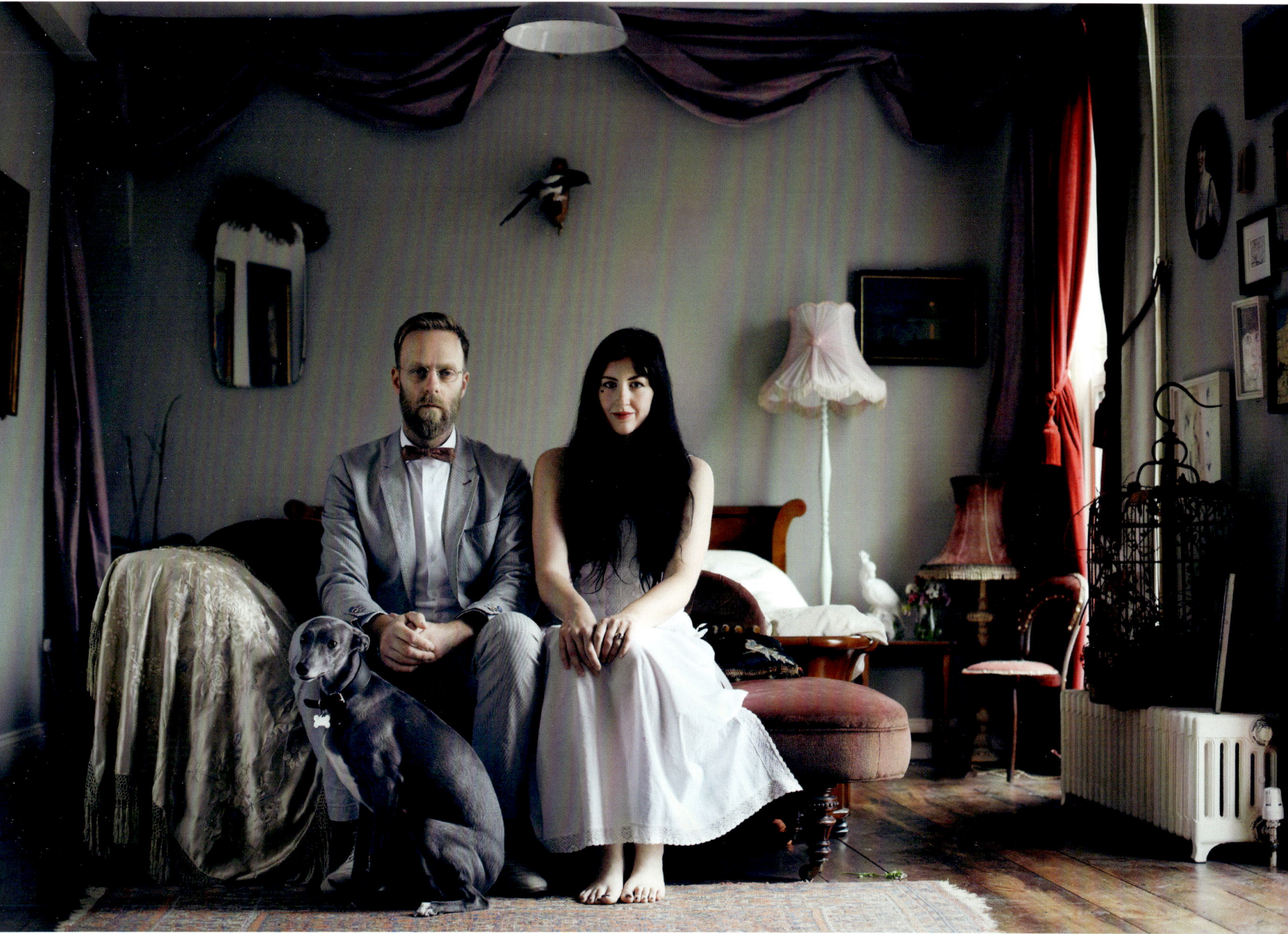

◑ JENNY LEWIS / HIGHLY COMMENDED

Polly and Stuart Pearson Wright
Hackney, London

My Hackney Studio project started as a celebration of the creatives
in my home borough. Each subject nominates the next. Two years
later and over eighty subjects and it feels more like the obituary of
an area. Half the artists have since been forced to move so I
realise I am capturing the end of an era.

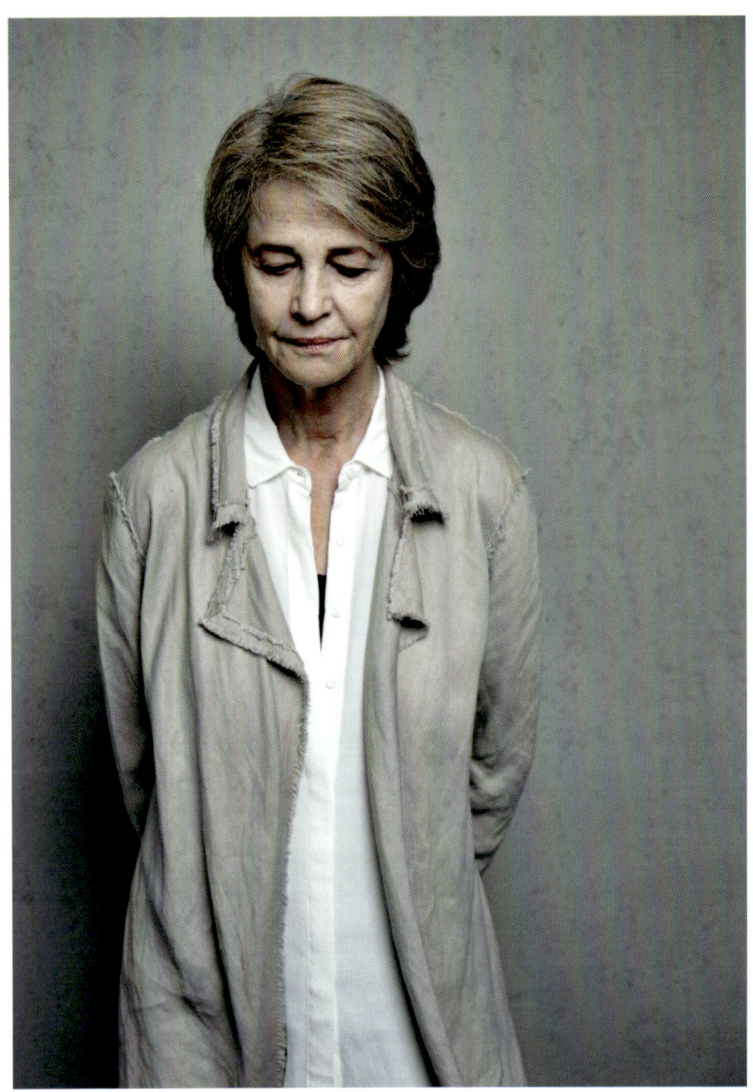

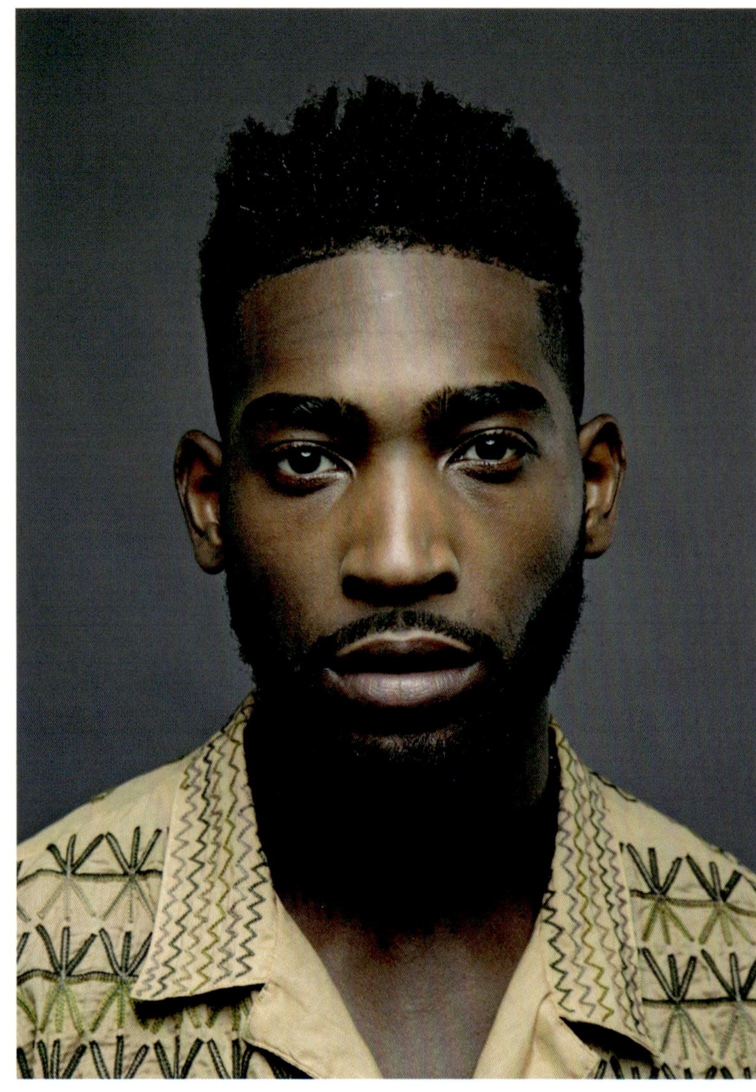

⬢ CHRIS MCANDREW / HIGHLY COMMENDED

Charlotte Rampling
London

I wanted to capture Charlotte's beauty in a reflective manner, asking her to look down and contemplate, which she was happy to do. I wanted a certain sadness to the image, which I think I achieved.

⬢ CHRIS MCANDREW / HIGHLY COMMENDED

Tinie Tempah
London

Tinie Tempah in the studio after nearly two hours getting ready. He had his barber do his beard from scratch with a cut throat razor and his hair re-twisted to perfection. It made for a slick looking shot with a 5 head set up which is what I love about working in the studio.

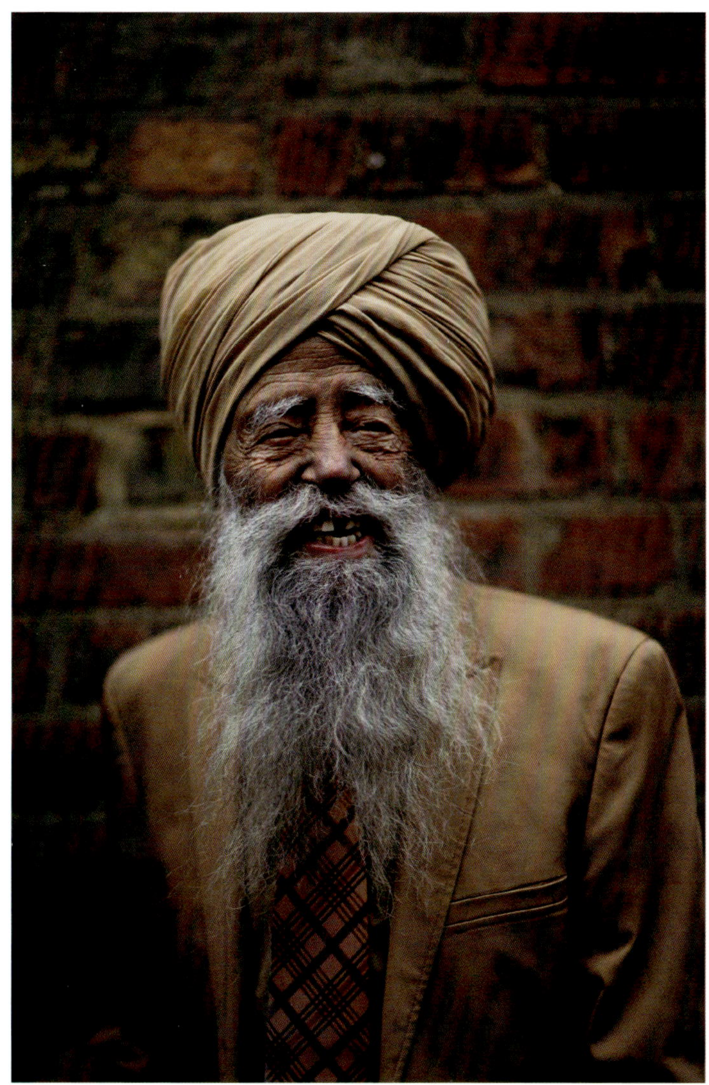

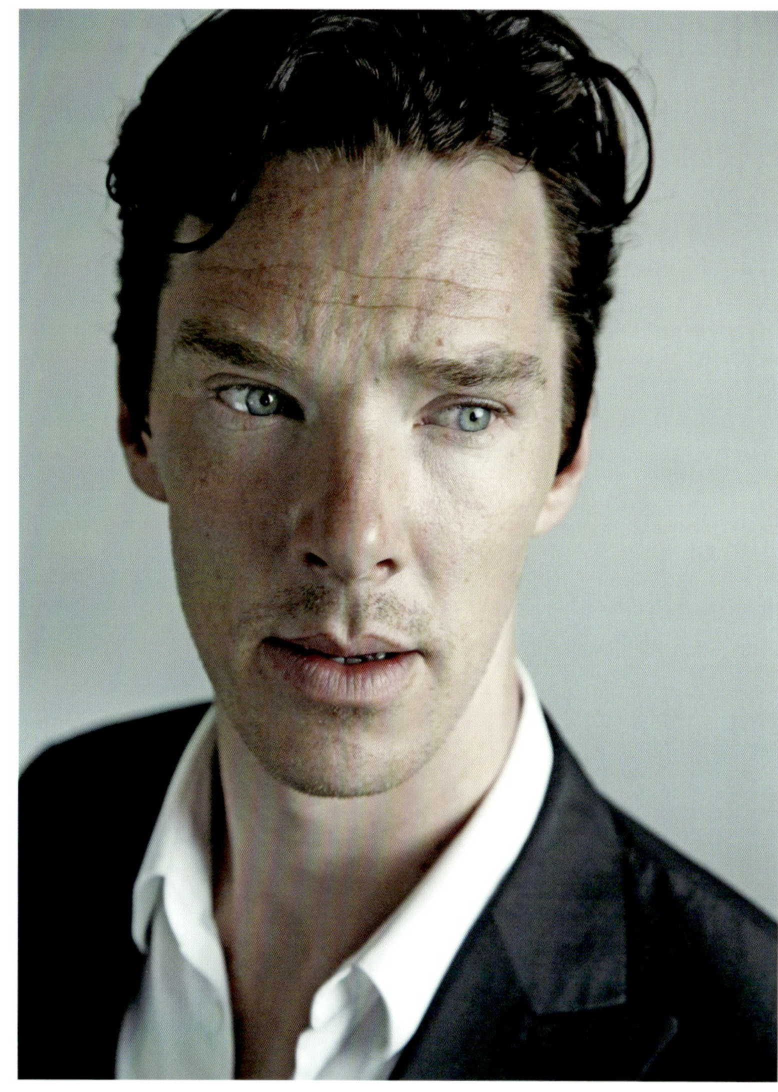

Fauja Singh BEM
East Ham, London

Fauja Singh retired from marathon running two years ago.
At 104 years old, Fauja is much loved and admired across the
world within the Sikh community. At the Vaisakhi parade, a
celebration of the Punjabi New Year and Harvest festival, in
east London, he agreed to give me a minute of his time, with
just a nod of approval. Meanwhile, his feet were being
touched by fellow Sikhs; like that of a worshipped deity.

Benedict Cumberbatch
London

Cumberbatch at the height of the Sherlock madness. He was
a fantastic subject to work with, someone who took direction
very well helping me get the image just as I wanted it. We shot
this upstairs at Kettners, Soho, in one of the empty spaces in
their vast building.

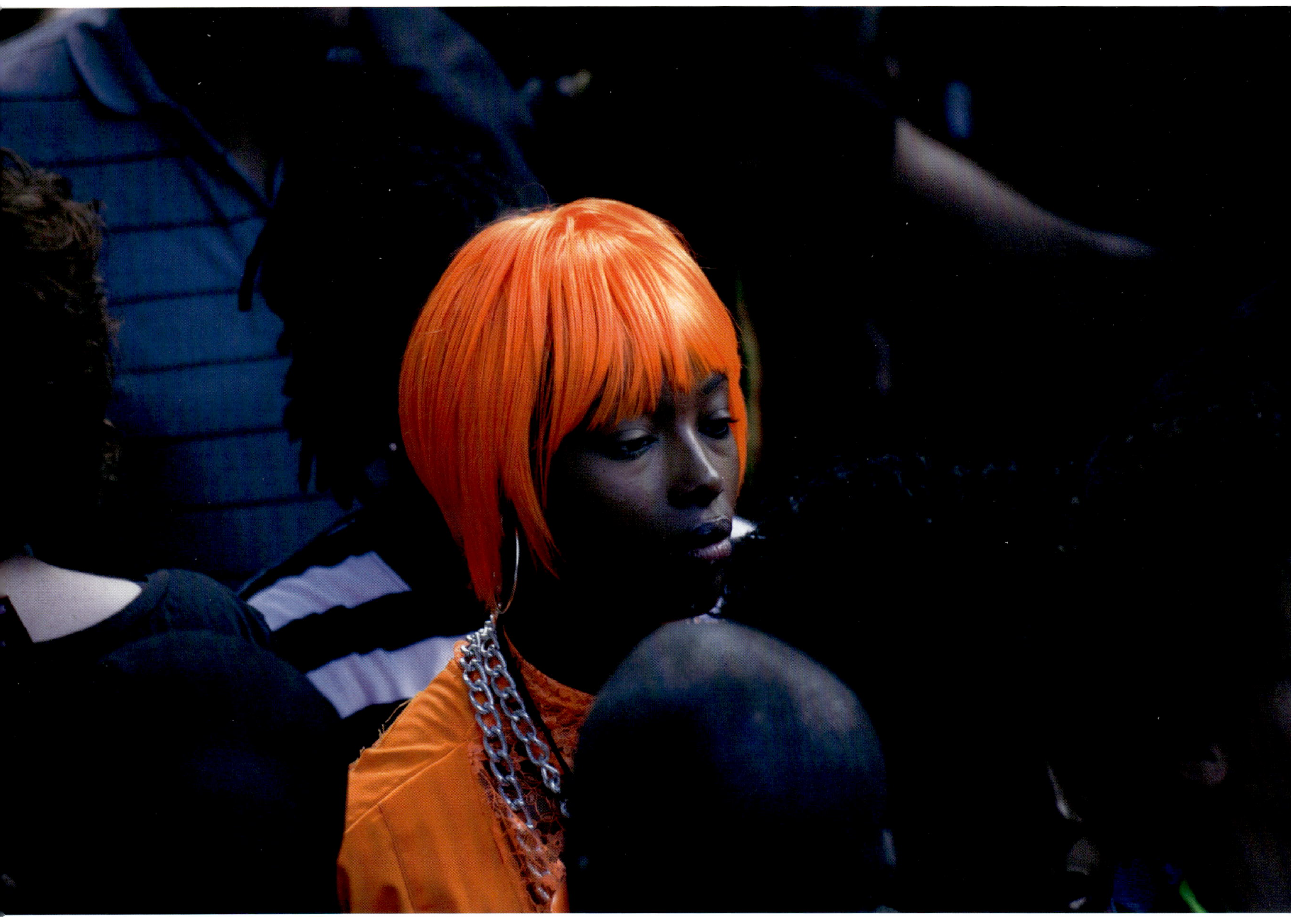

Notting Hill Carnival
London

It was my second day in London and I was living close to Notting Hill. I didn't
know anything about this event but I heard the music from my room and so I went
out with my camera to check what was going on. It was crazy out there. I stopped
on someone's door step and started to shoot from above. I saw this girl coming, I
waited for her, took the shot and then went back to the crowed street.

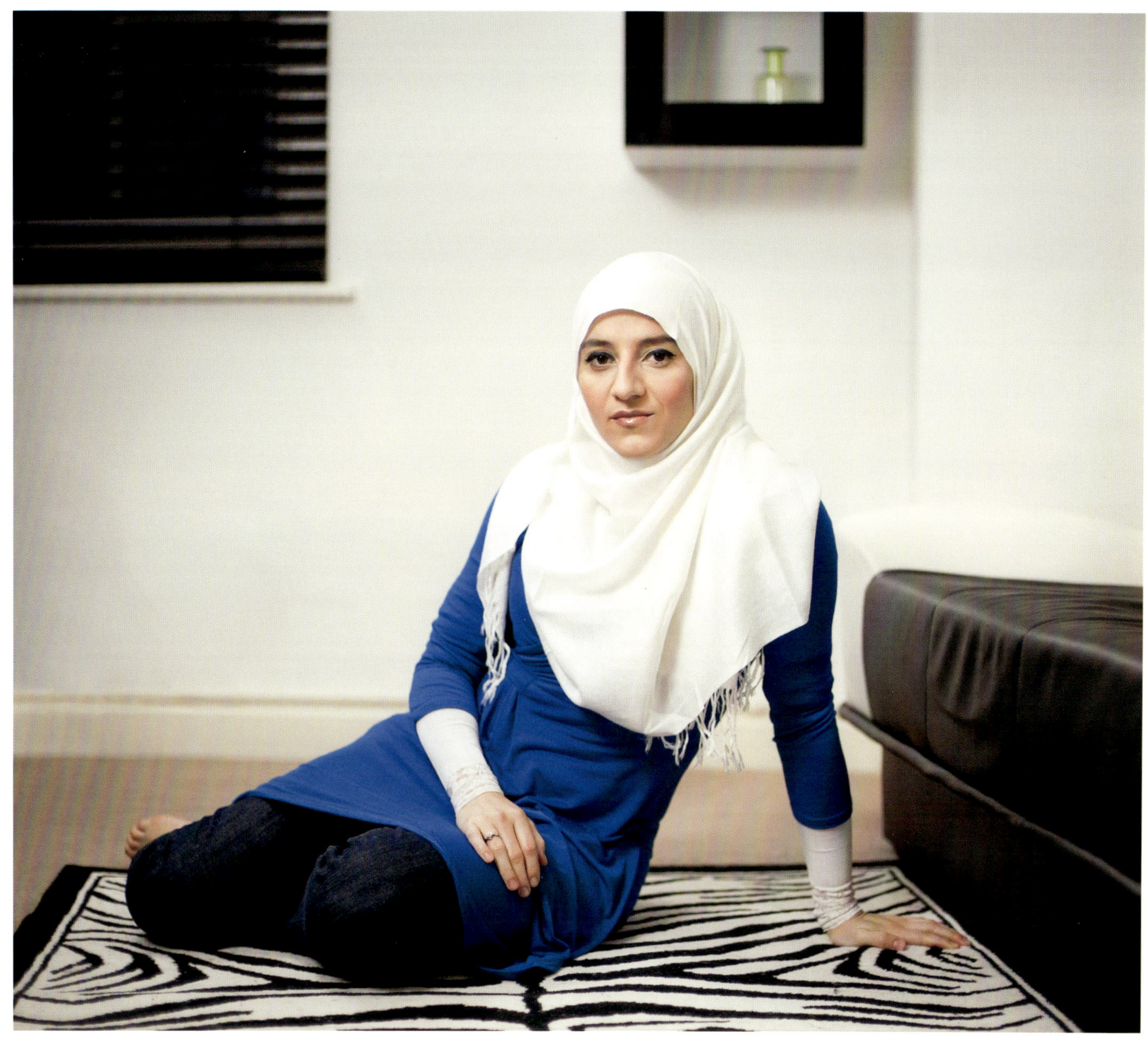

AMIT LENNON / HIGHLY COMMENDED

Khadijah
London

Khadijah has converted to Islam and has changed her name. She views herself as a modern Muslim, who wears fashionable clothes and teaches kick-boxing and martial arts. I photographed her in her home

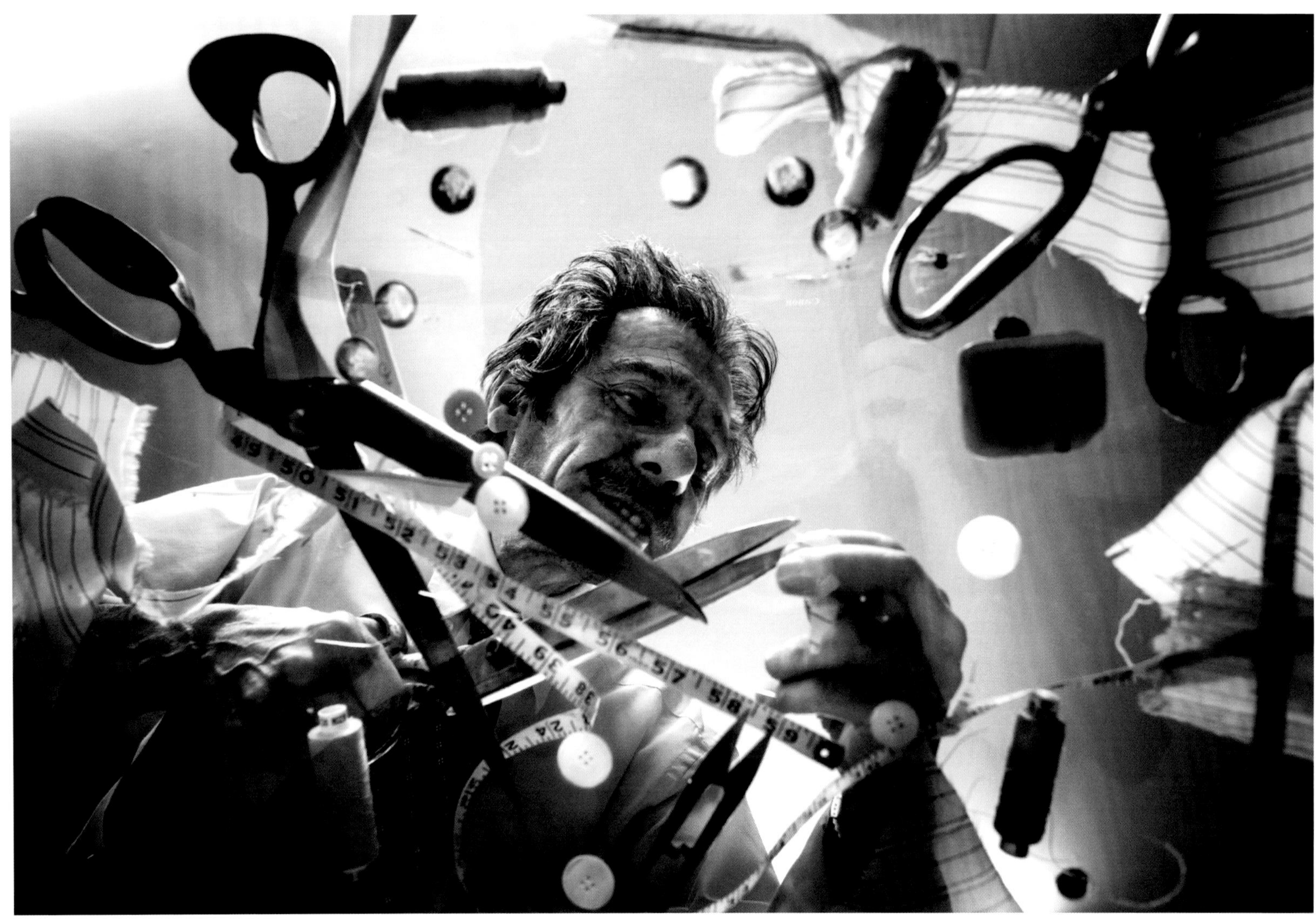

Tailor
Fitzrovia, London

This portrait took quite a long time to plan and make. I bought a
translucent sheet of plastic through which I took the portrait to
show the tailor working from this slightly unusual perspective.

The Welsh Dancer
Bridgend, South Glamorgan, South Wales

Gwerinwyr Gwent was formed in 1976 by eight people from the Gwent area who were interested in reviving the tradition of Welsh folk dancing. The name of the team can be translated as 'folk of Gwent'. Here a traditional Welsh Dancer poses before a practice dance in Bridgend, South Wales. From 'A loss of tradition', a photographic exploration of the demise of beloved British traditions.

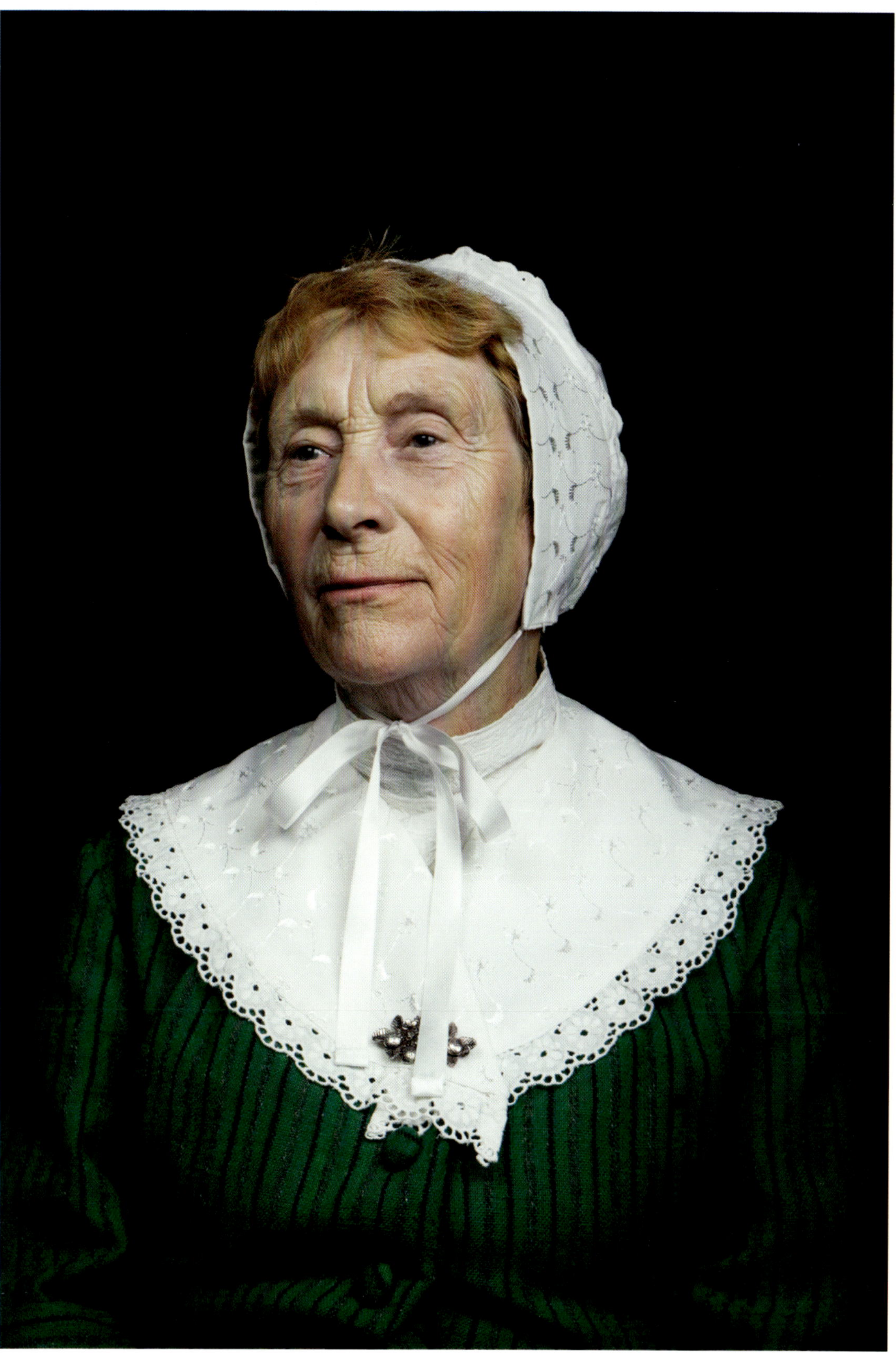

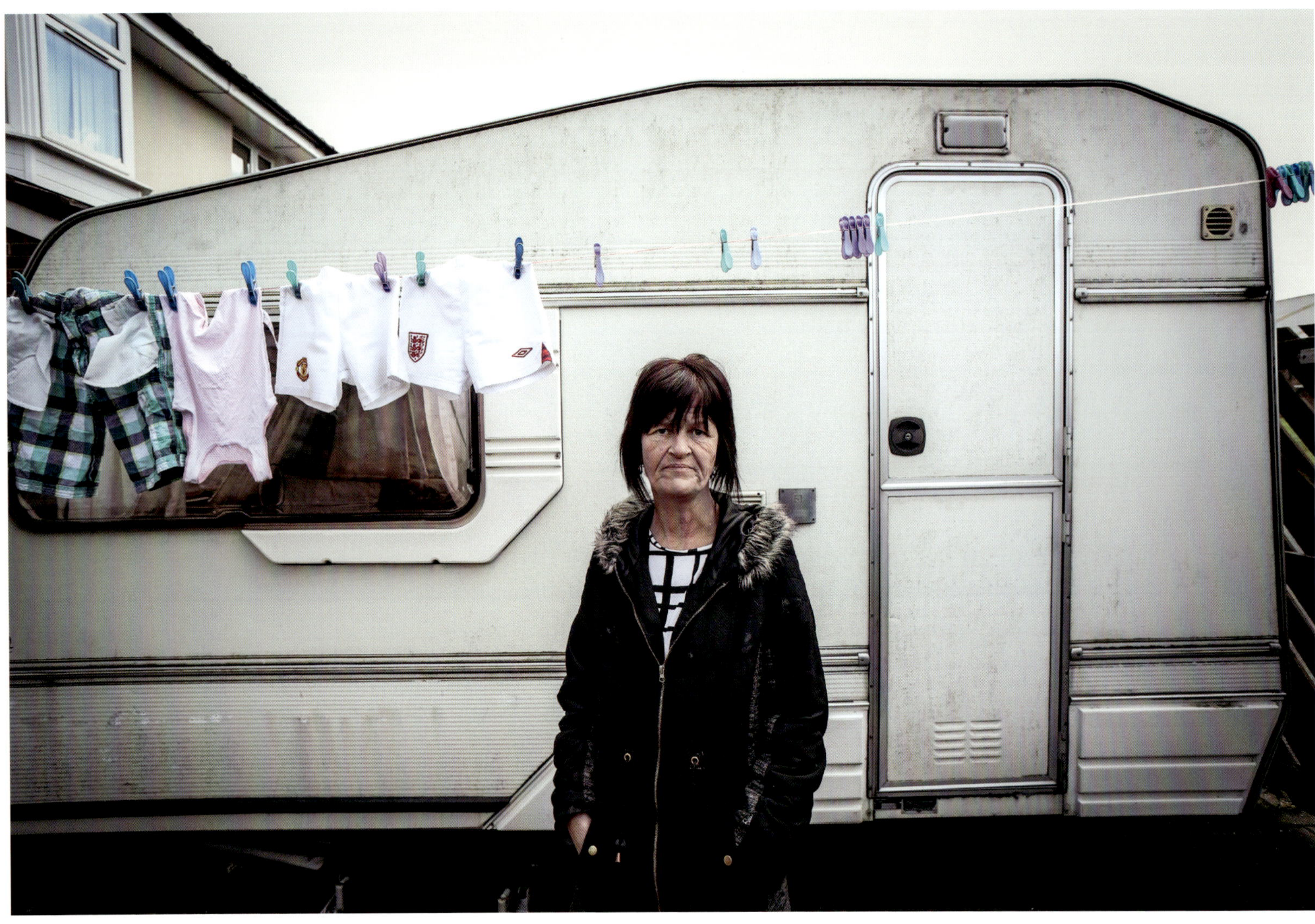

◐ STEVE MORGAN

Sue Griffiths
Tilery Estate, Stockton-on-Tees

Sue is a 50 year old mother of five who has lived on
the street for 20 years. The residents of the Tilery
Estate face many social problems including high
unemployment and low pay.

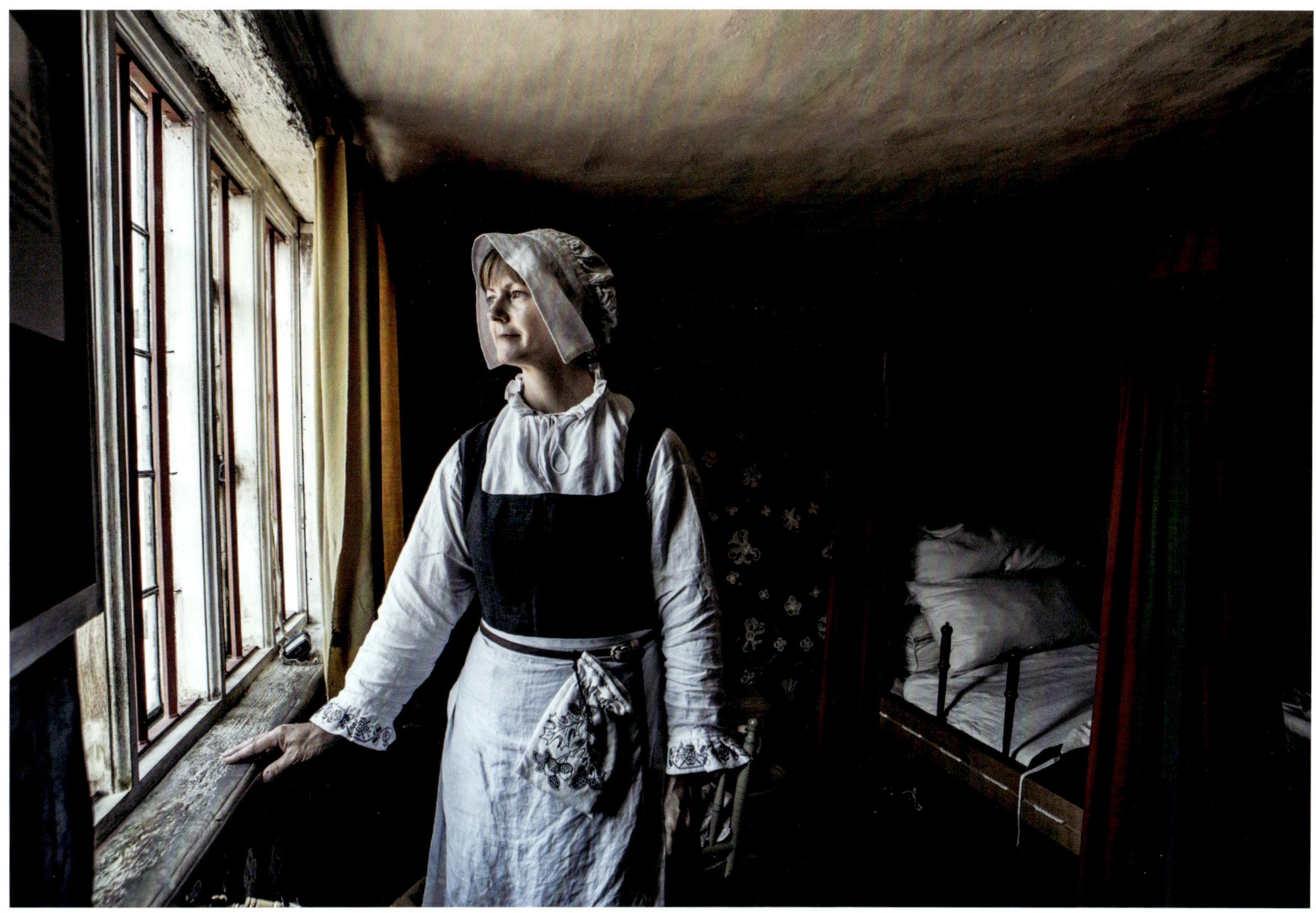

○ STEVE MORGAN

Shakespeare's Bedroom
Stratford upon Avon, Warwickshire

Actor and guide in the bedroom where William Shakespeare is
believed to have been born; Henley Street, Stratford upon Avon.
Period costumes help to convey a sense of place and history
for the many thousands of visitors. Taken for a feature on the
Shakespeare Way trail which may have been the walking route
The Bard took as young man to travel to London.

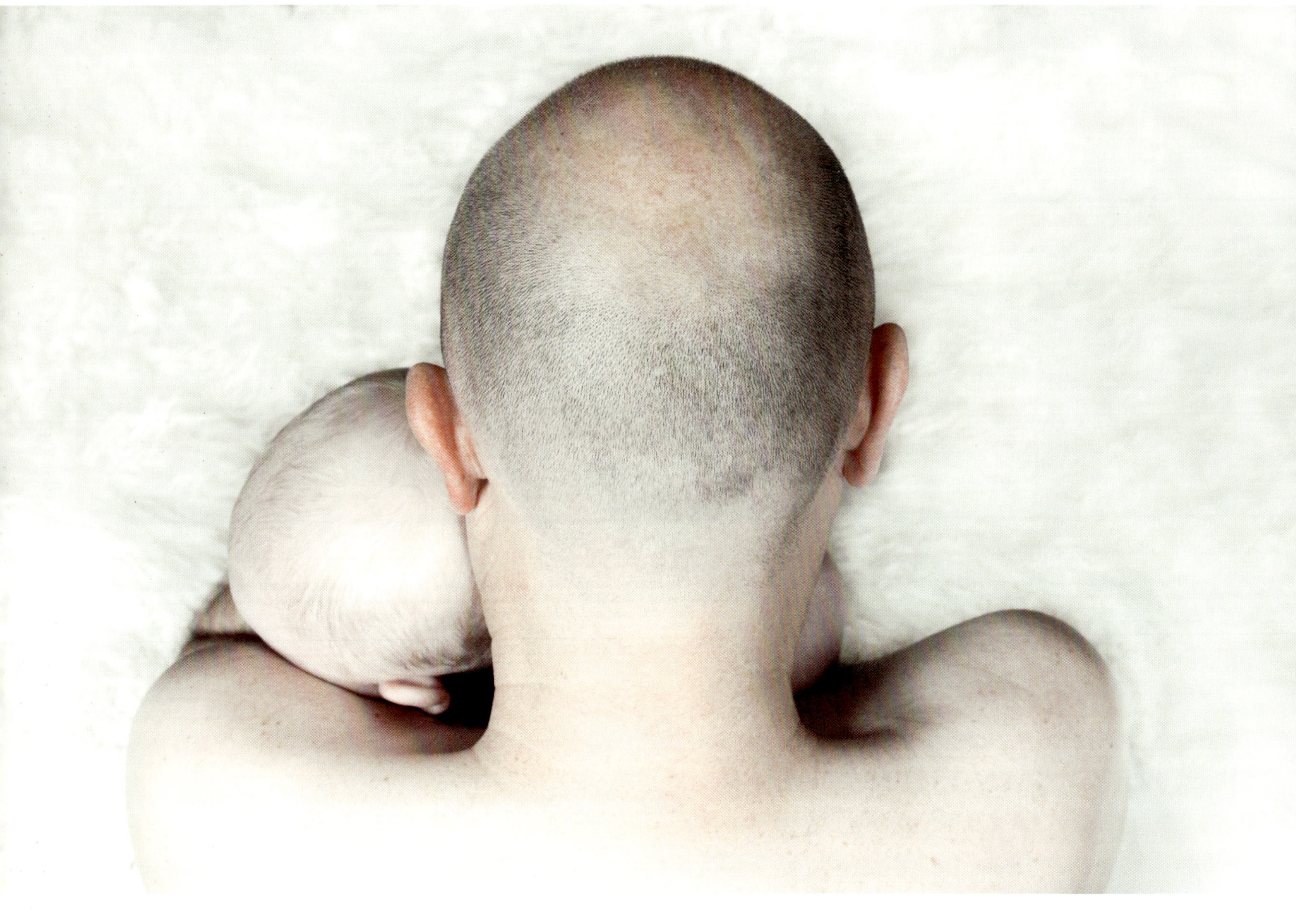

◔ JACKY CHAPMAN

Father and Son
London

This was one of the final images from a photo-shoot. I sought to capture the simplicity of two forms, showing tenderness and a loving bond between father and son, with no faces for distraction. Once shot, it reminded me of Bill Brandt's dynamic nudes on the beach. As Brandt once said "...the lens produced anatomical images and shapes which my eyes had never observed."

○ DANIEL LEWIS

Dame Zandra Rhodes
London

Dame Zandra Rhodes was a joy! I'd spent the day documenting her judging a national student design competition. At the end of the day she was happy enough to pose for me – all those colours had to be captured. My trusty favoured set up, used for opportunistic portraits, worked as ever. All I needed were three flash guns, a plain wall, Dame Zandra and 30 seconds of her time, which she gladly gave me.

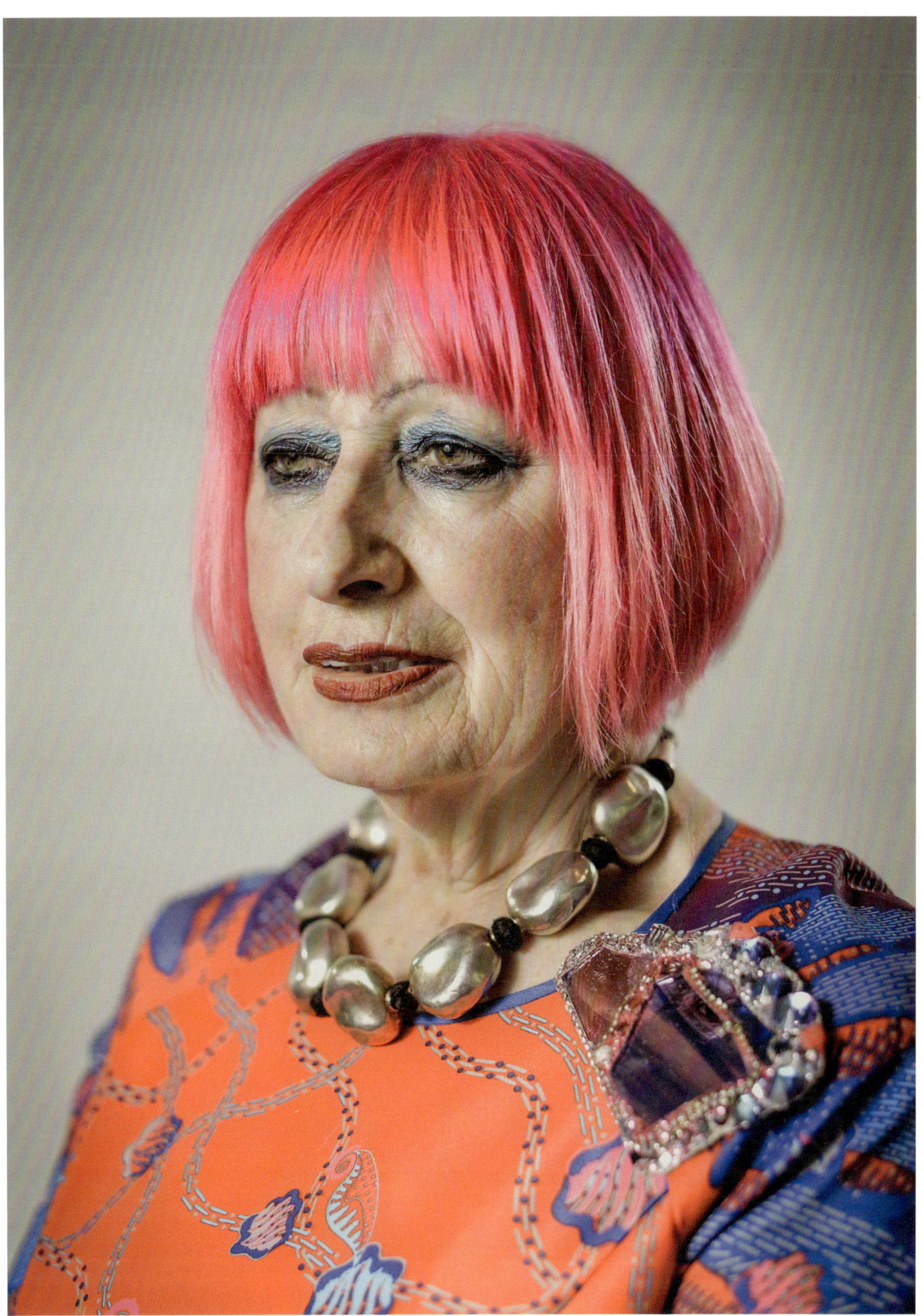

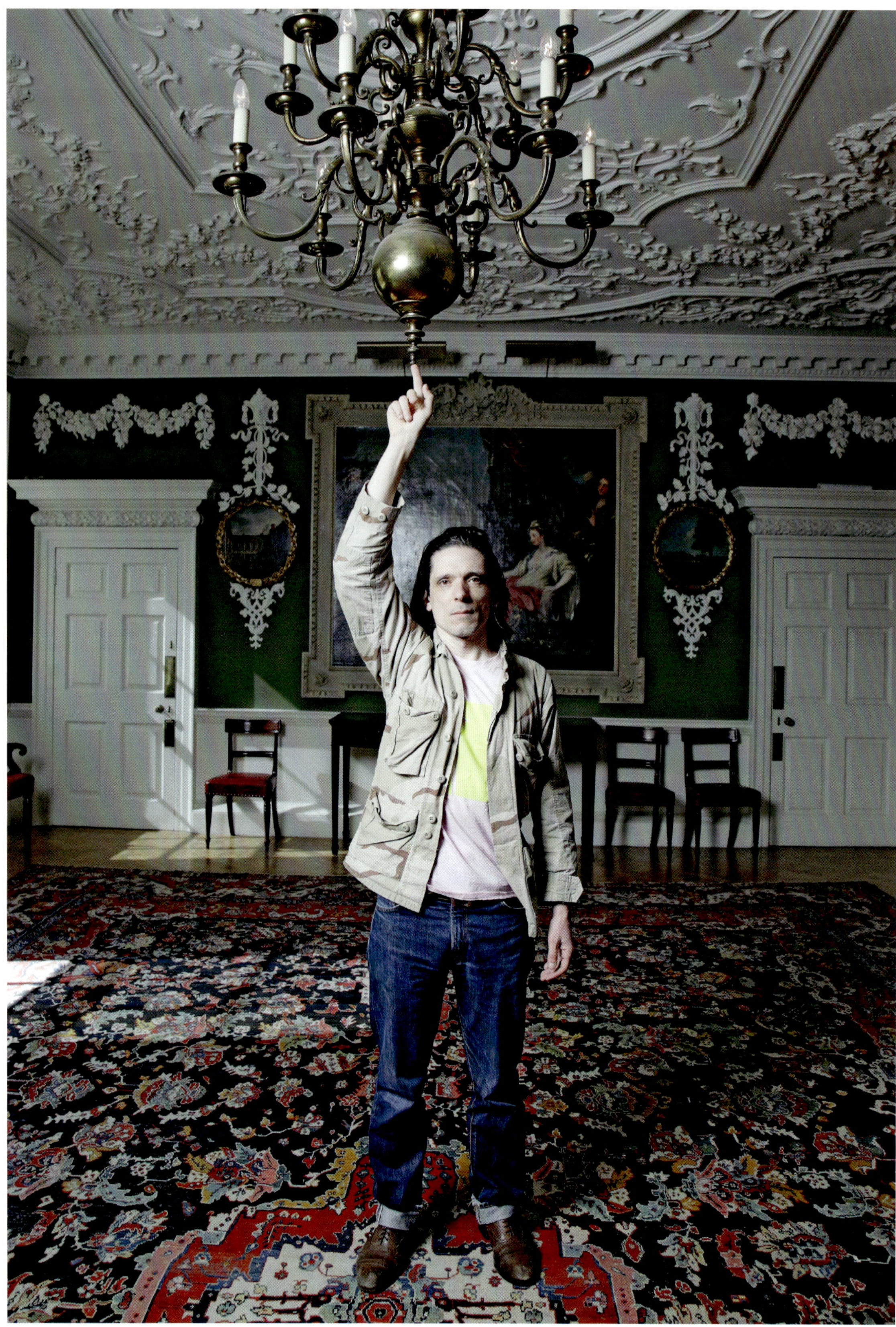

◖ CHRIS MCANDREW

Jeremy Deller
London

I liked the idea that it looked as if Jeremy was holding this massive ornate room up just with his finger so we gave it a go and it worked. We tried out a few variations and this was the shot I liked the best.

Jeremy Irons
London

This was one of those nail-biting photo shoots where the journalist and I were given only a few minutes with Irons during his lunch break whilst he was in rehearsals. The result? A handful of frames and an awful lot of praying! Shot for the Times Educational Supplement.

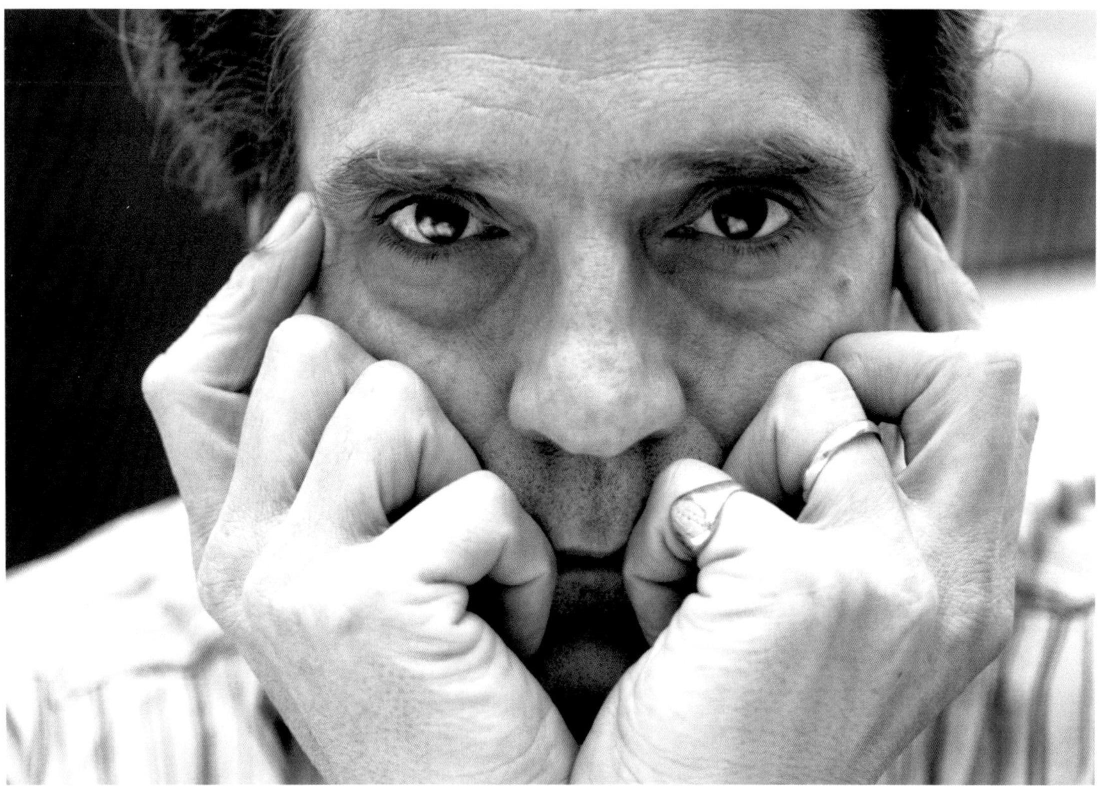

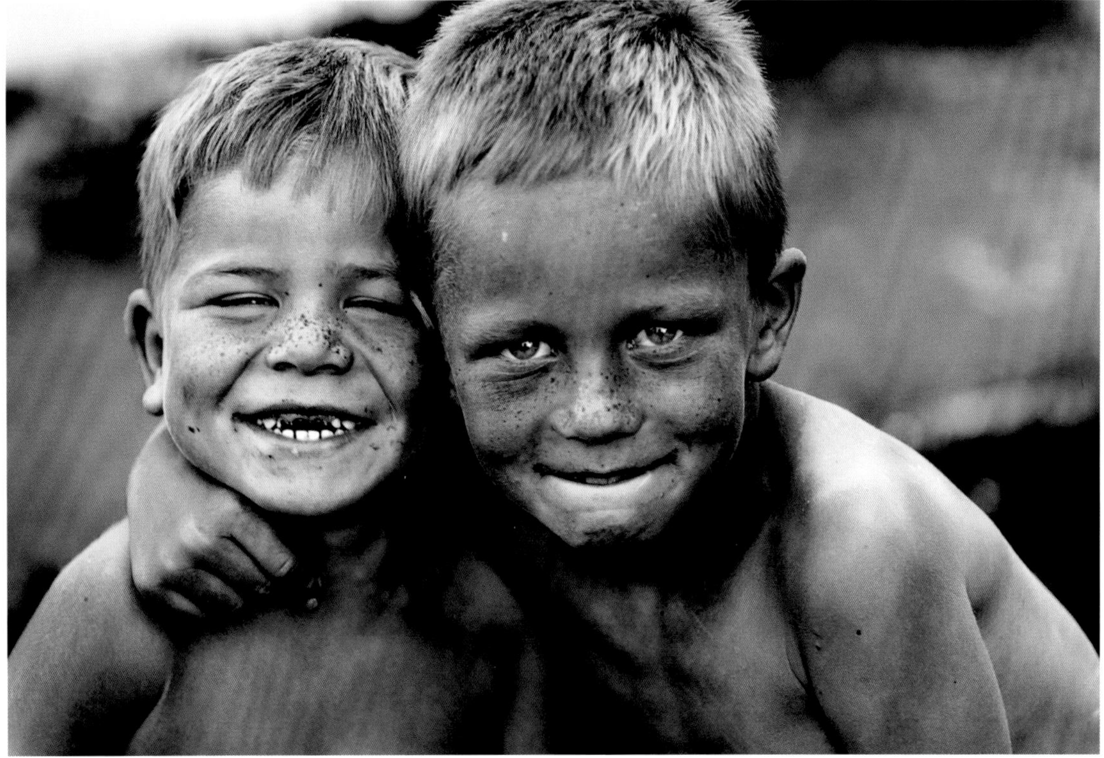

PAUL ANTHONY WILSON

Brothers
Seamer, nr Scarborough, North Yorkshire

I was photographing the 'Reading of the Charter' at the Seamer Horse Fair. These two brothers kept asking me to take their picture, the older boy grabbed the younger one in a head lock and made him laugh revealing his missing teeth, I couldn't resist and managed a couple of shots before they ran off chasing each other.

7
BRITISH WEATHER

We are blessed with four seasons that mould our landscape, coast, environment and communities. This category celebrates the great *British Weather* – a truly national obsession.

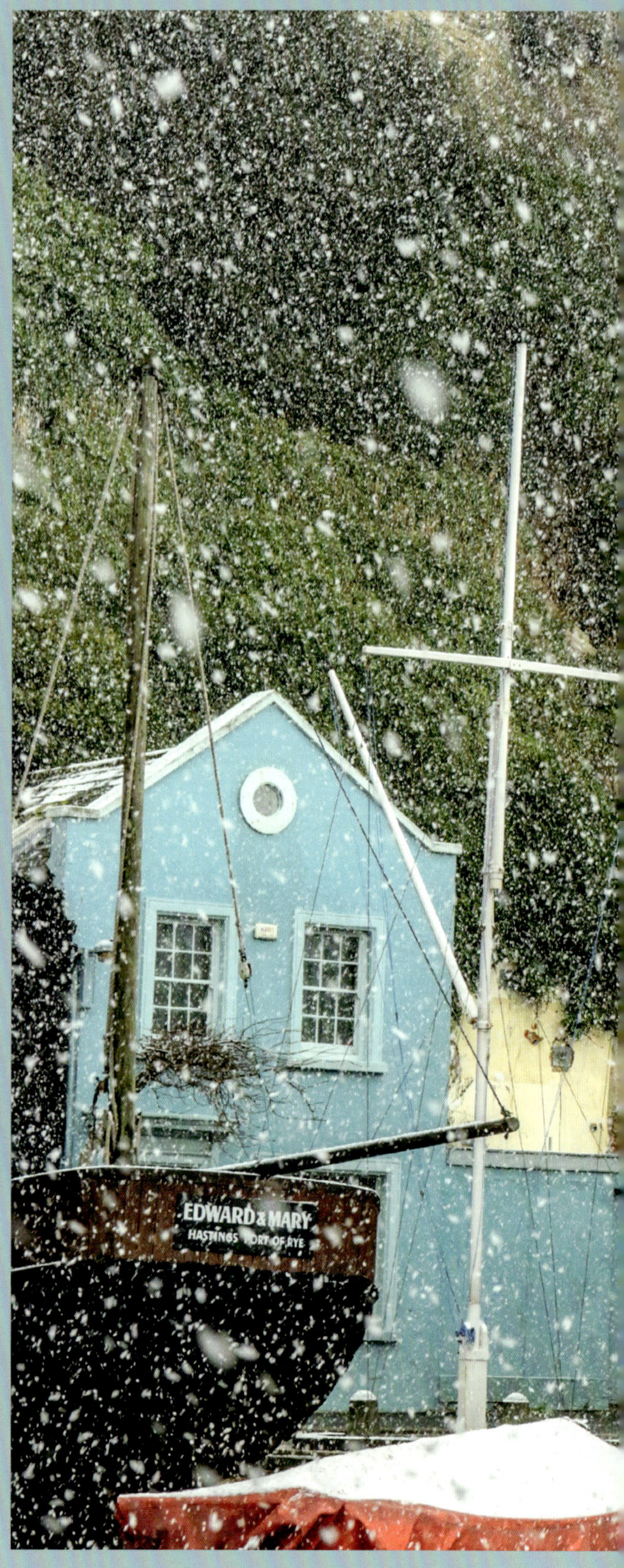

▷ CHRIS PARKER / WINNER

Snowing at Rock-a-Nore
Rock-a-Nore, Hastings, E Sussex

I love the old fishing net huts and boats at Rock-a-Nore and they provided the perfect background to capture this snow flurry.

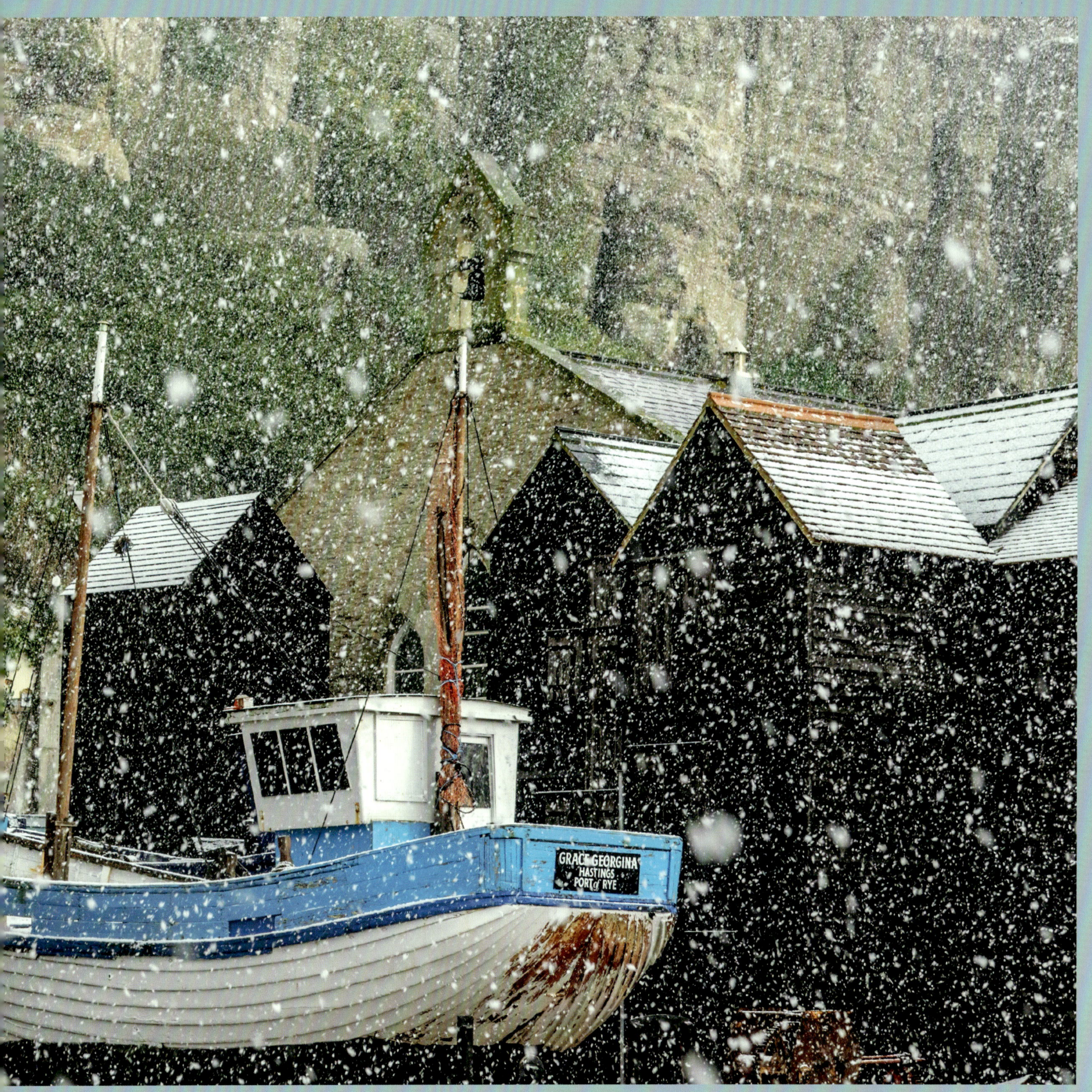

GRACE GEORGINA
HASTINGS
PORT of RYE

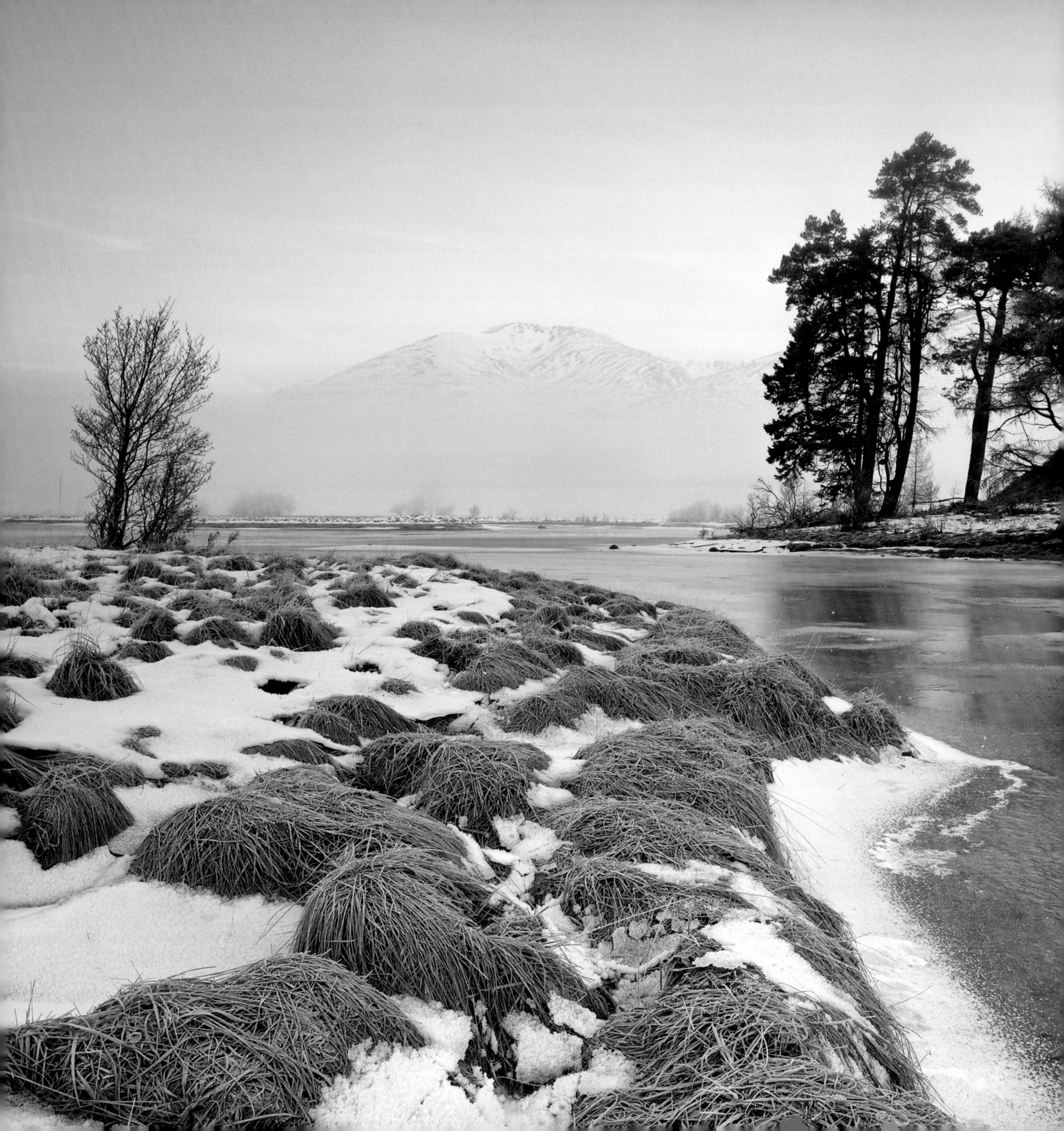

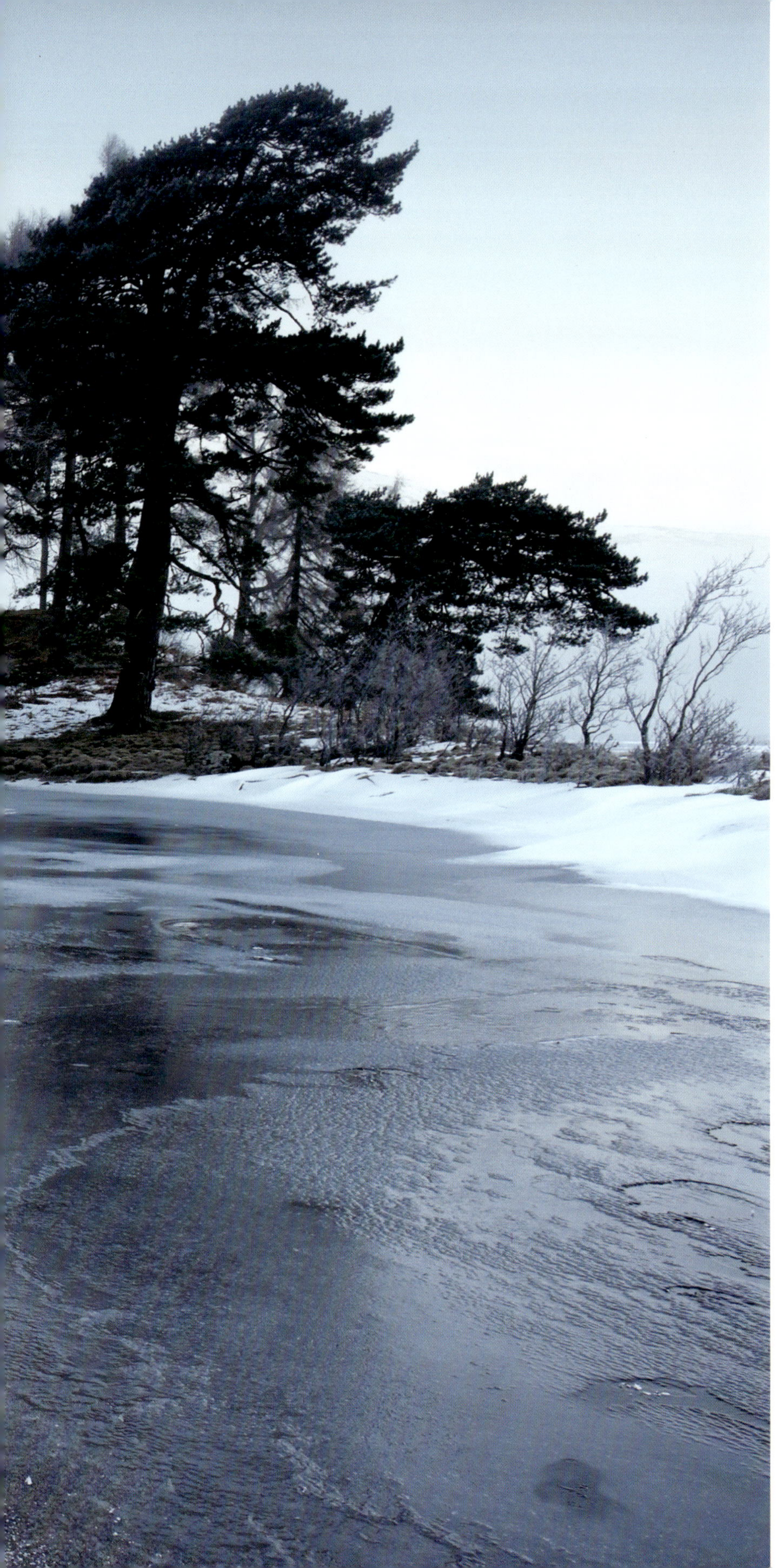

Frozen ground
Loch Tulla, Argyll, Scotland

This was a remarkably cold day with temperatures as low as minus eight. The ground was frozen and, despite the sunrise, both the loch and the normally boggy ground were also frozen. I camped here ready to walk the West Highland way and it marks the start of a cold, but rewarding hike.

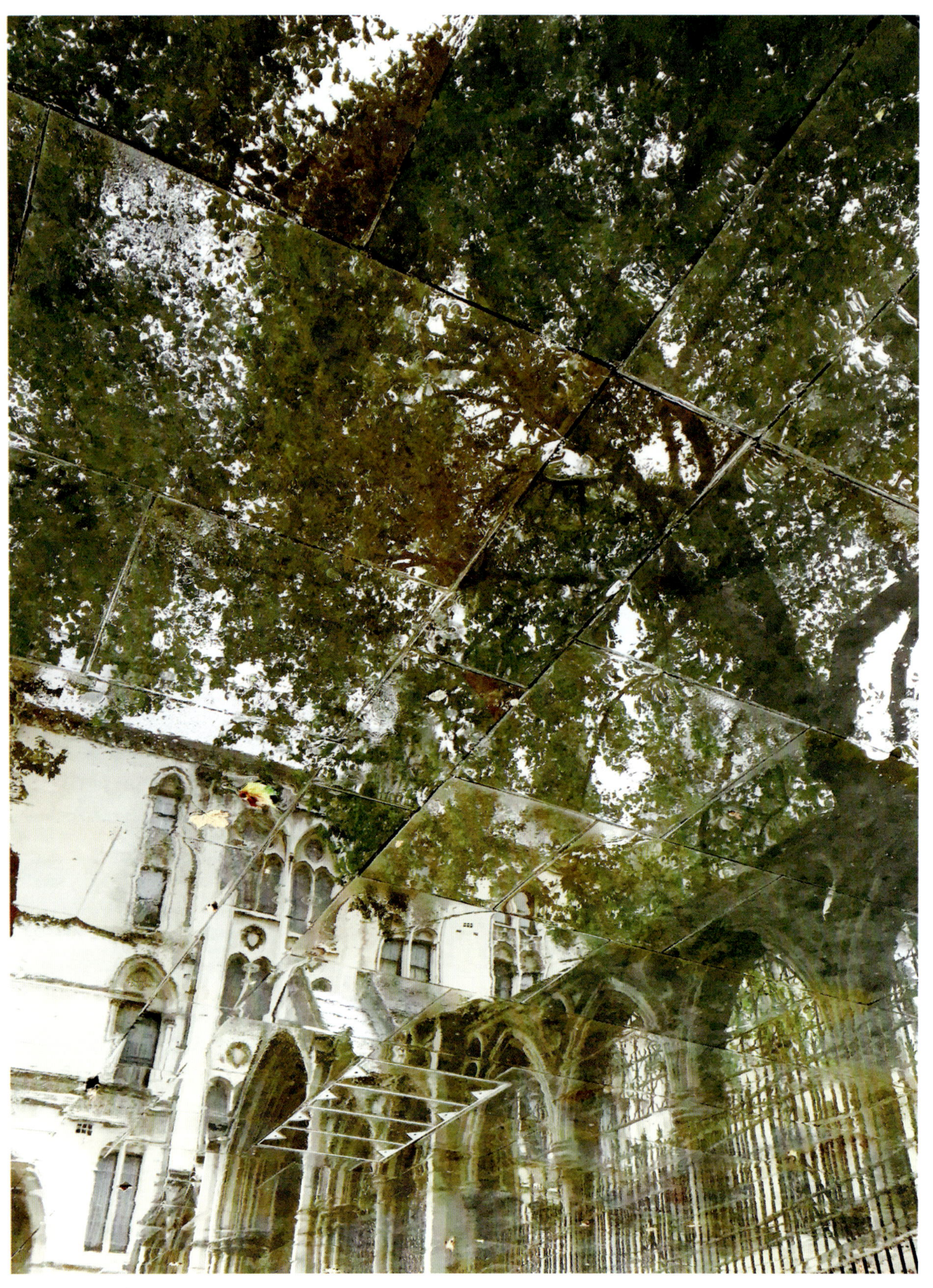

**Reflection of the
Royal Courts of Justice**
London

This photo was taken during
one lunch break. The rain was
steadily falling as I walked to
the bank when I happened
upon an unusually smooth
area of pavement which was
reflecting its surroundings
with stunning glassiness.
I was struck by the beauty
of the RCJ which had been
distorted by the water and
the structure of the pavement.
For me it captures the essence
of London in early Autumn.

GRAHAM EATON
HIGHLY COMMENDED

The Chapel and the sea
Porth Cwyfan, Aberffraw, Anglesey, Wales

I have photographed this tiny St Cwyfan's chapel many times, but always wanted to see it in a storm, with the sea over the causeway that links the tiny island to the mainland at low water. During a major storm I tried to photograph with wide angle, near to the island, but with so much spray, my equipment was instantly covered. So I retreated to a higher, inland viewpoint, and used a long lens. The Chapel was illuminated by the sun for about 30 seconds, but it adds scale to the enormous waves that were battering the coast. How many such storms has the Chapel survived? It is known to have existed since 1254.

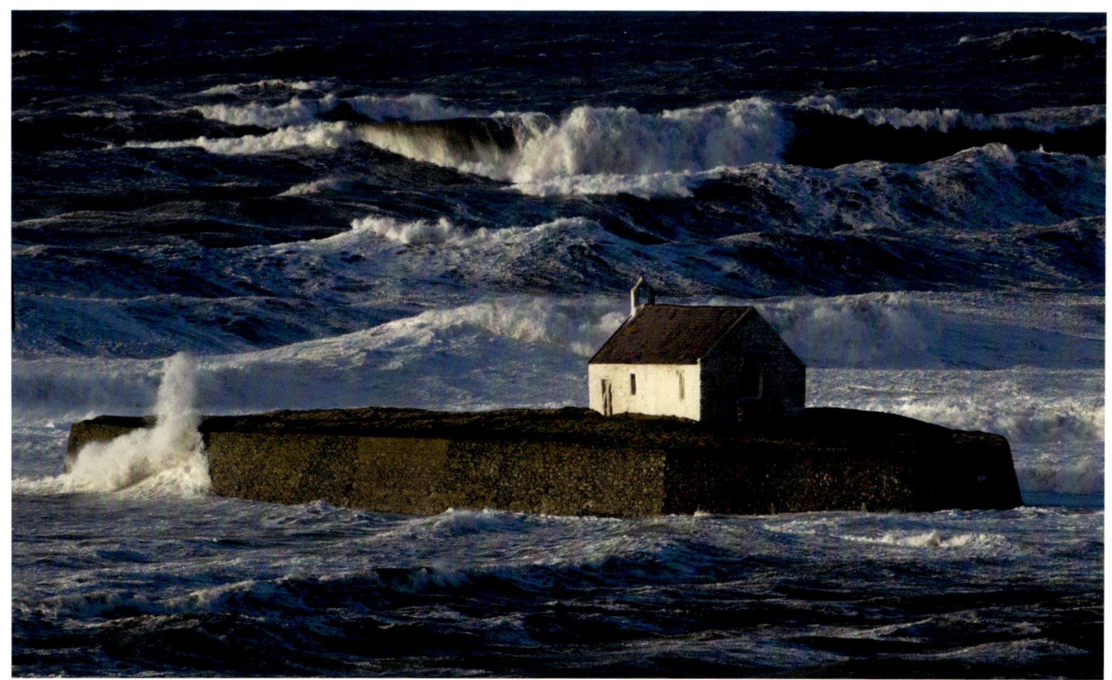

COLIN PAGE
HIGHLY COMMENDED

London
Greenwich Park

Despite the Summer rain, determined tourists enjoy the view of Canary Wharf from Greenwich Park. The photo was taken quickly while dodging a downpour.

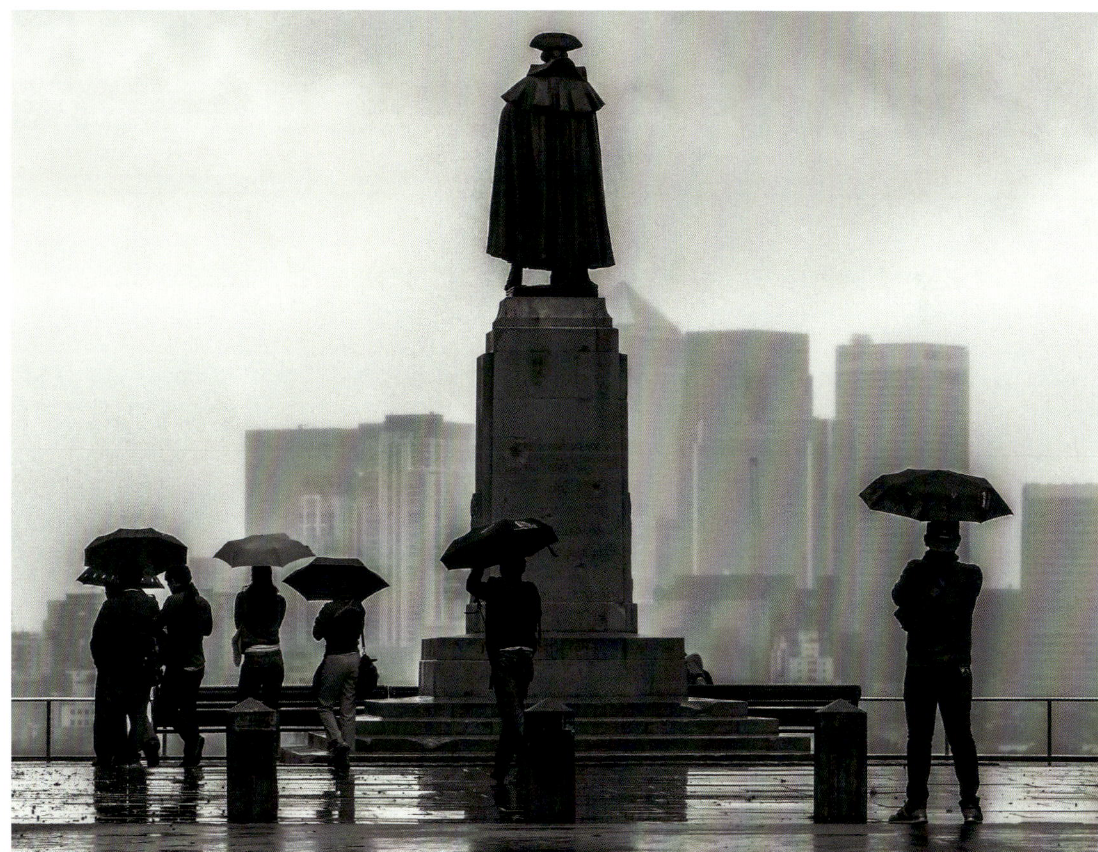

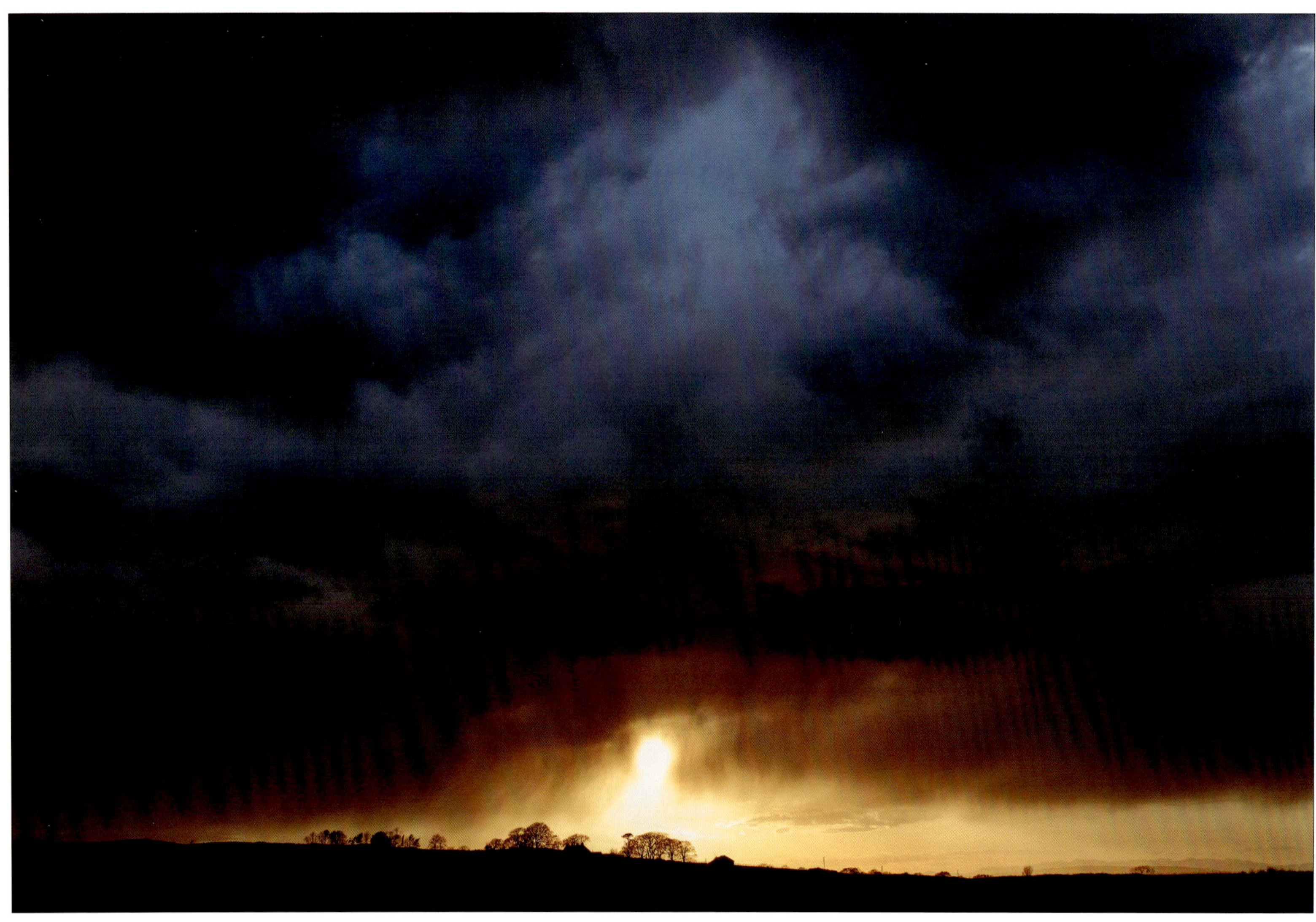

⬟ JON BROOK / HIGHLY COMMENDED

Armageddon approaches
Bentham, North Yorkshire

I was walking the dog and watching the gathering storm
looming above Lancaster, when suddenly the setting sun
burst under the clouds. The dog walk was curtailed and
I nipped inside to grab my camera.

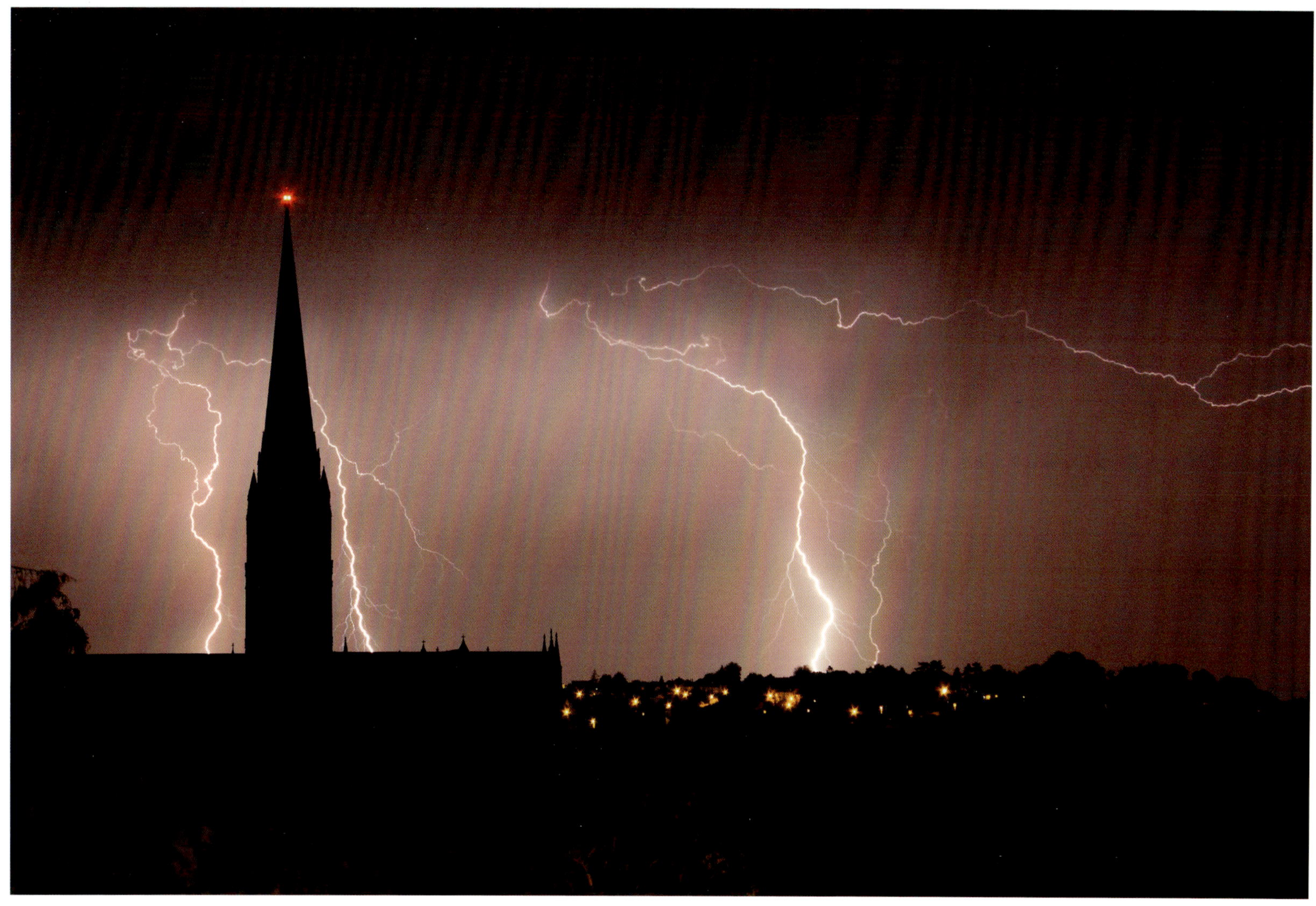

○ ANTHONY OLIVER / HIGHLY COMMENDED

Salisbury Cathedral in the storm
Salisbury, Wiltshire

This was taken during a night of severe thunderstorms across Southern England. Taken from my back bedroom it involved a bulb exposure and following the lightning to provide the necessary illumination to the image. The storm and subsequent image was taken on the night before my Father's funeral and has a particular significance to me for this reason.

⬡ CHAITANYA DESHPANDE
HIGHLY COMMENDED

Winter Pinks
London

I've taken images in Richmond Park in every
month of the year and so often the weather
has played a lead role in defining this majestic
Royal Park. I took this image in the winter
when if you're lucky you can be treated to
some beautiful dawn colours. The frost on
the ground was a bonus that morning.

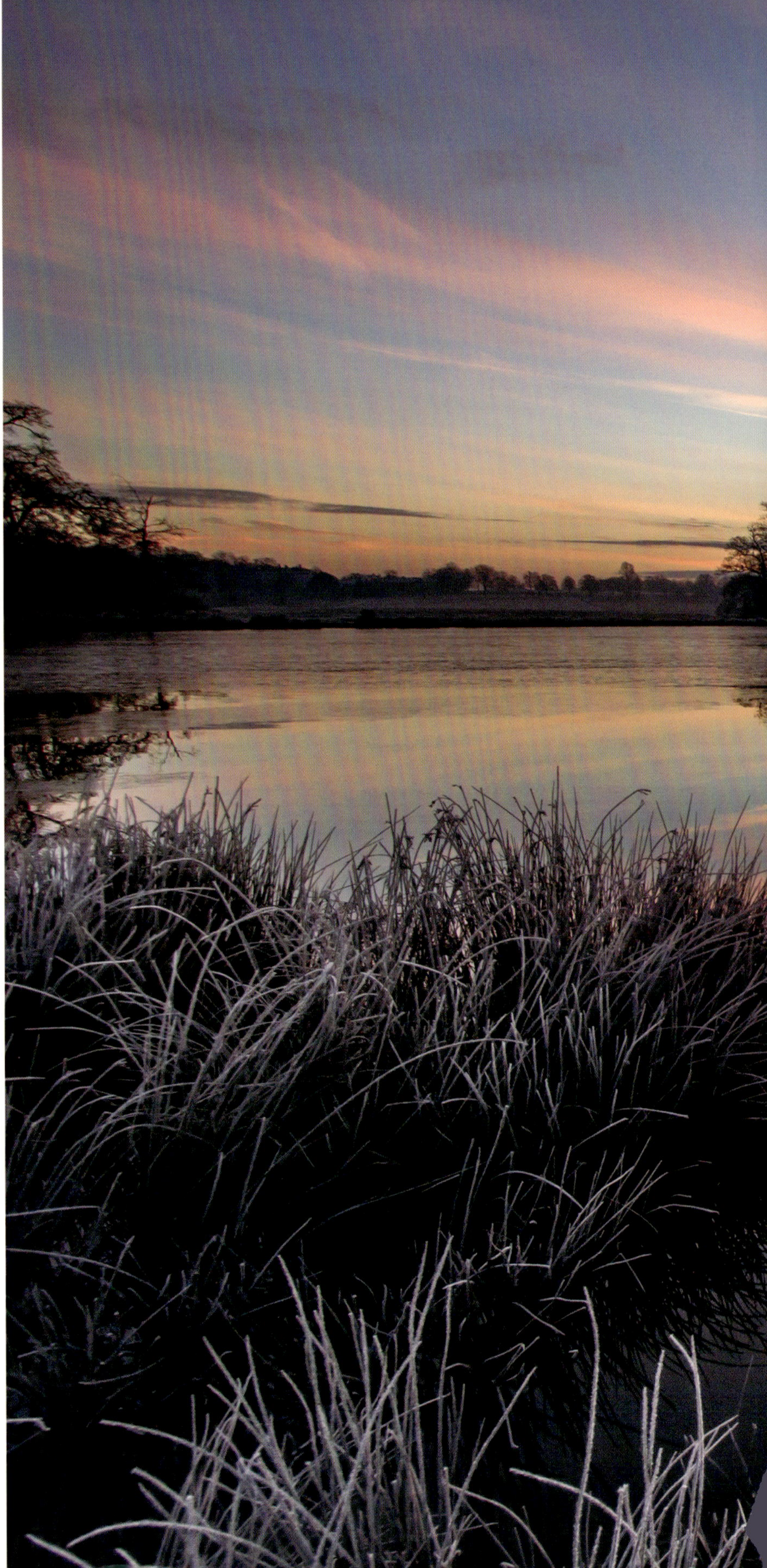

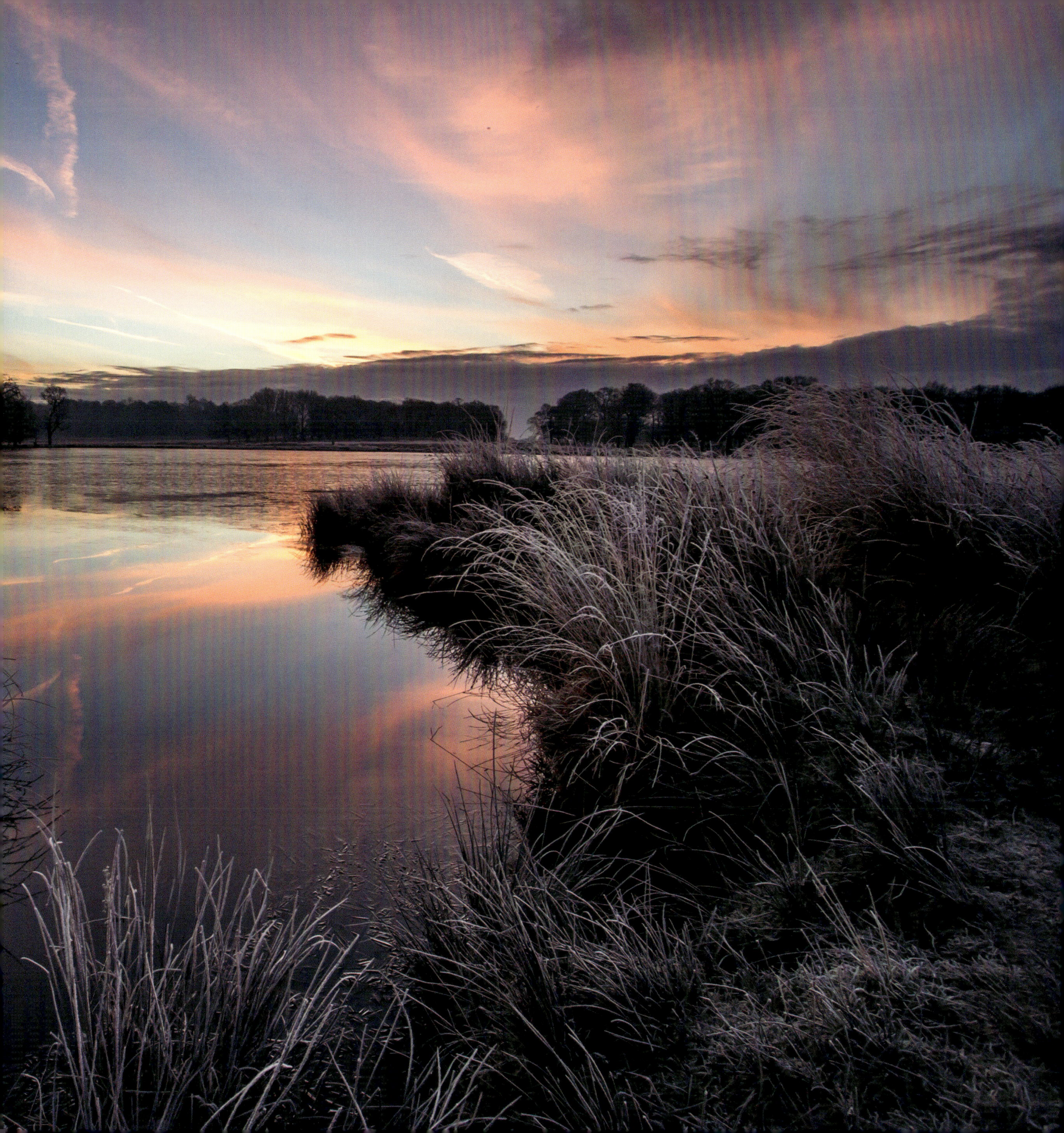

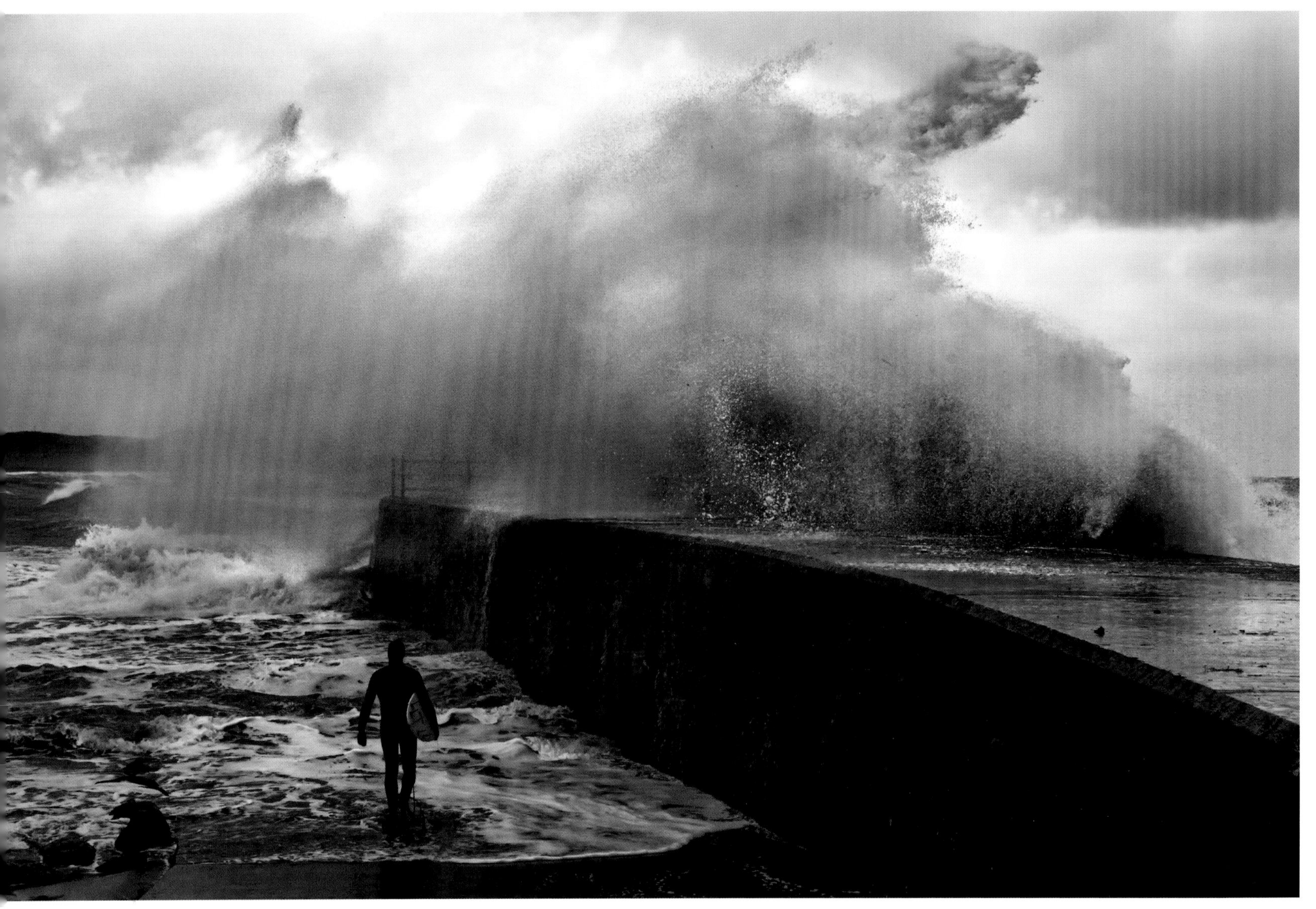

Into the cauldron
Criccieth, Gwynedd, Wales

I was photographing waves breaking over the harbour wall at Criccieth, during a strong easterly, when a surfer walked down the slipway, and into the water. Whilst I was trying to take photographs and to protect my camera from the spray, the thought of entering the cauldron was unimaginable but, to the surfer, it was just another day at the office.

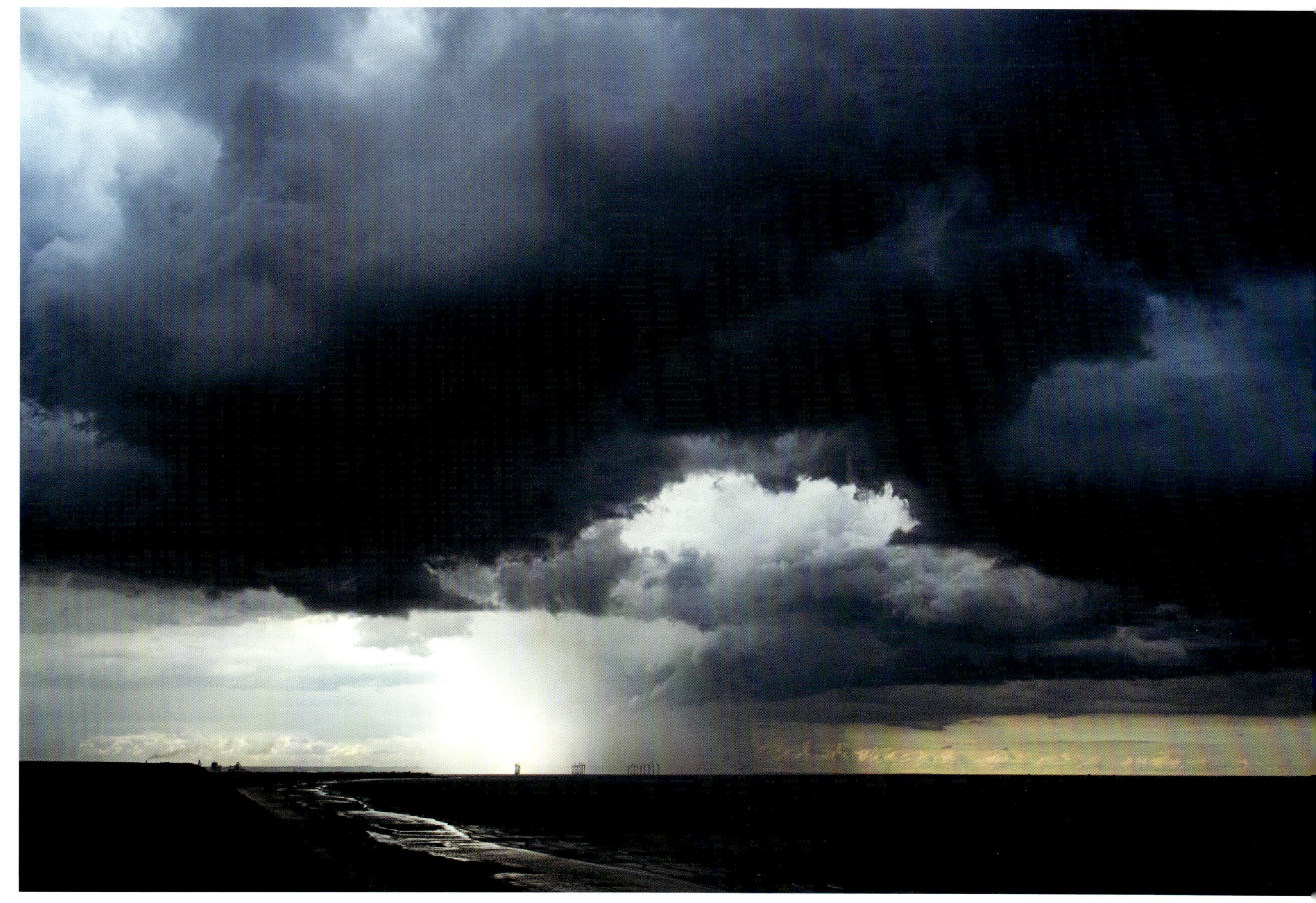

Storm Clouds over Teesside
Cleveland, taken from Saltburn

Large storm clouds form over Teesside as a rain squall passes over the energy offshore windfarm off the coast of Redcar. Living on the coast always brings interesting weather so, as I often do, I headed out during this weather to look for interesting pictures of the storm clouds.

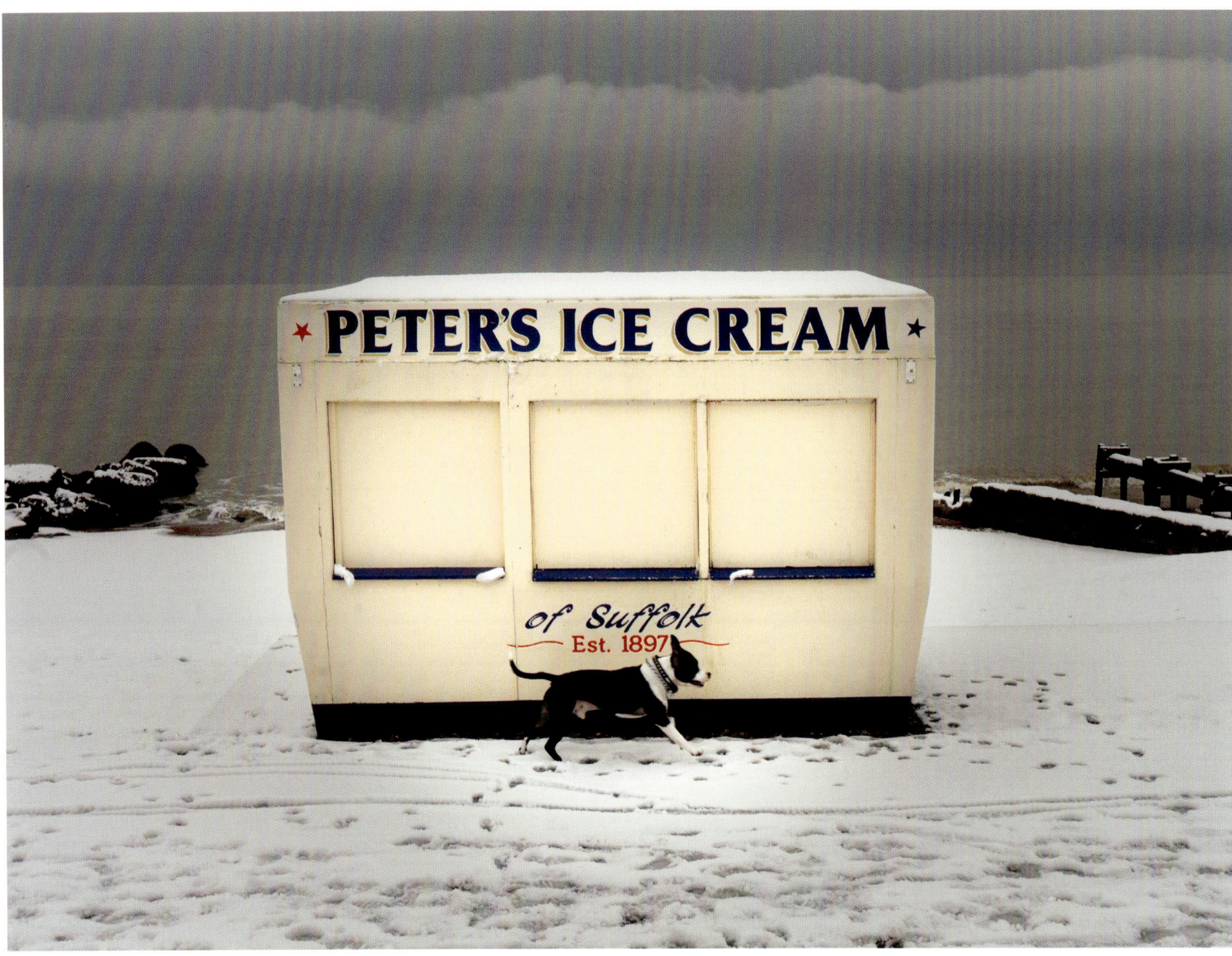

SARAH LUCY BROWN

The Ice Cream Hut
Felixstowe promenade, Suffolk

It was one of the coldest recent winters and there was heavy snowfall. I'm drawn to the ice cream hut throughout the seasons and knew it would make an engaging image. The beach was a blanket of white and the sky a dark grey. When the dog bounded past everything fell into place. It really made me smile. Taken for the East Anglian Daily Times and Ipswich Star newspapers.

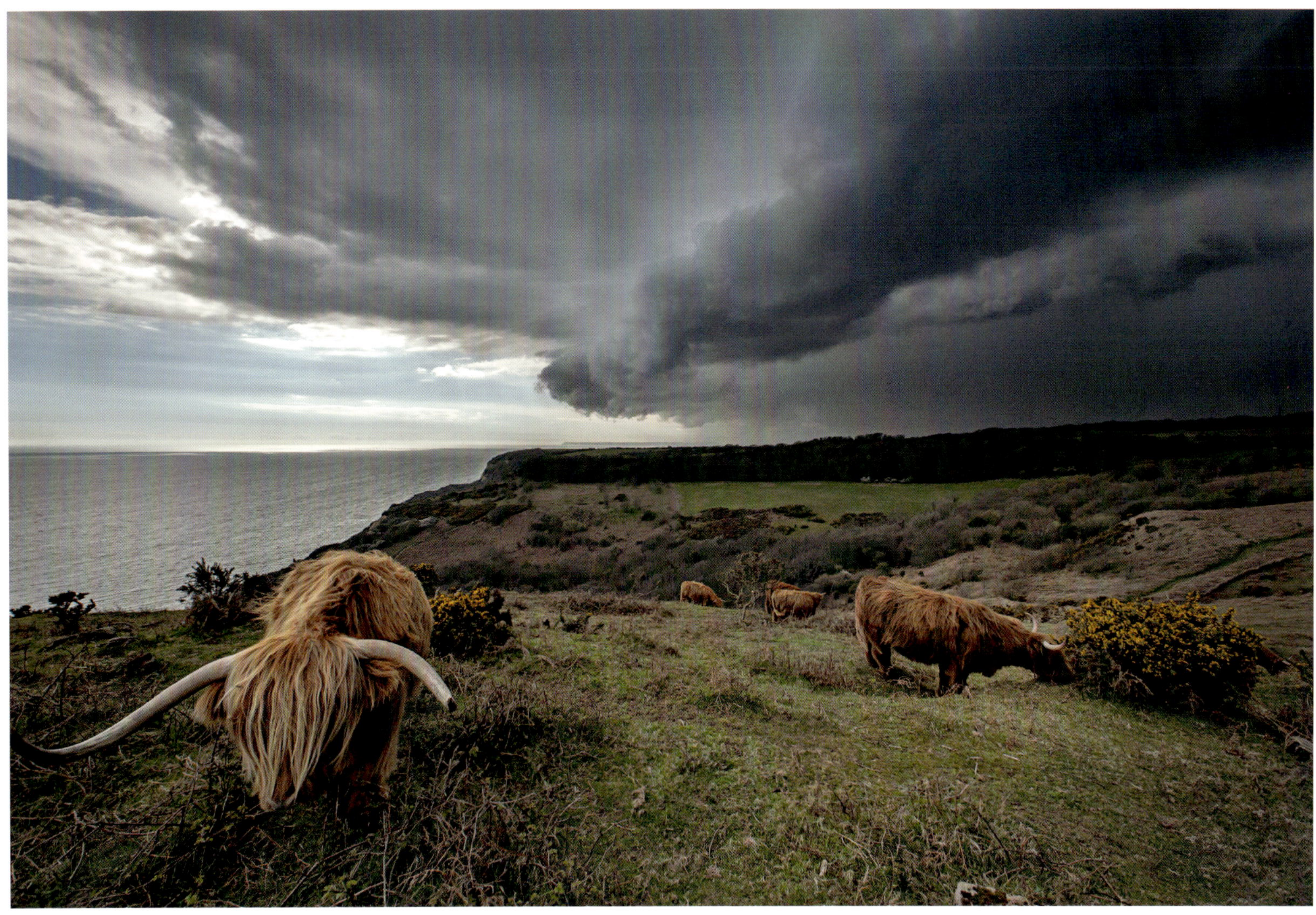

⬦ CHRIS PARKER

Highland Cattle
Warren Glen, Hastings Country Park, Hastings, E Sussex

Odd to discover Highland cattle along the south coast of England.
They had been 'borrowed' to munch their way through the evasive
bracken. I noticed the approaching storm and raced over to the site
to capture the drama.

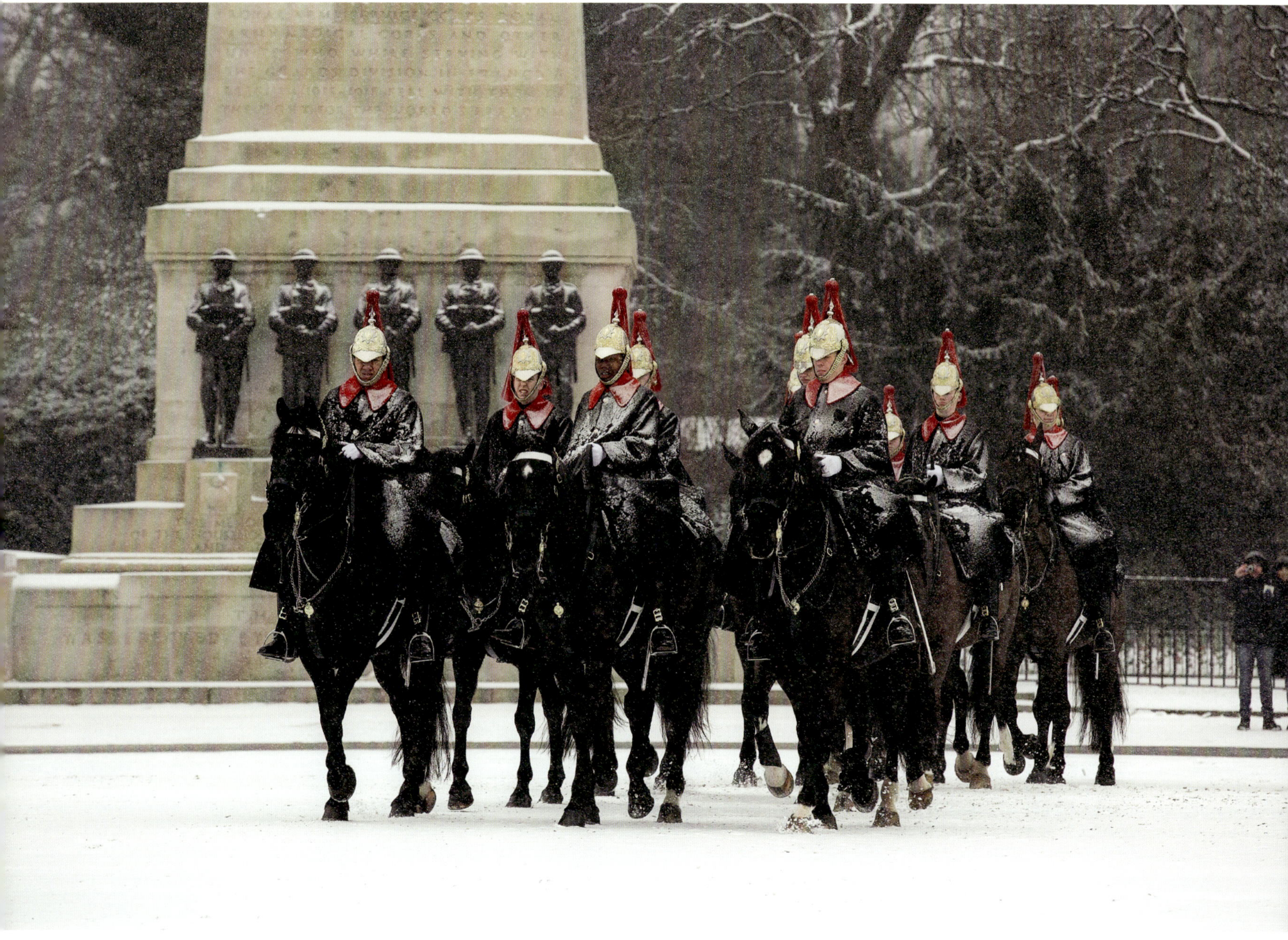

The Blues and Royals in the Snow
Horse Guards Parade, Whitehall, London

The Blues and Royals Household Cavalry changing the guard
at Horse Guards Parade on a snowy Sunday morning.

Three wheels on my wagon
Salisbury Cathedral Close, Salisbury, Wiltshire

This is one of a series of pictures that I took on a very snowy
January morning. The conditions were difficult for photographers
and pedestrians alike, and I struggled to keep my equipment dry
whilst composing images that portrayed the extreme weather
conditions. This image is extracted from a larger scene, but it
was the part that really caught my eye at the time.

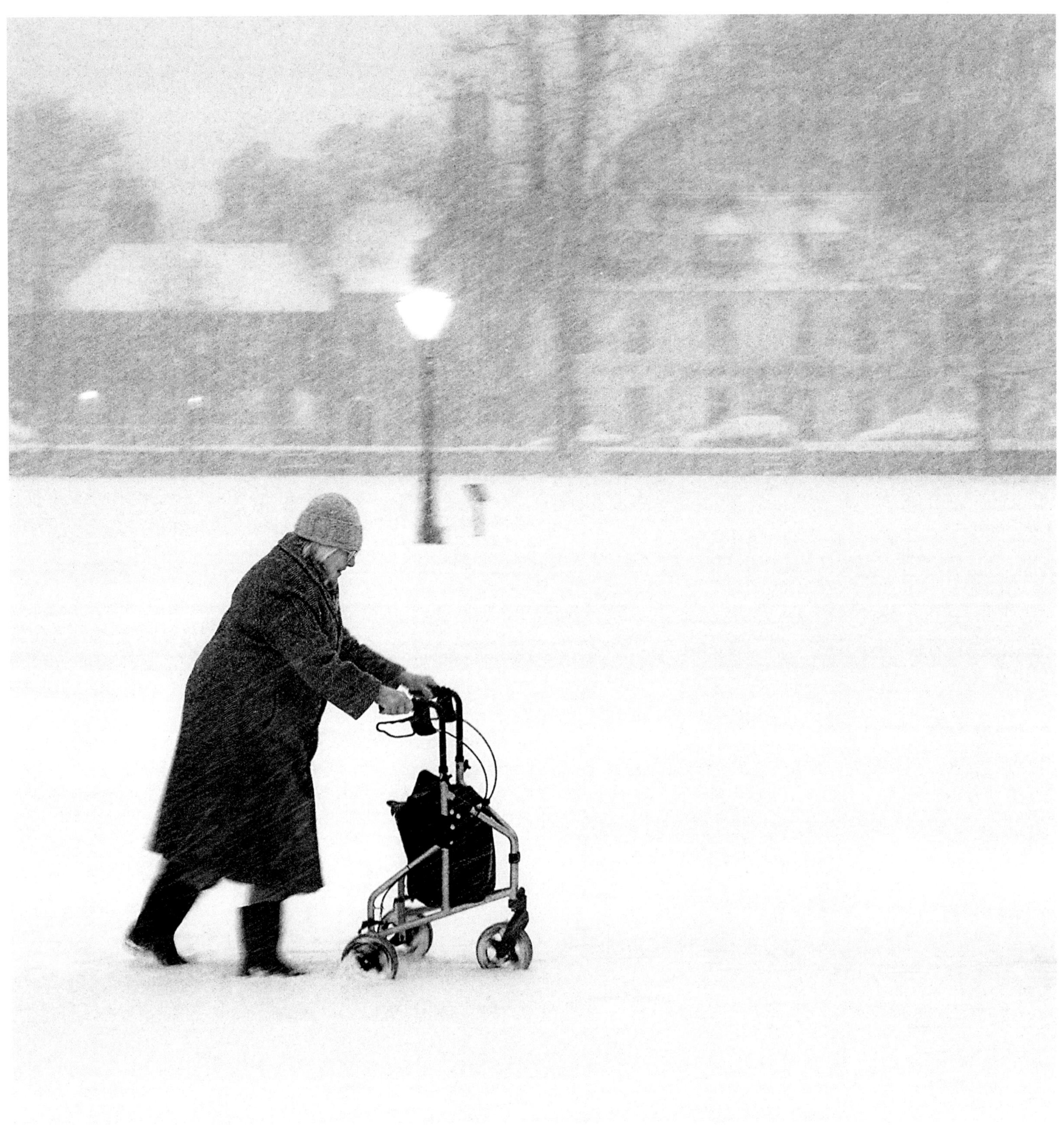

8

HISTORIC BRITAIN

Historic Britain celebrates our country's past, with images taken before the 1st of January 1990.

▶ JANINE WIEDEL / WINNER

Standing up against Apartheid
Trafalgar Square, London

The largest Anti-Apartheid march held in London. The protest was aimed at British Prime Minister Margaret Thatcher for her refusal to impose harsh enough economic measures against South Africa to force President Botha's government to end apartheid. Banners demanded the release of Nelson Mandela serving a life sentence for a 1964 conviction for plotting sabotage. The protest ended in violence with 114 demonstrators arrested and 3 protesters and 10 policemen injured. November 2nd 1985

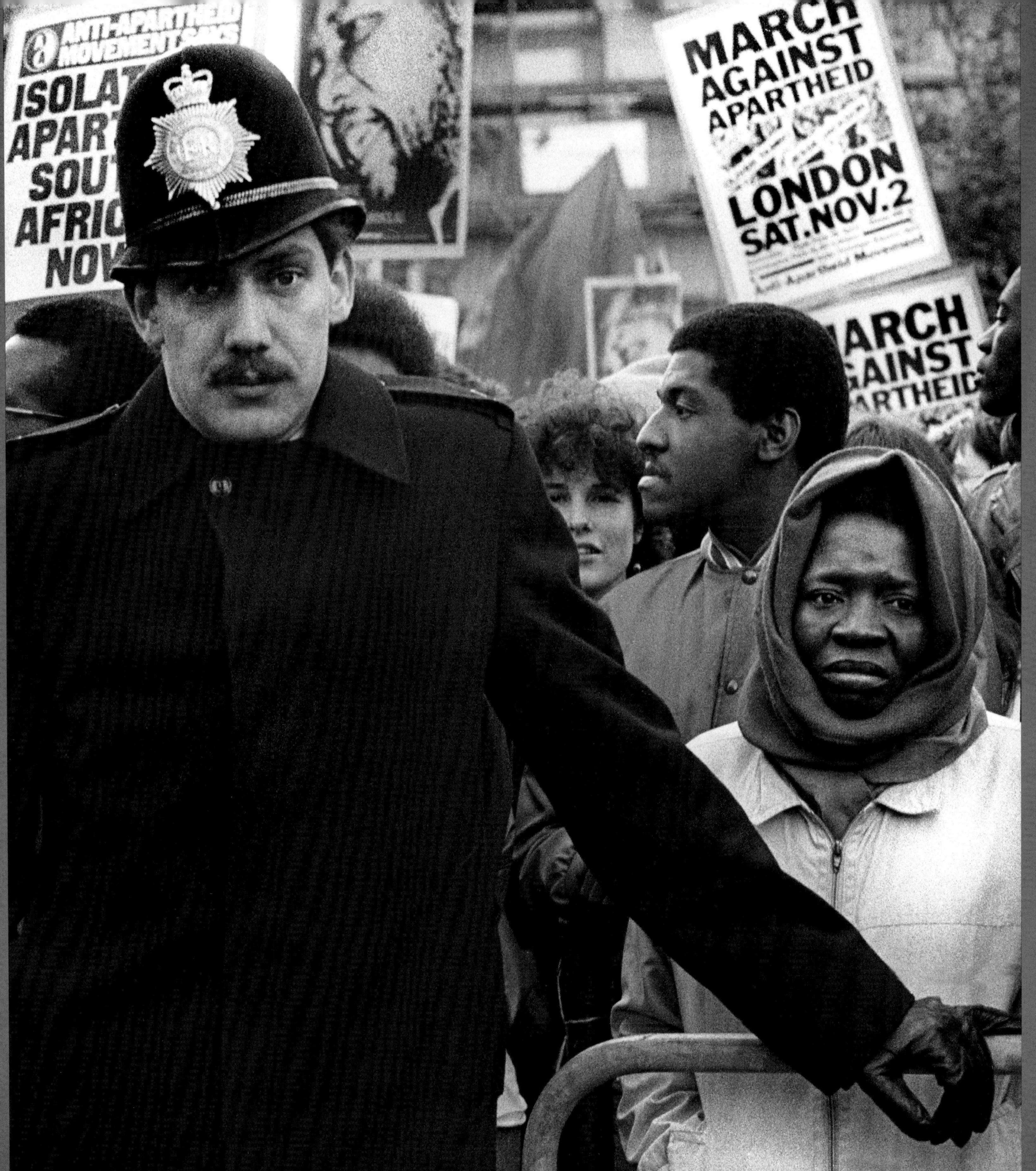
ANTI-APARTHEID
MOVEMENT SACS
ISOLAT
APART
SOUT
AFRIC
NOV
MARCH
AGAINST
APARTHEID
LONDON
SAT. NOV. 2
MARCH
AGAINST
APARTHEID

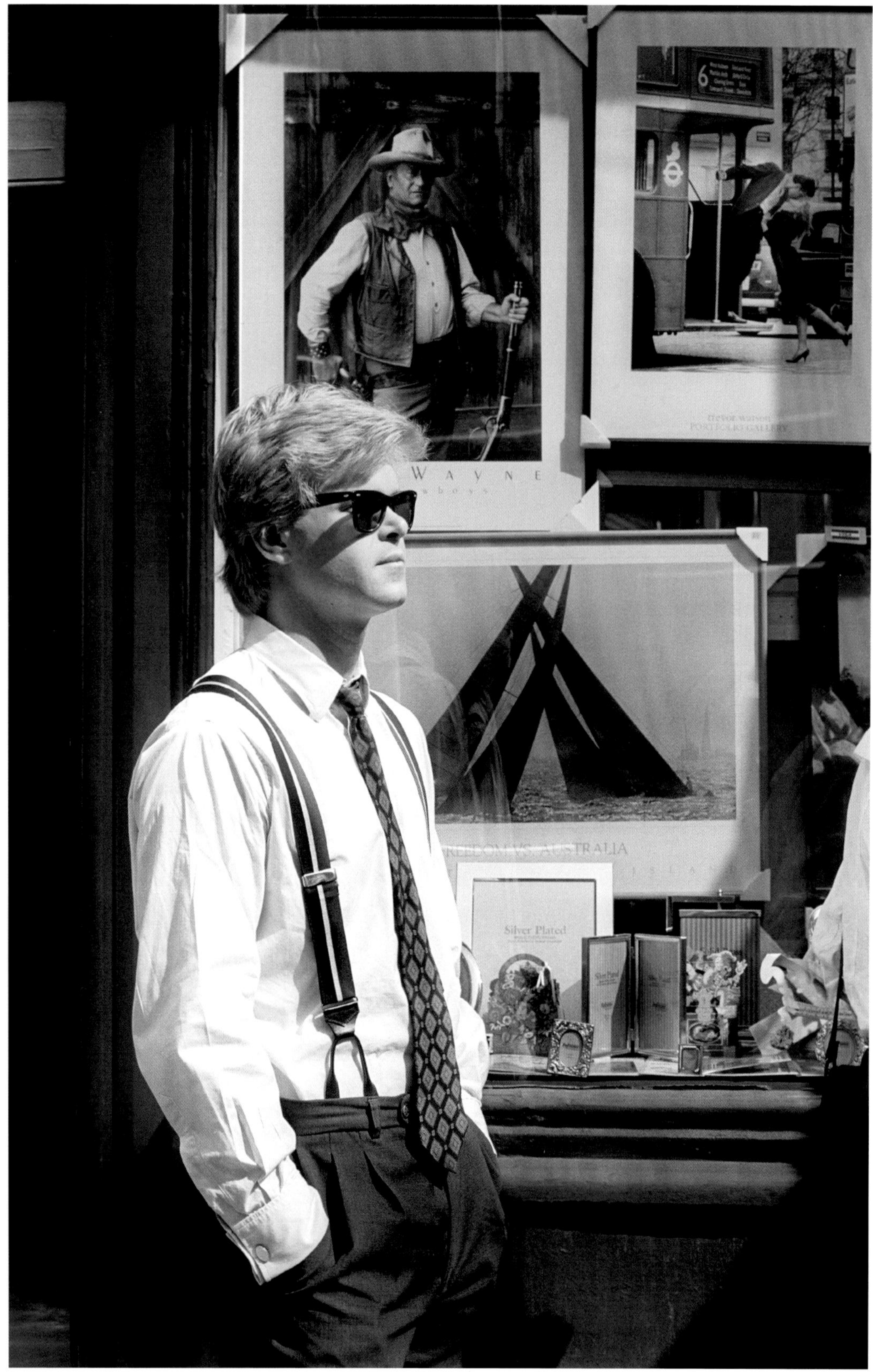

◐ JACKY CHAPMAN
HIGHLY COMMENDED

A future so bright...
London

Young professional donning braces and shades. Photographed in 1989 towards the end of the 'Yuppie' era. The 1980s saw the growth of the middle class and the creation of a large group of young urban professionals. I took this picture because of the play between the young confident male and the iconic image of John Wayne in the background.

**Vanessa Redgrave leading
Anti Vietnam War demonstration**
Grosvenor Square, London

I was a student of photography at Guildford School of Art, had borrowed a school camera, hitched into London and followed the demonstration. Somewhere, on the Charing Cross Road, I think, Vanessa turned, showing the letter to the US Ambassador. Leading the march with her was Tariq Ali and, over his shoulder, you can just glimpse a very young Richard Branson.

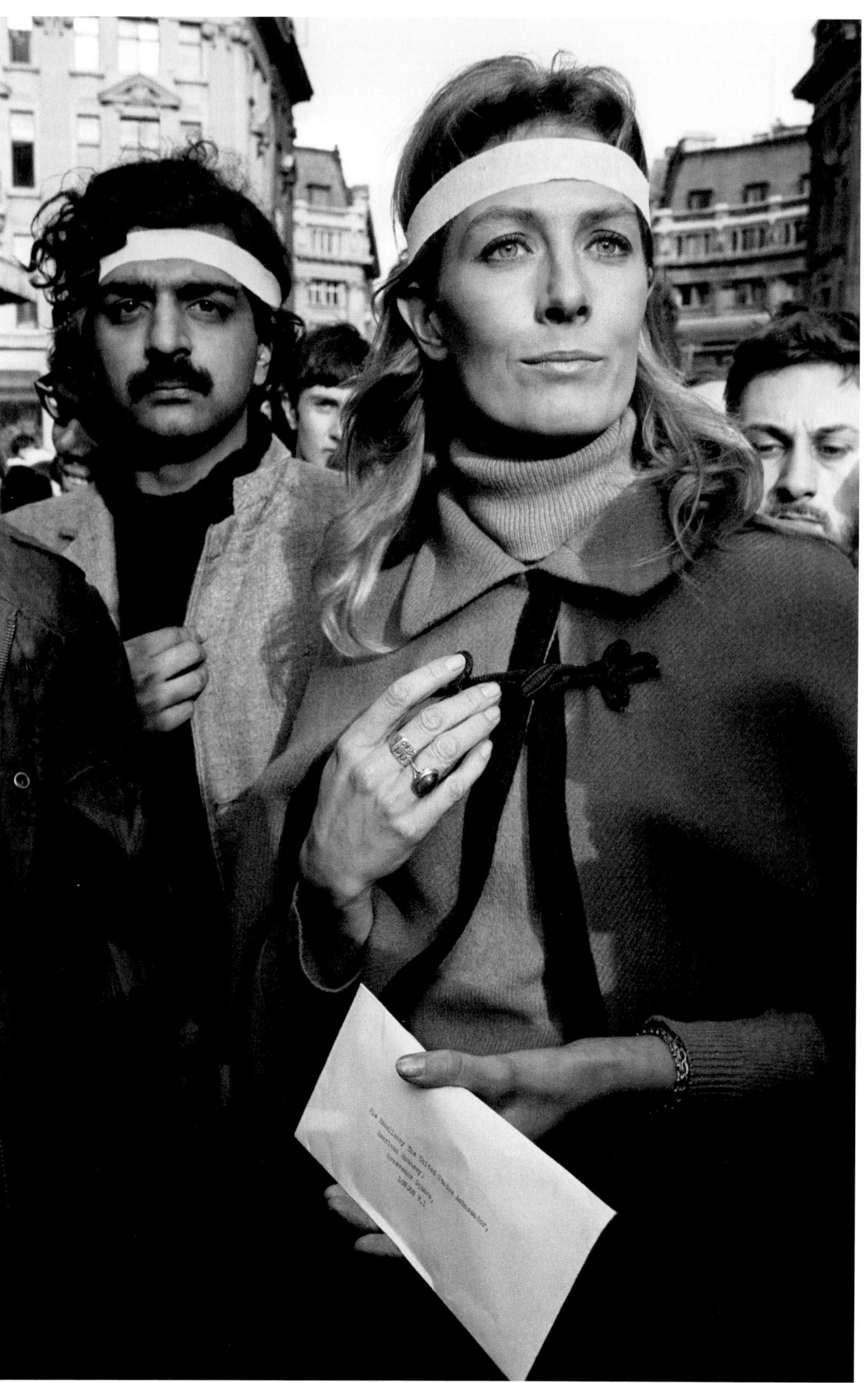

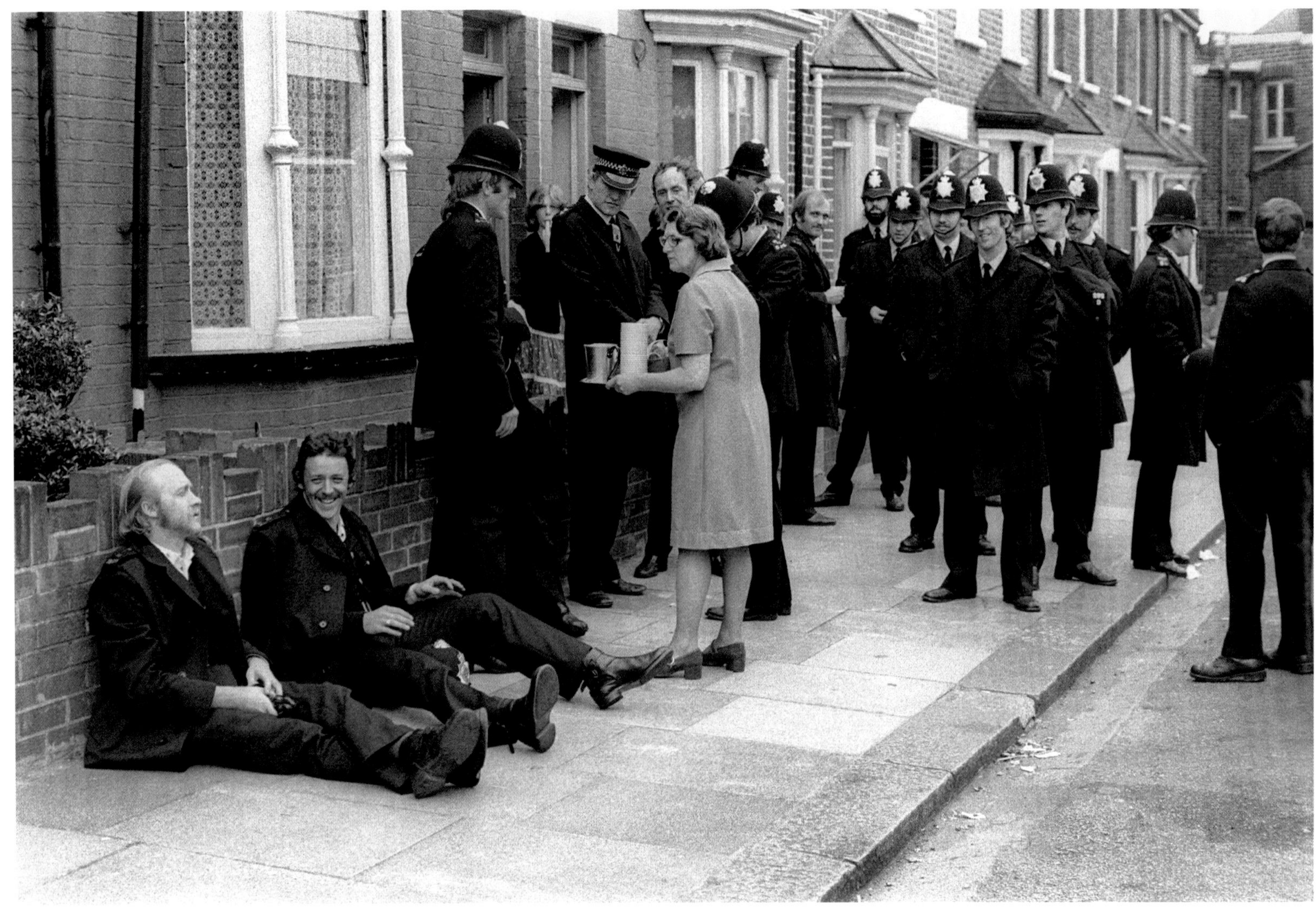

Tea for the Boys
Willesden, North London

The police had been battling the protestors during the Grunwick
Strike action. In the backstreets of Willesden they had discovered a
resting place with home brewed tea.

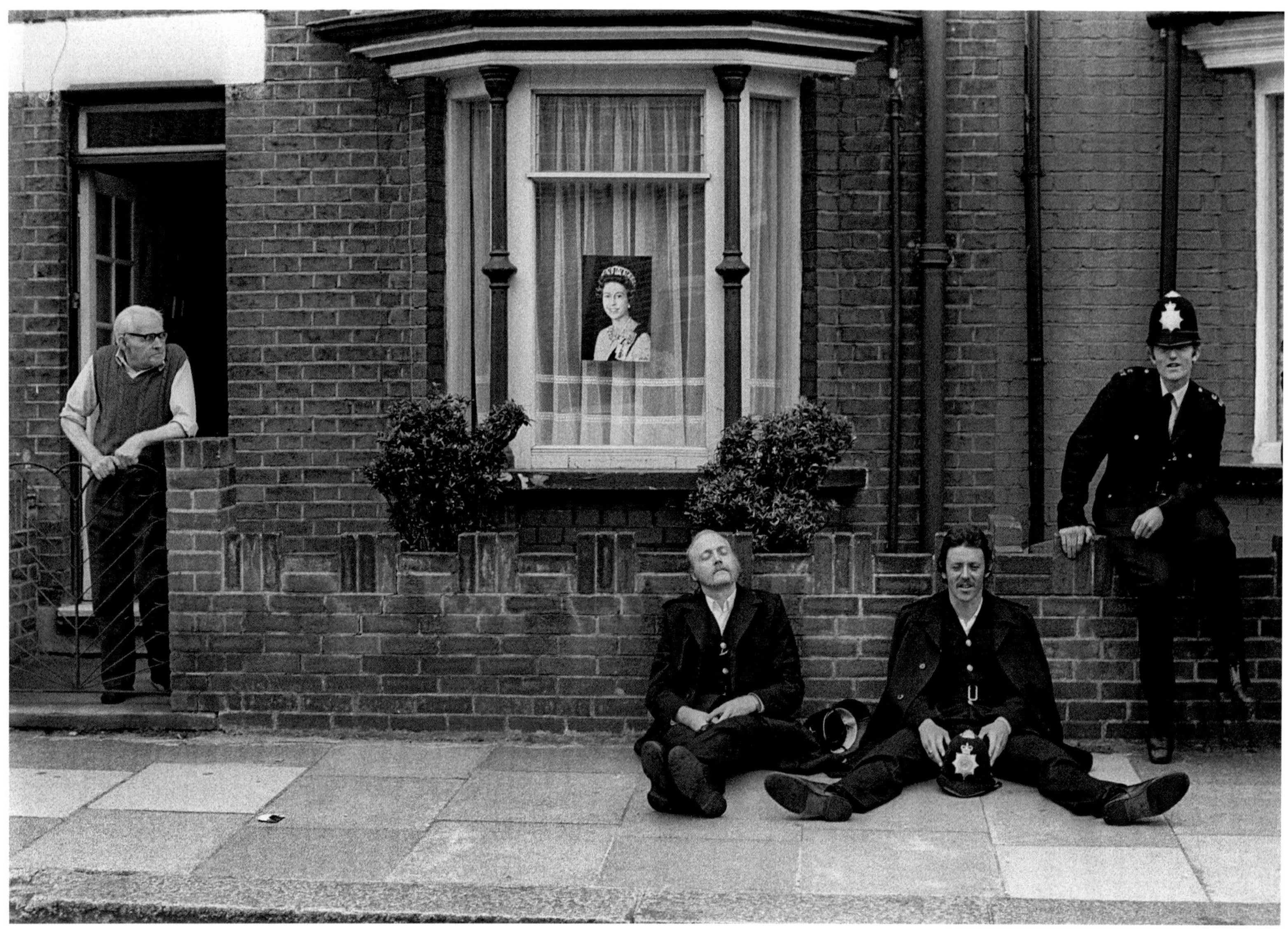

Resting with the Queen
Willesden, North London

I had been photographing the Grunwick demonstration and strike action. Wandering into a backstreet, I discovered the police recuperating from battling the protestors. This was also the year of the Queen's Silver Jubillee Celebrations.

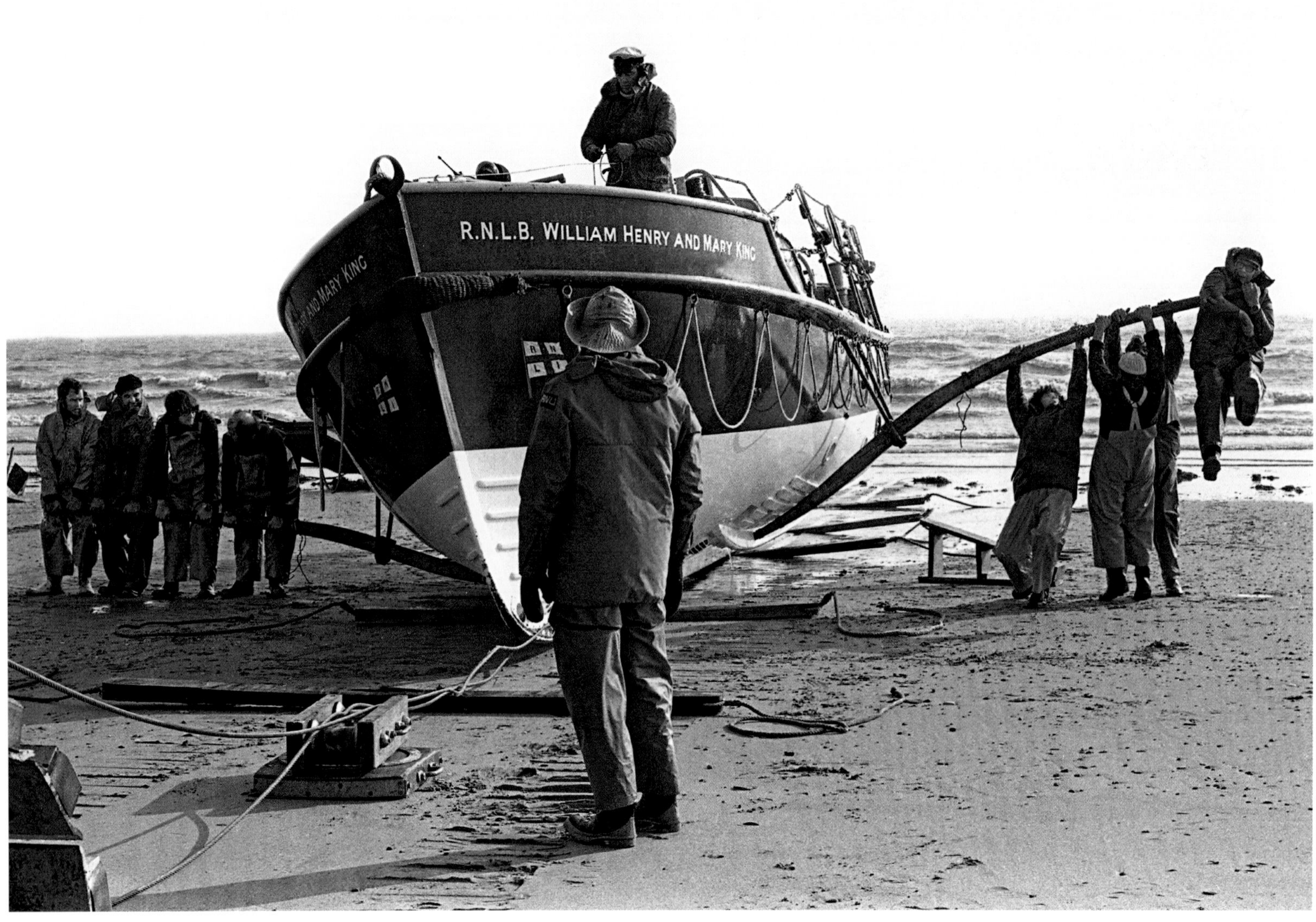

◓ PAUL BERRIFF / HIGHLY COMMENDED

Back on the Beach
Bridlington, East Yorkshire

The Bridlington lifeboat arrives back on the the beach after
returning from a callout. The lifeboat is driven at speed from the
sea onto wood planks placed on the beach. The shore crew then
keep the lifeboat level by using supporting beams attached to
the port and starboard sides of the boat. Once level the boat is
then winched by tractor onto a launch carriage ready for the
next call. 1972.

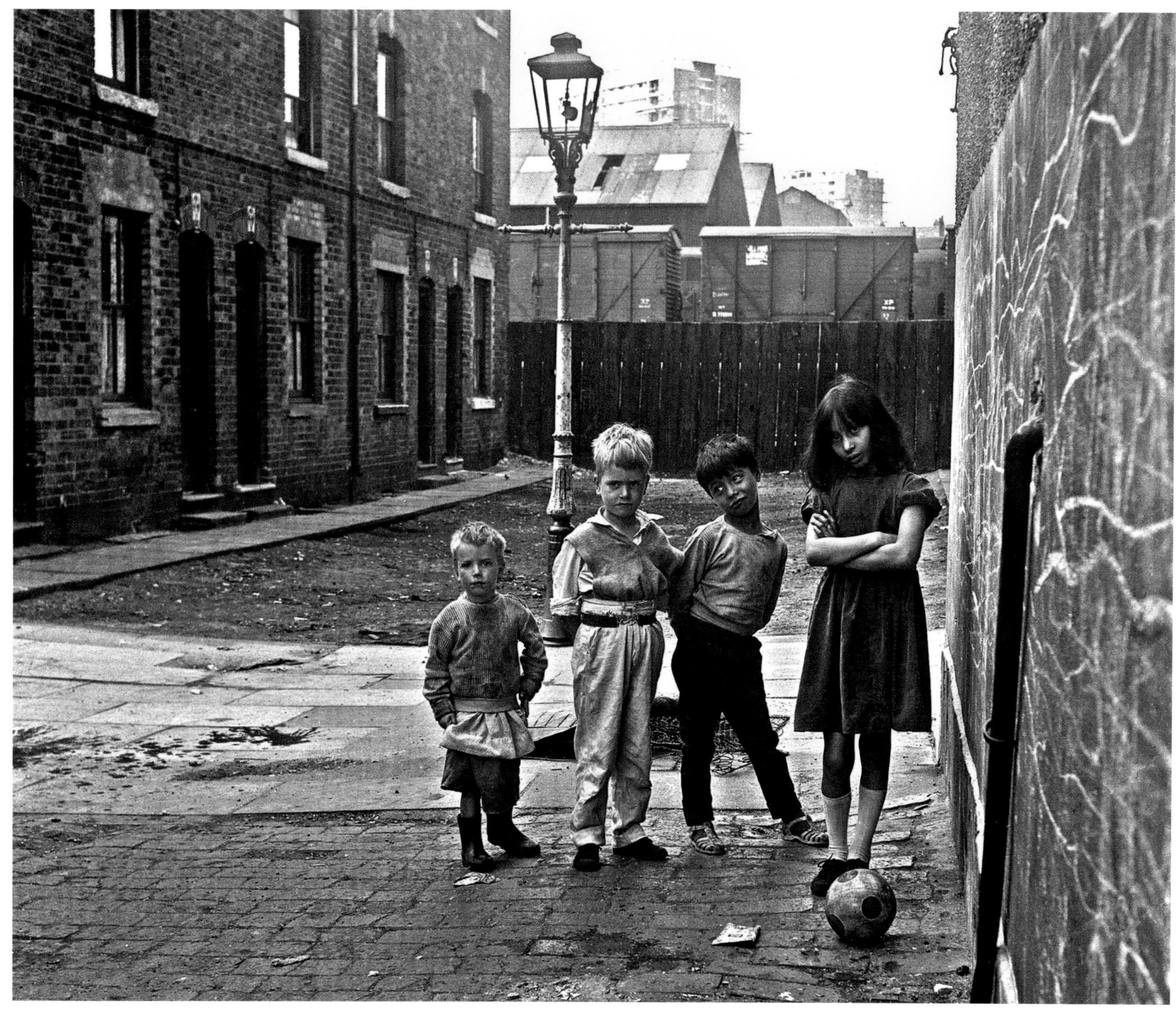

◑ PAUL BERRIFF / HIGHLY COMMENDED

Street Kids
Birmingham

Passing through the streets of Birmingham I noticed a group of children playing football.
Cobbles, gaslights and terrace houses have always appealed to me as being very
photogenic and any opportunity like this would not be ignored. I particular liked the
expressions on the children's faces and the clothing they were wearing. May 1963

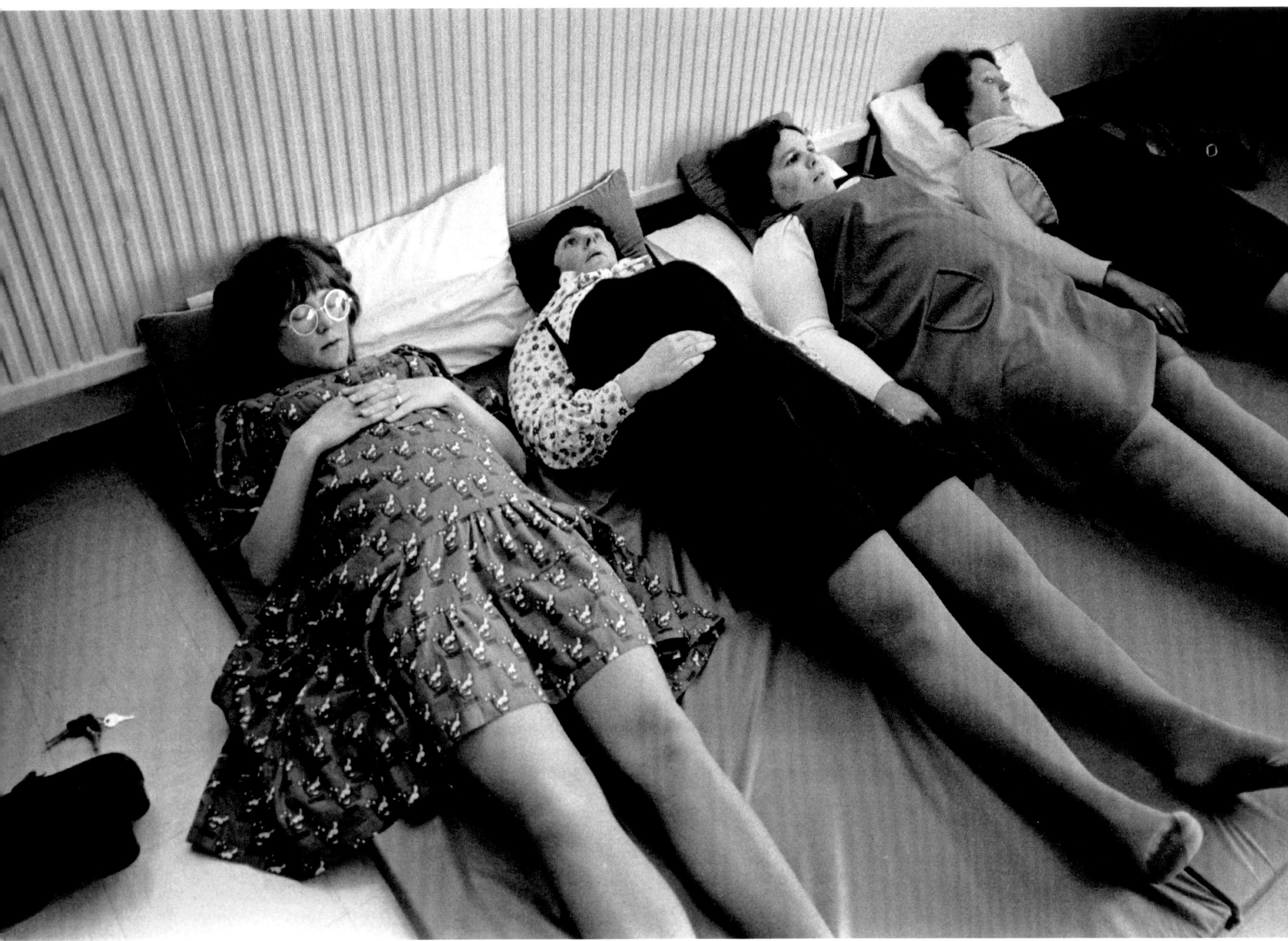

Ladies-in-Waiting
UK hospital

At a pre-natal class in a hospital, I noticed how relaxed this one
woman was, compared to all the others beside her. The picture was
taken in subdued daylight, which was coming in from the window
above them. 1986.

◎ DAVID JONES
HIGHLY COMMENDED

Medical Records
UK hospital

This image, taken in the days before computers, reminds us how all documents had to be typed or hand-written, and kept in folders, necessitating the need for massive archives of paper. This image shows a filing clerk going about her routine task of searching for patients' notes. The low-level lighting demanded the use of a wide-aperture lens, slow shutter speed, fast film and a steady hand. 1975

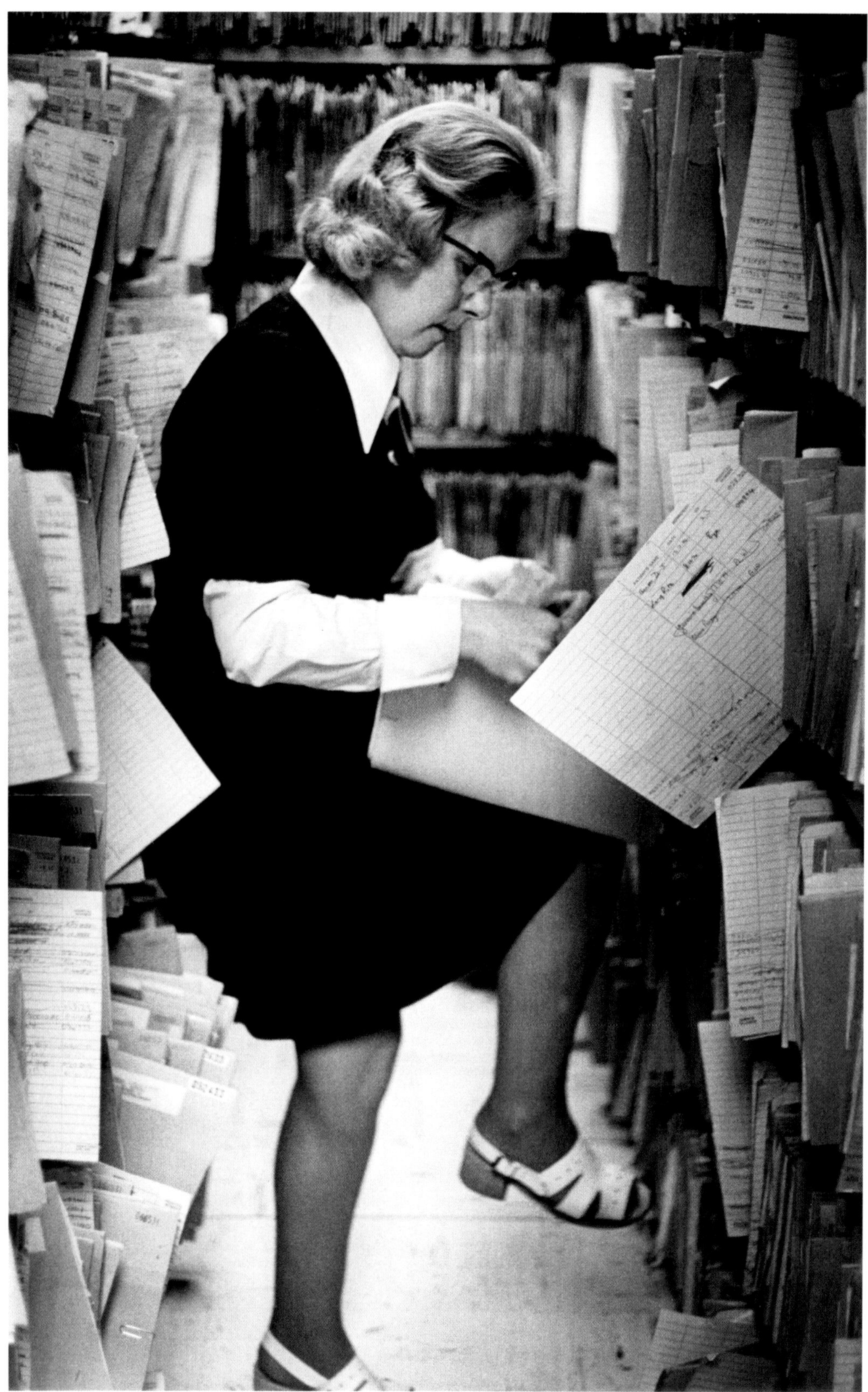

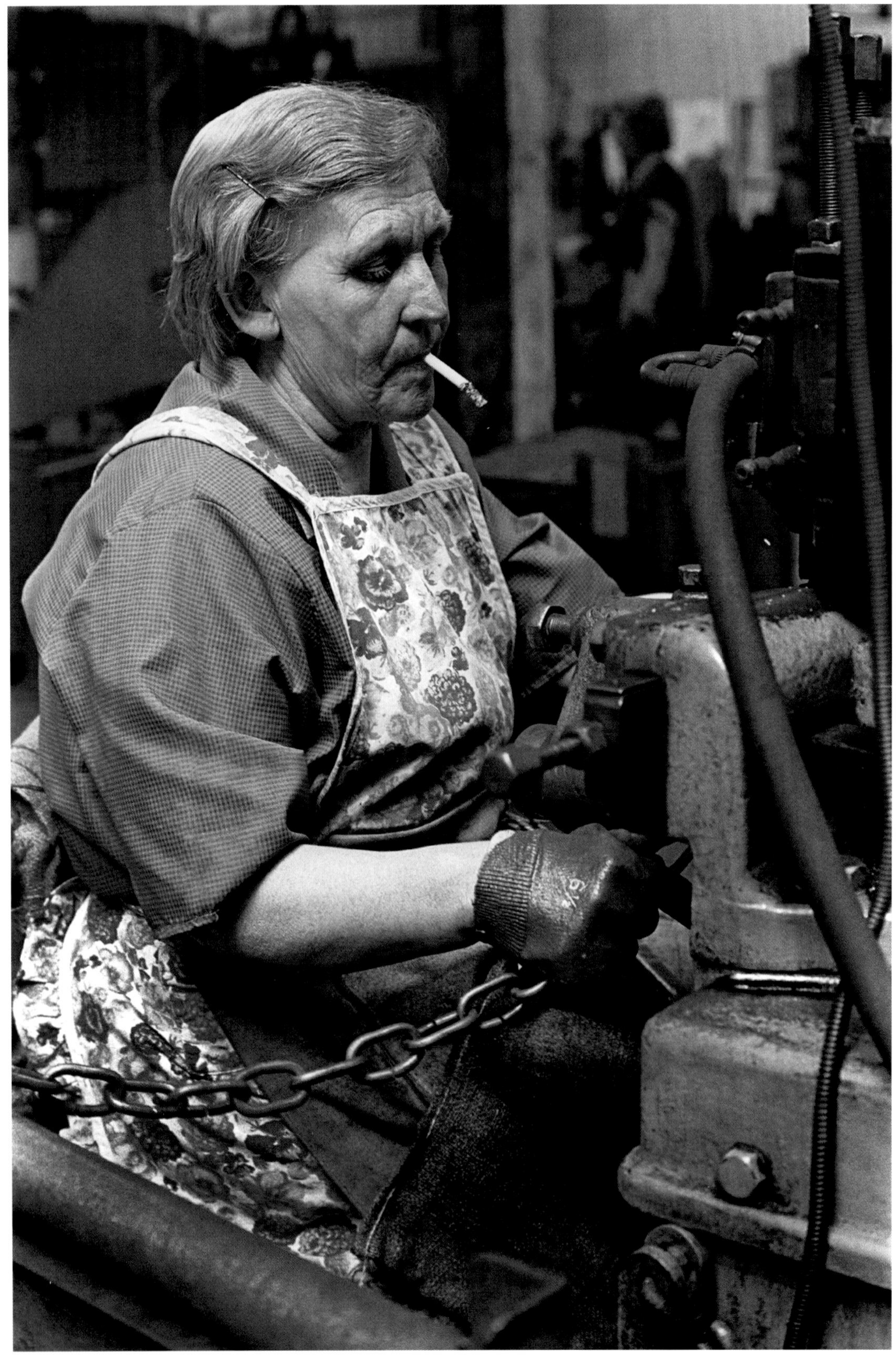

Eliza Tinsley Chain Works
The Black Country, West Midlands

This was taken in The Black Country in 1977 when I was working on 'Vulcan's Forge', a 2 year project funded by West Midlands Arts. A few years later, most of the Chain Workshops closed down and unemployment figures rose rapidly. Eliza Tinsley however managed to survive and after 150 years they are still major suppliers of chains and fittings. Traditionally, chain-making was work for women and children as the men were down the mines. 1977.

Waiting on the Verge
Cheadle, Staffordshire, West Midlands

I never did discover what they were
waiting for.

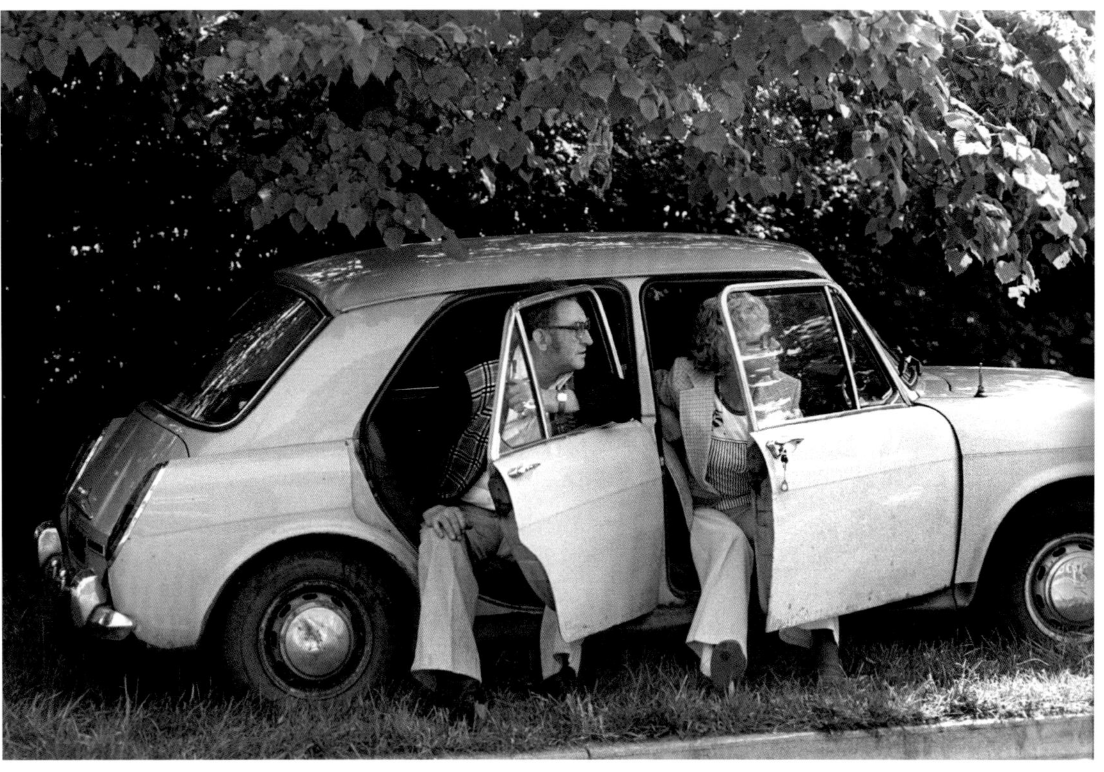

Off to Brighton
London

The annual London to Brighton Veteran
Car Run is the longest running motoring
event in the world. The first run was in
1896 and since it's revival in 1927 it has
taken place every year. All the cars that
enter must have been built before 1905.

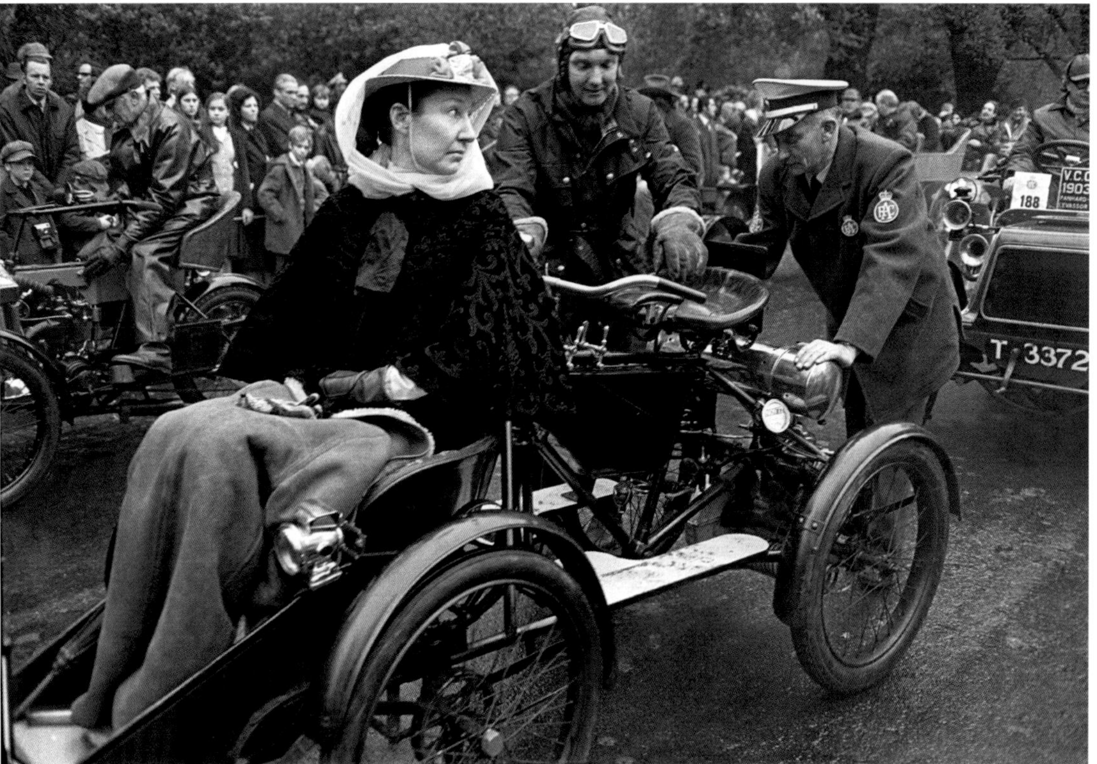

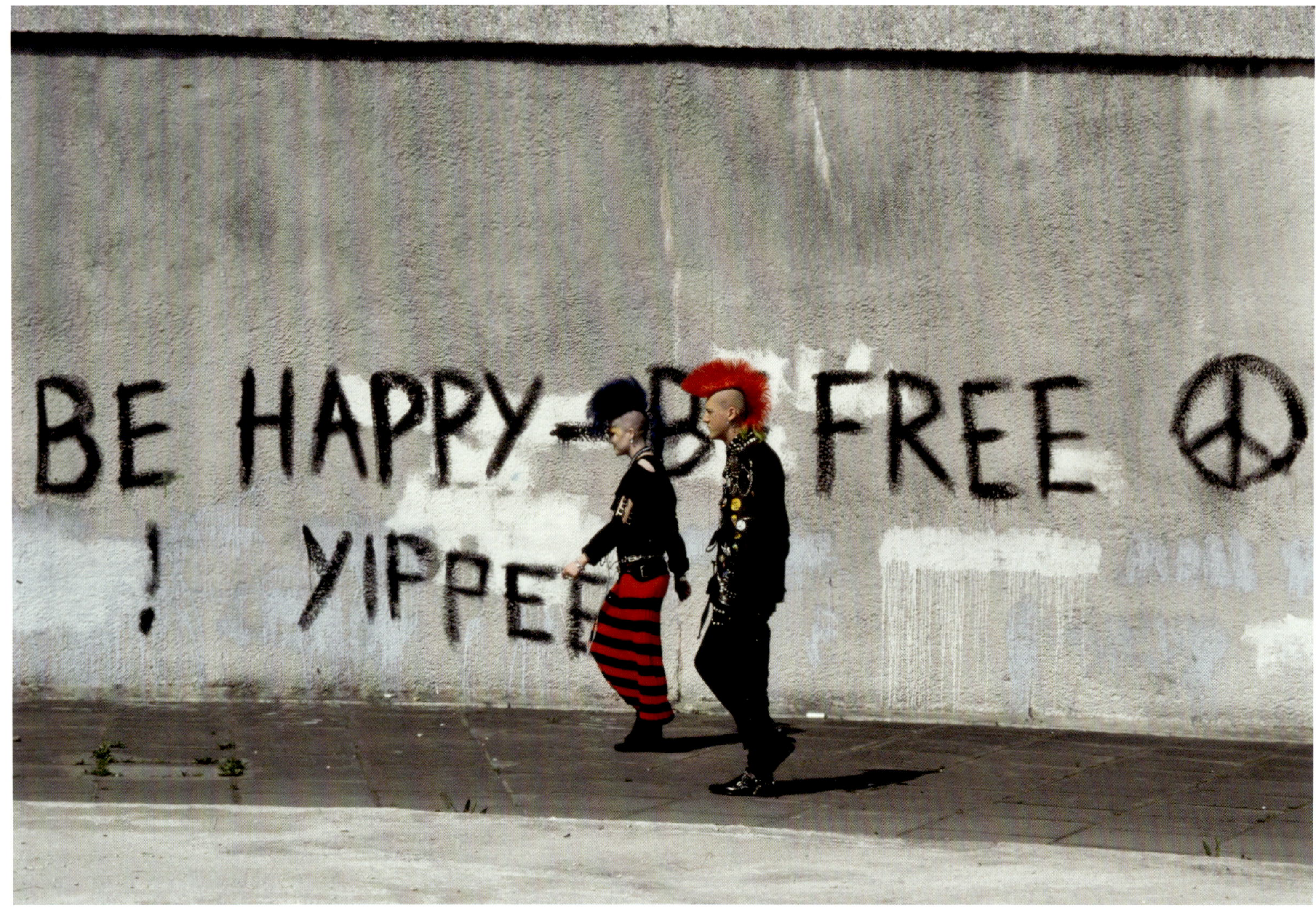

CHRIS PARKER

Be happy, Be free. Yippee.
London

By the 1980s punks were changing from the country's number one
enemy to tourist attractions on the Kings Road. Nobody epitomised
this more than Matt Belgrano, the postcard punk, with his red
Mohican hair. I photographed various punks during this period
and this is one of my favourites.

○ CHRIS PARKER

**Postcard punk Matt Belgrano
with a horseguard**
Horse Guards Parade, London

Wandering around London in the mid
1980s with the punk Matt Belgrano was
a challenging photo shoot. Crowds
gathered wherever we stopped but I
was determined to capture an iconic
image that represented the old and
new of London.

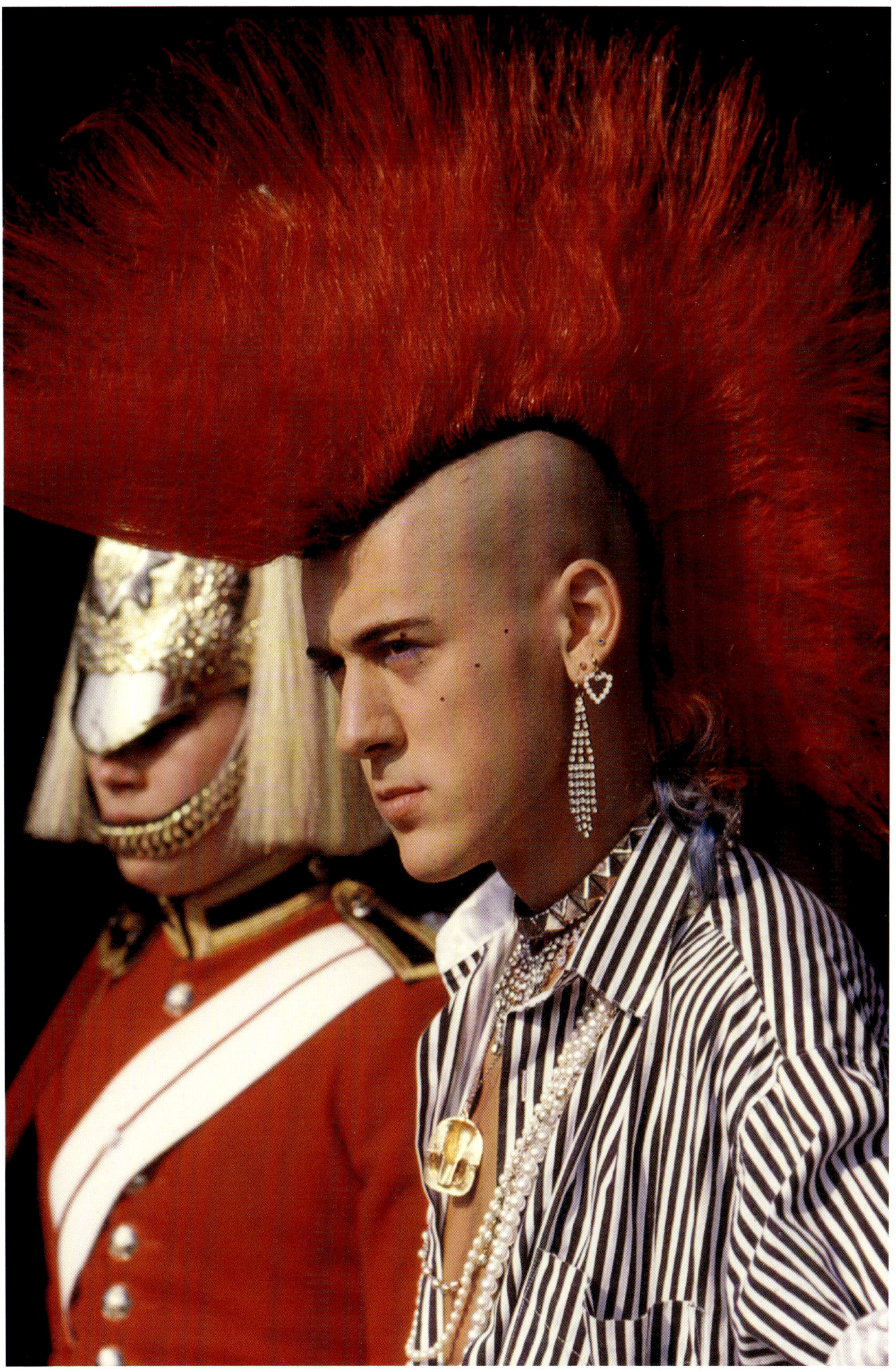

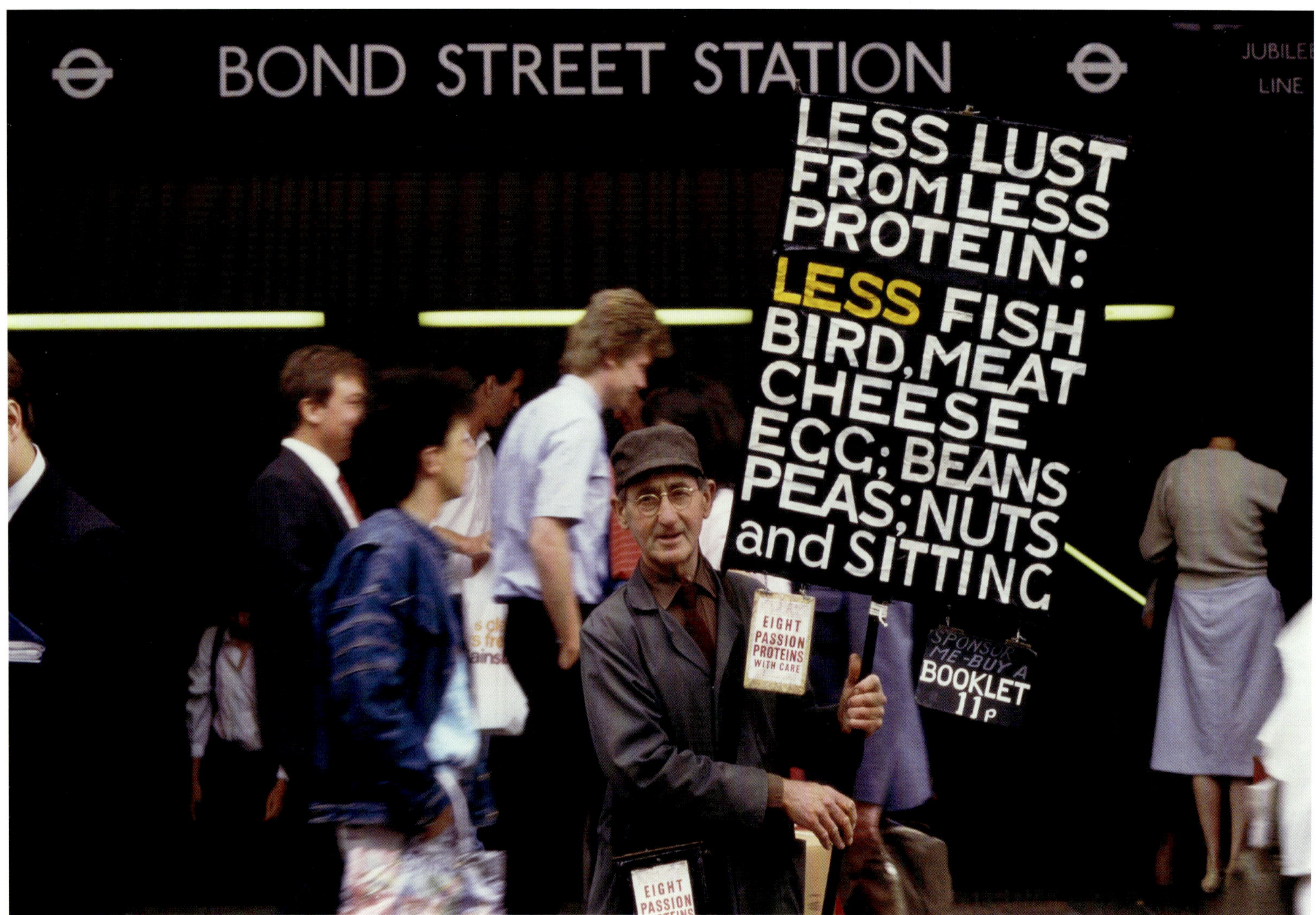

○ CHRIS PARKER

Stanley Green, Protein Man
Oxford Street. London

In the 1980s I used to see this gentleman wandering alone along
Oxford Street with his billboard come rain or sunshine. I admired
his perseverance despite the many rejections to buy his pamphlet
advocating 'Less Lust, From Less Protein'. Today he would be
surrounded by camera phone touting sightseers wanting selfies.

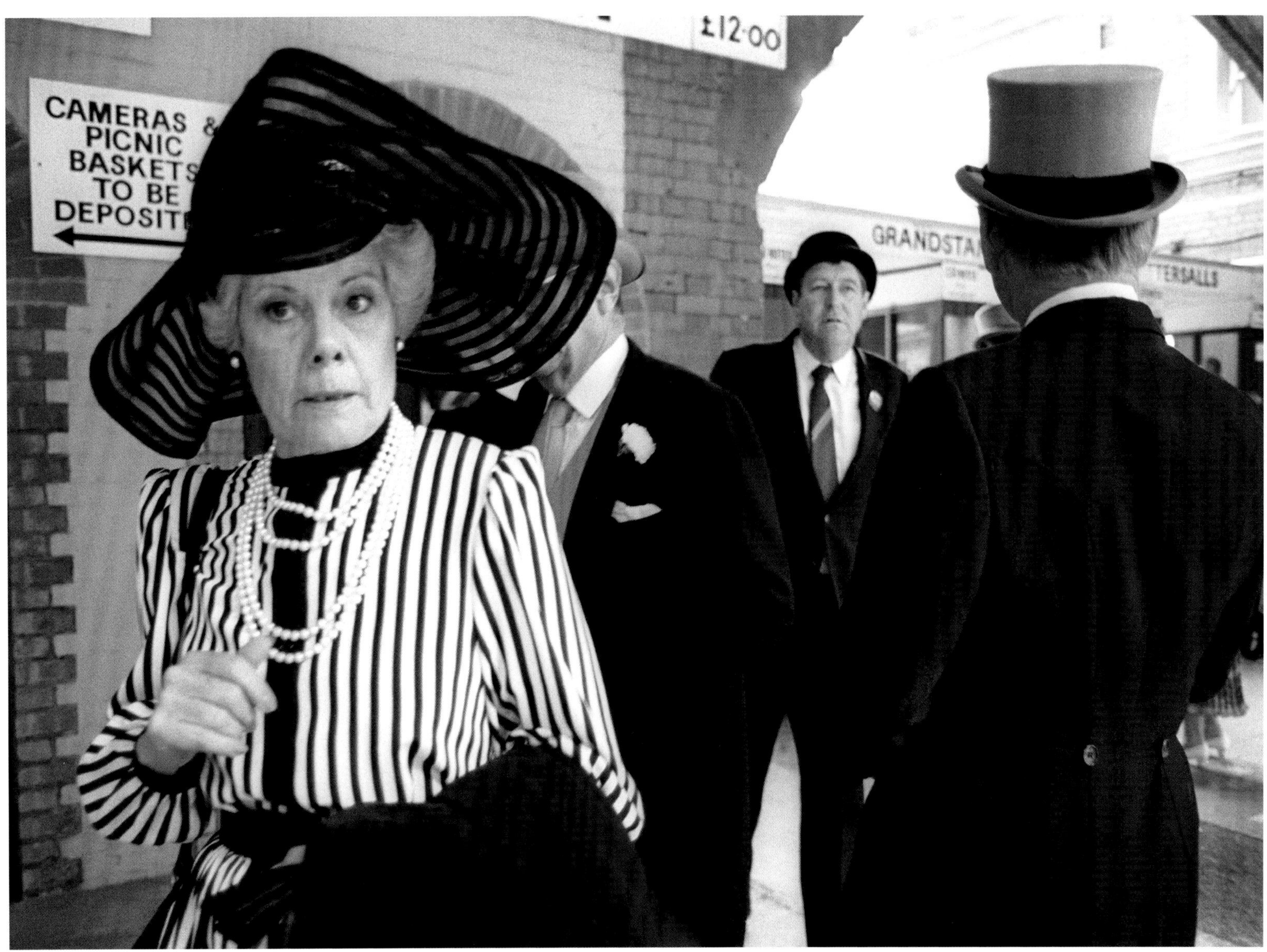

◔ JACKY CHAPMAN

Ladies Day
Ascot, Berkshire

During 1986, I documented Britain's diverse social classes. Royal
Ascot (dating back to 1711) and the Royal enclosure were obvious
candidates. I attended on the third day (traditionally Ladies Day)
where fancy hats, formal day dresses, top hats and tails are the
order of the day. 1986

9

DOCUMENTARY SERIES

The Documentary Series celebrates portfolios of images that tell the story of any subject or topic that conveys life in Britain.

○ DAN GIANNOPOULOS

Living with Dementia
South East London

Dennis is visited by his youngest daughter, Jane, on his last day in his family home where he's lived with his wife Ruby for almost 30 years. He will never return here. Dennis suffered a stroke in August 2008. The stroke triggered the onset of Vascular Dementia. After spending a number of months being cared for by his wife Ruby, the decision was made to transfer him to a care facility nearby.

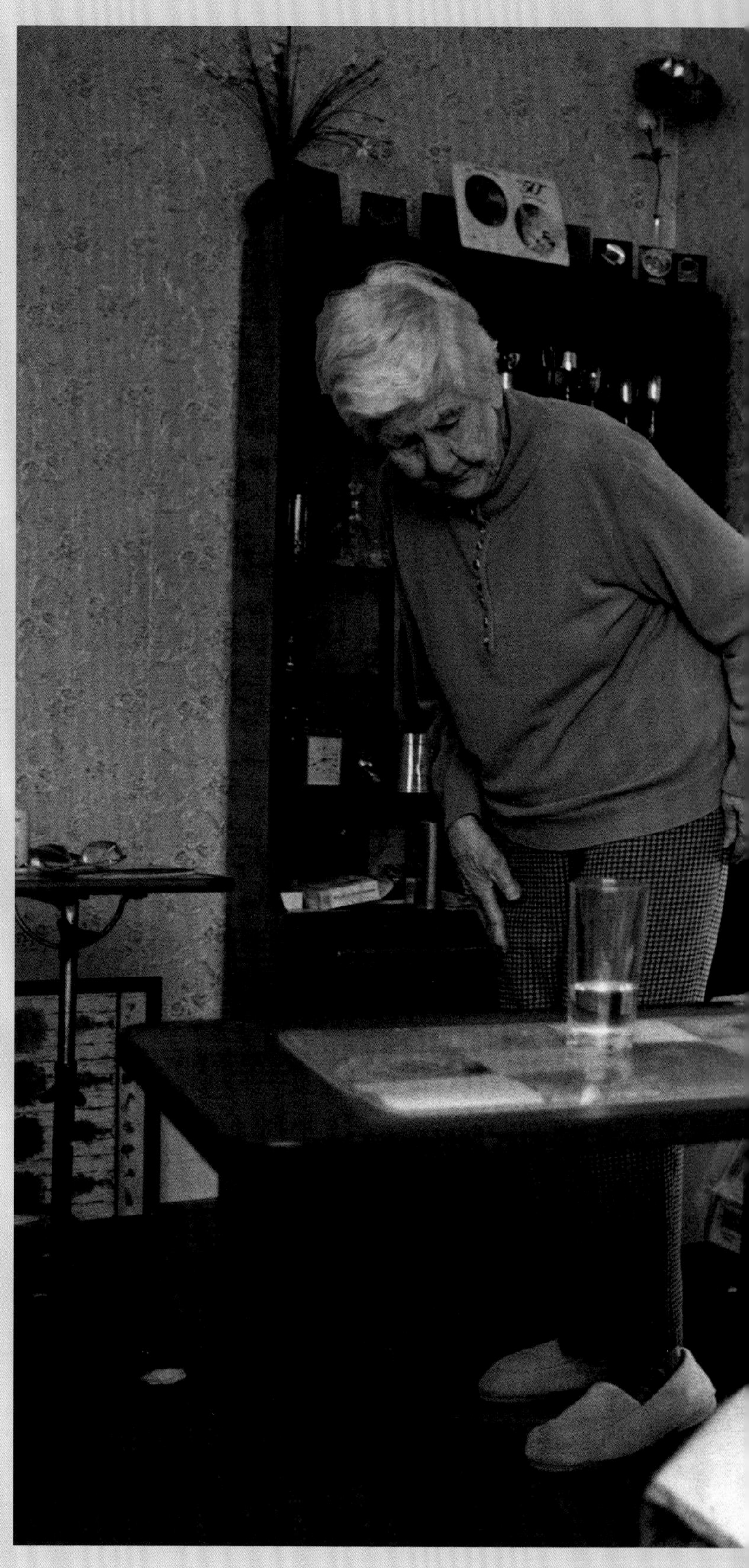

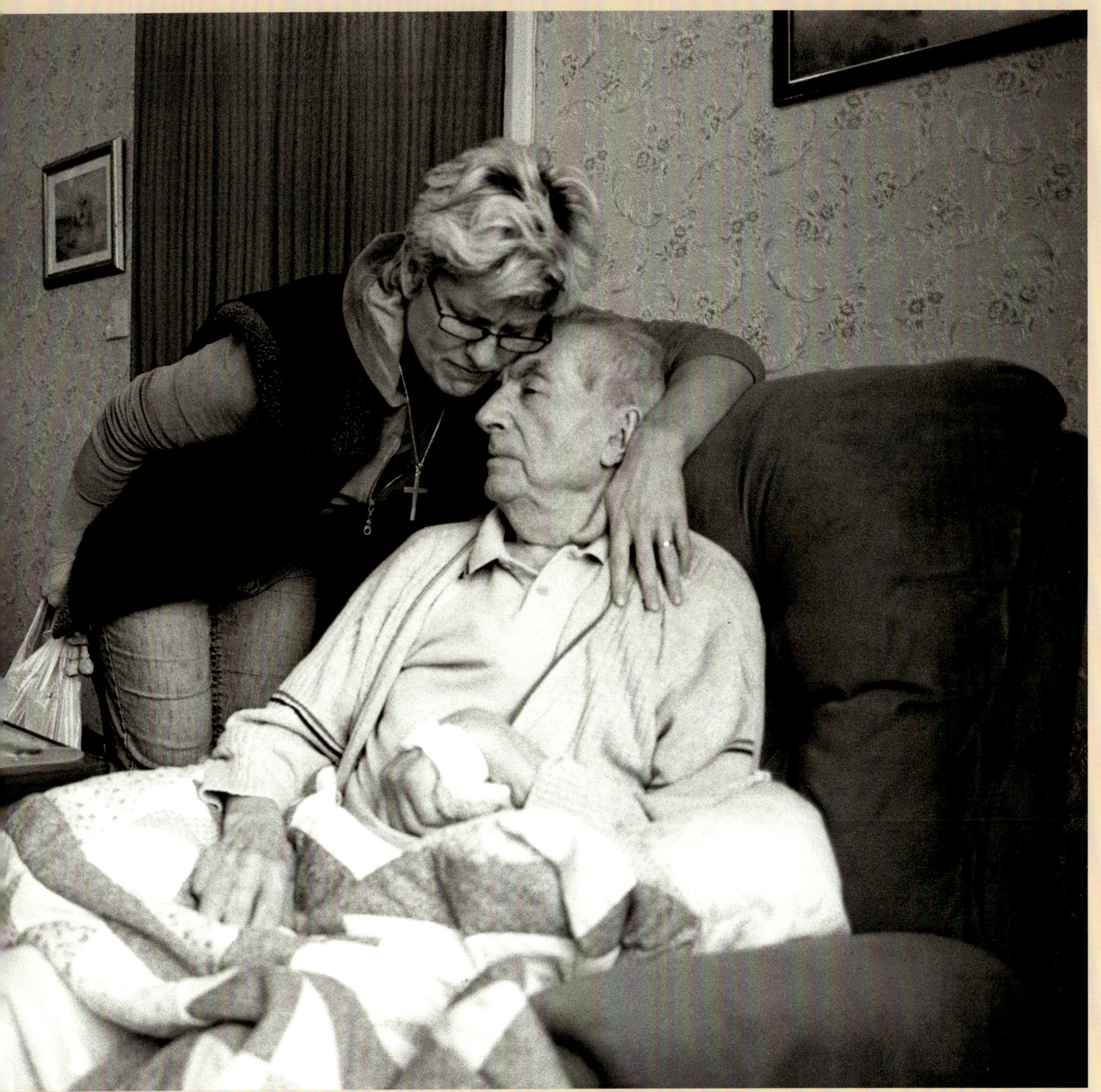

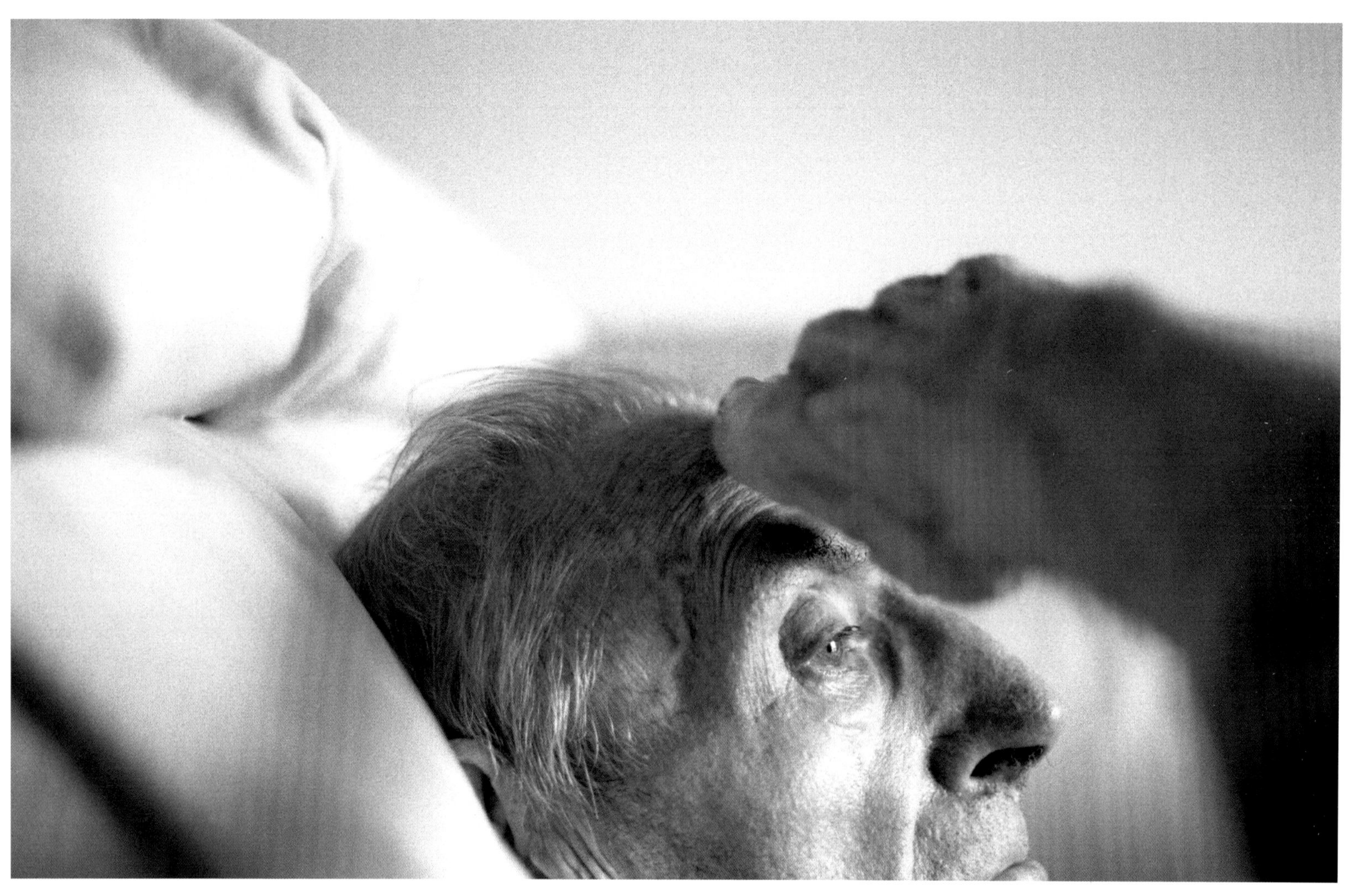

◓

Dennis looks out of his bedroom window. From his window
he can see the tops of trees in a nearby park. His family say
that when the summer comes they will take him outside to
sit under the trees.

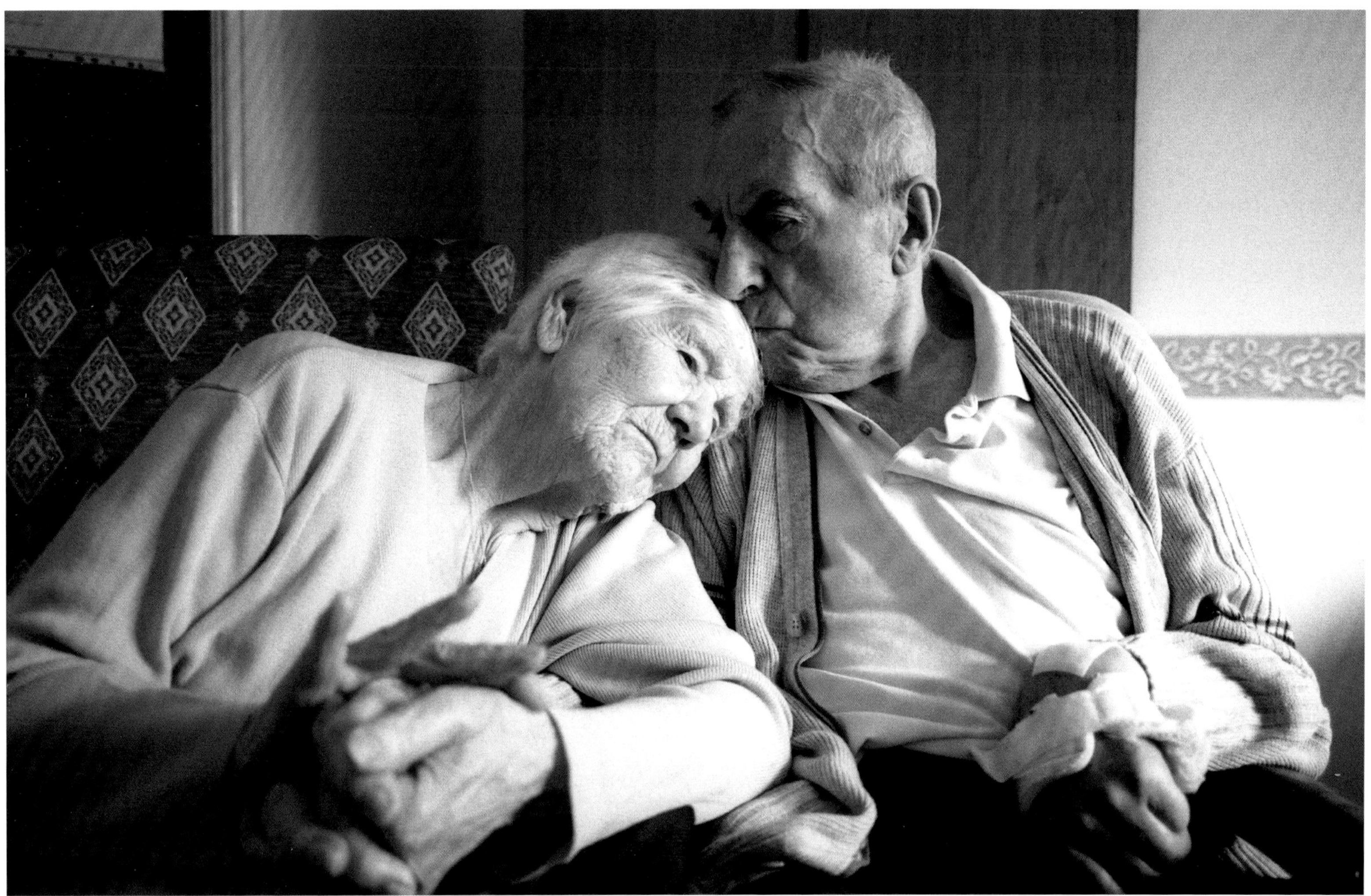

Dennis kisses Ruby during one of her daily visits to his care home. Throughout his deteriorating mental condition Dennis has never forgotten who Ruby is and remains as fiercely protective of her as ever.

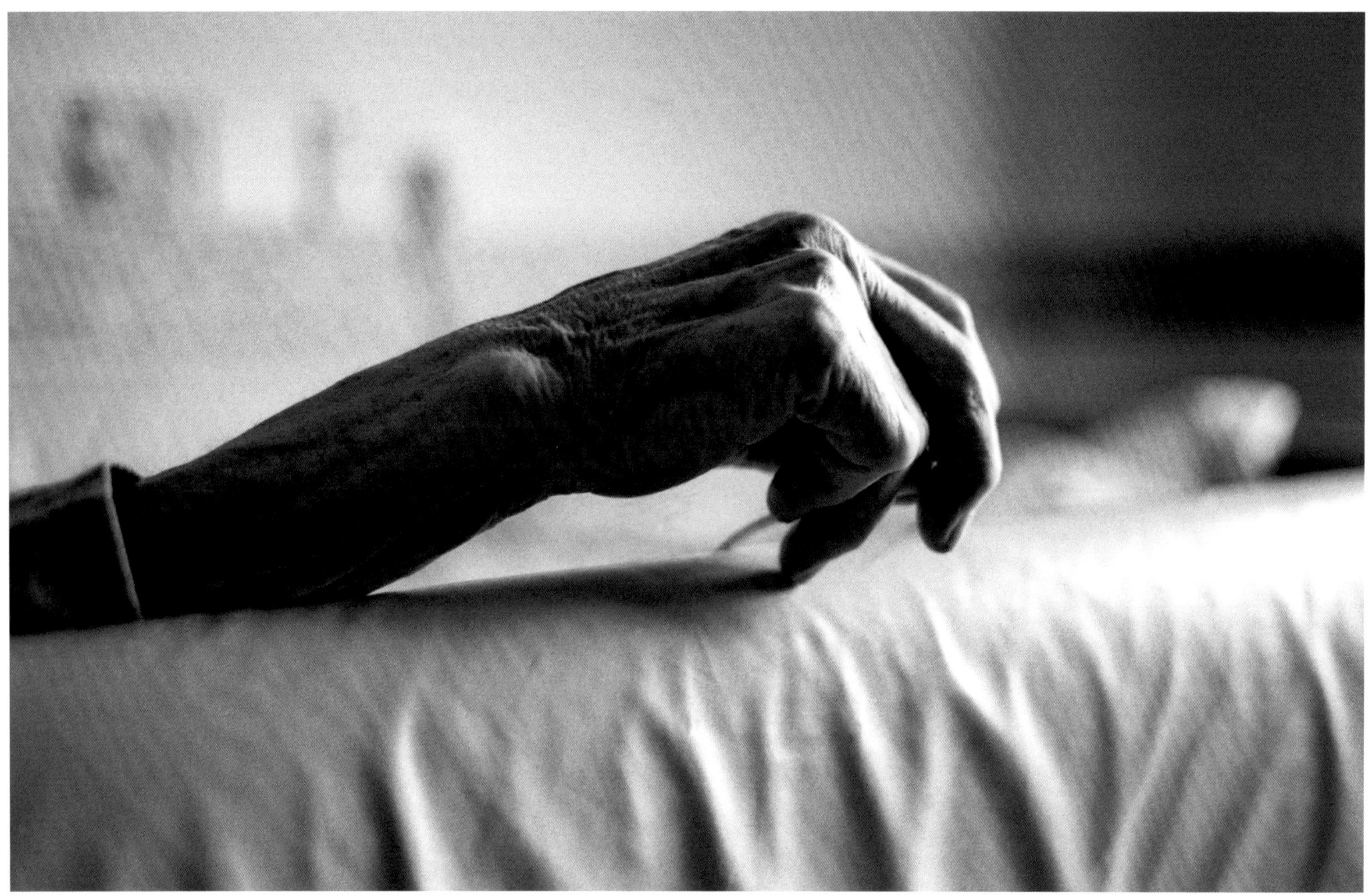

After over 2 months in residential care, physically, Dennis is
now half the man he used to be. He has been bed-ridden for
much of his time here.

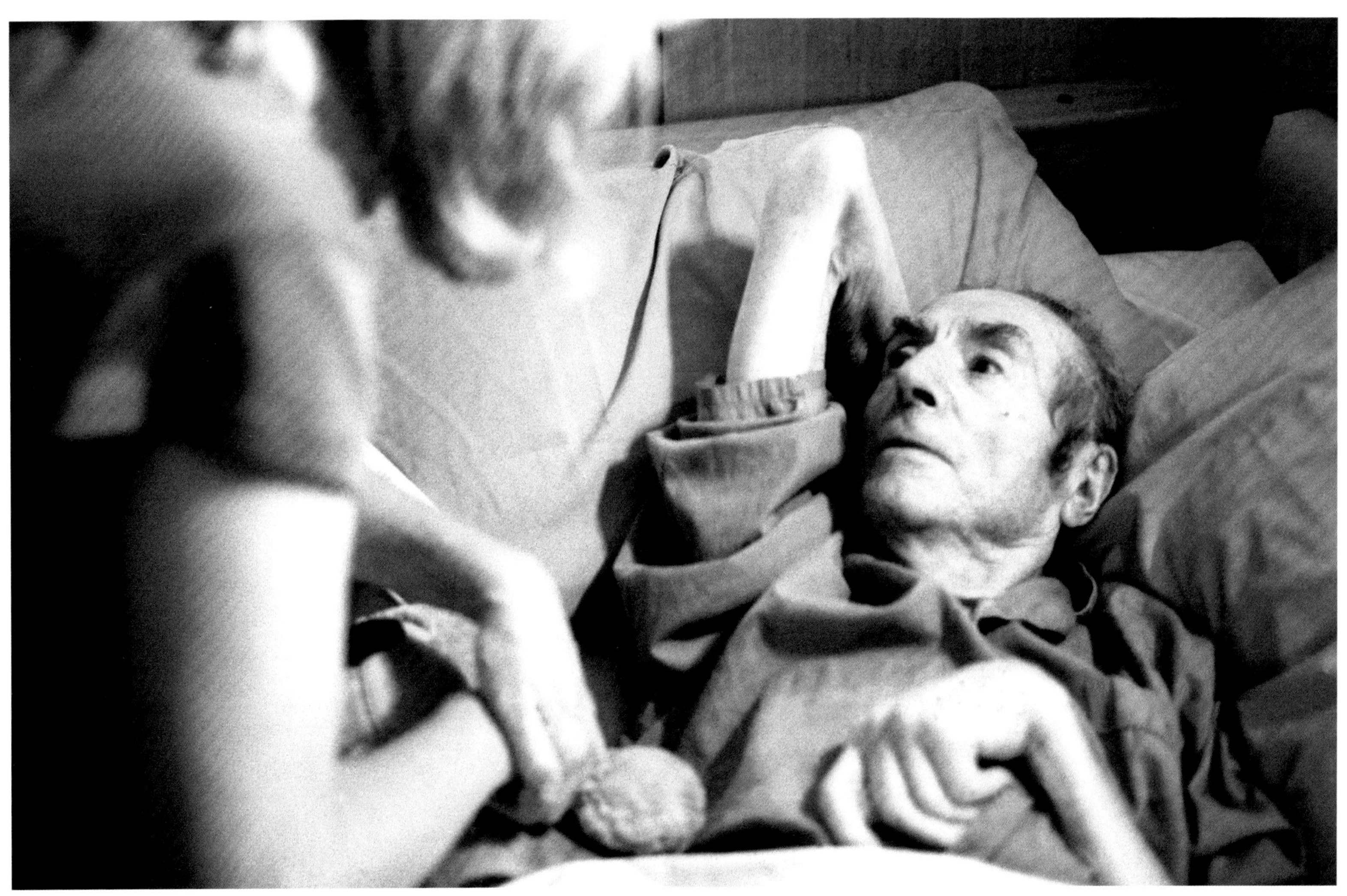

Dennis is visited by his daughter Susan on Father's Day in 2009. During his time in care, periods of lucidity have become less frequent. He now finds it increasingly difficult to remember and engage with his loved ones.

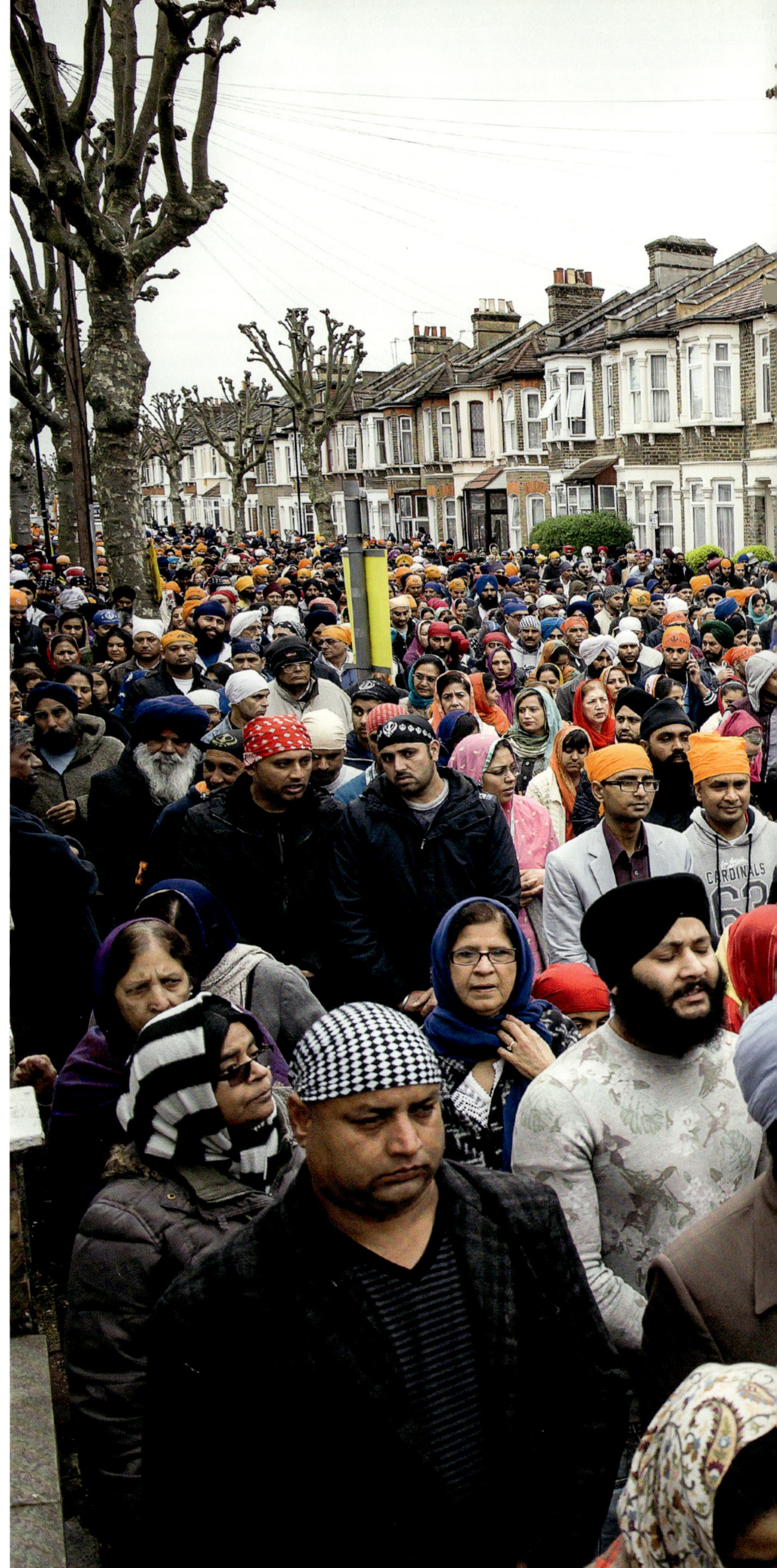

○ ANDREW BAKER

Vaisakhi Parade 2015
East Ham, London

The Vaisakhi Parade is hosted by various gurdwaras across London during April, the month of Vaisakhi. The festival marks several important dates on the Sikh calendar; including the harvest festival, Punjabi New Year and the year Sikhism became a collective faith in 1699.

Sikhs from across London join the procession following the Sri Granth Sahib through the east London streets.

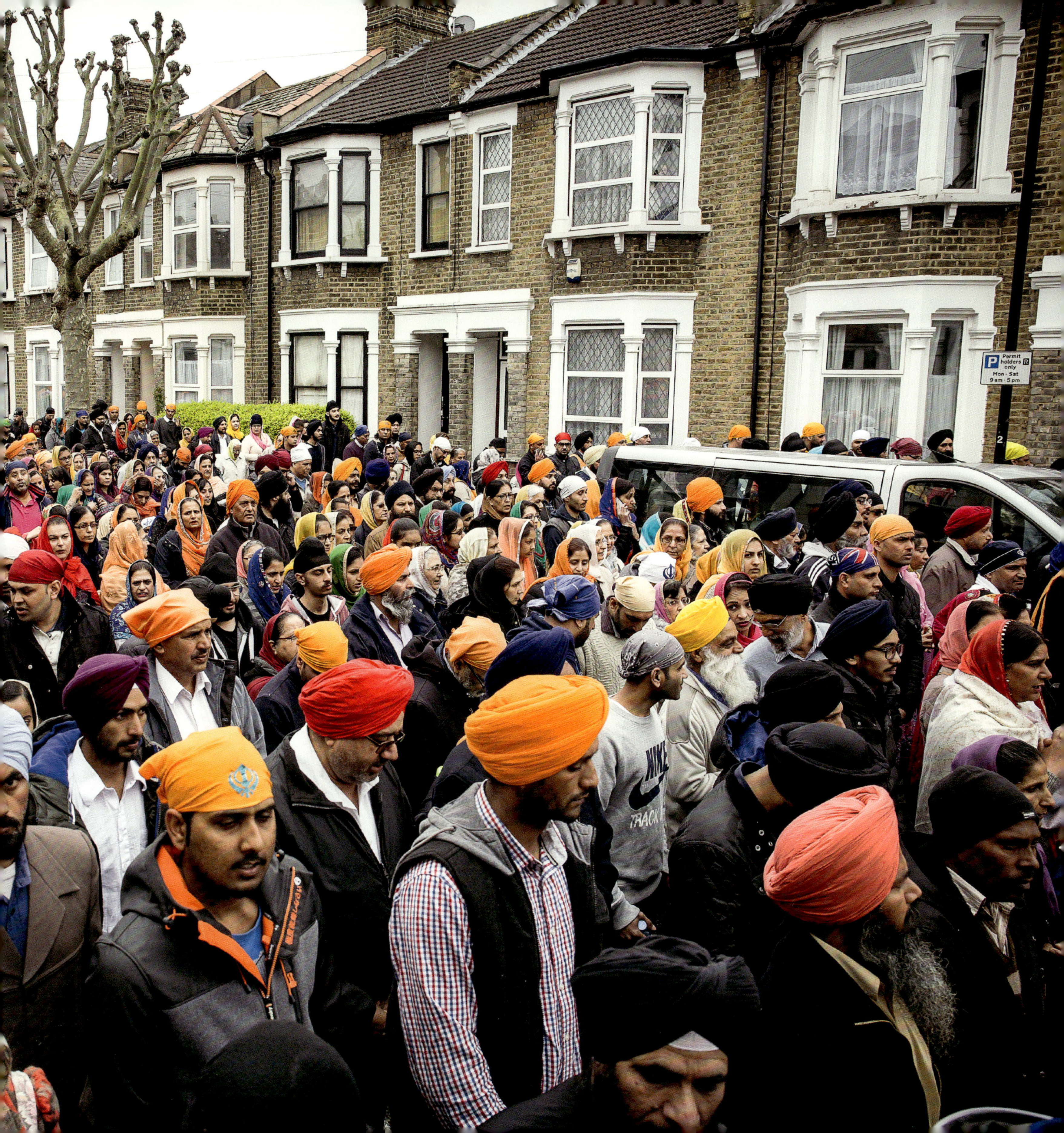

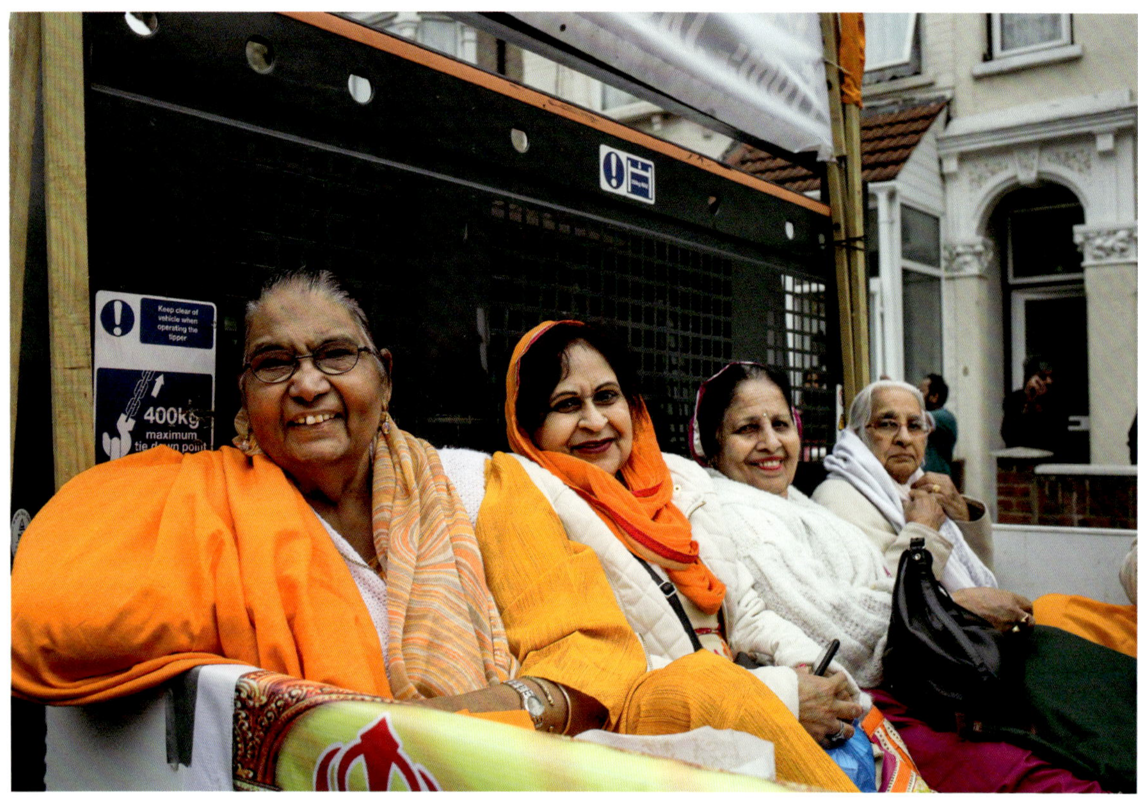

Elderly Sikh women make use of a builder's pick-up truck to take part in the procession.

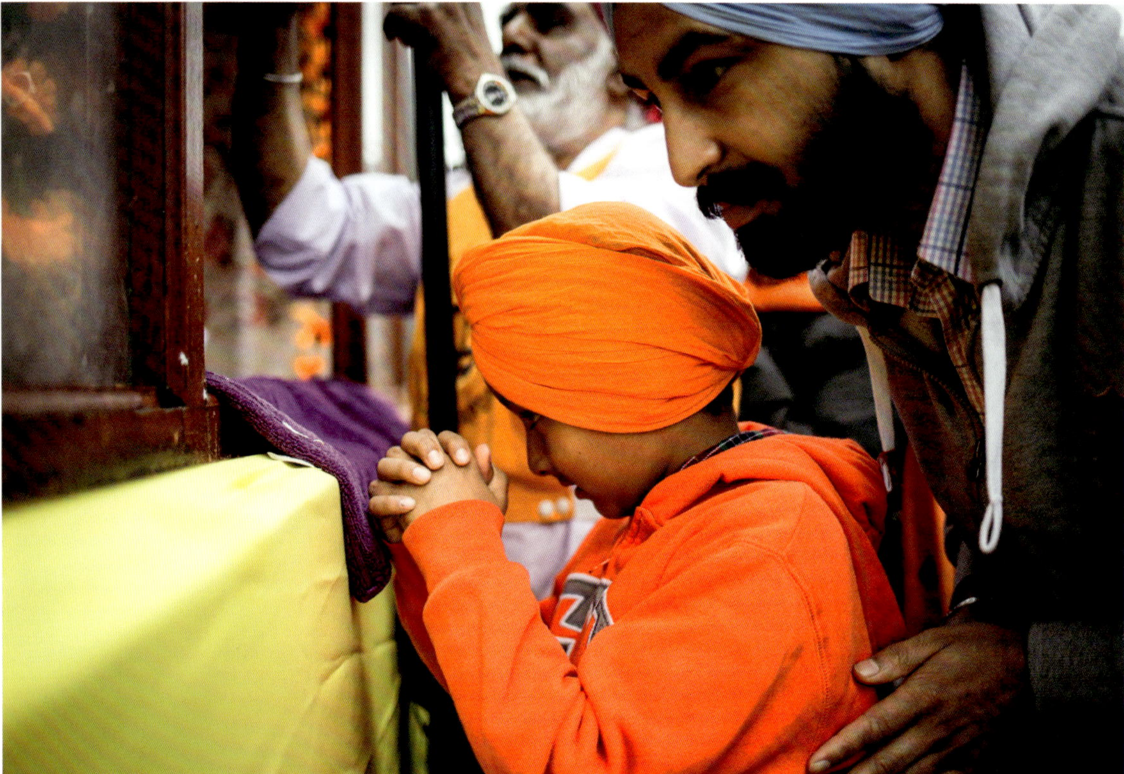

A young Sikh boy, with his father, bow in respect as the Sri Granth Sahib passes on the chariot.

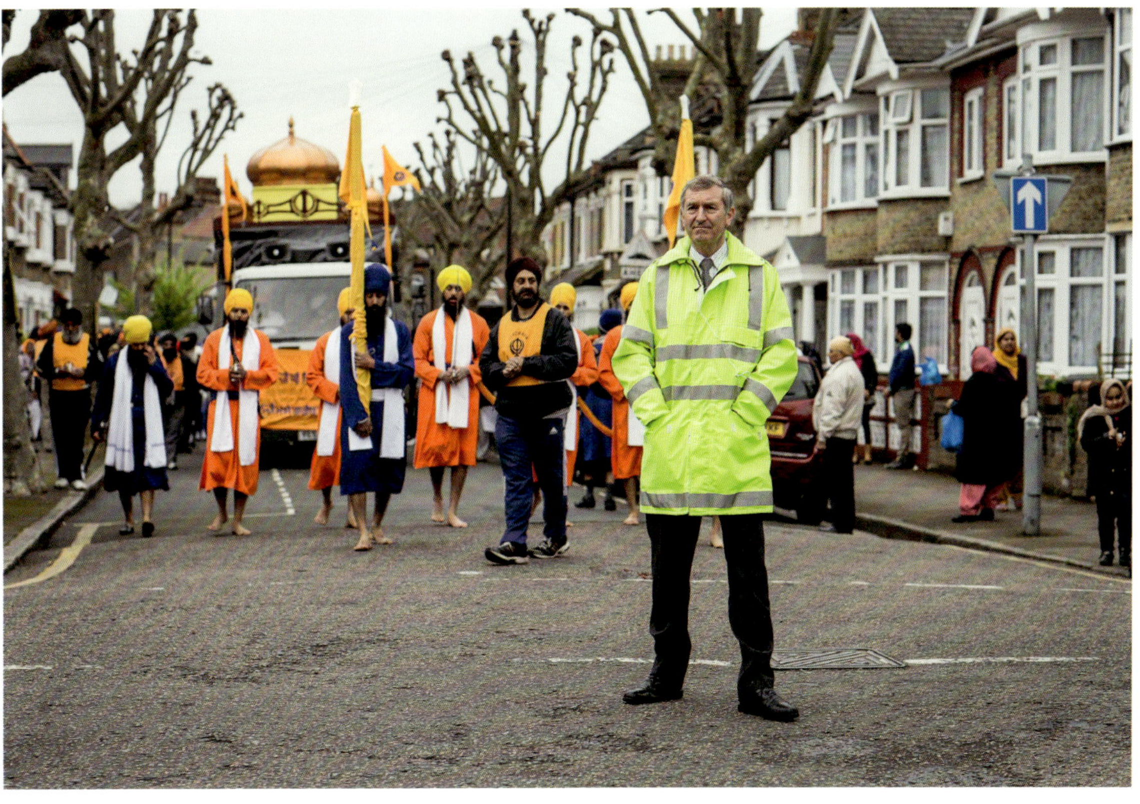

'The Man from the Ministry'. A council-appointed supervisor stands far in front of the procession.

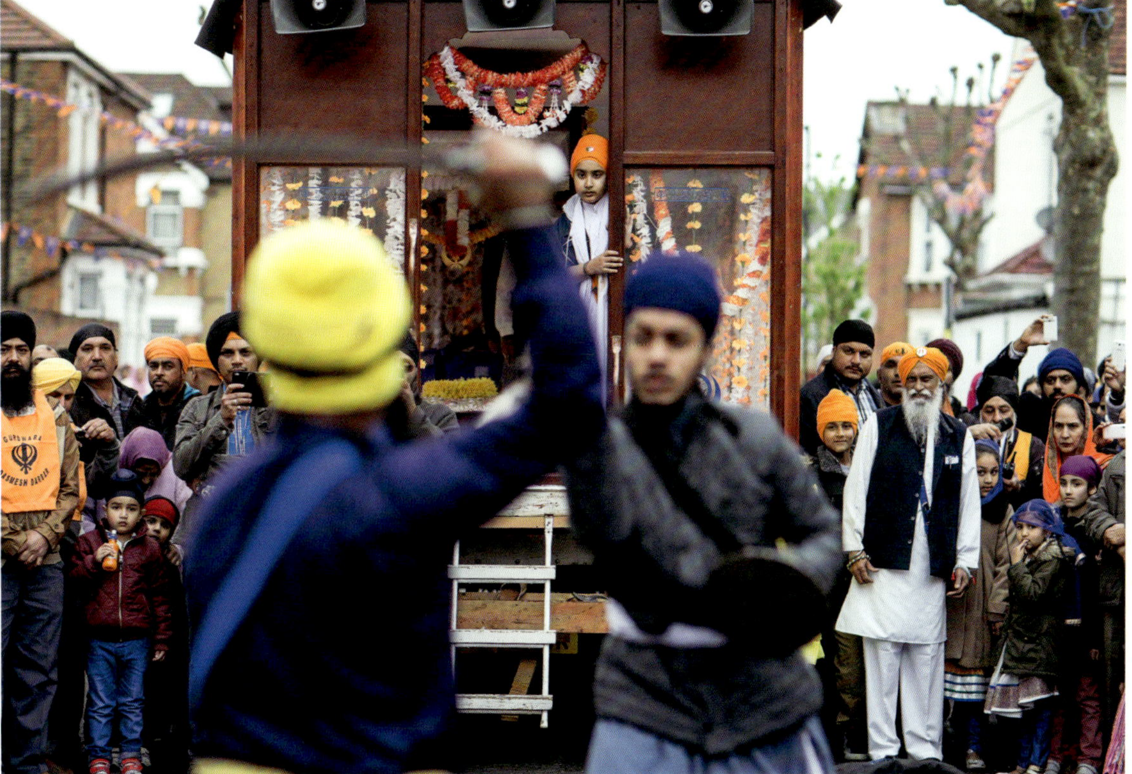

Sikh onlookers watch a choreographed fight performed by Punjabi warriors using authentic swords and shields from the Sikh faith's history.

Traditionally dressed Sikhs as the Panj Piaras
– 'the Beloved Five' – as they stand at the
forefront of the procession.

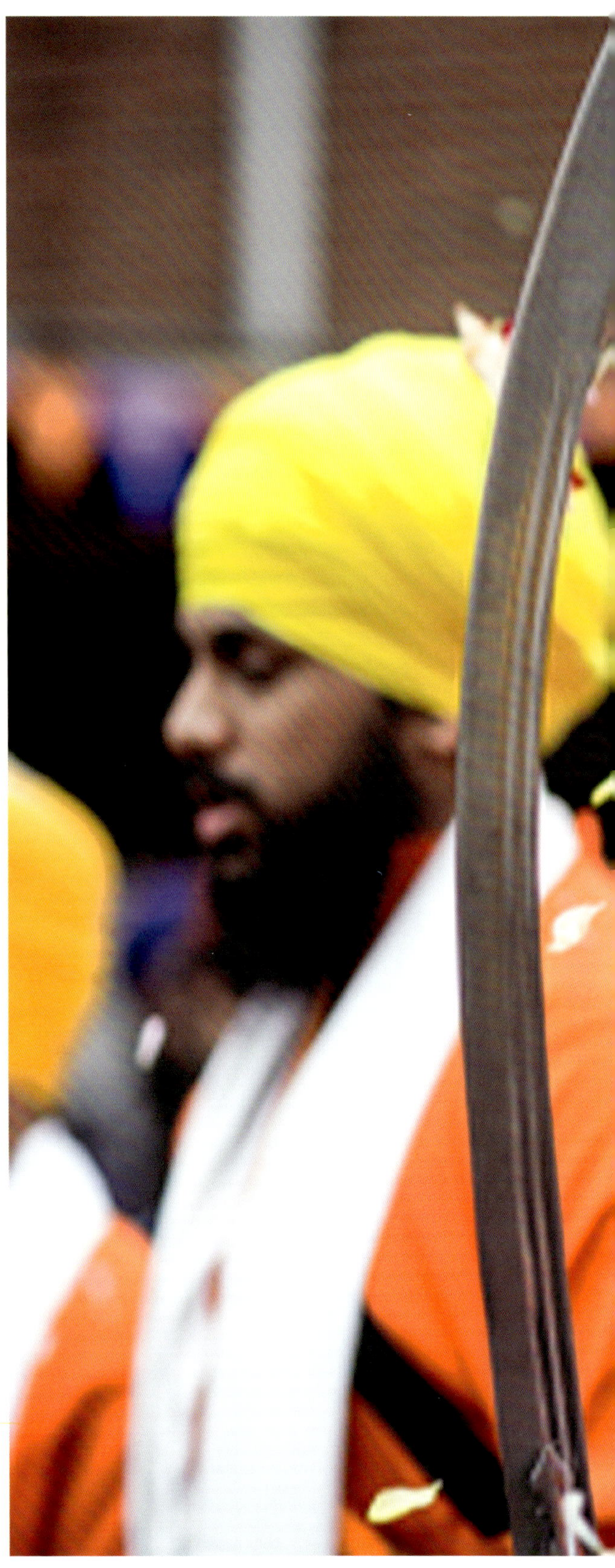

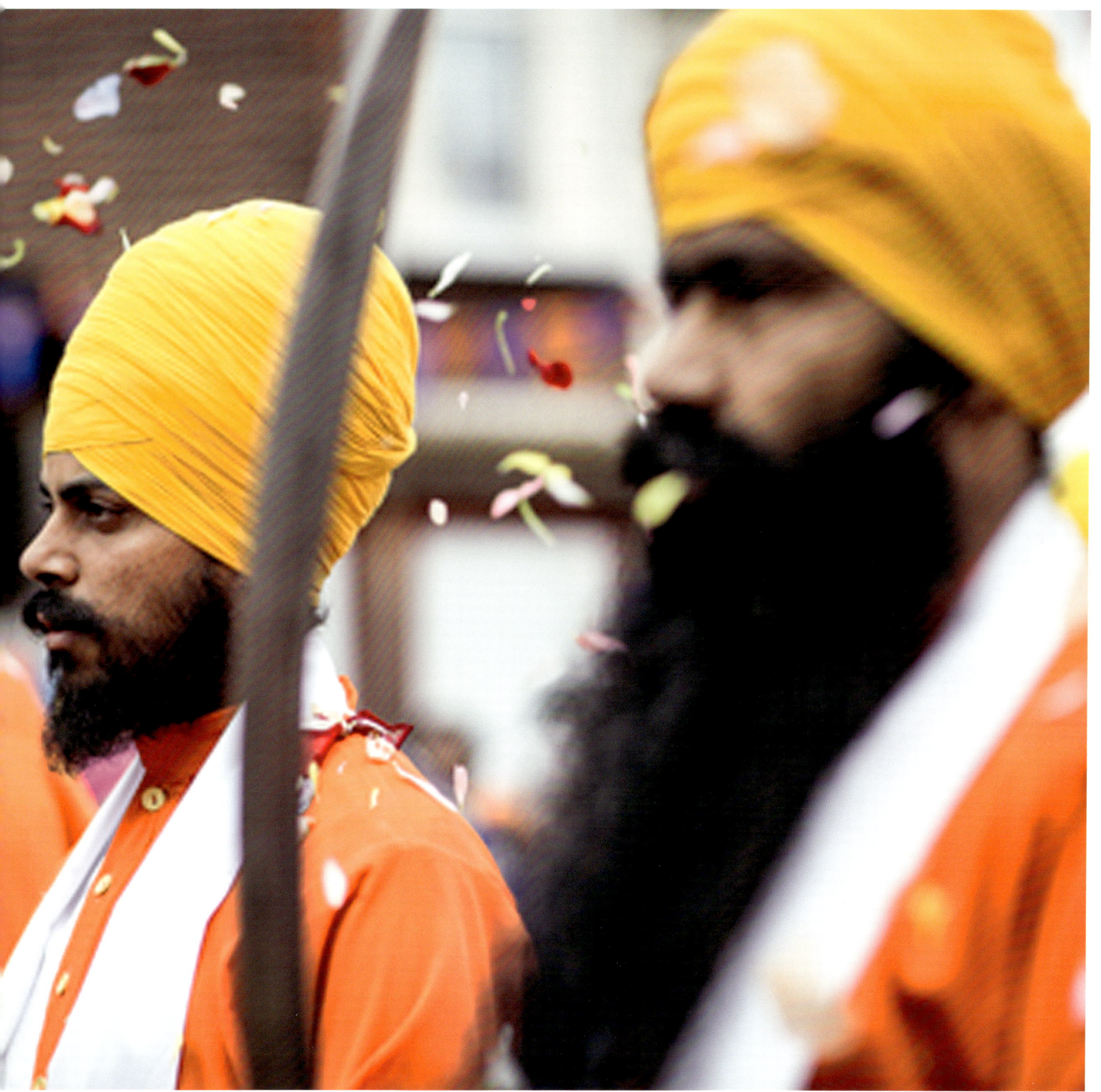

Nottingham

After being kettled into a side street by riot police in Nottingham's city centre, members of the far right group The English Defence League (EDL) become violent towards the gathered media. (My camera was punched into my face moments after the image was taken, leaving me with a bloody nose and a split eyebrow).

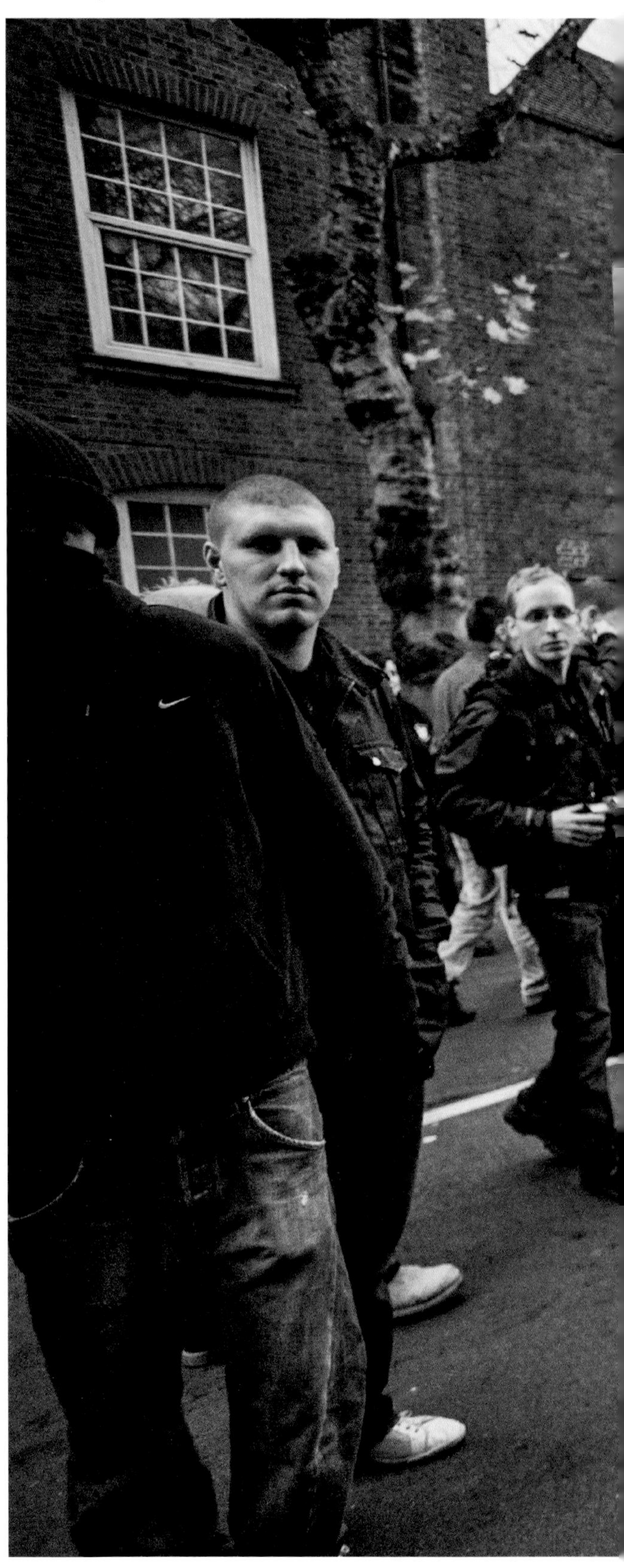

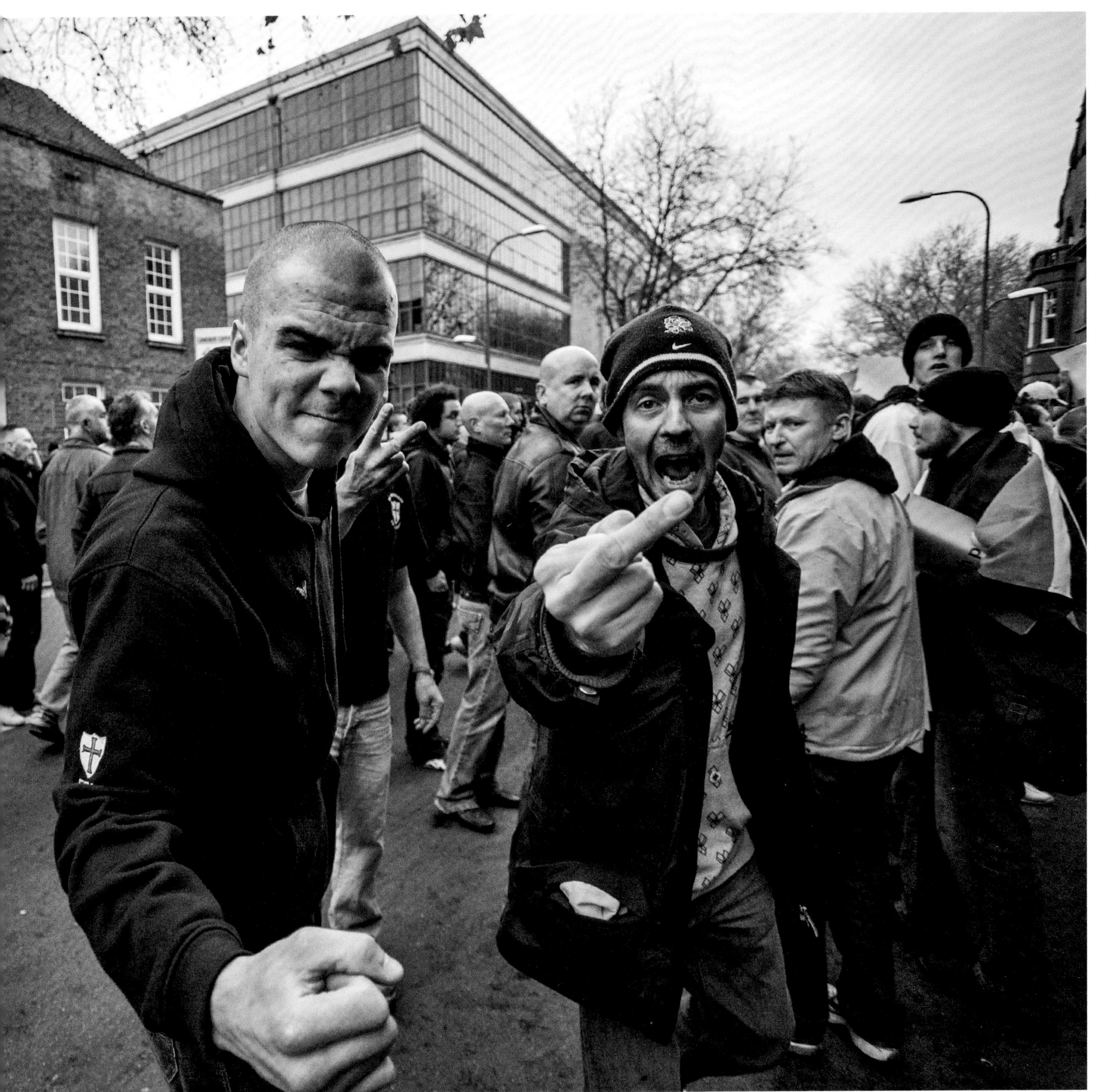

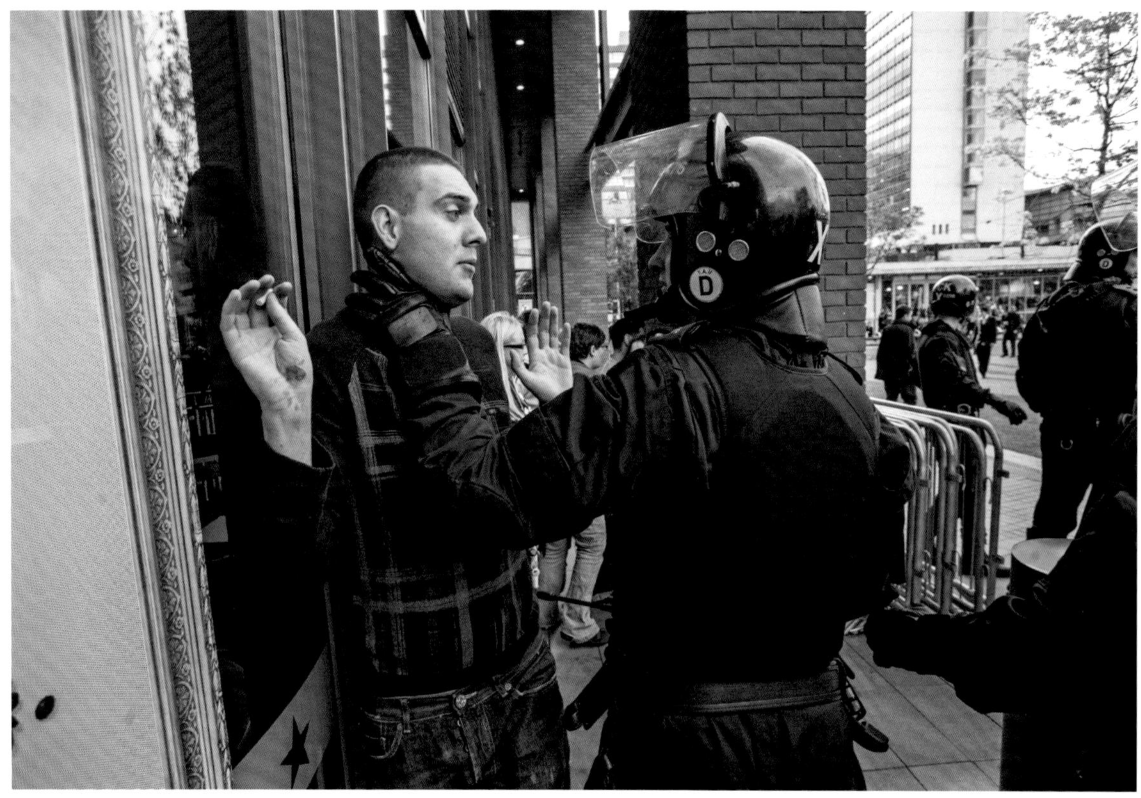

Manchester City Centre

A member of the English Defence League is held by police after breaking through a police cordon to a rival protest held by Unite Against Fascism (UAF).

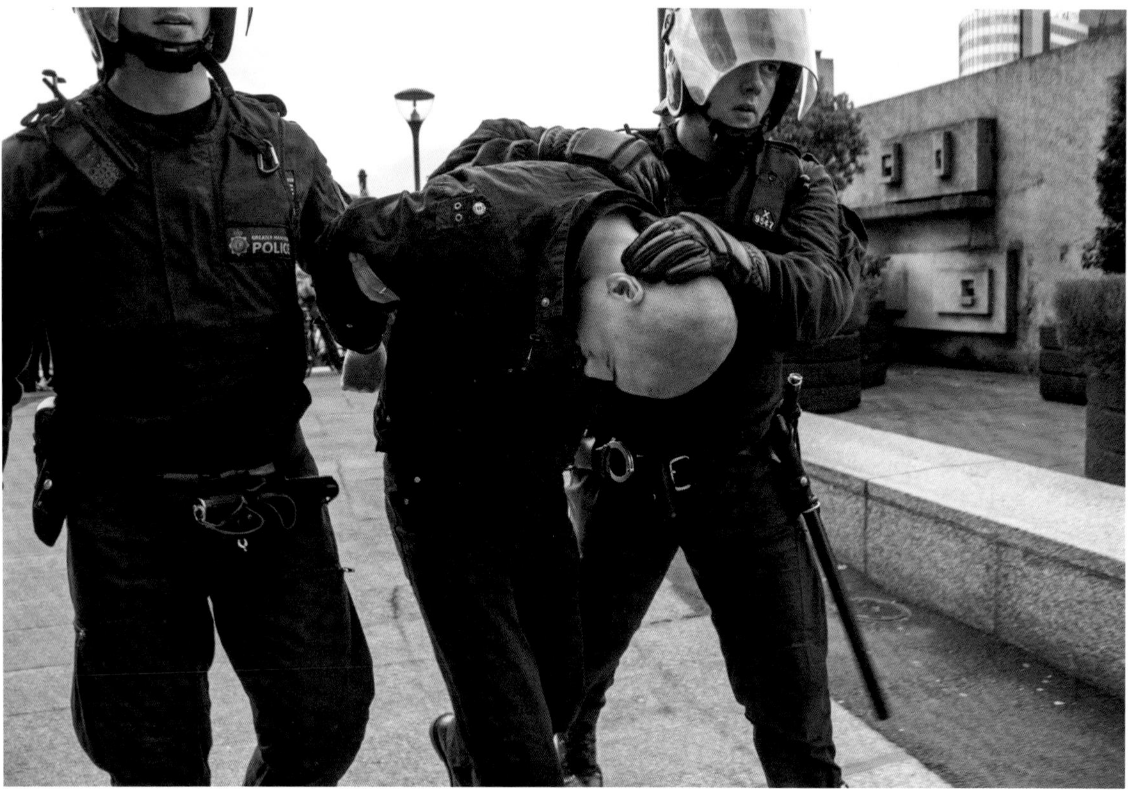

Manchester City Centre

A member of the English Defence League is arrested by riot police after throwing a projectile towards police lines during a violent demonstration in Manchester city centre.

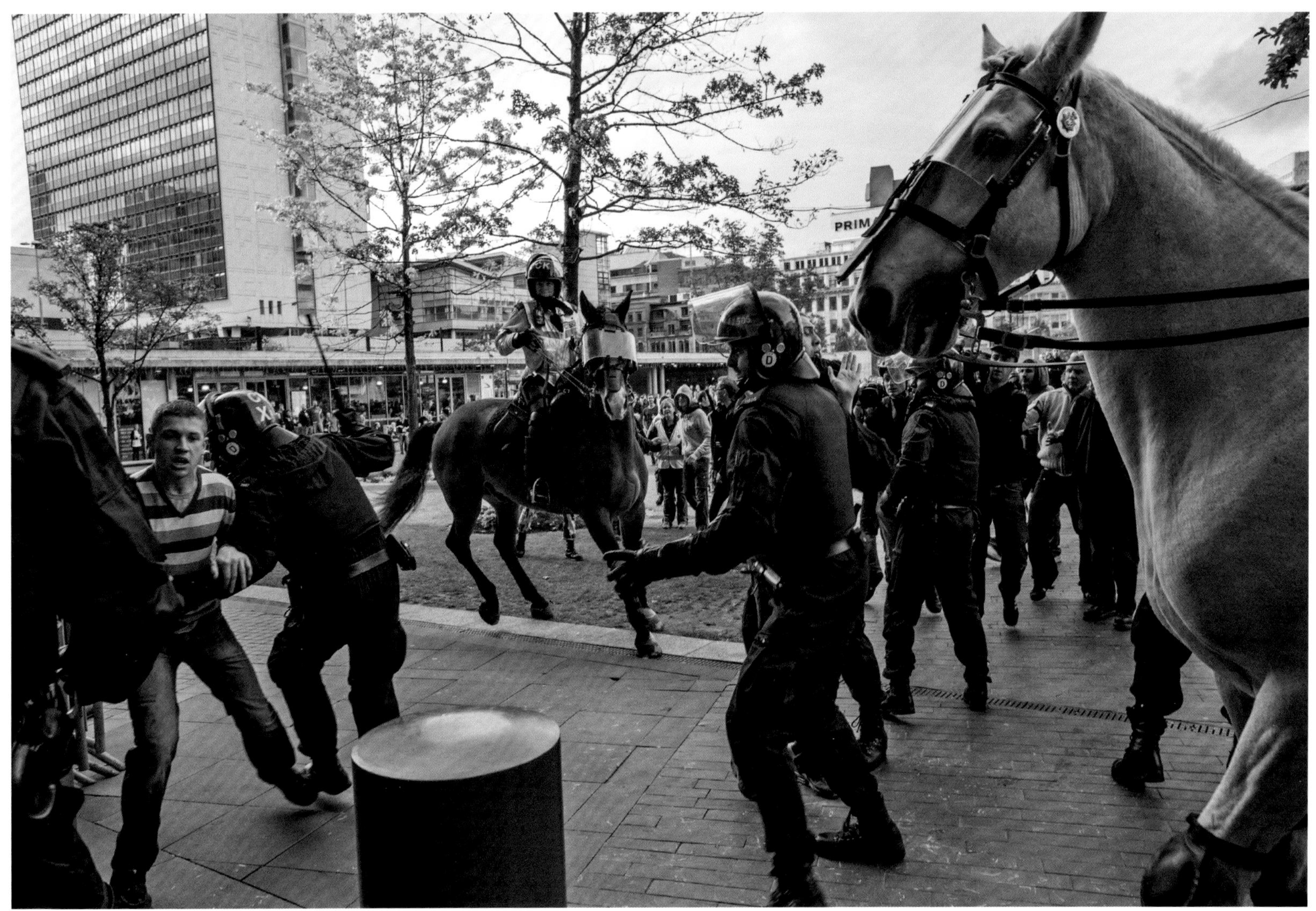

Manchester City Centre

A member of the English Defence
League is apprehended by police after
breaking through a police cordon.

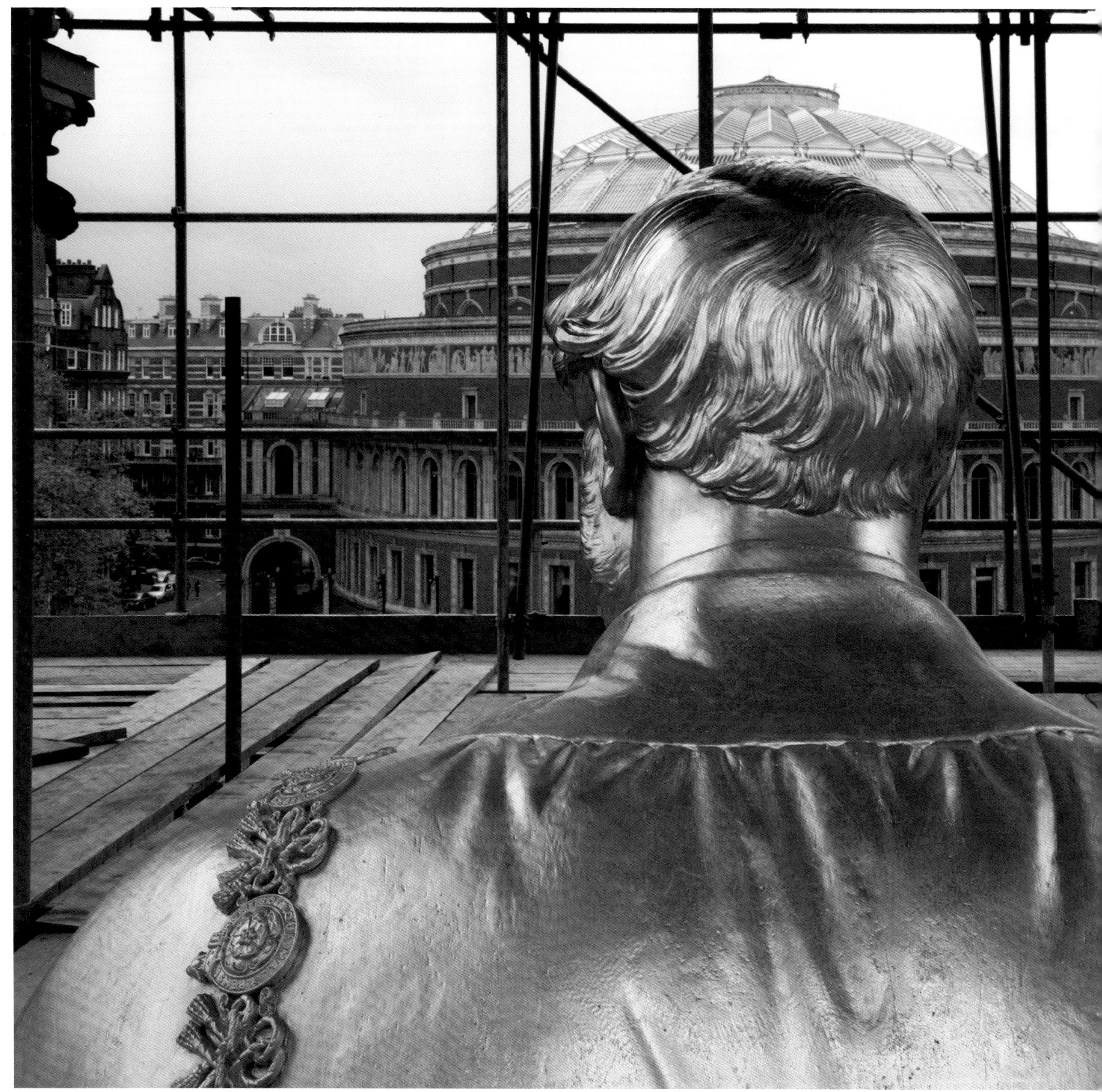

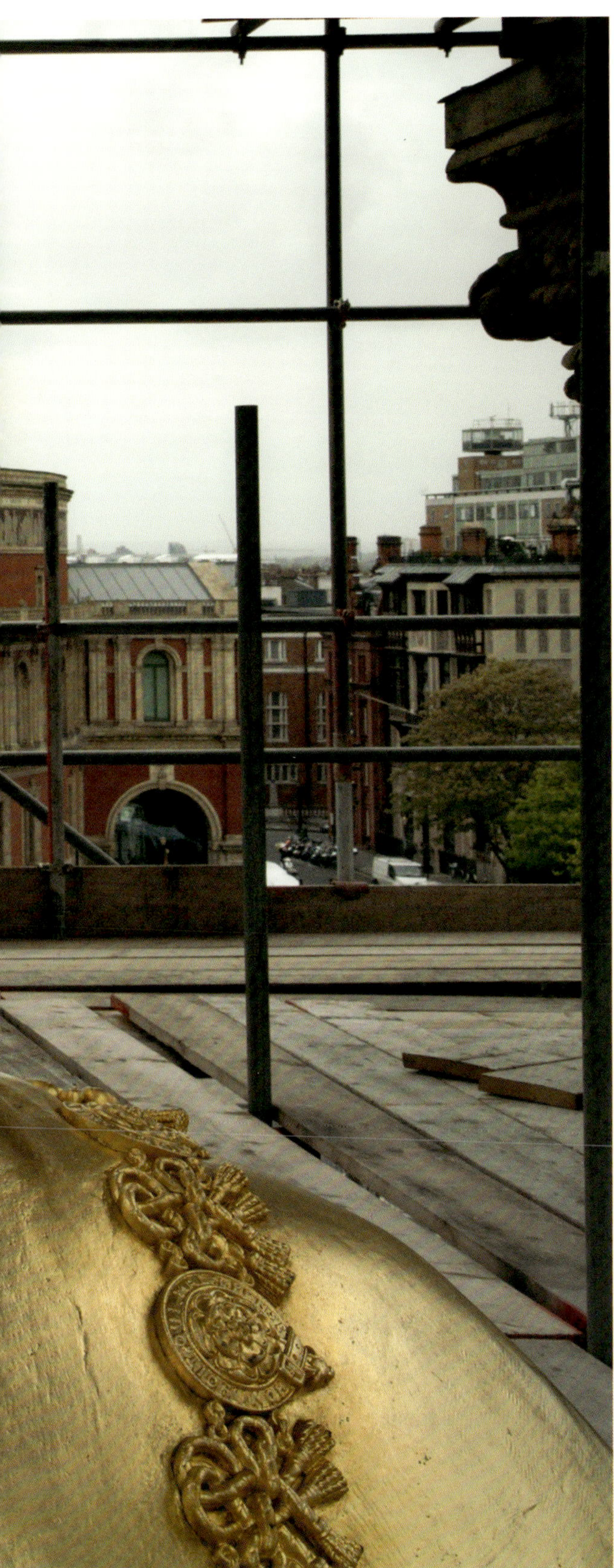

○ NADIA MACKENZIE

Albert Memorial / Royal Albert Hall
London

The Albert Memorial was commissioned by Queen Victoria as a tribute to her late consort, Prince Albert of Saxe-Coburg-Gotha. The High Gothic monument was completed in 1876, fifteen years after prince Albert died at the age of forty-two. I was commissioned to photograph the re-gilding project.

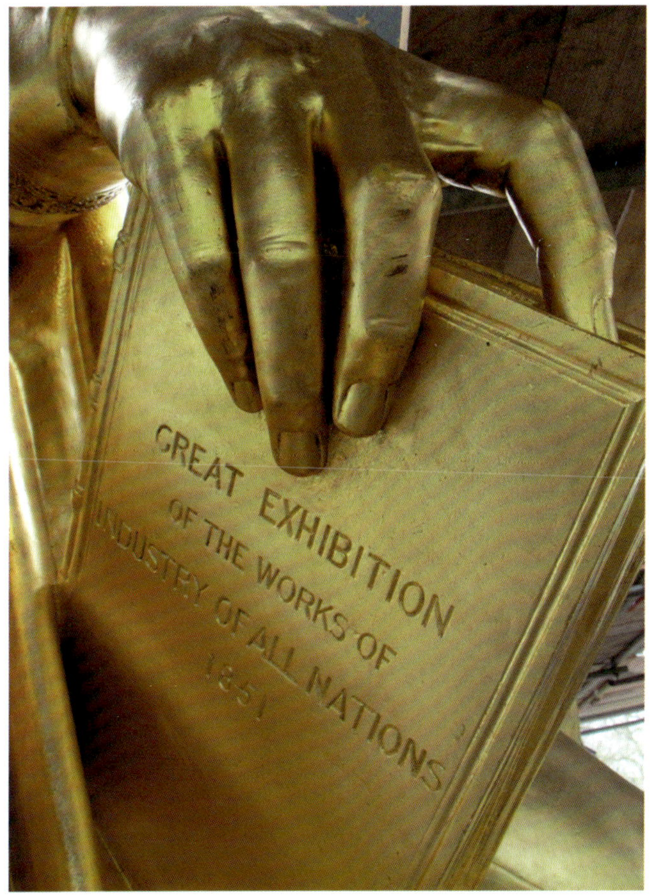

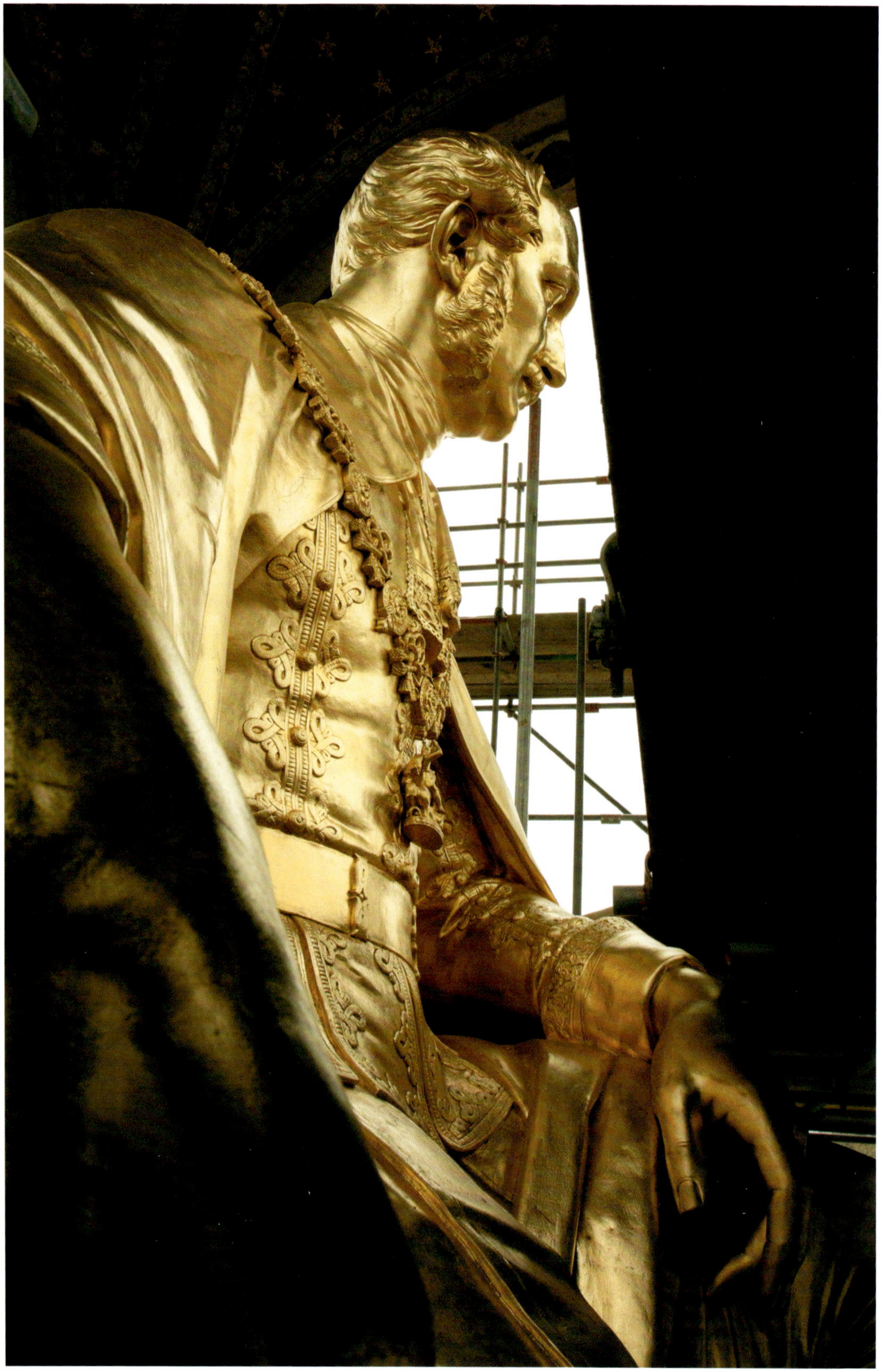

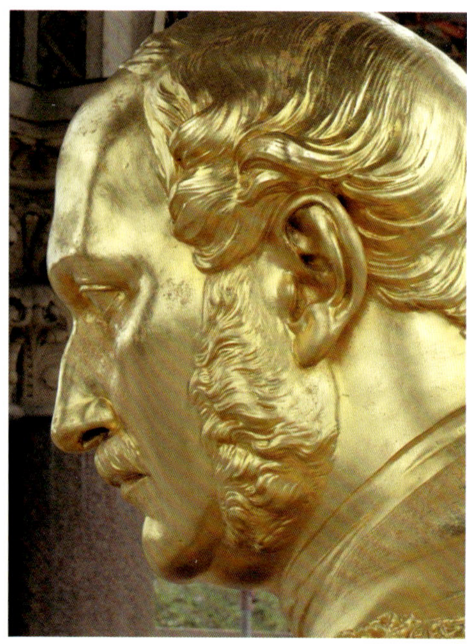

Albert Memorial / Royal Albert Hall
London

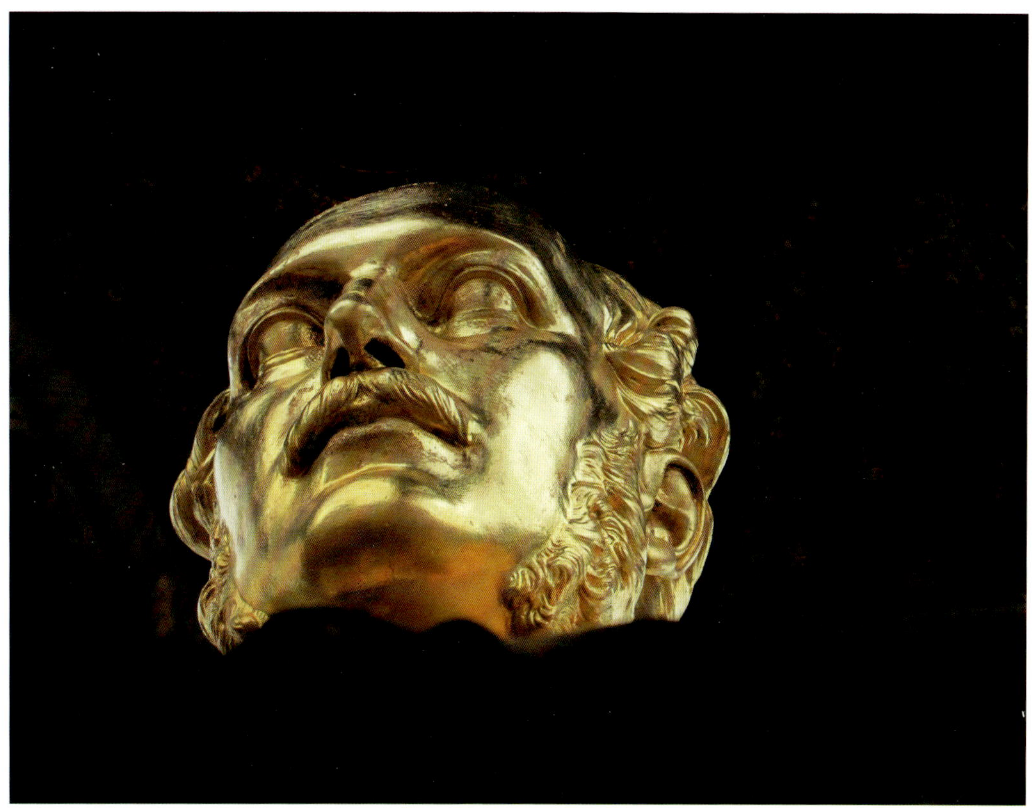

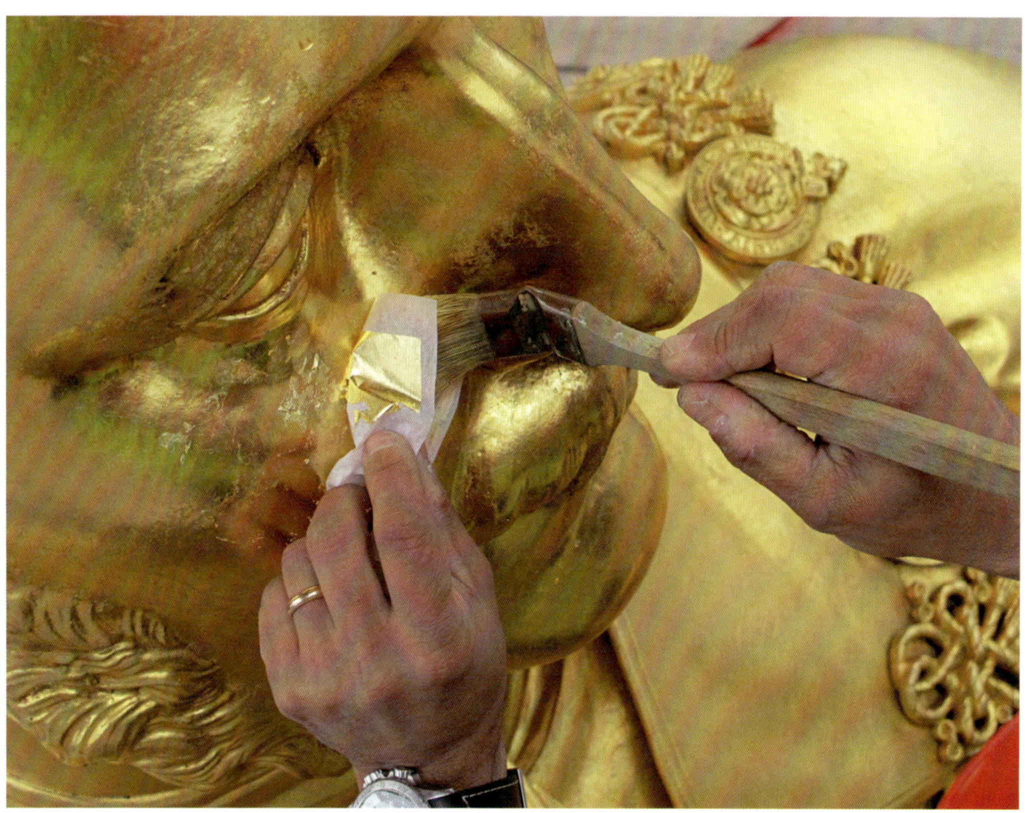

10

YOUNG PHOTOGRAPHER AWARD

▷ LUKE DRAY / WINNER

Protest at Parliament
London

Parliament is the heart and soul of Britain's democracy, and as such attracts demonstrations on a multitude of causes. On this occasion Parliament Square was the site of a pro-refugee gathering drawing hundreds of thousands in Autumn 2015.

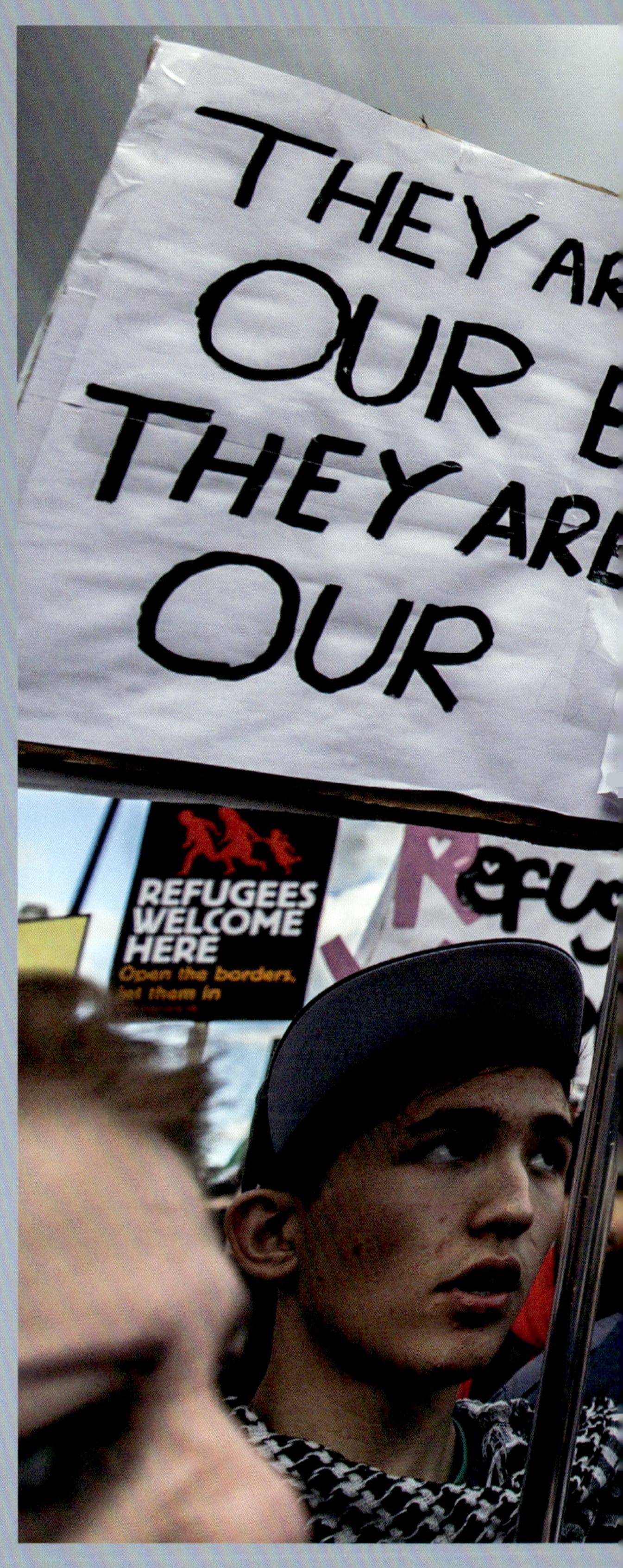

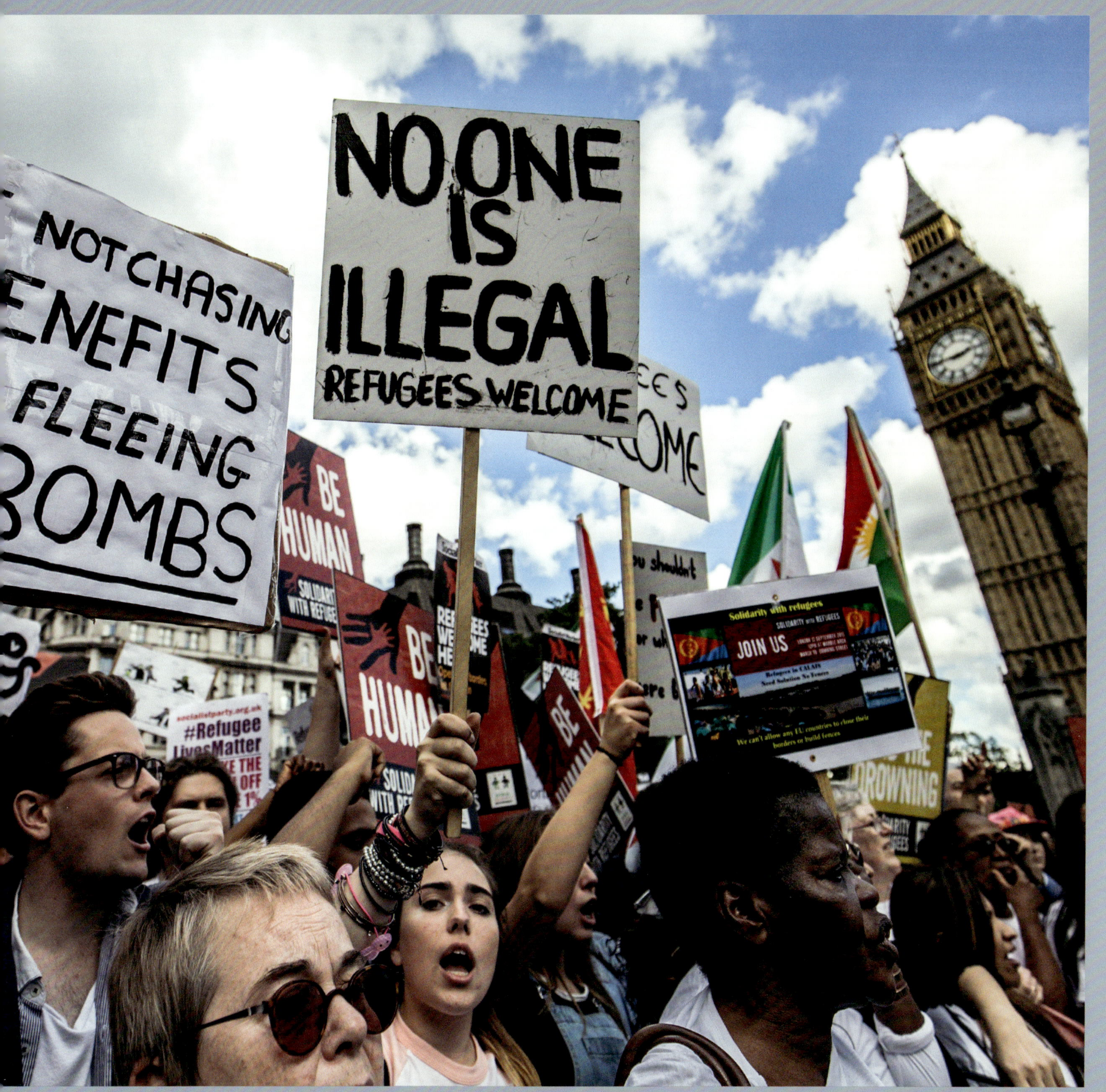
NOT CHASING
ENEFITS
FLEEING
BOMBS
NO ONE
IS
ILLEGAL
REFUGEES WELCOME
BE
HUMAN
SOLIDARITY
WITH REFUGEES
BE
HUMAN
SOLIDARITY WITH REFUGEES
#Refugee
LivesMatter
socialistparty.org.uk
Solidarity with refugees
SOLIDARITY with REFUGEES
JOIN US
Refugees in CALAIS
Need Solution No Fences
We can't allow any EU countries to close their
borders or build fences
DROWNING

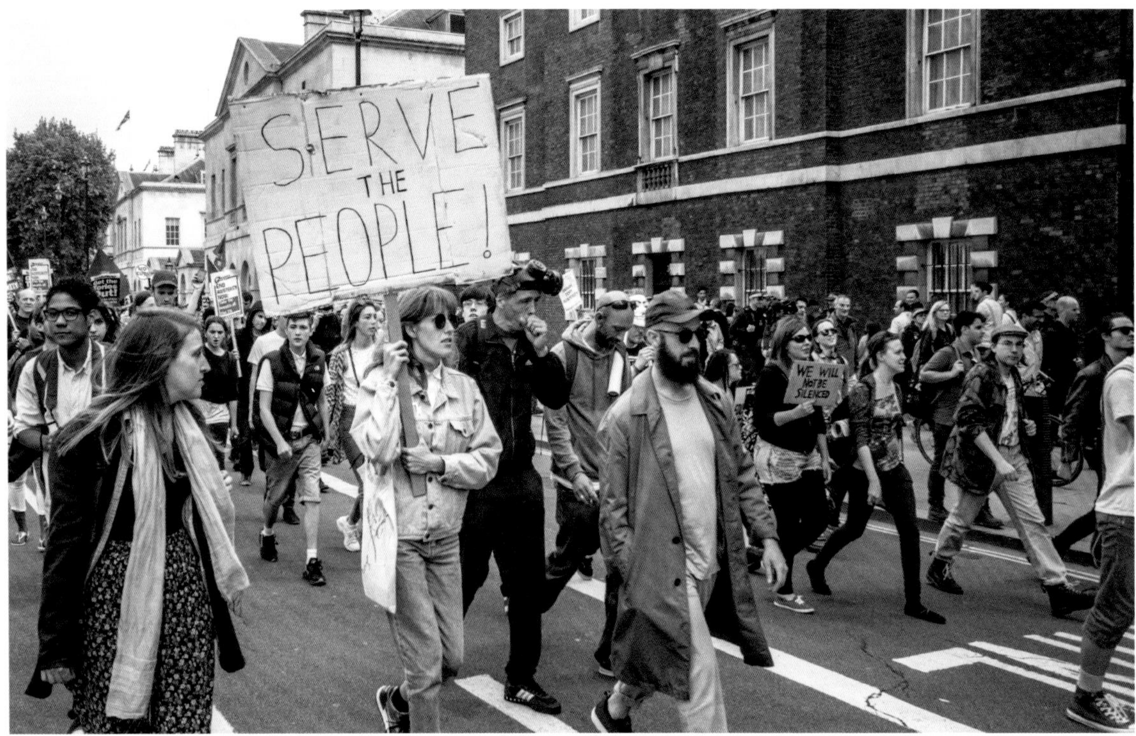

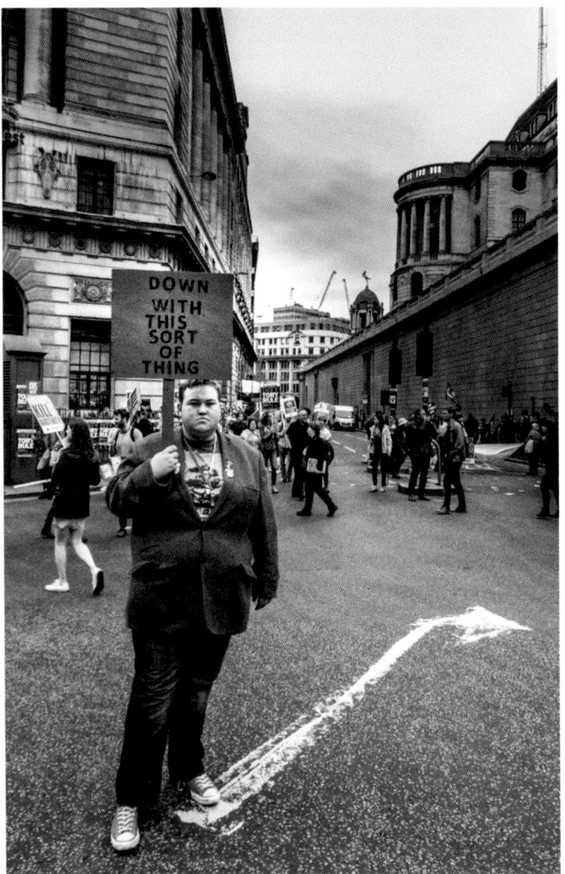

⬤
No Problems

The mainstream media often won't cover peaceful protests because they don't sell in print. This is a shame because some very creditable causes fail to get the attention they deserve.

◀
A Sign of the Times

Out of the many demonstrations I have covered, this placard sums it up: one sign fits all – a sign of the times.

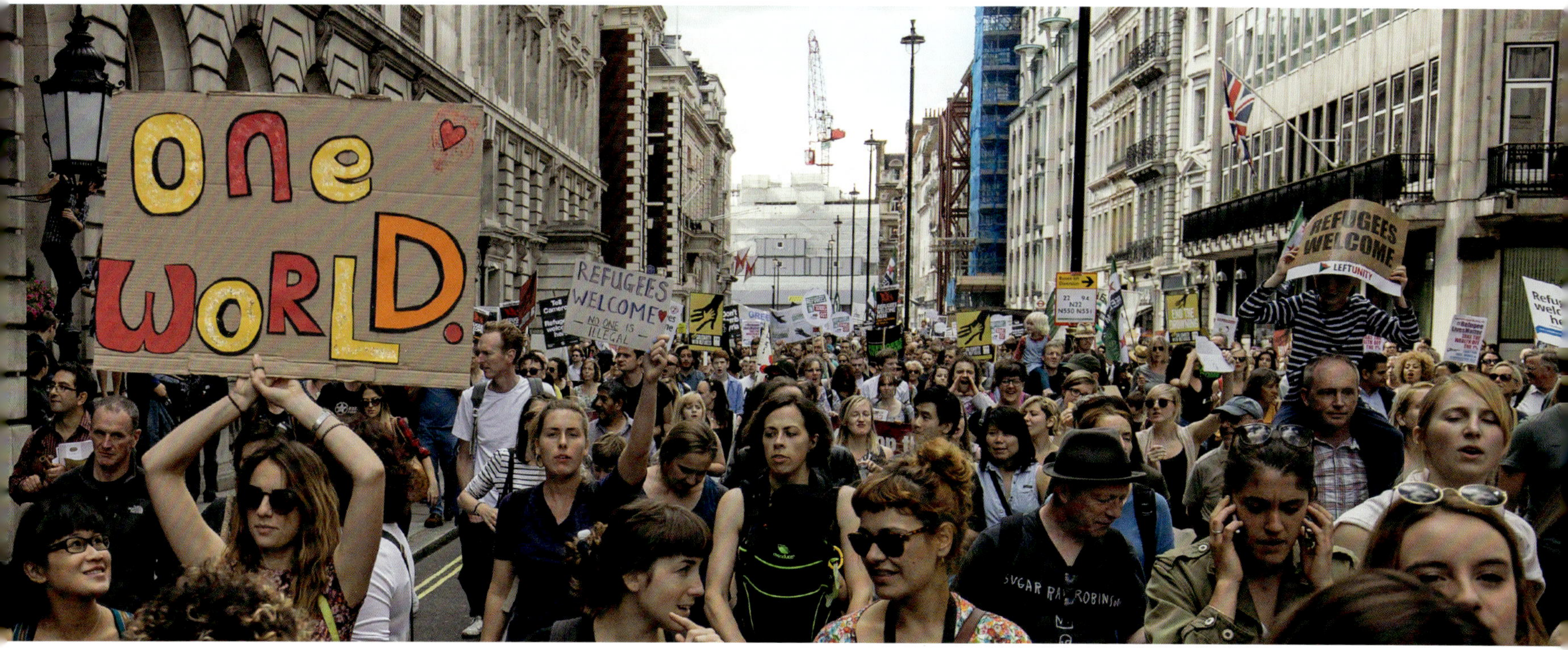

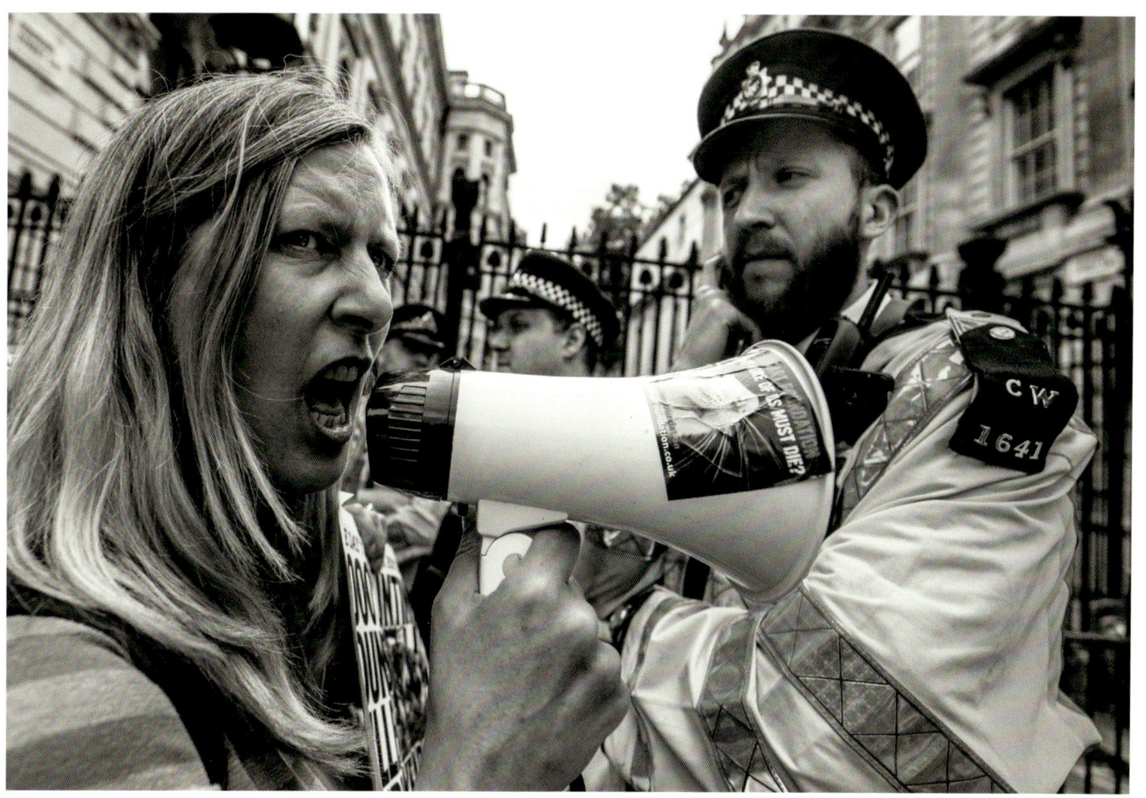

Refugees Welcome

The handling of the refugee crisis by the European Union sparked outcry. Thousands took to the streets showing their support for refugees.

The Voice of Protest: heard it all before

Here, the face of passion contrasts with the face of impartiality.

Save Me

Protesters gather outside Downing Street to urge the Prime Minister to back the ban on hunting with dogs.

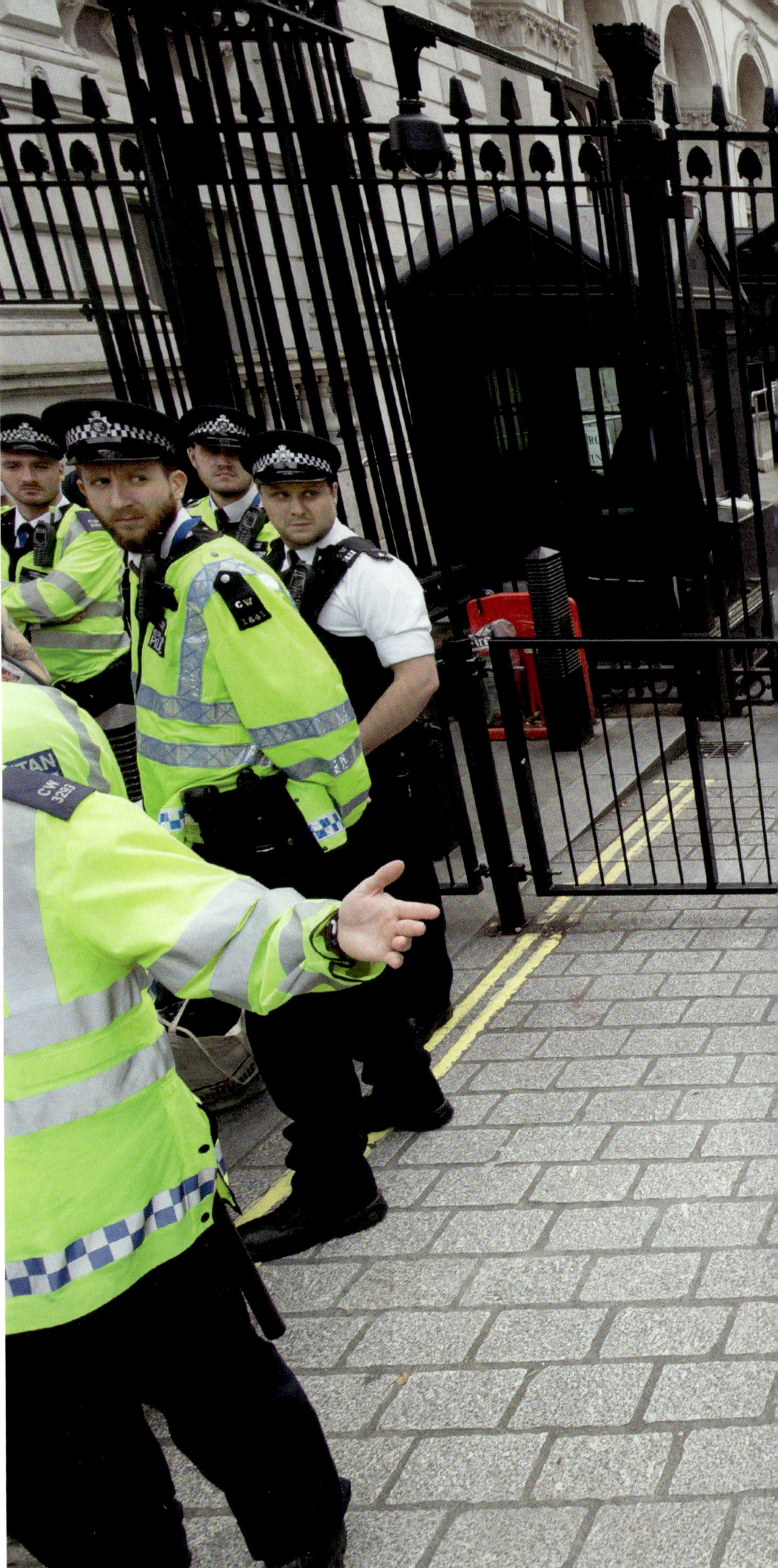

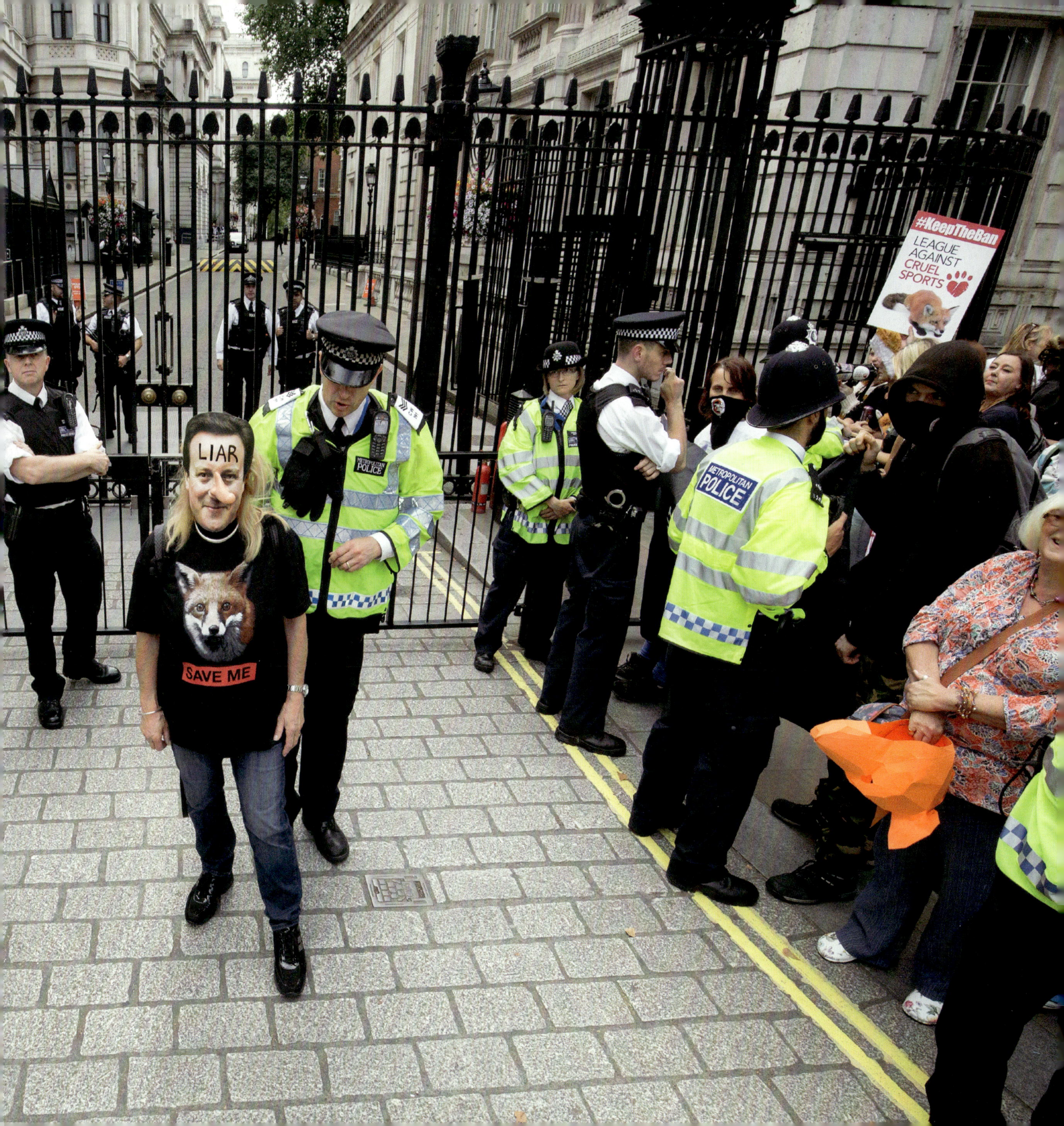

#KeepTheBan
LEAGUE AGAINST CRUEL SPORTS
LIAR
SAVE ME
METROPOLITAN POLICE
METROPOLITAN POLICE